AF683821

ROME'S EASTERN TRADE

ROME'S EASTERN TRADE

International commerce and imperial policy, 31 BC – AD 305

Gary K. Young

London and New York

First published 2001 by Routledge
11 New Fetter Lane, London EC4P 4EE

Simultaneously published in the USA and Canada by Routledge
29 West 35th Street, New York, NY 10001

Routledge is an imprint of the Taylor & Francis Group

© 2001 Gary K. Young
Typeset in Bembo by Keystroke,
Jacaranda Lodge, Wolverhampton
Printed and bound in Great Britain by Biddles Ltd,
Guildford and King's Lynn

All rights reserved. No part of this book may be reprinted or reproduced or utilised in any form or by any electronic, mechanical, or other means, now known or hereafter invented, including photocopying and recording, or in any information storage or retrieval system, without permission in writing from the publishers.

British Library Cataloguing in Publication Data

A catalogue record for this book is available
from the British Library

Library of Congress Cataloguing in Publication Data
Young, Gary K. (Gary Keith), 1963–
Rome's eastern trade : international commerce and
imperial policy, 31 BC–AD 305 / Gary K. Young.
p. cm.
Includes bibliographical references and index.
1. Rome—Commerce—Middle East—History.
2. Middle East—Commerce—Rome—History.
3. Rome—Commercial policy—History.
4. Commercial products—Middle East—History.
5. Rome—Economic conditions—30 B.C.–476 A.D. I. Title.

HF377 .Y68 2001
382′.09370394—dc21

ISBN 0–415–24219–3

DIS MANIBVS

DAVID J. BETTS

MAGISTRI ET AMICI

CONTENTS

ILLUSTRATIONS

Maps

Figures

Tables

PREFACE AND ACKNOWLEDGEMENTS

The study of the Roman East has been a field which has experienced a great surge in interest from scholars in recent years. Scholarly interest in the study of the Roman army, the societies of the East, and many other fields has increased dramatically since the publication of G.W. Bowersock's 'A Report on Arabia Provincia' in 1971, which issued a challenge to scholars to investigate this previously somewhat neglected area. One of the areas which has subsequently come under considerable attention is the study of the silk and spice trades of the Roman Empire, in which expensive goods were brought from such places as India, Arabia and Africa and carried into the Roman East, and thence to the markets of the empire.

While certain aspects of this field have come under investigation, especially that of Roman Egypt, there have been no recent attempts to determine the political effects of the trade upon the societies of the Roman East. Accordingly, this book is designed to investigate the long-distance trade in the Roman East in the light of recent research, and to study the political effects of this trade, both on the societies of the East and on the empire itself. This book is essentially a revision of my doctoral thesis. Although some areas have been altered in the light of recent archaeological investigations and historical research, the main argument of the thesis has been retained.

It is appropriate at this point to recognise the support of several individuals and organisations which have provided support of one form or another in the preparation of this work. First, I would like to thank my thesis supervisor, Dr Paul Gallivan, for the support and encouragement he has provided while this project was underway, as well as the other staff and students in the School of History and Classics at the University of Tasmania. I would also like to convey my thanks to the School for the provision of a Dunbabin travel grant, which allowed me to undertake a research trip to Egypt, Jordan and Syria as part of this project. In addition, I would like to thank Professors Steven Sidebotham, David Graf, David Kennedy, Dan Potts and Tom Parker for their provision of papers and helpful comments, and Drs Ghazi Bisheh and Fawzi Zayadine of the Department of Antiquities in Jordan for assisting me while I travelled in their country. Thanks must also go to Richard Stoneman and Catherine

Bousfield at Routledge for their support and encouragement, as well as to Frank Strk for Figures 4.3, 4.4 and 5.1. All other photographs are by the author.

Finally, I would like to thank my wife Helyn and my children James, Andrew and Caitlin for their patience and support while this book was being written. Without the help and support of all these people, this work would not have been possible. Each of them has contributed to the completion of my project, and must take credit for its good points, such as they are. The mistakes, of course, remain my own.

ABBREVIATIONS

The abbreviations used in this work correspond to those used in the standard works in the field. Abbreviations for ancient works are those used in *The Oxford Classical Dictionary*; those for journals and periodicals are those used in *L'Année philologique*. Corpora of inscriptions, ostraka and papyri are cited according to the following standards: for inscriptions, *Guide de l'epigraphiste* (Paris 1986), G.H.R. Horsely and J.A.L. Lee 'A Preliminary Checklist of Abbreviations of Greek Epigraphic Volumes' *Epigraphica* 56 (1994), 129–69, with modifications, and G.L. Harding *An Index of and Concordance of Pre-Islamic Arabian Names and Inscriptions* (Toronto 1978); for papyri and ostraka, J.F. Oates *et al. Checklist of Editions of Greek and Latin Papyri, Ostraca and Tablets* (*BASP* Supp. 7, 1992). *CAH* refers throughout to the second edition of the *Cambridge Ancient History*. Abbreviations used for specialist publications not covered in these lists are given below.

ANRW	H. Temporini and W. Haase (eds) *Aufstieg und Niedergang der römischen Welt* (Berlin 1972–).
Baalshamin III	C. Dunant *Le Sanctuaire de Baalshamin à Palmyre III: Les inscriptions* (Rome 1971).
ESAR	T. Frank (ed.) *Economic Survey of Ancient Rome* (Baltimore 1936–1939).
HHS	*Hou Han-Shou* (Annals of the Later Han Dynasty), as cited in F. Hirth *China and the Roman Orient* (Shanghai 1885).
IGLS	L. Jalalbert and R. Mouterde (eds) *Inscriptions grecques et latines de Syrie*, 21 vols (Paris 1929–).
Inv.	J. Cantineau, J. Starcky and M. Gawlikowski (eds) *Inventaire des inscriptions de Palmyre*, 11 vols (Beirut, Paris, Damascus 1930–).
NSIJ	V.A. Clark 'A Study of New Safaitic Inscriptions from Jordan' PhD Diss. (University of Melbourne 1980).
WH	F.V. Winnett and G.L. Harding *Fifty Safaitic Cairns* (Toronto 1978).

1

INTRODUCTION

General introduction

The long-distance trade in silk, spices and incense which was a feature of the eastern provinces of the Roman Empire has long attracted attention, both from scholars and in more popular literature. This is perhaps not surprising, as the images of camel caravans laden with silk and spices, fabulously rich 'caravan cities' and ships making the long and dangerous journey from the Red Sea to India and back in search of Indian pepper and other goods have often excited the imagination of scholar and lay reader alike. Indeed, a number of general studies of the eastern trade of the Roman Empire have already been made, which might bring one to question the need for this work.

Many of the studies of the trade completed earlier in the twentieth century, however, place great emphasis on a view of a strongly proactive Roman policy toward the trade. Indeed, many more recent writers have followed this tendency as well. These views have put forward such ideas that the Romans tried to promote or encourage the trade, and especially to force non-Roman 'middle-men' out of the trade and to concentrate the trade into Roman hands.[1] Such policies are envisaged as proceeding from the highest levels of government: on many occasions, commercial motives of this type have been posited as explanations for major military initiatives in the East, such as the annexation of the Nabataean kingdom in AD 106 or Trajan's Parthian expeditions. In addition, Roman officials at both imperial and provincial levels are seen as deliberately encouraging the trade in some areas by the provision of facilities, or redirecting trade routes in order to weaken the commerce in other areas. One recent study, while retreating from such an extreme view of Roman involvement in the trade, has still suggested that the provision of facilities for the commerce is indicative of a direct imperial interest in the commerce and of a proactive trade policy proceeding from the imperial court.[2]

Such views, however, have not been left unchallenged. In one particularly significant work on the topic, M.G. Raschke has questioned many of the assumptions which have been made about the Roman commerce with the East.[3] His reappraisal of the commerce has emphasised the fact that the 'middlemen' involved in the trade were usually Romans or Roman subjects, and consequently the views which emphasise attempts to remove non-Roman 'middlemen' should be rejected. Similarly, it has been shown that the vast majority of Roman foreign policy initiatives in the East can be better understood as stemming from military aggression and aggrandisement rather than from any economic motives.[4] While emphasising this view of imperial policy, however, scant attention has been paid to the political influence of the trade at a lower level: that is, in the communities of the Roman East itself. Some work, indeed, has been done on the significance and political effect of the trade on the Nabataean kingdom and Palmyra,[5] but this has generally been done against the background of the proactive view of Roman policy toward the trade. Even in the absence of any 'trade policy' from the imperial or provincial governments, however, we might expect to see local authorities acting to exploit and encourage the commerce through their own communities.

Accordingly, in the course of this work it is proposed to study closely the various routes and communities involved in the commerce, and the commodities in which the trade was carried on. This book will examine each individual area in which the eastern trade was active. First, the effect of the commerce on the actions of the Roman government will be examined, whether such actions come from the emperor, provincial governors or local authorities. After this, the significance of the trade to the relevant local communities will be examined by a study of the things which can be discovered about the people involved in the commerce, and the way in which local authorities acted toward the trade and its practitioners.

This work does not intend to be a comprehensive history of the eastern trade in the Roman East. Rather, it tries to collect and examine evidence for the existence of various trade routes coming into and passing through the Roman East, and their effect on Roman imperial policy in the area and on local political formations within the Roman eastern provinces. For the purposes of this study, the 'East' is defined as the territory covered by the provinces of Syria, Mesopotamia, Palaestina, Arabia and Egypt, as well as client kingdoms in this general area (see Map 1.1). The period of the study is roughly from the accession of Augustus in 31 BC to the abdication of Diocletian in AD 305. This period covers what we might call the 'classical' period of the Roman eastern trade, which really ended with the fall of Palmyra in AD 272. The extension of the period under study to AD 305 allows the examination of some of the effects of this fall, without going too far into the late Roman/Byzantine period, which saw a significant recovery of the trade as well as important

Map 1.1 The Roman Near East (*opposite*) – showing the approximate boundaries of Roman provinces as they were in AD 118–161, from the abandonment of Trajan's Parthian conquests to the commencement of Lucius Verus' eastern campaign.

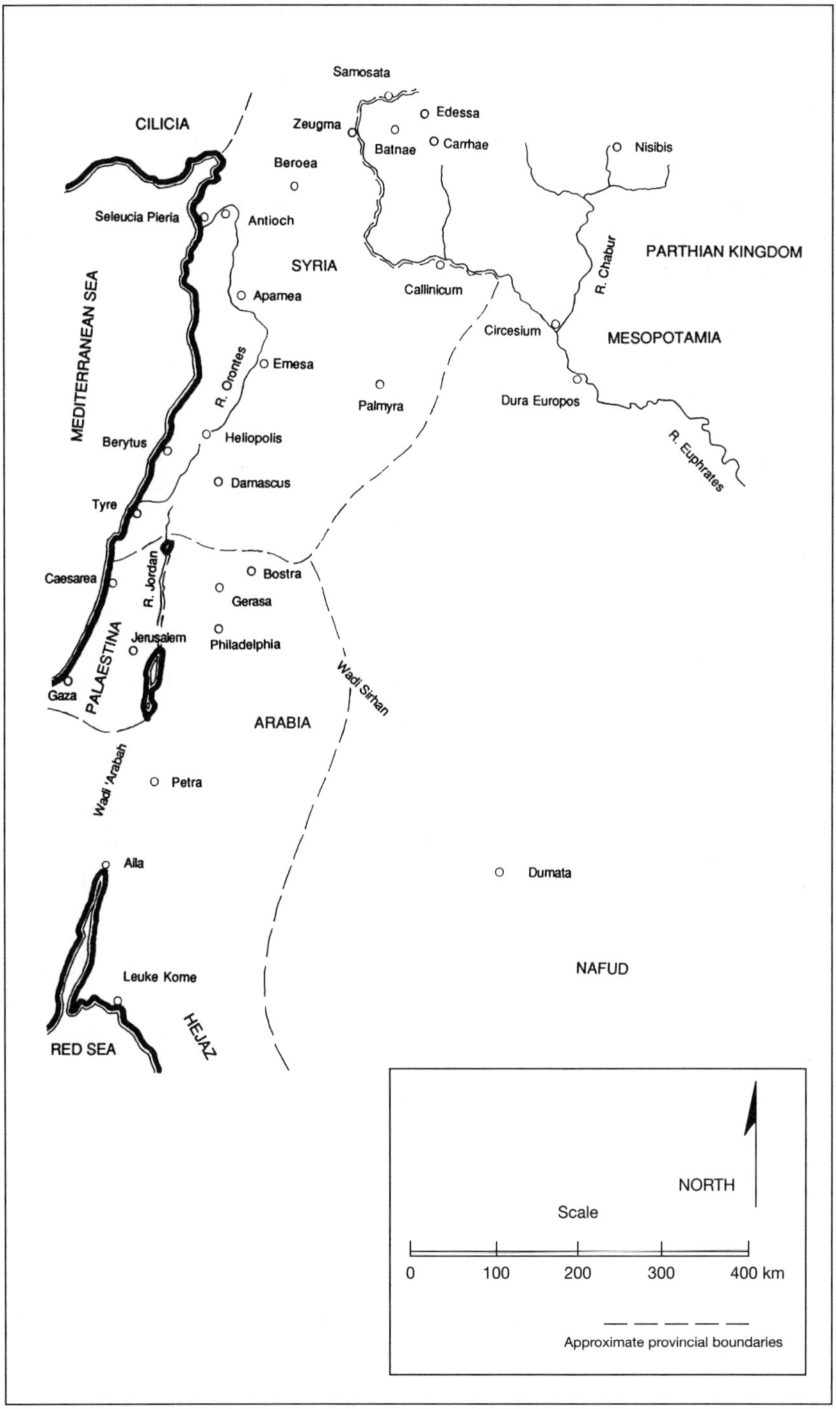
Samosata
CILICIA
Zeugma
Edessa
Batnae
Carrhae
Nisibis
Beroea
Seleucia Pieria
Antioch
SYRIA
PARTHIAN KINGDOM
R. Chabur
MEDITERRANEAN SEA
Apamea
Callinicum
Circesium
MESOPOTAMIA
R. Orontes
Emesa
Palmyra
Dura Europos
Berytus
Heliopolis
R. Euphrates
Damascus
Tyre
Caesarea
R. Jordan
Bostra
Gerasa
Jerusalem
Philadelphia
PALAESTINA
Wadi Sirhan
Gaza
ARABIA
Wadi 'Arabah
Petra
Aila
Dumata
Leuke Kome
NAFUD
HEJAZ
RED SEA
NORTH
Scale
0
100
200
300
400 km
Approximate provincial boundaries

changes in the government's treatment of it, and therefore warrants its own separate study.

In the first chapter, the Introduction, some basic background essential to the study and understanding of the trade is set out. After this general introduction, the wide variety of source material which will be used in this study is briefly surveyed, followed by an overview of the trade within the Roman Empire, concentrating on the demand for eastern goods in Rome, the types of goods which were imported, and what can be known about the volume and general conduct of the trade within the empire.

Chapter 2 focuses on one of the best attested areas of the trade, Roman Egypt. First, the types and sources of the various goods of the Red Sea trade are studied, followed by an examination of the manner in which the trade goods were conveyed from the Red Sea coast through Egypt and then into Alexandria, before their shipment to the markets of the empire. After this, the various participants in the Egyptian trade are examined, both private individuals and government officials, and a likely motivation for the involvement of the Roman government in the trade is presented. Finally, changes which occurred to the trade over the course of the period under study are documented, and a series of conclusions about the trade in Egypt reached.

The same general outline is followed in Chapter 3, the study of the trade in Roman and pre-Roman Arabia. In this chapter, however, the study will be divided into two broad sections: that which deals with the trade in the Nabataean kingdom, and that which deals with the commerce in the Roman province of Arabia, which succeeded the Nabataean realm in AD 106. Particular emphasis will be given to ideas of a deliberate Roman weakening of the Nabataean kingdom and their relevance to Roman government policy with respect to the trade. Possible motives for the Roman annexation of the kingdom and the considerable military buildup which took place along the Arabian frontier after the Roman takeover will be considered.

A similar outline is once again followed in Chapter 4, which is devoted to the study of the commerce of Palmyra. Special attention, however, is given to the high degree of importance that the trade held in Palmyra and to some of the effects which the commerce may have had on Palmyra's political organisation and society. While much of the information which we have dealing with the eastern trade in Syria comes from Palmyra, it is clear that some commerce passed through northern Syria and along the Euphrates river as well, bypassing Palmyra altogether. These routes form the subject matter of Chapter 5, which gives special attention to the matter of Roman relations with Parthia and the question of whether or not the eastern trade had any influence on these relations.

Having then examined the eastern trade in all the major areas, Chapter 6 turns to an investigation of the imperial attitude toward the commerce, drawing on fresh evidence as well as that which has been covered in the regional studies. Attention is given to possible influences on the government attitude to the commerce, including on the one hand the Roman attitude toward *luxuria* and *mollitia*, two vices which the Romans saw as related to the use of luxury goods, and on the other hand the significant tax revenues which the government was able to extract from the commerce. Chapter 7 then forms a conclusion to the whole study, focusing on the nature of the trade, the effects of the trade on the imperial government and its policy in the East, and finally on the trade's significance to political formations in the communities of the Roman East.

The Appendices mostly provide greater information on topics noted in the text. Appendix A lists prices for various commodities in the trade as listed in Pliny the Elder's *Historia Naturalis*, and a brief comparison of these prices with the prices of staples and regular wages to give some idea of the relative expense of the items. Appendix B deals with the silver content of Nabataean coins, which is relevant to the question of whether or not the Nabataean kingdom experienced an economic slump in the first century AD, and whether or not this was related to the trade passing through the kingdom. Charts of Roman currencies over the same period are provided for comparison. Appendix C deals with those inscriptions which mention an independent Palmyrene military organisation in the years prior to the Palmyrene rebellion against Rome in the third century, while Appendix D describes the changes in Palmyra's political situation from AD 251 to AD 267.

A note on the sources

The study of the long-distance trade of the Roman East cannot depend on only one or two historical sources, but must take into account a wide variety of literary, archaeological, epigraphic and other material. Indeed, there is no one pre-eminent source to which we can turn in this study. Instead, we are forced to rely on more or less peripheral comments in works devoted to other subjects: only in two cases, the *Periplus Maris Erythraei* and the Palmyrene corpus of caravan inscriptions, could we truly say that we have a primary source actually devoted to the subject in hand. Nonetheless, there is a wide variety of works which touch on the topic from time to time, although the scattered and diverse nature of the evidence warrants some caution.

Literary sources

As already mentioned, the *Periplus Maris Erythraei* is the only literary source which has the spice and silk trades as its primary subject. As a result, this merchant's handbook for the Egyptian Red Sea trade is invaluable, providing not only copious information on the trade routes and ports of call in India, Africa and Arabia which Egyptian based ships used, but also lists of goods traded at each port. The very nature of this book also inspires confidence in the truth of its accounts: it is a workmanlike, practical manual for the merchant of the Red Sea trade, never intended as a work of literature, and thus we may reasonably expect the accounts it provides to be accurate.[6]

This view of the *Periplus* is strengthened still further when an examination is made to see what can be learned about its author. Although the writer does not name himself, the *Periplus* is apparently the work of a merchant with considerable first-hand experience of the trade, as is shown at several points in the text.[7] By his references to Egyptian months and, at one point, his mention of 'the trees we have in Egypt',[8] it is evident that he must have been a Greek-speaking resident of Egypt.[9] It is clear then that his work was intended as a guide for other merchants like himself who intended to be involved in the Red Sea trade. Accordingly, the information it provides can probably be relied upon to reflect at least the view of the trade that an Egyptian merchant would have held at the time. In the absence of strong evidence to the contrary, it would seem reasonable to accept the *Periplus*' accounts and descriptions at face value. Although its emphasis is on the Egyptian trade, it can also provide some interesting insights into the trade in Arabia and further afield.

There has, however, been a long-standing dispute over the date of composition of the work, which has some potential impact upon its reliability. Most scholars date the work to the middle of the first century, which would make it a primary source of great importance, as this was the time at which the Red Sea trade seems to have peaked. Others, however, have contended that the work dates from the third century, and is consequently of lesser importance in any study of the trade.[10] The date would actually appear to be settled by a comment within the *Periplus* itself, which refers to a king at Petra named Malichus.[11] As Nabataean chronology is now well established, we can be sure that Malchus II reigned in Petra AD 40–70, and therefore we can date the *Periplus* to the same period.[12] Similarly, the *Periplus*' reference to 'Charibael, king of the Homerites and Sabaeans'[13] has been identified as a Hellenised reference to the king Karib'il Watar Yuhan'im I, king of Saba and dhu-Raydan, who reigned in the first century AD and probably before AD 70.[14] Some, however, would still try to put forward a later date, although their arguments have been effectively refuted by Dihle.[15] On the whole, it seems eminently reasonable to allot the *Periplus* to the middle of the first century AD, and consequently to regard it as a first-hand source of pre-eminent importance for the study of the Egyptian Red Sea trade.

Other literary sources are more peripheral to the subject, but still often make useful references to the eastern long-distance trade. In this category the ancient geographers are of particular importance. Strabo (63 BC–AD 24) and Pliny (AD 23–79), and to a lesser extent others, record a great deal of useful information and frequently make direct reference to the eastern long-distance trade. Although their records are generally secondary and thus may well be somewhat distorted, this is not always the case. Strabo, for example, provides some first-hand accounts of Roman Egypt and a generally reliable account of the expedition of Aelius Gallus to Arabia Felix through his friendship with

Gallus. Generally speaking, the geographers can provide useful information, although it is probably not wise to accept uncritically what they have to say unless it is confirmed by another source. Unfortunately, on many occasions we find that no such other source is available, and in the absence of any confirmatory evidence we have little choice but to accept the statements of Strabo or Pliny.

There are also some accounts of value in the works of ancient historians, most notably Diodorus Siculus and Josephus. While Diodorus, who wrote in the first century BC, deals with the period before this study, he nonetheless gives some information about the origins and early history of the Nabataean kingdom which helps in the understanding of the importance of the aromatics trade which passed through that realm. Likewise, the work of Flavius Josephus, written toward the close of the first century AD, occasionally makes reference to a point of interest that can be helpful. Nonetheless, the long-distance trade is not his primary concern and thus the information he provides is often peripheral. All of these works can be very helpful when taken as a whole: often one source can be used to fill in a blank left by the others, and by this means a reasonable picture can emerge. Similarly, later historians such as Appian and Cassius Dio occasionally provide snippets of information which can be utilised. Yet another literary source which can be of use is the work of Latin poets, many of whom make helpful references to the use of various goods of the eastern trade.

Beside these ancient literary works, there are some ancient itineraries and maps which can be of use. One which merits particular mention is the *Parthian Stations* of Isidore of Charax, an account of the late first century BC. Despite the fact that this work has been described as the record of the overland trade route through the Parthian kingdom from Antioch, along the Euphrates river, and thence over the Iranian plateau,[16] nowhere in the text itself is this stated or even implied. This account does, however, provide a list of the *stathmoi* or 'stations' along a route traversing the Parthian realm, though without specifying whether these were commercial caravanserais, military stations, or points along the royal mail route of the Achaemenid kings, all of which are possibilities. It consists basically of a list of place names along a route, with distances supplied between most of the stations (especially those along the Euphrates), and occasionally distances from the starting point (Zeugma on the Euphrates) or some other reference point. Although this work is brief, and it is unwarranted to call it an account of the trade route along the Euphrates, it nonetheless provides us with a useful record of the 'natural' route between Roman Syria and the East. Even though we cannot say that Isidore's work was written with commercial activities in mind, it is nonetheless safe to say that merchants would have made use of this route.

Literary sources are an important but limited resource for the study of the long-distance eastern trade of the Roman Empire. While there are some very valuable first-hand accounts, most notable among which must be the *Periplus*

Maris Erythraei, much of the literary material dealing with this topic is of a secondary nature. While such evidence can still be of great value, we should nonetheless for this reason approach it with some caution. Fortunately, however, there are other forms of evidence which allow us to fill out and expand on the information given by literary sources.

Papyri and ostraka

Papyri and ostraka have also provided important information on the eastern commerce. The bulk of the evidence in this category is, as one might expect, from Egypt. The preponderance of Egyptian evidence with regard to papyri and ostraka is a function of the peculiar climate and conditions of that country, which have resulted in the preservation of a great deal of perishable evidence which would have been destroyed in other places. Thus, for the Egyptian trade especially, we have what is potentially a very valuable resource of contemporary documents.

Perhaps one of the most significant archives is the collection of ostraka from Coptos in the Nile valley which has come to be known as the 'Archive of Nicanor', the records of a family engaged in the caravan trade between Coptos and the Red Sea ports.[17] Although this family does not appear to have been involved in the actual transport of eastern merchandise across the Eastern Desert, they were certainly involved in the supplying of the Red Sea ports and the imperial quarries in the region with foodstuffs and other essentials. This archive reveals important information about the supplying and maintenance of these ports, as well as about the lines of traffic and about many of the participants in the eastern trade.

Other papyrus collections have also come to light in the recent excavations of various Red Sea ports. One of the most significant of these is the collection of papyri and ostraka from the excavation of Quseir al-Qadim, published separately to the excavation reports.[18] As with the Nicanor archive discussed above, these papyri do not tend to contain specific references to the Red Sea trade, but are concerned more generally with the everyday needs of the population at Quseir al-Qadim. In addition, this collection, along with other papyri discovered in the region, provides an insight into the system used to garrison the Roman military posts in the desert.

Apart from these major collections, many other papyri from Egypt are useful in the discussion of the Red Sea trade. Some of these come from other published collections, while others have been published in isolation. Several provide extremely important information about the trade, as they deal specifically with items of the commerce, the merchants involved, and many other important matters.[19] With reference to the Egyptian Red Sea trade in particular, it would not be unreasonable to suggest that the evidence from papyri and ostraka is of great significance.

In other areas affected by the eastern trade, however, this is not the case. The volume of papyri preserved outside Egypt is far smaller, and so we simply do not have this resource available to us in such places as Syria and Arabia. Nevertheless, some peripheral information is supplied by collections of papyri which have been discovered in Judaea and at Dura Europos. While not directly dealing with the caravan trade or its participants, these nevertheless do provide useful information in some areas.

While outside Egypt the importance of papyrological evidence is somewhat limited, within Egypt its importance cannot be overestimated. In addition, the conclusions which can be reached concerning the trade in Egypt might in many cases be applied to the commerce in other regions. Though many writers continue to emphasise the 'uniqueness' of Egypt, there are, in many cases, significant parallels with the situation elsewhere in the East. Thus, not only in Egypt, but elsewhere too, the papyrological evidence for the eastern long-distance trade of the Roman Empire assumes great significance.

Inscriptions

Inscriptions have been found to be very useful in the study of the eastern long-distance trade. It is certainly true that the 'epigraphic habit' was well entrenched in the Roman East, as indeed it was in most other areas of the Roman Empire. The tendency to inscribe matters of importance to both cities and to individuals means that we might expect to find references to the eastern trade, especially in those places where the commerce was of some significance in the life of the city concerned.

Nowhere is this tendency better expressed (with respect to the eastern caravan commerce) than at Palmyra. The numerous commemorative inscriptions of this city are for the most part published in the eleven volumes of the *Inventaire des inscriptions de Palmyre*, while others are published in separate excavation reports or journal articles.[20] Most of these inscriptions are, uniquely in a city of the Roman East, in Aramaic, while those in especially prominent public places tend to be Greek-Aramaic bilinguals. A great many of them refer directly to the caravan trade of Palmyra,[21] usually commemorating the successful return of trading expeditions to the Arabian Gulf. In so doing, they provide a unique primary resource for this trade: indeed, with very few exceptions, it is the only evidence we have for the study of this particular aspect of the eastern commerce of Rome. Important details concerning the organisation of the caravans and the routes they took are revealed in the inscriptions, while other inscriptions in the corpus which do not directly mention the trade nonetheless reveal details of the way Palmyra tended to the needs of the trade in such areas as military protection. In addition, the very prominence afforded the 'caravan inscriptions', many of which are still *in situ* at important locations in the city, is itself an important testimony to the great significance of the caravan trade at Palmyra and the unique effects the trade appears to have had on the political life of that city.

By comparison with the richness of the Palmyrene archive, other collections of inscriptions pertinent to the eastern long-distance commerce must inevitably seem rather poor. Nonetheless, other inscriptions are frequently able to contribute to our understanding of this commerce and its effects. There are, for example, several epitaphs and commemorative inscriptions erected by persons involved in the trade at one point or another which give some insight into the types of people that these merchants were. While not conveying much information about the trade as such, these inscriptions can reveal valuable information about the social standing of the dedicator, as well as other information.

Particularly notable in this area are the inscriptions which have been found on the roads between the Egyptian Red Sea ports and the Nile valley.[22] While not especially detailed, these inscriptions nonetheless provide some important information about the periods during which various roads were used, and help to supply more information about individuals known from other sources, such as some of the people mentioned in the Archive of Nicanor discussed earlier. In the Red Sea area as elsewhere, especially Arabia, Roman military inscriptions can be of great value in determining the position and purpose of various Roman military postings. As will be seen throughout the course of this book, such military postings are frequently associated with the caravan trade. Another important collection of inscriptions which is often overlooked is the corpus of pre-Islamic Arabian inscriptions from the Syrian and Jordanian deserts, often referred to as the Safaitic and Thamudic inscriptions.[23] While these do not deal directly with the caravan trade, they nevertheless provide an insight into aspects of the political and social situation in Arabia during the Roman period.

It is thus very clear that epigraphic evidence must be allotted a very important place in the study of the long-distance eastern commerce of the Romans. Indeed, in the case of the trade which passed through Palmyra, such a study would be completely impossible if it were not for the evidence of the Palmyrene inscriptions. Although in other areas the epigraphic evidence might not possess the same relative importance, it nonetheless is able to provide illuminating evidence concerning many aspects of the trade, and the institutions of the Roman East which were significant to the trade.

Archaeology

The nature of the eastern long-distance trade means that in many cases there are few physical remains which can be studied in order to learn more about the commerce. Nonetheless, in several cases archaeological work has been of considerable use in this study, in the form of both field studies and intensive excavations. The increasingly important role of archaeological data in modern historical inquiry is amply illustrated by a study such as this, where a wide variety of sources must be employed in the absence of any authoritative work on the subject from the ancient world. Data from archaeological explorations can be used to supplement written records when they are present, and often to provide information where no other evidence is available.

Field surveys have been useful in providing information in several areas of this study. One significant example is the case of the Roman military sites in the Arabian desert, which for the most part have not been excavated but have received attention from surface sherding, field surveying and other techniques. This has been most helpful in understanding the nature of the Roman military presence in this region, a factor which is itself related to the significance of the spice trade in the area. Similar surveys have been carried out on the roads between the Nile river and the Egyptian Red Sea coast. The information gleaned from this work has been very useful in studying the amount of military investment the Romans were prepared to make in protecting the caravan traffic.[24] Thus, surface surveys have been of great help in certain areas of the study, particularly those areas where the Roman army was involved in some way in the caravan traffic.

However, we need to sound a note of caution when dealing with the results of surface surveys. Often, the impressions gained by such surveys can be overturned when intensive investigations of the same area are carried out. In one example pertinent to this work, the date of some forts and roads in the Negev had to be revised after excavation, as the excavation showed the forts to have been occupied at times the initial surface survey had indicated they were abandoned. This, as will be seen, had significant ramifications for the study of the aromatics trade passing through Petra.[25] Nonetheless, in the absence of any intensive excavation or other dating criteria in most other cases we would seem to have little choice but to accept the dates provided by the surveys, unless there is a compelling reason to reject them.

Excavation of various sites concerned with the spice trade has with few exceptions yielded little information except in recent years, most probably due to the limited remains such a trade would leave behind, coupled with the extensive amount of 'background noise' in a large ancient site. Thus, even if there were physical remains of the long-distance eastern trade in major cities of the Roman East, it may very well be impossible to distinguish them from the artefacts of general trade and commerce in the city. Thus, excavations of such sites as Petra, Palmyra, Alexandria and others, though these places were heavily involved in the eastern trade, have yielded comparatively little information on it.

This problem, however, has been overcome to some extent in recent excavations of sites primarily involved with the Red Sea trade. Several sites on the Egyptian Red Sea coast, such as 'Abu Sha'ar, Quseir al-Qadim and Berenike, have been excavated in recent years,[26] and the information gained in these excavations has been very useful in the study of the Red Sea trade (see Map 1.2). In these sites, the problem of 'background noise' is far less severe, as the long-distance trade appears to have been a primary occupation of these communities. Thus, artefacts concerned with the trade are far more easily identifiable, and their lessons can be learned far more readily. Due to the recent

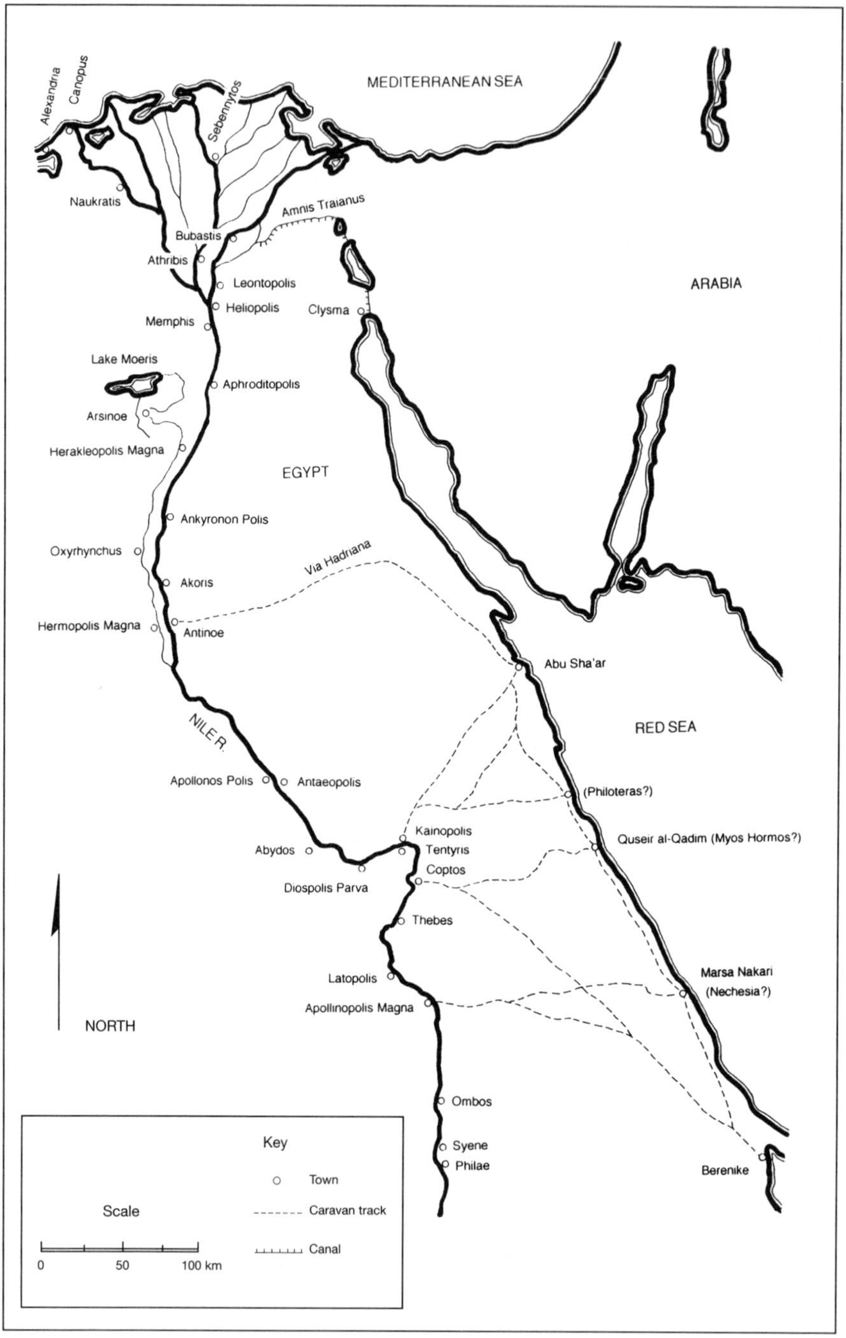

Map 1.2 Roman Egypt

date of these excavations, we are still forced to rely on preliminary reports as the final reports are still in preparation and in some cases cannot be expected for many years. Nonetheless, the excavation of these sites, together with some information which has been gained from other excavations in the area, add a great deal to our understanding of the eastern long-distance trade.

Thus it can be seen that archaeology has been a vital source of information in the investigation of the eastern long-distance trade of the Roman Empire. Both field surveys and excavations have provided illuminating evidence for this study, and it is felt that this provides a good example of the potential role of archaeology in future historical undertakings. This is particularly the case in studies such as this one, where the available evidence is so widely scattered, and it is usually desirable to have some confirmation of a statement in an ancient source before we accept it. Archaeology can, in many cases, provide just such a confirmation. In addition, archaeological information can often stand on its own, although, as with all other sources, it is preferable to have another source to confirm and to contextualise the archaeological data. All things considered, however, archaeology has been of great help in conducting this study, and it would be clearly most unwise to omit it from the preparation of any similar work.

Summary of the evidence

Some points are worthy of note in conclusion. One which will probably not have escaped the reader's notice is the preponderance of Egyptian evidence. With the exception of the Palmyrene inscriptional corpus, the majority of the significant sources of information are found within Egypt, and it is possible that this may lead to an unwarranted bias toward the Egyptian trade in the study. While we must certainly remain alert to this possibility, there is really very little which can be done about it. From time to time it may be possible to apply conclusions reached from Egyptian evidence to other areas of the trade, and when this is possible it will be done. Nonetheless, for the most part we must simply accept that our study will be necessarily weighted toward those areas where a larger volume of evidence is available. We must, however, always remember that a preponderance of surviving evidence in one area does not necessarily translate to a greater significance of that area in the ancient world.

It is abundantly clear that the study of the eastern long-distance trade is dependent upon a wide variety of sources. What is equally clear, however, is the fact that no single source of information is sufficient to supply all the evidence for this study. Rather, it has been necessary to collate evidence from a number of sources in order to explore virtually any aspect of the trade. However, much as we might wish for more comprehensive information, it is felt that this wide evidential base is a strength, not a weakness of this study. Rather than try to concentrate upon one source of information, simply using others to 'fill the gaps' where necessary, it is unapologetically proposed to adopt a holistic approach in this work, in which many sources of information are used in arriving at such conclusions as are possible. Indeed, this would seem to offer the historian wider avenues of opportunity for the investigation of his or her subject, although necessarily complicating the task somewhat. In the case of this study in particular, such an approach is the only one which promises a profitable result, given the scattered and varied nature of the sources. It is felt that this methodology will allow positive and significant results from what at the first sight might seem to be a confusing and limited pool of available evidence.

Items of the eastern commerce

It is not proposed in the course of this book to undertake a systematic survey of the origins of the various items of the eastern trade, as the respective provenances of the goods presumably had little consequence upon the political significance of the commerce. Nor indeed is it intended to attempt to catalogue all the items of the trade. Such surveys do exist, and they have shown that the majority at least of these items can be identified with reasonable accuracy.[27] As far as this study is concerned, however, the items of the trade are of significance only when first received by Roman traders, and these points will be explored in the chapters relating to the trade in various areas of the empire.

The trade in silks, spices and other such goods of the eastern commerce could never of course have arisen if there had been no demand for such goods in the Roman Empire. Frequently this commerce is described as a trade in luxuries, arising out of 'decadent' tastes and desires, especially at the height of Roman power and wealth under the empire.[28] However, we should be careful about applying such terms as 'luxury goods' indiscriminately to these items, or assigning the demand for them wholly to a Roman taste for *luxuria*. In an examination of the references to these goods as they were used in Rome, it will soon be found that there is no readily available category to which we might assign them. Some goods were indeed luxury goods, but on many occasions these commodities and others had medicinal or religious applications. Therefore, as will be seen, it is incorrect to call Rome's long-distance trade with the East a 'luxury' trade, as items of a religious nature for example would certainly not have been regarded as luxury items by the Romans, expensive though they might be. Rather, we should examine the different ways in which the various goods were used at Rome, and try to determine what conclusions can be drawn from this information regarding the market for such merchandise.

Genuine luxury goods

There were, nonetheless, several items which the eastern trade brought to Rome solely to appeal to the Roman taste for luxury goods. Although we must be careful about the moralising stance taken by many Roman writers, it is still not unfair to suggest that the upper echelons of Roman society had a pronounced taste for various luxury items. *Luxuria* was a vice against which writers from the republican period on had railed, with apparently little effect. There seems to have been a steady market for luxury goods from relatively early in the republican period, and it is during this period that the first literary complaints about eastern luxuries and corrupt 'luxurious' living are found.[29] Despite the lack of easy communication with this region during the republican period, many of these goods came from the East. However, judging by the literary references there appears to have been a dramatic increase in the availability of eastern goods early in the Augustan period, no doubt due to the recent Roman subjugation of the Eastern Mediterranean and the newly established peace which allowed the merchants free access to the markets of Rome. For example, such goods are frequently mentioned in the poems of Propertius and Ovid.[30] Of course, there is significant debate as to the 'reality' of the world described by the Latin erotic poets;[31] by itself, this poetry could not be taken to indicate a significant demand for luxury goods at Rome. However, by the very fact that these items can be named with reasonable expectation that the reader will understand the reference, these poems certainly *do* show a certain degree of familiarity with the goods among the readership of the works.

Such references show that such goods were well known and used in this period, and that in many cases their uses were unashamedly for the pursuit of *luxuria*. Some of the goods, for example, consisted of items for the production of clothing and adornment. In this category are found silks, decorated cotton, pearls and various gemstones, as well as other decorative materials such as shells, tortoiseshell, coral and ivory. Other items which can be identified from the ancient writers were used chiefly as perfumes and unguents, including nard and aloe. A further category which can be identified under this heading is that of culinary items, such as pepper, cinnamon, cassia and others, most of which could also be used in the manufacture of perfumes, ointments and unguents. Also a part of the commerce, although presumably in far smaller quantities, were such exotic items as tigers and ostriches.

All of these items, of course, had to be brought at great expense over long and difficult trade routes, and were priced accordingly by the time they reached the consumer in the Roman Empire. Although prices are very difficult to determine in many cases, and no doubt varied from time to time, we can nevertheless gain a general knowledge of the kind of prices paid for these goods. Pliny gives some prices which were presumably those current at Rome in his time: for example, he quotes prices of between 4 and 15 *denarii* per pound for various types of pepper,[32] 40–75 *denarii* per pound for nard leaves,[33] and 300 *denarii* per pound for a trader's grade of cinnamon.[34]

It is thus quite clear from these figures that the luxury goods traded at Rome could be quite expensive, and were presumably regularly consumed only by the richer members of society. Such prices were not, however, prohibitive: they would have been low enough to allow most of the wealthier classes of Romans to use these goods. Indeed, given the fact that most people would have used only small portions of such valuable spices, even those of lower economic status may have made use of them occasionally. Expensive though they were, they were not so expensive as to make them the exclusive preserve of the very rich: probably a reasonable cross-section of Roman society would have been able to make use of at least some of these goods.[35]

Goods of a religious nature

Although the Arabian aromatics such as frankincense and myrrh are often taken with the goods described in the previous section as 'luxury goods', one should in fact be careful to make a distinction in the case of these incenses. While there is no doubt that they were expensive (as will be seen), the importance of incense in religious observance means that we must consider the Arabian aromatics a category entirely separate to the luxury items described in the previous section. A wide range of Roman and other literary references show clearly that frankincense and myrrh were predominantly considered to be items of religious significance rather than luxury goods.[36] These incenses had been burned in honour of the gods at temples and at funerals for centuries, both in Roman religious practice as well as in Hellenistic and Near Eastern cults.[37]

Despite this, the use of incense at funerals was not immune to excess: the commerce in Arabian incense certainly seems to have been enhanced by society's tendency to *luxuria* in the imperial period. Pliny describes this excess in the use of funerary incenses, implying that much more of the incense was in fact used in funerals than was used in other religious rituals, and that the volume of incense so used had more to do with extravagance than it did with religious necessity:

> beatam illam fecit hominum etiam in morte luxuria quae dis intel-lexerant genita inurentium defunctis. periti rerum adseuerant non ferre tantum annuo fetu quantum Nero princeps nouissimo Poppaeae suae die concremauerit. aestimentur postea toto orbe singulis annis tot funera, aceruatimque congesta honori cadauerum quae dis per singulas micas dantur!
>
> The luxury of men even in death makes it (sc. Arabia) fortunate, in burning to the dead the things which they understood were made for the gods. Good authorities state that Arabia does not produce as much in a year as the Emperor Nero burnt for his consort Poppaea in a day. After that, let the number of funerals throughout the whole world in one year be reckoned, and that which is piled up in heaps to the honour of corpses, but given to the gods in single grains![38]

The trade in Arabian incenses cannot therefore be entirely divorced from the luxury trade, as Pliny in the above quote specifically cites the tendency to use excessive amounts of incense at funerals as a case of *luxuria*.[39] Nonetheless, it should be noted that Pliny decries only the extravagance with which the incenses were burned, not the validity of the practice of burning them to the gods or (presumably in lesser quantities) at funerals.

Access to these incenses would have been generally confined to the wealthier strata of Roman society, but again they were not so prohibitively priced as to prevent some use by the less well off. Pliny records prices for both frankincense and myrrh: frankincense was sold at between 3 and 6 *denarii* per pound, depending on the grade, while myrrh fetched between 12 and 16.5.[40] Thus, while these prices were not as expensive as many of the luxury commodities outlined previously, they were still reasonably high. Especially when the large quantities implied by Pliny are taken into account, the market at Rome for Arabian incenses such as frankincense and myrrh must have been a lucrative and sizeable one.

Goods used for medicinal purposes

As well as luxury goods and goods which were used for religious purposes, abundant literary evidence points to the use of items of the eastern trade in the manufacture of medicines.[41] One of the most comprehensive of the ancient treatises which deal with the medicinal uses of various items of the eastern trade was the *De Materia Medica* of Dioscorides, which dates from approximately AD 65. In the course of this work, Dioscorides describes the use of several Arabian and Indian spices, either on their own or as an ingredient in a compound medicine, for the treatment of assorted ailments. Some of these included myrrh and oil of myrrh, cinnamon and cassia, nard, malabathron and several others,[42] all of which were commodities of the eastern trade.

These goods were especially prized for their perceived properties as antidotes to poison, which made them useful for cleansing wounds, defeating infections and as a preventative against poisoning.[43] Indeed, eastern spices were major ingredients in Crateuas' famous antidote which he administered to King Mithridates of Pontus to prevent poisoning,[44] and which was said to have been so effective that when Mithridates actually wanted to poison himself to prevent capture he was unable to do so. Similarly, Theophrastus noted the power of pepper as an antidote.[45] While it is not the place of this work to comment on whether or not these remedies actually are medically effective, it is quite clear that they were regarded as being so in the Roman world. Thus, it seems that the medicinal properties of these goods would have made some contribution to the demand for goods of the eastern trade in the Roman and Hellenistic worlds. While it is impossible to tell what proportion of these goods might have been used for medicinal rather than 'luxury' purposes, the existence of a medicinal demand over and above the demand for these goods purely as luxuries must affect the common view of the trade as a 'luxury' commerce.

Also worthy of note is the fact that the items which were used for medicinal purposes were not necessarily specifically imported for that purpose. In many cases the items used in the manufacture of medicines were the same as those used for religious purposes or used in the manufacture of perfumes and other luxury items. It is thus, as has already been noted, not possible to divide the goods sharply between their categories of use: myrrh, for example, was used as an ingredient in perfume, an incense burnt at funerals and in honour of the gods, and as an ingredient in medicines.

Thus, the term 'luxury trade' is not a useful one when dealing with Rome's long-distance eastern commerce. The items could be put to many purposes, but they had in common the fact that they were easily transportable and the object of a considerable demand, which made it worthwhile to ship them such vast distances. Without such a demand, the trade as we know it from Roman times would never have been possible. Moreover, the relatively high prices recorded by Pliny for some of these items show clearly that even in the Flavian period, after the trade had been strongly established for many decades, the demand and market for such goods were still very strong. This demand indicates that, regardless of the route taken by a trader or the amount of tax he had to pay, he could be assured of a good price for his wares in Rome.

An overview of the trade in the reign of Augustus

While it is true that the trade in aromatics, spices and other such goods was particularly prominent during the Roman period, it nonetheless had existed long before the Romans came on the scene. Many ancient societies of the East participated in the trade, and commodities such as frankincense, myrrh and cinnamon were known and valued many centuries before Roman traders became acquainted with them. Thus, when the Romans finally took complete control of the Eastern Mediterranean region after 31 BC with the surrender of Ptolemaic Egypt, they acquired territories in which the long-distance trade with the East was already well established.

The routes of the south

For the greater part of the first century BC, long-distance trade into what became the Roman East was largely confined to the southern region, as the political situation in the north prevented much traffic along the Euphrates route. The rivalry between the Parthian state and the Seleucid realm, followed by the political disintegration of Syria in the early first century BC, had made the Euphrates region a dangerous place. As a result trade, or at least that for which we have physical and literary evidence, had tended to pass through the relatively stable Ptolemaic and Nabataean realms to the south.[46]

These kingdoms exploited this situation to their advantage and gained considerable income from the proceeds of the trade. The commerce through the Nabataean kingdom seems, as far as can be discerned from the literary evidence, to have dealt only in aromatics from southern Arabia. In the first century BC Diodorus Siculus mentions that the Nabataeans became wealthy due to their trade in Arabian incense,[47] and there is no indication from any source that they were involved in such commerce as that in silk or Indian spices. It is important to bear this in mind, because it has sometimes mistakenly been assumed that overland trade from southern Arabia existed in competition with that along the Euphrates.[48] In fact, the Arabian incense, which originates in southern Arabia, could not have been bought along the northerly route, as a quick glance at the map will reveal.[49] A clear distinction must be made at the outset between the trade in Arabian incense, which originated in southern Arabia and travelled either overland through the Arabian peninsula or by sea to Egypt, and the trade in Indian spices and in silk, which passed either overland up the Euphrates route or by sea from India to Egypt.

Before the arrival of the Romans, the Ptolemies had begun to exploit the trade with both India and Arabia by the construction of ports along their Red Sea coast. The sea trade was well established by the end of the Hellenistic period,[50] but Strabo indicates that the volume of the commerce was not anywhere near as large as after the Roman takeover.[51] The trade with both the Arabian peninsula and with India was greatly facilitated by the discovery of the use of the monsoon winds, which enabled the ships trading with India to travel there directly instead of being forced to make a long and dangerous coasting voyage. Prior to this, it appears that few ships made the trip directly, the cargo that did make the journey being transhipped from Indian and Arab ships at one of the southern Arabian ports. The *Periplus Maris Erythraei* mentions a time when there were no direct sailings from Egypt to India, but all cargo was transhipped at Eudaimon Arabia (Aden):

> Εὐδαίμων Ἀραβία, εὐδαίμων δὲ ἐπεκλήθη, πρότερον οὖσα πόλις, ὅτε, μήπω ἀπὸ τῆς Ἰνδικῆς εἰς τὴν Αἴγυπτον ἐρχομένων μηδὲ ἀπὸ Αἰγύπτου τολμώντων εἰς τοὺς ἔσω τόπους διαίρειν ἀλλ' ἄχρι ταύτης παραγινομένων, τοὺς παρὰ ἀμφοτέρων φόρτους ἀπεδέχετο, ὥσπερ Ἀλεξάνδρεια καὶ τῶν ἔξωθεν καὶ τῶν ἀπὸ τῆς Αἰγύπτου φερομένων ἀποδέχεται.
>
> Eudaimon Arabia was called 'fortunate', being once a city, when, because ships neither came from India to Egypt nor did those from Egypt dare to go further but only came as far as this place, it received the cargoes from both, just as Alexandria receives goods brought from outside and from Egypt.[52]

After the discovery of the monsoon by Greek seamen, Mediterranean ships made the sailing directly, and south Arabia's role in the trade between Egypt and India was reduced to that of a watering point.[53] However, Arabia's most lucrative trade, that of myrrh and frankincense, was unaffected by this development as these commodities were cultivated within Arabia itself. Thus, there is no reason to believe that the wealth of the southern Arabian kingdoms was dramatically affected by the discovery of the monsoon. The date of the monsoon's first use by Greek sailors has been much disputed,[54] but its use was clearly well established by the time of the writing of the *Periplus*. In addition, Strabo's mention of a vastly increased trade between Egypt and India after the Roman annexation of Egypt would certainly seem to indicate that the monsoon was known and used in his time.

There has arisen a notion among some scholars that there existed before the Greek exploitation of the monsoon some sort of South Arabian 'thalassocracy'. Such views state that the Arabians, exploiting their knowledge of the monsoon, grew wealthy from Indian trade, which they jealously kept to themselves by concealing the use of the monsoon from western seamen.[55] The evidence put forward for this theory consists of items of alleged western provenance found in India and the Far East dating from times before the known exploitation of the monsoons by the Greeks. It is concluded from this that the items must have been carried by Arab ships exploiting the monsoon. These items, however, are all spurious or else their presence is capable of far simpler explanation.[56] Indeed, even if the items do in fact date from this time they are not proof of Arab use of the monsoons: they could have been carried there by the earlier coasting trade mentioned in the *Periplus* and not necessarily by ships using the monsoons at all.

Another argument which is occasionally put forward to support this theory is the fact that cinnamon, which today comes from the Far East, is mentioned in western sources earlier than any Greek contact with India. This is then taken as proof that the Arabs must have been carrying this commodity to the West well before the Greeks could have been.[57] However, it should be noted that all ancient literary sources state that cinnamon was a product of Arabia or Somalia,[58] and thus the most likely explanation is that the spice known as cinnamon in ancient times was not the same commodity as the Asian product we know as cinnamon today.[59] Even if the ancient cinnamon *did* come from the Far East, of course, there still remains the possibility that it was transported by a limited coasting trade: it is still no proof of a Sabaean 'thalassocracy' or even a monopoly on the eastern trade before the Greek discovery of the monsoon winds.[60] Clearly, there is no proof of a great south Arabian maritime hegemony in the years prior to the Greek exploitation of the monsoons.

Indeed, the *Periplus*, by contrast, shows the kingdoms of southern Arabia enjoying a high degree of wealth and influence *in the first century AD*, with their ports busy and full of traders:[61] this situation most probably arose because of the Roman trade in incense with these regions. These kingdoms are described as having possessions on the coast of Africa and in the islands of the Red Sea. Thus Azania, the east coast of Africa from Oponê to Rhapta, was under the rule of the king of the Himyarites and Sabaeans,[62] while Dioscurides (the island of

Socotra) was ruled by the king of the Frankincense-bearing Land (Hadramaut).[63] Thus, to the extent that there ever was a southern Arabian 'thalassocracy', it would appear to have been alive and well in the first century AD.

This would also appear to be confirmed by the archaeological investigation of the area. Excavations at the southern Arabian ports of Kanê (modern Qana) and Moscha Limen (Sumhuram) have revealed that these ports were both developed in the early part of the first century AD.[64] This would appear to indicate an *expanding* maritime trade in Arabia at this time, not one in decline. The view that Arabia suffered as a result of the Roman direct trade with India is clearly not supported by either the picture of this region found in the *Periplus* or the archaeological record.

The routes of the north

While, as has been discussed, most of the 'international' trade that was undertaken at the time of Augustus' accession went by what Rey-Coquais describes as the 'routes of the South',[65] there is evidence that the more northerly routes along the Euphrates were at least known, even if the political situation precluded their use to any great extent. These routes were, according to Strabo, fraught with great difficulties for the traveller because of the exactions of nomadic chieftains along the route, who had perhaps gained in ascendancy after the Seleucids lost control of this area.[66] He stated that for this reason merchants tended to risk a journey into the desert rather than to travel along the river:

> διαβάντων γὰρ ἡ ὁδός ἐστι διὰ τῆς ἐρήμου μέχρι Σκηνῶν, ἀξιολόγου πόλεως ἐπὶ τοὺς τῆς Βαβυλωνίας ὅρους ἐπί τινος διώρυγος ἱδρυμένης. ἔστι δ' ἀπὸ τῆς διαβάσεως μέχρι Σκηνῶν ἡμερῶν πέντε καὶ εἴκοσιν ὁδός. καμηλῖται δ' εἰσι, καταγωγὰς ἔχοντες τοτὲ μὲν ὑδρείων εὐπόρους, τῶν λακκαίων τὸ πλέον, τοτὲ δ' ἐπακτοῖς χρώμενοι τοῖς ὕδασι. παρέχουσι δ' αὐτοῖς οἱ Σκηνῖται τήν τε εἰρήνην καὶ τὴν μετριότητα τῆς τῶν τελῶν πράξεως, ἧς χάριν φεύγοντες τὴν παραποταμίαν διὰ τῆς ἐρήμου παραβάλλονται, καταλιπόντες ἐν δεξιᾷ τὸν ποταμὸν ἡμερῶν σχεδόν τι τριῶν ὁδόν.

> For after the river-crossing the road is through the desert to Scenae, an important city on a canal near the boundaries of Babylon. From the river-crossing to Scenae it is a journey of twenty-five days. There are camel drivers on the road who maintain caravanserais, some well supplied with water, mostly with cisterns, and some where they use water brought in from other areas. The Scenitae are peaceful and moderate in their levying of tolls, for which reason travellers avoid the country by the river and strike out through the desert, leaving the river on the right for a journey of about three days.[67]

Thus, Strabo gives evidence for the use of this route by merchants (those paying the tolls are called 'merchants' a few lines later) in the mid-first century BC.[68] This route appears, according to Strabo's description, to have crossed the Euphrates and then passed through the desert between the Tigris and Euphrates until Babylonia was reached.

Whether this abandonment of the Euphrates route was long-term or merely temporary is difficult to say. The route down the Euphrates was certainly in use, and is described by Isidore of Charax in his *Parthian Stations*. While it is possible that Isidore may have gained much of his information from merchants who used the route,[69] the route is nevertheless not explicitly described as a commercial one. It may be that, even in Isidore's time and later, merchants sometimes preferred to use the route between the Tigris and Euphrates, avoiding the expensive exactions to be found along the Euphrates.[70] It was no doubt the case that following the Euphrates removed much of the need for caravanserais and watering points, but it may still be that the presence of towns and military establishments, particularly in time of war, made the strategically important Euphrates route too expensive and dangerous for commercial purposes. However, it has to be said that the Euphrates route would be the most natural for anyone wanting to traverse this region, and if it were at all possible this would be the route that the traveller would choose. The route described by Strabo would probably be used only when necessity demanded it,[71] such as during the time of the disintegration of the Seleucid kingdom.

The route which later came into such prominence, that which crossed the Syrian desert via the oasis of Palmyra and thence to the Euphrates, seems unknown to both Strabo and Isidore,[72] and so it is possible that it did not yet have its later prominence. Appian, however, mentions the existence of Palmyra in 41 BC in describing an attack by Mark Antony upon that city. In this account, Appian mentions that the Palmyrenes were merchants involved in carrying goods from within the Parthian realm to Rome:

> ἔμποροι γὰρ ὄντες κομίζουσι μὲν ἐκ Περσῶν τὰ Ἰνδικὰ ἢ Ἀράβια, διατίθενται δ' ἐν τῇ Ῥωμαίων.
>
> For being merchants they carry Indian and Arabian goods from Persia and sell them in the lands of the Romans.[73]

The Palmyrenes had evidently already begun their mercantile activities which were to lead them to such wealth in the centuries to come. Moreover in this, the only literary reference to Palmyra's role as a trading centre, we find one of the few clues to the nature of the goods being carried: they were Indian and Arabian goods which were brought from within Persia. Whatever evidence there may be for a 'Silk Road' and a coherent trade in silks with China at a later date (which will be discussed), there is certainly none for the first century BC. The goods being carried through Palmyra, and thus most likely along the Euphrates route and Strabo's route as well, were Indian and Arabian goods, most probably spices and aromatics. Moreover, it is clear that these goods were being carried from Persia, that is from within the Parthian realm. This trade was thus not in any kind of competition with that passing through the Nabataean kingdom, which as we have seen was derived from southern Arabia.

The trade in eastern goods within the Roman Empire

The transportation of raw goods into the empire is of course only one part of the story. Once the goods had entered Roman territory, a process of manufacture, reprocessing and resale took place before the goods reached their intended market. The evidence seems to indicate that there was a large group of merchants engaged in the purchase of goods coming into the eastern part of the empire and in the subsequent reprocessing of the goods and eventual sale to the consumer.

Many of the imports into the Roman East consisted of raw, unfinished items. Generally, however, the goods were not sold to the consumer in this form. There is, for example, evidence of a considerable reprocessing industry in Roman Italy, especially in Campania. In Capua there existed an area called Selapsia, frequented by the *unguentarii* who bought, sold and manufactured perfumes:[74] many of the ingredients of these perfumes no doubt came from the eastern trade. This kind of reprocessing seems to have added a considerable amount to the value of the items imported in the eastern commerce. This is demonstrated by the vast difference in price between raw silk and reprocessed silk in Diocletian's price edict, a list of maximum prices issued by the Emperor Diocletian in AD 301. Although the document is late, the difference in price is not likely to be markedly different in the earlier period.[75] It is probable that many of the goods which were finally purchased for consumption in Rome or in other markets throughout the empire had undergone some similar form of reprocessing since their arrival in the East. This is very important to bear in mind, as it implies that the bulk of money which was spent on the goods may very well have gone not to foreign traders or 'middlemen', but rather to those who traded in and reprocessed the goods within the empire itself.

Once they had undergone this processing, these goods were then conveyed to the final point of sale, which could have been anywhere throughout the whole empire. However, a great quantity of goods would no doubt have been conveyed immediately to the place where the greatest demand existed, which in the early imperial period was the city of Rome itself. These goods were especially a feature of the markets of the *Via Sacra* in the late republican and early imperial periods,[76] as several primary references attest (see Figure 1.1).[77] Although of course not all luxury goods were of eastern provenance, many of the goods sold in these stalls probably came from the East. Indeed, Dio records that the *horrea piperataria* (pepper warehouse) built by Domitian on the current

Figure 1.1 The *Via Sacra* in the Forum, Rome. This was an area associated with the sale of eastern commodities

site of the Basilica of Maxentius and Constantine was a 'storehouse of Egyptian and Arabian wares'.[78] It may well be, considering the long association of the *Via Sacra* area with the sale of luxuries, that Domitian's construction merely restored the earlier function of a market for eastern luxuries to this area after it had been appropriated by Nero for the approach to his *Domus Aurea*.[79] In any case, the presence of a substantial permanent structure largely devoted to the sale of eastern goods at Rome indicates a considerable demand and market for eastern goods at Rome, and probably also throughout the empire.

The volume of the trade

With such a proliferation of people involved in the commerce, and with such evidence as we have for a strong demand for the goods of the long-distance eastern trade, it would appear that the trade was a sizeable and profitable venture. Indeed, given the vast amount of capital that would be required to undertake a journey to the East, participation in the eastern commerce must have been very profitable, in order to justify the risk and expense involved.[80] Nevertheless, despite the general impressions which we can gain from the ancient sources concerning the relative prominence and significance of the trade, any attempt to divine precise statistics for the trade seems difficult if not impossible.

Pliny does in fact give some figures for the volume of the trade, but these figures cannot be taken as reliable. In one instance, Pliny states that the amount of money being sent out to India to pay for goods imported from that country was 50 million *sestertii* per year; in another location, he tells us that 100 million *sestertii* were expended upon all imports from India, China and Arabia.[81] On several occasions scholars have used Pliny's figures as a basis for calculating the exact volume of the trade.[82] In reality, however, these figures are difficult to use for this purpose, for they do not specify whether this was the actual amount of money which found its way to India or if it was the total retail cost of the items in Rome: no doubt two very different amounts, as we have seen.[83] In all probability the figures given by Pliny are very vague estimates, owing more to Stoic moralising on the cost of luxury than to imperial customs receipts or various other sources which have been suggested.[84]

Nonetheless, even though the figures given by Pliny do not in fact possess the precision which they seem to imply, they still give an idea of the scale of the commerce. Even though we cannot know absolute quantities, it is apparent that the eastern long-distance trade of the Roman Empire was conducted on a considerable scale, and supplied a sizeable demand for its goods among the upper classes of Roman society. Indeed, the literary sources indicate that there was a strong upsurge in the volume of the commerce almost immediately upon the Roman takeover of the whole Mediterranean basin in 31 BC. The establishment of peace after the disruption in the previous centuries appears to have had a dramatic and immediate effect on the demand for spices, aromatics and so forth.

Such an increase is seen clearly in the geographers' accounts, as well as in the Augustan poetry mentioned in the previous section. Strabo mentions the fact that the number of ships sailing to India from Egypt had increased considerably only a few years after the Roman annexation of Egypt:

> ὅτε γοῦν Γάλλος ἐπῆρχε τῆς Αἰγύπτου, συνόντες αὐτῷ καὶ συναναβάντες μέχρι Συήνης καὶ τῶν Αἰθιοπικῶν ὅρων ἱστοροῦμεν ὅτι καὶ ἑκατὸν καὶ εἴκοσι νῆες πλέοιεν ἐκ Μυὸς ὅρμου πρὸς τὴν Ἰνδικήν, πρότερον ἐπὶ τῶν Πτολεμαικῶν βασιλέων ὀλίγων παντάπασι θαρρούντων πλεῖν καὶ τὸν Ἰνδικὸν ἐμπορεύεσθαι φόρτον.
>
> When Gallus was prefect of Egypt, having accompanied him and ascended to Syene and the borders of Ethiopia, we found that even one hundred and twenty ships were sailing from Myos Hormos to India, but under the Ptolemaic kings only a very few dared to sail and to trade in Indian goods.[85]

At another point, Strabo mentions that only twenty ships (presumably these figures mean the number of ships per year) had sailed for India under the Ptolemies.[86] Moreover, it is worth noting that this increase in trade must have occurred within a very few years of the Roman takeover. Strabo mentions that he took this trip during the prefecture of Aelius Gallus, thus placing it prior to 25 BC.[87] Similarly, Pliny mentions that due to demand and increased sales a second harvest of frankincense each year had been instituted in southern Arabia.[88]

It thus seems clear that there was a great increase in the volume of trade immediately after the cessation of the Roman civil wars and the unification of the Mediterranean basin under a single government. The consequent peace and prosperity greatly increased the market for the goods. With their extant knowledge of the monsoon and the resultant greater ease and lower costs of trading with the East, the merchants of the Indian Ocean were in a position to service and exploit this new opportunity. Thus, the combination of a strong market and the means of effectively servicing that market is more than enough to explain the vigour and prosperity of the spice and incense trade under the Roman Empire.

2

THE RED SEA TRADE IN EGYPT

The Egyptian Red Sea trade is perhaps the best attested, and some might say the most significant, area of the eastern trade of the Roman Empire. The Red Sea had been used for trade even in the Pharaonic period, during which expeditions had been sent to 'Punt' (probably Somalia) and to Arabia. However, it was only, to a limited extent, in the Ptolemaic period, and then in the Roman era that the trade began to reach as far as India on a regular basis. For the Hellenistic and Roman periods, considerable literary, archaeological and papyrological evidence has come to light which allows us to form an adequate picture of the commerce. While we cannot determine the volume of trade carried, it would seem clear from the evidence available that the trade was a substantial and profitable one in Roman times. Accordingly, it is proposed to examine both the history and nature of the Egyptian Red Sea trade, coupled with studies of the participants in the commerce and some possible effects of the trade on Roman Egypt. By this means, it is hoped that we can arrive at some understanding of the broader significance of the commerce with respect to the inhabitants of Egypt, the local military and the imperial government.

Although, as we have seen, the commerce in the Red Sea underwent rapid expansion during the reigns of Augustus and his successors, the precedents for this trade were laid well before the arrival of the Romans. The Ptolemaic kings established ports on the Red Sea and built protected roads connecting them to the Nile valley, although it is likely that their interests originally lay in obtaining war elephants and gold, not in encouraging trade with India and Arabia.[1] However, the existence of these ports and roads and the high value of the goods which could be obtained in such overseas trade would certainly have encouraged entrepreneurs to make trading voyages to these places.[2] This commerce was greatly facilitated by the discovery of the use of the monsoon as discussed earlier,[3] but even with this assistance it would seem that in the absence of peace in the Mediterranean, the trade could not develop fully until the beginning of Augustus' reign.

Routes and commodities of the Red Sea trade

Unlike most other areas of Rome's trade with the East, we are fortunate with respect to the Red Sea trade in that we have an accurate, contemporary account of the commodities with which this commerce dealt, and the lines upon which these goods were conveyed.[4] The *Periplus Maris Erythraei*, written near the middle of the first century AD, records many significant details about the commerce. Other sources such as Pliny the Elder can tell us something, in addition to the contributions made by archaeology, epigraphy and papyrology. These sources reveal a rich and complex trade in goods from India, Arabia and Africa arriving at the Red Sea ports, and a significant quantity of goods as well as gold and silver bullion being exported from the Roman Empire in exchange.

The trade with India

Probably the most significant line of trade to Roman Egypt, based upon the fact that the bulk of the text of the *Periplus* is devoted to describing it, was the commerce with India (see Map 2.1). To reach India, the ships left the Red Sea ports in July in order to catch the monsoon which would convey them directly to India without the need for the long and dangerous coasting voyage.[5] The monsoon would convey the ships to India, according to modern sailing times, in about twenty days,[6] leaving plenty of time before the return trip could commence to catch the north-east monsoon: according to Pliny the ships left India for the return journey in December or January.[7]

There seems to have been a choice of two major areas to which the ships could go in India. One was to India's north-west coast, to two ports referred to in the *Periplus* as Barbarikon and Barygaza. The *Periplus* gives a record of the goods that were brought to these ports as well as the merchandise which could be obtained in them. It relates that there was a market at these ports for wine, glass, metals, coral, textiles, as well as Roman money and frankincense, which must have been picked up in Arabia during the outward journey to India. In return, traders could buy there perfumes such as bdellium and nard, precious stones of various types, ivory, cotton cloth and silk, which would have been brought there overland from China.[8] As will be seen later, the Roman merchants of Egypt were not the only traders from the West in these ports: many Palmyrene inscriptions refer to ships travelling to 'Scythia', which was the name given to this region.[9] Thus, it seems that this region was a major trading area for the Roman trade with the East by two different routes: one from Palmyra and one from Egypt. As a source of silk, especially, this region would have been extremely significant: indeed it has even been suggested that Scythia was *the* major source of silk for the Roman Empire,[10] although this would be impossible to prove given the absence of any figures for the volume of trade. Nonetheless, it does make it quite clear that the silk trade was not dependent upon Parthian co-operation or subject to a Parthian monopoly, as some scholars of the silk commerce have alleged.[11]

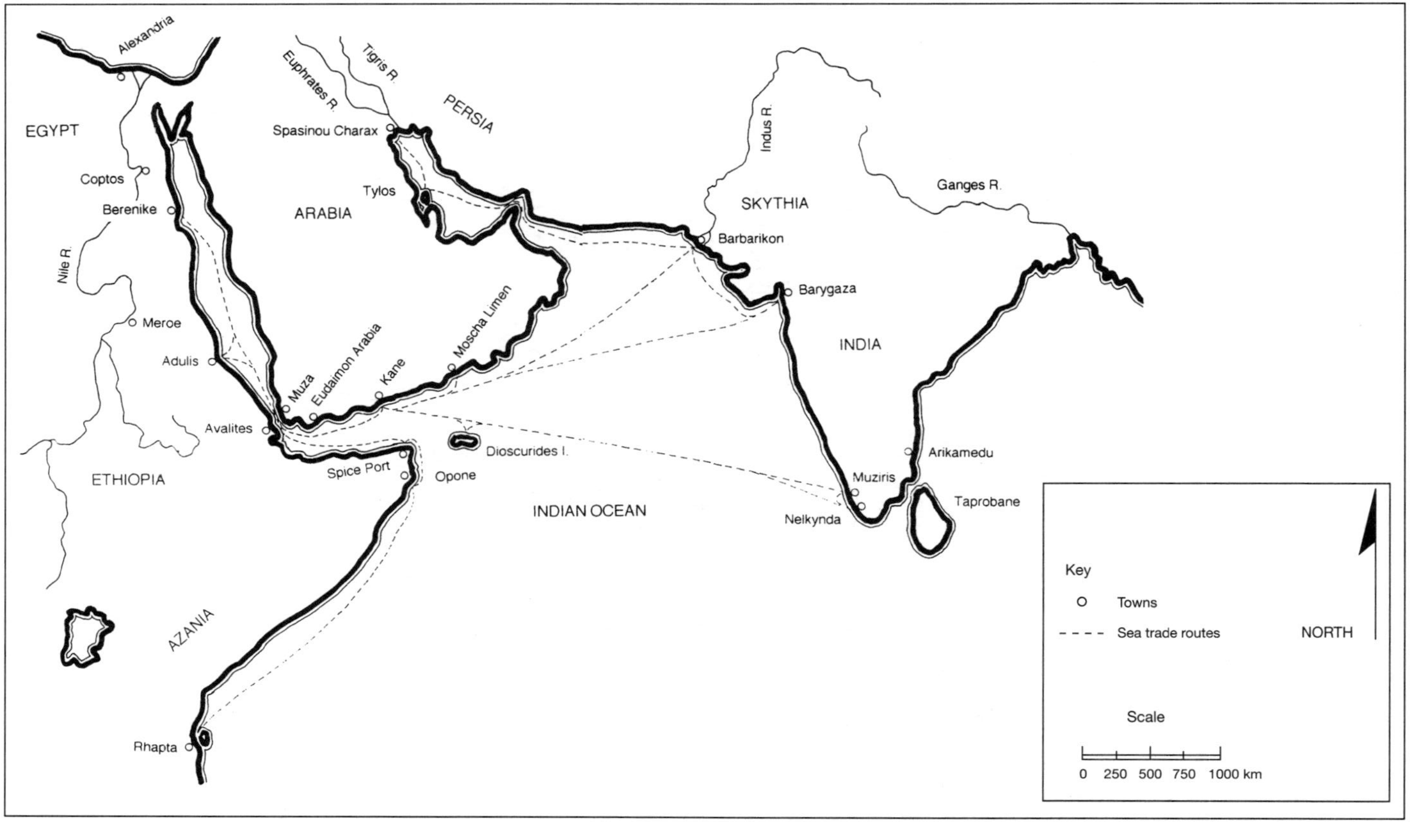

Map 2.1 The Indian Ocean in Roman times – showing the major maritime routes as described in the *Periplus*. Geographical terms are those used in the *Periplus*

Many ships, instead of travelling to Scythia, took a more direct route across the Indian Ocean, which took them to the southern part of the Indian subcontinent. The most important ports in this region were Muziris and Nelkynda.[12] While it is true that Pliny considered Muziris an undesirable destination due to piracy in the region and the necessity of using smaller boats to offload and take on cargoes,[13] the prominence given to the port in the *Periplus* indicates that it received a substantial part of the trade. The chief goods obtainable in this region were pepper and malabathron, with some nard, Chinese silks and gemstones. By the prominence given it in the *Periplus*' account, however, it appears that pepper was the chief export of the region.[14] For the most part, these goods were purchased with Roman money: the *Periplus* states the main item brought into these ports was 'a large amount of money'.[15] This is confirmed by the discovery in southern India of several hoards of Roman coins. Approximately 6,000 *denarii* have been found in this region of southern India, along with some *aurei* and other coins. Most of the silver coins are two specific types of Augustan and Tiberian issues, probably showing that the Indians preferred these types of coins, not that this was the peak of trading activity.[16] These hoards immediately bring to mind the complaints voiced by Tacitus and Pliny concerning the outflow of Roman wealth to India;[17] whether or not these hoards really do represent a dangerous outflow of coins, or whether the Romans thought such an outflow existed, will be discussed later in this book.[18]

Another feature of the port of Muziris worthy of note is the possible presence of a Roman 'merchant colony' there. The main evidence for this comes from the *Tabula Peutingeriana*, a medieval map which had a Roman prototype, and which depicts the Roman world as it was in the first century AD.[19] This map shows a building marked as *Templum Augusti* (Temple of Augustus) at Muziris.[20] Such a structure would have been built only by subjects of the Roman Empire, and presumably ones who were living in Muziris or who spent a significant proportion of their time there.[21] This is supported by two other pieces of evidence. In one case, a papyrus detailing a loan for the purpose of purchasing goods from India mentions 'the loan agreements at Muziris': the loan had therefore presumably been contracted in Muziris with a Roman resident there,[22] in order to purchase goods for the return trip.[23] The other piece of evidence comes from the *Periplus*. In describing the imports into this port, the author lists among the goods mentioned earlier:

> σῖτος δὲ ὅσος ἀρκέσει τοῖς περὶ τὸ ναυκλήριον διὰ τὸ μὴ τοὺς ἐμπόρους αὐτῷ χρῆσθαι.
>
> Enough grain for those concerned with shipping, because the merchants do not use it.[24]

The merchants who do not use grain who are mentioned here are presumably Indians who would have eaten rice; 'those concerned with shipping', by contrast, are probably resident westerners.[25] That these are not just the crews of Roman ships in the area would seem to be indicated by the fact that this is the only statement of this type in the *Periplus*: presumably, therefore, the situation at Muziris was different from that found at other ports. Thus, it would seem that the pepper and malabathron trade from southern India was lucrative enough to encourage Roman merchants to settle in the area. Of course, the trade may well have been lucrative enough in other areas of India too, such as at Barygaza and Barbarikon, but perhaps the local rulers prevented the establishment of such a colony at those places.

There is also some evidence of another Roman merchant colony in India. At the site of Arikamedu, on the south-eastern coast of India, there is considerable archaeological evidence of a group of resident westerners during the early centuries AD.[26] The most recent research indicates that the main period of contact between Arikamedu and the Mediterranean was from the first century BC until the end of the first century AD.[27] In addition, the discovery of a coin of Constantine and some Tamil-Brahmi inscriptions datable on palaeographic grounds to the third century may indicate that it was re-inhabited during the third and fourth centuries.[28] Indeed, the apparent decline of the site at the end of the first century AD may well have had more to do with rising sea levels at the site rather than the health or otherwise of western trade with the region.[29]

At the port, evidence has been uncovered of many items of Mediterranean manufacture, including pottery, wine vessels and garum jars.[30] While these goods may well have been destined for consumption by the westerners at the site, they may also have been sold to the Indians as part of the Red Sea trade. From this evidence, as well as the references to export goods in the *Periplus*, it is clear that the trade between Rome and India was in many cases a reciprocal one, with goods passing in both directions.

The evident existence of an active western trade station at this location on the east coast of India is very interesting, given the general lack of interest that the author of the *Periplus* seems to have toward the east coast of India.[31] Indeed, the *Periplus* seems to imply that the strait between Sri Lanka and India was the furthest point normally reached by western vessels trading with India,[32] and this was most probably due to the fact that western vessels large enough to withstand the monsoon winds which they used to reach India would not be able to negotiate the shallow straits in this area.[33]

The probable explanation for the existence of the station at Arikamedu is that the western merchants there were involved in the forwarding of the eastern coast goods to such places as Muziris and Nelkynda, where the western ships could pick them up.[34] The *Periplus* states that Gangetic nard and malabathron were forwarded by local ships from the mouth of the Ganges river to Muziris and Nelkynda, where western ships took on the loads for the journey to Egypt.[35] The western merchants of Arikamedu may well have been involved in the forwarding of such goods to their associates in the west coast ports.

In addition to the sea traffic in local craft, some of this forwarding may have been done by an overland route across the southern tip of the Indian peninsula. Most of the Roman coin hoards in India which were mentioned earlier are to be found on a communication route between the east and west coasts of the peninsula.[36] Possibly, then, Roman trade passed by this route also.

Trade in the East beyond India

Another place in this area which was involved in the Red Sea trade is the island of Sri Lanka, known to Greeks and Romans as Taprobanê. The author of the *Periplus* mentions the existence of Taprobanê, but it is apparent from his account that he is not using first-hand descriptions, as he greatly exaggerates the island's size and does not state that western ships called there.[37] While according to Pliny, knowledge of the island had existed in the Mediterranean world from the time of Alexander, direct contact began during the principate of Claudius.[38] He recounts the events by which this occurred:

> hactenus a priscis memorata. nobis diligentior notitia Claudi principatu contigit legatis etiam ex ea insula aduectis. id accidit hoc modo: Anni Plocami, qui Maris Rubri uectigal a fisco redemerat, libertus circa Arabiam nauigans aquilonibus raptus praeter Carmaniam, XV die Hippuros portum eius inuectus, hospitali regis clementia sex mensum tempore inbutus adloquio percontanti postea narrauit Romanos et Caesarem. mirum in modum in auditis iustitiam ille suspexit, quod paris pondere denarii essent in captiua pecunia, cum diuersae imagines indicarent a pluribus factos. et hoc maxime sollicitatus ad amicitiam legatos quattuor misit principe eorum Rachia.
>
> Thus far is known by the ancient writers. We however gained greater knowledge when during the principate of Claudius an embassy actually came from that island. It came about in this way: a freedman of Annius Plocamus, who had gained the contract for the Red Sea tax from the treasury, while sailing around Arabia was carried by the north wind past Carmania, and on the fifteenth day made the port of Hippuros there (i.e. in Sri Lanka). There he was kept by the kind hospitality of the king for six months, learning the language and afterward speaking of the Romans and Caesar. The king gained admiration for Roman honesty because the denarii which were on the captive were all equal in weight, although their diverse images showed they were coined by different persons. He, wishing friendship because of this, sent four envoys, the chief of whom was Rachia.[39]

Despite this allegedly first-hand evidence, the account which Pliny then proceeds to give of the island is wholly fanciful. Nonetheless, Roman contact with Taprobanê does appear to date from around this time, as coins from the reign of Nero have been found there. There are, however, only a few coins from this early period: the bulk of the Roman coin deposits in Sri Lanka come from the fourth century and later until well into the Byzantine period, when there appears to have been a strong trade between Sri Lanka and the Mediterranean world.[40] In the period with which we are dealing, by contrast, there seems to have been only relatively limited contact. For the most part, it appears that western ships went no further than the southern tip of India until the fourth century.

Of course, there were a few limited exceptions to this general rule, and a few intrepid merchants may have gone much further in search of profitable commerce, perhaps even as far as China. Much of the evidence for this comes from Chinese court records, which mention both visits of Chinese emissaries to the Parthian court and Chinese knowledge of the Roman East (which will be dealt with later),[41] as well as visits of Roman traders to South East Asia and China. Raschke generally downplays the reliability of these records,[42] but recently Graf has defended their reliability and the earlier interpretations of Hirth and others.[43] Nonetheless, the very existence of Chinese knowledge of Rome, however distorted, implies that there must have been some form of contact, and the records of Roman sea voyages to China and South East Asia may well be true. Given that the sea voyage to India was a regular occurrence in this period, it would perhaps be unsurprising if a few sailed further east on at least one or two occasions in search of profit.

The most famous of these accounts is found in the *Hou Han-Shou*, or Annals of the Later Han Dynasty, which cover the period AD 23–220 and which were compiled in the fifth century AD.[44] These annals record that in AD 166 an embassy from the king of *Ta-ch'in* who was named *An-tun* arrived from Annam (Vietnam) and sent gifts of ivory, rhinoceros horn and tortoiseshell to the Han court.[45] Hirth identified *Ta-ch'in* as the Chinese name for the Roman East and *An-tun* as the Chinese rendering of Antoninus, as the emperor at that date would have been Marcus Aurelius.[46] While scholars are in general agreement that the 'embassy' was in fact simply a group of traders rather than a legitimate embassy,[47] their existence nonetheless provides evidence of Roman merchant activity in the area of South East Asia.

Such activity is also attested in later Chinese records. The *Liang shu* records some of the events of the period after the collapse of the Han Dynasty in 220, although the date of composition in the later seventh century AD renders its accuracy on earlier matters somewhat questionable.[48] Nonetheless, the record it gives is worth noting. These annals record that in AD 226 one Ch'in Lun, a merchant from *Ta-ch'in*, arrived in *Chiao-chih* (the Han province of northern Vietnam) and was sent on to the court of the Wu emperor at Nanjing.[49] These same annals also state that merchants from *Ta-ch'in* were active in parts of Cambodia and Vietnam.[50] These accounts are also reflected in one second century classical source: Ptolemy's *Geography* describes the 'Golden Chersonese', usually identified as the Malay peninsula, and beyond that the port of Kattigara, which he states was visited by a Greek seafarer named Alexander, who was most probably a merchant.[51]

The evidence of the Chinese annals and of Ptolemy is perhaps confirmed by some archaeological discoveries, although they represent only isolated artefacts and cannot be taken as solid evidence of Roman contact. Nonetheless, the discoveries of Roman gold medallions from the reigns of Antoninus Pius and (probably) Marcus Aurelius at the trading port of Oc-eo, near Ho Chi Minh City in Vietnam,[52] give greater credibility to the Chinese and Roman sources which speak of Roman trading activity in South East Asia, especially in the Antonine period. In addition, other more recent finds of Mediterranean artefacts in Thailand, Vietnam, Malaysia and Indonesia give added support to the existence of some kind of contact between these areas and the Roman Empire.[53]

Thus, while the evidence from Ptolemy, from Chinese records and from the discovery of isolated Roman artefacts in South East Asia could never be taken independently to confirm the existence of Roman trade activity in South East Asia, together they may be considered to provide at least a case to answer. This is further strengthened by the fact that all the sources seem to highlight the Antonine period, which is perhaps why these visits are not mentioned in the *Periplus*. It would seem likely, therefore, that in the Antonine period and later, some Roman traders began to fare further than India and Sri Lanka and commenced trading activity in the region of Indo-China. From here, some of them may have ventured as far as China, although such contacts were presumably rare as they would otherwise not have attracted mention in the Chinese court annals.

Nonetheless, the bulk of Chinese goods imported into the West probably continued to be bought by Roman merchants in India, simply due to the complexities and time involved in a voyage any further than the western coast of India. Despite this, however, some enterprising individuals seem to have made just such journeys, and their achievement deserves recognition.

The trade with Arabia

Far closer to home was another important line of trade, which dealt with the kingdoms of southern Arabia. While these kingdoms were passed by ships sailing to India, the *Periplus* treats Arabia and India as separate lines of trade since the voyage to these two different destinations had to be made separately. The *Periplus* records that merchants wishing to sail for Arabia should depart in September,[54] in order to arrive at the time of the frankincense harvest, whereas the ships sailing to India had already left in June and would not commence the return journey until December or January.

The first major port of call in Arabia was Muza, located within the realm of the king of the Himyarites and Sabaeans.[55] This port provided a market for various articles of cloth and metalwork, as well as wine, grain and money.[56] In return, traders could pick up myrrh, which was no doubt the chief crop,[57] as well as some marble and goods brought to Muza from Somalia in Arab boats.[58] The author also mentions that the traders of Muza participated in trade with Barygaza, but this must have been for local consumption as the list of commodities which could be obtained in Muza provided in the *Periplus* does not contain any Indian goods, only local and African products.[59]

Beyond Muza along the southern coast of the Arabian peninsula lay the harbours of Ocelis and Eudaimon Arabia, which appear to have been only watering stations rather than ports of trade at the time of writing of the *Periplus*.[60] However, this situation appears to have changed in later years, when the two ports became centres of trade. Ptolemy records both of these places as *emporia*,[61] so by his time they must have become active trading ports. When this occurred Ocelis and Eudaimon Arabia presumably traded in the same goods as did Muza, that is myrrh and some local marble.

The next ports, and the last major ones in Arabia, were Kanê and Moscha Limen, both in the territory of the 'Frankincense-bearing Land'. As one might expect from such a title, the chief item of merchandise available at these ports was frankincense, both grown locally and imported from Somalia. In addition to this, at Kanê merchants could obtain aloe and some goods brought across from Africa.[62] Kanê appears to have been the main port of trade for this kingdom, as the *Periplus* states that all the frankincense in the land was brought there: Moscha Limen received only boats sent on there from Kanê, as well as boats which were returning from India late and wintered at Moscha.[63] At both Kanê and Moscha Limen the frankincense trade was a monopoly of the king of the Frankincense-bearing Land: we should not, however, suppose that such a monopoly extended to all the frankincense grown in Arabia, but simply to that which was grown in this particular kingdom.

This picture of trade as revealed in the *Periplus* has been broadly confirmed by archaeological investigations in the Hadramaut. Remains of Roman goods have been found at several widely scattered sites throughout the region, indicating that the trade goods were fairly widely distributed. Such remains include amphorae, which were probably used to transport wine, as well as other pottery.[64] In addition, the excavations at Qana (Kanê) in Yemen have uncovered the remains of a building which was used as a storehouse for incense.[65] The evidence provided by these remains seems to confirm the existence and vitality of trade contacts between the Mediterranean and south Arabia in this period.

It is evident from the *Periplus* that the chief items of consideration in the Arabian trade were the locally grown incenses of frankincense and myrrh. There may have been a little transit trade in items of Indian provenance, but not enough to attract the attention of the writer of the *Periplus*. The profits to be gained in Arabia, both by the Arab traders and those from Egypt, were to be found in the incense traffic, not in transit trade. The prosperity of Arabia was assured as long as there was a demand for its local incenses, and the health or otherwise of the Roman trade with India had no bearing on the situation of the kingdoms of southern Arabia. The incense trade with Arabia seems to have been a very significant portion of the trade entering Egypt, although perhaps it was somewhat secondary to the trade with India, judging by the relative portions of the *Periplus* devoted to each of these lines of trade.[66]

The trade with Africa

The other line of trade which is described in the *Periplus* is that which was conducted along the east coast of Africa. The first ports used by traders to be found in this area south of Berenike on the Egyptian Red Sea coast were Ptolemais Theron, followed by Adulis, both of which were under the rule of a King Zoskales, who appears to have ruled from Axum. These ports, located on the Eritrean coast of the Red Sea, offered a market for various items from Egypt, mostly clothing and other manufactured goods, and they exported chiefly ivory and tortoiseshell. Ships wishing to reach these ports departed Egypt in September.[67]

After these ports came those the author called the 'far-side' ports; that is, the harbours of the northern coast of Somalia.[68] These included Avalites, Malao, Mundu and, on the eastern coast of Somalia around Cape Gardafui, the Spice Port and Oponê.[69] These ports offered a market for basically the same things as the Ethiopian ports of the Red Sea but exported frankincense, myrrh and cassia along with ivory and tortoiseshell. In addition to the quantities of these goods which went to Roman Egypt, some were also exported to the ports of southern Arabia on the opposite shore of the Red Sea. Other goods were imported to them from Barygaza in India, although it is not specified whether this trade took place in Roman ships or Indian and Arab vessels. Ships departing Egypt for these ports did so in July.[70]

South of Oponê, on the east coast of Africa, lay the territory called Azania. The furthest point south on this run which was regularly reached by ships from Egypt was the port of Rhapta, which was on the coast of modern Tanzania, possibly in the vicinity of modern Dar-es-Salaam.[71] Ivory, rhinoceros horn and tortoiseshell were the chief exports of this region, which was also in continual contact with the southern Arabian kingdom of the Sabaeans and Himyarites, to which the region was tributary. The *Periplus* indicates that seafarers from Roman Egypt ventured no further than this point.[72]

The trade route along the eastern coast of Africa, while seemingly secondary to those to Arabia and India, was evidently still of some importance to the merchants of Roman Egypt. However, the merchants with the greatest involvement in this region seem to have been those of southern Arabia, a territory which had strong political and economic ties with Africa, especially the coasts of Somalia and Azania. Nonetheless, the traders of Roman Egypt appear to have been welcome in these ports too; there was clearly no monopoly of the trade active in any of these harbours.

Indeed, the complete absence of any monopolies on any items is quite apparent when we study the trade described in the *Periplus*, especially that of Arabia and Africa. Instead, we see an entirely free exchange of commodities, with no attempt at restriction apparent anywhere. For example, it appears that Roman shippers could purchase items of African provenance in the ports of southern Arabia, as was mentioned earlier. However, it is clear from the description of the trade in Africa that they could also go to the African ports themselves and pick these things up there as well: there is clearly no exploitative Arab monopoly in existence here. In one case, it is stated that the king of the Frankincense-bearing Land controlled the output of frankincense from his kingdom, not allowing any of it to be exported except through the port of Kanê.[73] This amount included some aromatics brought to Kanê over the water from the 'far-side' ports; yet, as we have seen, shippers from Roman Egypt could purchase frankincense directly from the Somalian ports.[74] Clearly the king's monopoly extended only to his own realm: traders were able to pick up African frankincense either in Kanê or in Somalia, as they pleased. The overall impression gained is that wherever a ship arrived, it would be able to pick up a cargo of the local merchandise, and that any monopolies that existed were very local in nature. The evidence for government interference and control in the trade, whether from the Roman government or the Arabian kingdoms, is non-existent outside their respective territories.

One last possible line of trade by which African goods may have entered Roman Egypt is, strictly speaking, not a part of the Red Sea trade at all. The kingdoms of Ethiopia, Meroe and Axum, as well as other regions of the African interior, would probably have found it easiest to communicate with Egypt by means of the Nile river, and thus some of the products of the region noted above may have entered Egypt through Syene.[75] There are a few ancient literary references which indicate that this was the case. Philostratus records that bullion, linen, ivory and spices were to be found at the border between Egypt and Ethiopia, to which point the Ethiopians brought these goods.[76] In addition to this, Juvenal mentions that ivory entered the empire at Syene,[77] which must indicate that it was transported by means of the Nile valley. Indeed, Pliny relates that the Ethiopians navigated the Nile down to Syene by means of collapsible boats with which they portaged the cataracts of the river.[78] Although he does not specify that this was a line of trade, it would seem reasonable that this was the means by which the goods of Ethiopia mentioned by Philostratus and Juvenal were conveyed into Egypt. There is of course no way of knowing the relative proportions of this trade compared to that which entered Egypt by way of the Red Sea, but it is at least clear that some goods of African provenance entered Egypt through the Nile valley.

Commerce in the Red Sea

The Red Sea trade flowing into Egypt in the Roman period was clearly very active and varied. Goods from India such as spices and Chinese silk were imported, along with incense from Arabia and ivory from Africa. We are fortunate indeed that the *Periplus* is able to provide us with such a comprehensive account of the trade routes and the goods available in the Red Sea commerce. Moreover, as we have seen, this account is supplemented in many cases both by other literary sources and by archaeological investigations. By these means, we are able to build up a fairly clear picture of this trade: certainly this understanding is clearer than that which we have from other areas of Rome's eastern trade.

Another point which is worthy of mention is that the picture the *Periplus* paints of the Red Sea trade shows a commerce substantially free of government interference and regulation, whether it be Roman or foreign. There was some regulation of the commerce by the Roman government, but this was chiefly concerned with the collection of taxes and took place only within the empire. As far as can be told, outside the empire traders were perfectly free to go where they liked and pick up whatever goods they preferred, controlled only by very limited local direction. There is no direct Roman control evident in the lands of the Red Sea, let alone further afield, and similarly there is evidence of only limited and local Arab attempts to control the trade in the Red Sea. All things considered, it seems that the merchants of the Red Sea trade purchased their cargoes and brought them to Roman Egypt in what was essentially an unfettered free market.

The Red Sea trade in Egypt under the Julio-Claudians and the Flavians

The goods conveyed in this commerce passed through one of the Red Sea ports before or after their journey up the Nile valley. In the second century AD, Claudius Ptolemy listed six ports from north to south along the Red Sea littoral: Cleopatris, Myos Hormos, Philoteras, Leukos Limen, Nechesia and Berenike (see Map 2.2).[79]

The Red Sea ports

The first of these ports, variously called Cleopatris, Arsinoë or Clysma, was located at the modern site of Suez.[80] While archaeological investigations have shown this site to be a Ptolemaic foundation, it appears that in the Roman period Clysma was not used significantly as a port of trade until the second century at the earliest,[81] and thus it will be discussed later.[82] Similarly, the port of Philoteras may have been of limited significance in Roman times, as it is not mentioned in the other sources which speak of the Roman Red Sea trade.

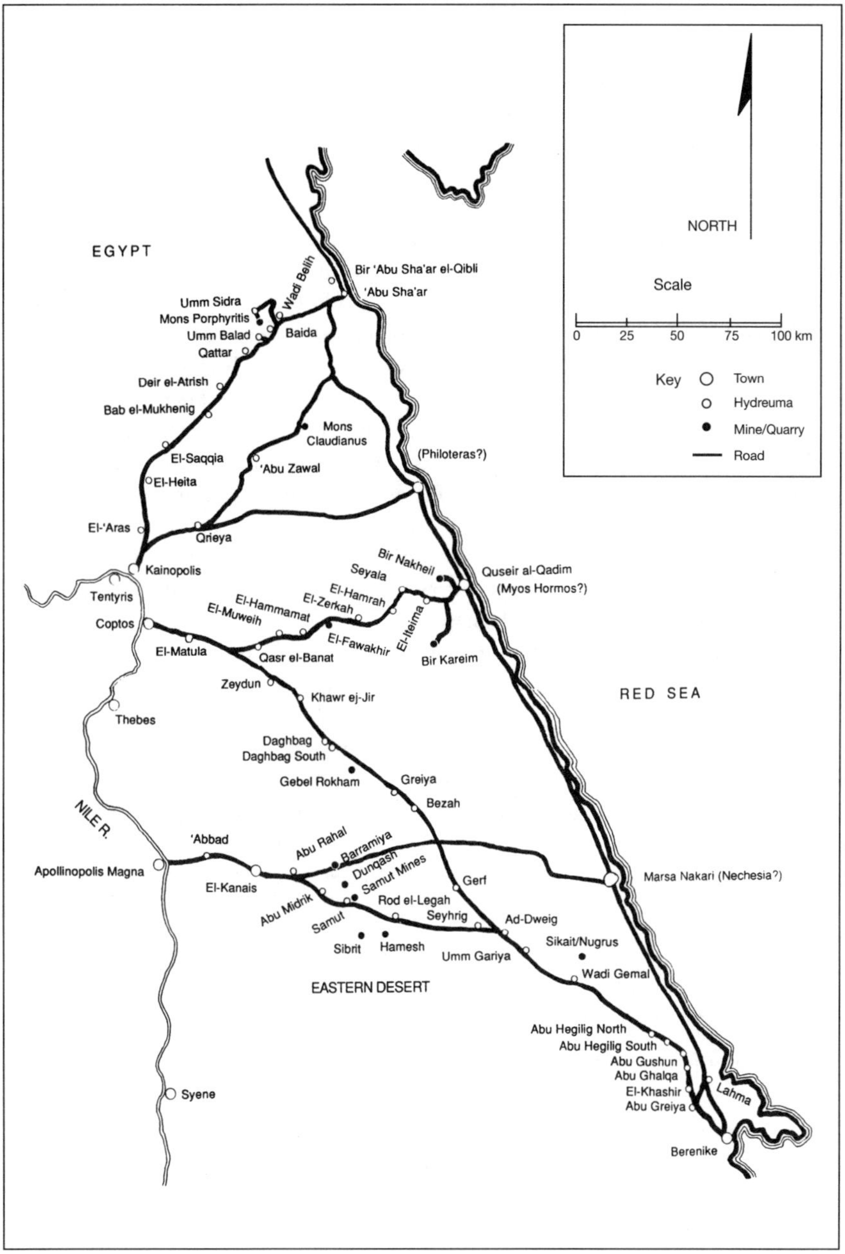

Map 2.2 Roman roads and forts in the Egyptian Eastern Desert

Source: This map is based on those in R.E. Zitterkopf and S.E. Sidebotham *JEA* 75 (1989), 159; S.E. Sidebotham and R.E. Zitterkopf *Expedition* 37. 2 (1995), 40; S.E. Sidebotham *Berenike* 1997 (1999), 366.

Indeed, it has never been precisely located and thus it is impossible to say what its period of use may have been.[83]

The next port in Ptolemy's list after Cleopatris, however, is of great importance in the Augustan period. Myos Hormos was, according to several sources, one of the most significant ports of the Red Sea trade in the early Roman imperial period. It and Berenike are the only two Egyptian ports mentioned in the *Periplus* as being active ports of trade at the time of writing,[84] and Strabo too describes only these ports as the ones involved in trade, saying that in his time Myos Hormos had the greater reputation.[85] It is clear from this that, whatever significance other ports may have had in the Red Sea trade, Berenike and Myos Hormos were, at least in the first century, the only ones of any great importance. While Strabo, as noted, says that Myos Hormos had a greater importance in his own time, it would seem from the reference to both ports in the *Periplus* that neither port ever succeeded in entirely eclipsing the other.

The location of Myos Hormos is a vexed question.[86] For many years the most probable contender was the site of 'Abu Sha'ar, where there are the remains of a Roman fort and a town, causing many to locate Myos Hormos at this site.[87] However, recent excavations at 'Abu Sha'ar have revealed that there was no activity at this site until the third century,[88] and consequently it must be rejected as a possible location for Myos Hormos.

The site of Quseir al-Qadim, *c.* 150 km south of 'Abu Sha'ar and lying at the end of a fortified Roman road from Coptos, was excavated between 1978 and 1982 by a team from the Oriental Institute of the University of Chicago.[89] Based upon the co-ordinates given by Ptolemy and on some documentary evidence from the site, the excavators identified Quseir al-Qadim as Leukos Limen.[90] The documentary evidence for this identification consists of a papyrus fragment and an ostrakon found during the excavation. The former consists of what appears to be a list of soldiers' names, on the reverse of which is found what seems to be the name and title of the addressee. This line, with restorations by the publisher, reads:

> Seren[o c]ura[(tori)] Le[uci Limenis]
>
> To Serenus, the *curator* of Leukos Limen.[91]

This restoration seems quite reasonable and thus this papyrus seems to refer to a military official known as the *curator Leuci Limenis*, presumably the commander of a small garrison there. In addition to this an ostrakon found at Quseir bears the abbreviation Λευκ, which is assumed to have been an abbreviation for Leukos Limen.[92] To these might also be added a piece of ceramic found in the Wadi Hammamat on the road from Coptos to Quseir al-Qadim bearing what seems to be the destination εἰς Λυ[, again possibly referring to Leukos Limen.[93] Thus, there is at least a *prima facie* case for regarding Quseir al-Qadim as the site of Ptolemy's Leukos Limen.

This identification, however, is not without its difficulties. Some scholars have in recent years advocated the idea that Quseir al-Qadim is, in fact, to be equated with Myos Hormos,[94] and thus the port of Leukos Limen (which is not mentioned in the *Periplus*) is to be sought somewhere to the south of Quseir. There are, however, some objections to this. Sidebotham has stated that Quseir could not be Myos Hormos due to the apparent lack of any Ptolemaic remains there:[95] Strabo's sources Agatharchides and Artemidorus wrote of Myos Hormos, showing it must have existed in the Ptolemaic period, whereas the evidence from pottery sherds at Quseir al-Qadim revealed no evidence for occupation earlier than the reign of Tiberius.[96] It should be noted, however, that by no means all of the site was excavated and evidence for Ptolemaic use of the site may still await discovery. In addition, at the beginning of the twentieth century Weigall reported some blocks of a Ptolemaic temple at this site.[97] While these remains were not found during the archaeological excavations at Quseir al-Qadim, it may be that the stones were robbed and re-used at the modern town of Quseir, 8 km further south.[98] Ptolemy's co-ordinates, too, need not be considered conclusive: his work in this region was only approximate and possibly dependent upon the observations and logs of others.[99] Against this, the *Periplus* records the distance from Berenike (the site of which is secure) to Myos Hormos as 1800 stadia,[100] which is exactly the distance between Berenike and Quseir al-Qadim. Clearly, there is at least no reason to reject the identification of Quseir al-Qadim with Myos Hormos out of hand. What then is the evidence which can be adduced to make this identification, and can it be considered any more conclusive than that which is used to identify Quseir with Leukos Limen?

Quseir al-Qadim is connected to the Nile valley by a Roman road well provided with fortified watering places and watchtowers.[101] Indeed, of all the routes which cross the Eastern Desert from the Nile to the Red Sea, that which crosses from Coptos to Quseir seems to have been the most important, or at least the best protected. The road is equipped with stations approximately every 16–18 km, whereas that from Coptos to Berenike has stations 30–40 km apart.[102] Bernand's study of the inscriptions found along this road show clearly that it was active and the fortified points were operational in the early Roman imperial period.[103] Of the graffiti on the road, three can be securely dated to the reign of Augustus, ten to that of Tiberius, one each for Claudius, Nero and Titus, two for Domitian, four of Hadrian and one each of Antoninus Pius and Maximinus Thrax.[104] Thus, it is clear that this road was in extensive use throughout the first century AD and later, coinciding with the apparent period of greatest activity at Quseir al-Qadim. It is clear that the road and the port are related, and that a major reason for the existence of this significant road from Coptos to the Red Sea coast was to connect the port at Quseir al-Qadim to the Nile emporium of Coptos.

This fact, however, would seem to pose insuperable problems for the identification of Quseir as Leukos Limen. All our sources speak of only two ports active in the Red Sea trade at this time, these two being Myos Hormos and Berenike. Indeed, the *Periplus* calls these two the only 'designated' harbours in Egypt,[105] by which is meant a harbour with guards to protect merchants and their ships.[106] Similarly, the Archive of Nicanor mentions both Myos Hormos and Berenike, but makes no mention of Leukos Limen.[107] The question then that must be asked is this: if Quseir al-Qadim is Leukos Limen, why is it situated at the end of the most significant Roman road in the Eastern Desert of Egypt and yet considered too insignificant to be even mentioned by the *Periplus*, and too unimportant for the Nicanor family to have bothered with doing business there? Casson attempts to resolve this difficulty by stating that Leukos Limen (by which he means Quseir al-Qadim) must have flourished *after* the writing of the *Periplus*.[108] However, this will not do, as the epigraphic and archaeological evidence from both the road and the port itself make it clear that it was operational in the time of Tiberius, well before the writing of the *Periplus*.[109] By far the simplest explanation is that the site of Quseir al-Qadim is in fact Myos Hormos. This would account for the significant facilities on the road which connects it to the Nile valley and its intense activity as a trading port during a time when all our sources refer to only two ports active in the Red Sea trade, Berenike and Myos Hormos.

The identification of Quseir al-Qadim with Myos Hormos is also strengthened by its physical similarity to Myos Hormos as described in the classical authors. There are two main accounts describing the harbour; one is that of Agatharchides of Cnidos, which is later also cited by Diodorus Siculus. Agatharchides' account reads:

> πλησίον δὲ τῆς λίμνης εὐμεγέθει πεδίῳ βεβηκὸς ὄρος ἀναφαίνεται μιλτῶδες, ἄλλην μὲν οὐδεμίαν ὑποδεικνύον ἰδιότητα, χροιὰν δὲ τοιαύτην ἀπὸ τῆς κορυφῆς σημαῖον τῆς ἄκρας, ὥστε τῶν ἀτενιζόντων τὰς ὄψεις ἐπὶ πλέον βλάπτεσθαι. ἐφεξῆς δὲ λιμὴν μέγας ἐκδέχεται, ὅς πρότερον μὲν Μυὸς ἐκαλεῖτο ὅρμος, ἔπειτα δὲ 'Αφροδίτης ὠνομάσθη. ἐν οἷς καὶ νῆσοι τρεῖς εἰσὶ προκείμεναι, ὧν αἱ μὲν ἐλαίαις πεπύκνωνται, μία δὲ ἧττον μὲν δασεῖα, τῶν δὲ μελεαγρίδων ἐκτρέφουσα πλῆθος.
>
> Near the lake on a large plain there appears a red mountain, which shows no other peculiarity but shows the same colour from the very peak of its heights, so that the eyes of those who stare at it intently for too long are harmed. Next is a great harbour which was formerly called mussel harbour, but later was named Aphrodite's. In it there are three islands, of which two are covered with olives, and the other is less thickly wooded, but has a great flock of birds called guinea-fowls.[110]

A similar account, clearly referring to the same harbour, is found in Strabo. Strabo, citing Artemidorus, reveals also that the harbour possessed a winding entrance:

πλησίον ὄρος ἐστὶν ἐν πεδίῳ μιλτῶδες· εἶτα Μυὸς ὅρμον, ὅν καὶ 'Αφροδίτης ὅρμον καλεῖσθαι, λιμένα μέγαν, τὸν εἴσπλουν ἔχοντα σκολιόν· προκεῖσθαι δὲ νήσους τρεῖς, δύο μὲν ἐλαίαις κατασκίους, μίαν δ' ἧττον κατάσκιον, μελεαγρίδων μεστήν·

Nearby there is a red mountain in a plain. Then comes mussel harbour, which is called Aphrodite's harbour, a large port which has a winding entrance. Nearby there are three islands, two covered with olives, while one is less covered and is full of guinea-fowls.[111]

These passages, then, give a reasonably clear description of the appearance of Myos Hormos. Unfortunately, there are no sites along the Egyptian Red Sea coast which would seem to answer this description. 'Abu Sha'ar perhaps comes closest, as the islands of the Gebel Zeit archipelago are found offshore. However, it has been pointed out that there are more than three islands in this group,[112] and it should also be noted that 'Abu Sha'ar lacks the mountain mentioned in both accounts. In addition, the identification of 'Abu Sha'ar with Myos Hormos must clearly be rejected due to the archaeological evidence mentioned earlier which shows no evidence of occupation until the third century AD.

Although today Quseir al-Qadim does not have a natural harbour, being marked only by a small bay in the coastal reef, satellite images have revealed that the coastline in the area has changed dramatically over the years.[113] These photographs show that what is currently a small indentation in the reef was once a deep, curved channel which led into a lagoon which has now silted up completely. In this lagoon lay three islands, corresponding to the three islands in the classical sources.[114] In addition, Gebel Hamrawein, the highest mountain in the region, is composed of red granite and thus corresponds to the 'red mountain' described by Agatharchides.[115] Quseir al-Qadim can be seen to answer the descriptions of Myos Hormos given by the classical geographers, further strengthening its identification with that port.

What then of the papyrus and ostraka which appear to refer to Leukos Limen and were found at Quseir al-Qadim? The most obvious point is, of course, the fact that simply because two of these pieces were found at Quseir, it does not necessarily follow that Quseir was the place they were referring to. Indeed, the ostrakon marked λευκ does not have to refer to a place at all,[116] as the word simply means 'white' and could be referring to some item of merchandise. It might be noted that there were also ostraka discovered at Quseir which could refer to Myos Hormos,[117] yet these are not adduced as proof for the identification of Quseir al-Qadim. It has been suggested that Leukos Limen may be the site of a fort further south on the Red Sea coast,[118] which might account for documents referring to such a site being found at Quseir al-Qadim. Messages and consignments passing from the Nile to a site south of Quseir would naturally make use of the Coptos–Quseir road, passing through Quseir al-Qadim on their way south. Alternatively, although Ptolemy lists the two sites separately, he may have in fact confused his sources and Leukos Limen and Myos Hormos could be two names for the same place, or two localities in the same general area. In any case, the evidence as it stands would seem to be most consistent with the identification of Myos Hormos as Quseir al-Qadim, with Leukos Limen perhaps to be identified with some minor site on the coast south of Quseir.

The next port south, Nechesia, has not been positively identified. However, the University of Delaware survey of the Eastern Desert has uncovered early and late Roman sherds at the site of Marsa Nakari, together with evidence of a road connecting this port to Edfu.[119] Sherding of sites on this road showed that it had been in use from the Ptolemaic period through to the late Roman period. Thus, it is quite possible that this is the site of ancient Nechesia. Excavations commenced at the site in 1999, and it is hoped that the results of these will assist in identifying the site.

Concerning the site of Berenike there is no such confusion. This site has been identified as that of Foul Bay, inland from the cape of Ras Banas, and confirmed by inscriptions at the site. This port was initially founded by Ptolemy II in the third century BC , but came into its most significant period of use in the Roman period, especially in the first century AD. When Strabo wrote it would seem that Myos Hormos had been the more important port, as this is the port to which he refers most frequently in connection with Indian and Arabian trade.[120] By the time of the writing of the *Periplus*, however, it appears that Berenike may have been the pre-eminent port, as all the distances and sailing times given in the work are calculated from Berenike rather than Myos Hormos.[121] There are natural advantages to Berenike which may explain this. Even though Berenike is considerably further by land from Coptos, this disadvantage may well have been offset by the longer time it would have taken to sail to Myos Hormos. The winds in the northern Red Sea are predominantly northerlies, and ancient ships with their square rig would have found it difficult to beat against such winds. Thus, Berenike's position as the southernmost of the Egyptian Red Sea ports may well have given it a decisive advantage.[122]

However, it is possible that this natural advantage was offset in the early years by a lack of facilities at the port, which may have been corrected during the reign of Tiberius. This might explain the early pre-eminence of Myos Hormos and the rising significance of Berenike in the first half of the first century AD. The excavations at Berenike have shown that there was construction of some harbour works during this period, including what appears to have been a sea wall built in the earlier part of the first century AD.[123] Moreover, after this work was done, Berenike seems to have maintained its position of pre-eminence, as the archaeological record indicates that the port continued in extensive use throughout the Roman period.[124]

The predominant position of Berenike throughout this time is apparently confirmed by the fact that it appears to have been the administrative centre for the whole region east of the Nile valley. This whole region, in the first century AD at least, was under the authority of a governor who was called the *praefectus montis Berenicidae* or similar titles.[125] This official was in charge of the ports, as is indicated by his title,[126] but there is also indication from inscriptions at the quarries in the Red Sea mountains that he was the overall supervisor of the mines and quarries of the area as well.[127] Thus, it seems that this official was responsible for the control of all the sources of imperial income from the Eastern Desert, both from the mines and from the customs duties payable on the Red Sea trade.

The conduct of the Red Sea trade at these ports must have brought a wide variety of officals, traders and transporters there. In particular, the activities of the agents of various shippers and merchants present at the ports, as is attested in several papyri which will be discussed in the next section, show clearly that these Red Sea ports, despite their remoteness, could be very active communities. There is also the possibility that items for export may have been manufactured at these ports, although conclusive evidence of this has not yet been found in the Berenike excavations. There is some indication of metal and glass production, although it is not immediately apparent whether this was for local consumption or for export.[128]

The desert roads

Once the merchandise of the Indian and Arabian trades had been landed at one of the Red Sea ports, it had to be conveyed overland by a system of fortified roads to the Nile valley. There are several routes which cross from the Red Sea coast to the Nile valley, and several of these were provided with significant fortifications during the Ptolemaic and early Roman period.

The northernmost of these desert routes is the one which runs from Kainopolis on the Nile to the site of 'Abu Sha'ar on the Red Sea. As has been discussed earlier, however, there does not appear to have been any traffic from the port at 'Abu Sha'ar in the first century AD, as the remains at that site date from the fourth century and so cannot have been used in the early Roman period. It is reasonable to conclude that the road from the Nile to 'Abu Sha'ar was, in the first century at least, intended for the carriage of the stone from the imperial quarries at Mons Porphyritis and other mining settlements along the route, not for the carriage of Red Sea commerce.

The next route south, that which runs between Coptos on the Nile and Quseir al-Qadim on the Red Sea, does seem to have been involved in the Red Sea trade. This route is clearly one of great significance, as the *hydreumata* on the road are much closer together than on other roads, at an average distance of 16 km.[129] As was mentioned above, the evident importance of this road strengthens the case for the identification of Quseir al-Qadim as Myos Hormos, because a port of such significance in the ancient literary sources would presumably have warranted a significant road. The road is indeed very well furnished with *hydreumata* and watchtowers, particularly in the more mountainous and remote eastern section of the route.

In contrast with the stations on the 'Abu Sha'ar–Nile route, the forts on the Quseir–Nile road do not have any outside animal barracks, nor are there any wheel-ruts on the road itself.[130] This is significant as it allows us to delineate somewhat the two different purposes of the roads. The road from 'Abu Sha'ar to the Nile has animal barracks at several of the stations and wheel-ruts in places along the road indicative of the use of heavy-wheeled transport, showing that quarrying was the main activity on the road in the early imperial period. By contrast, on the Quseir–Nile road, animal barracks are absent and there is no evidence of wheeled transport ever being used on the road. Thus, this particular route seems to have been used by smaller caravans of pack-animals rather than the large draught teams which would have been required for the traffic from the stone quarries.[131] Given the presence of the Red Sea port of Quseir al-Qadim at the end of this route, which was in use in the early imperial period, it would seem likely that a major part of the traffic on this road was the conveyance of trade goods to and from the Red Sea. The cargoes of spices and silk were very valuable but relatively small, and it would have been a perfectly manageable arrangement to have brought the animals inside the forts when overnight stops were made.

The road from Coptos to Berenike appears to be similar in its construction and facilities. This road, the only one of the Red Sea roads described in the ancient literary sources,[132] was surveyed by a team from the University of Delaware between 1990 and 1995, during which time numerous classical sites were located, and the *hydreumata* mentioned in the ancient sources were identified.[133] The pottery from this route indicates that it was chiefly in use between the first and seventh centuries AD,[134] approximately the same period that the port of Berenike was active.

Another route from Berenike to the Nile, which departed the Coptos route at Wadi ad-Dweig and reached the Nile at Edfu, seems to have been the preferred route during the Ptolemaic period. According to the pottery and inscriptional evidence, however, this route was not used to any great extent in Roman times, apart from soon after the Roman annexation.[135] It is possible that the Romans consolidated the traffic between Berenike and the Nile on the Coptos to Berenike road at approximately the same time as their improvements to the port at Berenike mentioned earlier. This is perhaps confirmed by a Latin inscription from Coptos which mentions renovations being carried out at numerous sites along the Coptos–Berenike route in the reign of Tiberius, the same time period as the reconstruction of the port at Berenike itself. After a long list of names and Roman military units, the text reads:

> Per eosdem, qui supra scripti sunt,
> lacci aedificati et dedicati sunt: Apollonos hydreuma VII k. Ianuar.,
> Compasi k. Augustis,

Berenicide XVIII k. Ianuar.,
Myoshormi idus Ianuar.
castram [*sic*] aedificauerunt et refecerunt.

By the same men who are written above, the wells were built and dedicated: Apollonos hydreuma seven days before the kalends of January, Compasi on the kalends of August, Berenike eighteen days before the kalends of January; at Myos Hormos on the ides of January they built and refurbished the fort.[136]

This inscription, dated in the early imperial period,[137] would seem to indicate that there was considerable construction activity on the Coptos–Berenike road, as well as some fortification work at the ports of Berenike and Myos Hormos themselves at that time. This then may have been the time at which the port at Berenike was upgraded, and the commercial traffic from Berenike was redirected to travel along the road to Coptos rather than the earlier Ptolemaic route to Edfu.

Another route which traversed the Eastern Desert has only recently been recorded, and appears to have been in use from the Ptolemaic period through to the late Roman. This route left the Nile at Edfu and reached the Red Sea coast at Marsa Nakari.[138] This site (as was discussed earlier) may be the site of the port of Nechesia. The results of further forthcoming surveys of this route are eagerly awaited.

Coptos

Having traversed the Eastern Desert, most of the cargoes of goods from the Red Sea now arrived in the Nile city of Coptos, which acquired an extremely significant place in the Red Sea commerce. As has been noted above, the Romans seem to have consolidated the routes crossing the Egyptian desert so that those from Berenike and Myos Hormos at least terminated at Coptos. This may have been so that the Romans could effectively monitor and control the traffic, and specifically to ensure that the caravans traversing the route paid all the taxes and various *portoria* which they were required to pay.[139] Movements of both goods and persons in Egypt were very heavily regulated throughout the Roman period, and it would be very surprising if the traffic from the Red Sea were to have been an exception.

This role for Coptos is reflected in our evidence. The first is in a papyrus which is quoted in full later in this work.[140] This papyrus, *P. Vindob.* G 40822, is a double-sided document, the verso of which provides a list of goods from India, no doubt the shipment described on the other side of the document, in connection with the 25 per cent customs duty which was imposed on all imports. The recto, however, gives a considerable amount of detail concerning the financing of a commercial expedition to India and of how such an expedition was conducted.[141] This document mentions the existence at Coptos of a warehouse for the receiving of customs duties. Here, goods brought from the Red Sea ports were to be placed under the seal of their owner until such time as they were loaded aboard a freighter for the journey down the river to Alexandria:

> [εἰς τὰ]ς ἐπὶ Κόπτου δημοσίας παραλημπτικὰς ἀποθήκας καὶ ποι–
> [ήσω ὑ]πὸ τὴν σὴν ἤ τῶν σῶν ἐπιτρόπων ἤ τοῦ παρόντος αὐτῶν
> [ἐξουσία]ν καὶ σφραγεῖδα μέχρι ποταμοῦ ἐμβολῆς.
>
> to the public customs-house at Coptos, and I will place (them) under the authority and seal of you or of your agents or of whoever of them is present until the loading on the river.[142]

The exact nature of the tax payable at Coptos is not specified, nor is it mentioned whether or not all trade passing through Coptos had to be placed in this warehouse, or only that which came from the Red Sea ports. In any case, it appears that all goods arriving at Coptos from the Red Sea were interned in the customs-house under the seal of their owner until the duty was paid, whereupon the goods were released to their owners for transportation down the river. We do know that this tax was *not* the 25 per cent duty payable on all imports of the eastern trade, as this same papyrus mentions the payment of that duty at Alexandria. However, it is quite likely that some local customs duty was enforced at this point, as indeed such duties were imposed at many points on the journey through Egypt. The duty at Coptos seems to have been a particularly important one, though, as it required the goods to be impounded until the money was paid. According to the account of the journey from the Red Sea to Alexandria contained in *P. Vindob.* G 40822, such impoundment is mentioned as taking place only twice: at Coptos and at Alexandria.

One duty that may have been payable at this point (although probably not the only duty) is the toll recorded in the inscription which has become known as the Coptos tariff. This particular tax appears to have been levied by an official known as the *arabarch* under orders from the *praefectus montis Berenicidae* upon users of the roads between Coptos and the Red Sea.[143] The tariff probably represents a toll collected by the military which was designed to pay for the maintenance of the Eastern Desert roads and military stations along them.[144] In the tariff, numerous different types of road users are mentioned, together with the tolls appropriate to that class of user:

> ἐξ ἐπιταγῆς . . .
> . . . ὅσα δεῖ τοὺς μισθ[ω]–
> τὰς τοῦ ἐν Κόπτῳ ὑποπείπτον–
> τος τῇ ἀραβαρχίᾳ ἀποστολίου πράσ–

σειν κατὰ τὸν γνώμον[α] τῇδε τῇ
στήλῃ ἐνκεχάρακται διὰ Λουκίου
'Αντιστίου 'Ασιατικοῦ ἐπάρχου
ὄρους Βερενείκης·
κυβερνήτου 'Ερυθραικοῦ δρα–
χμὰς ὀκτὼ. . .,
πρωρέως δραχμὰς δέκα,
[φυλ]άκου δραχμὰς πέντε,
[να]ύτου δραχμὰς πέντε,
[θε]ραπευτοῦ ναυπηγοῦ δραχμὰς
πέντε, χειροτέχνου δραχμὰς
ὀκτὼ, γυναικῶν πρὸς ἑταιρισ–
μὸν δραχμὰς ἑκατὸν ὀκτω,
γυναικῶν εἰσπλεουσῶν δρα–
χμὰς εἴκοσι, γυναικῶν στρατι–
ωτῶν δραχμὰς εἴκοσι,
πιττακίου καμήλων ὀβολὸν ἕνα,
σφραγισμοῦ πιττακίου ὀβολοὺς δύο,
πορείας ἐξερχομένης ἑκάστου
πιττακίου τοῦ ἀνδρὸς ἀναβαίνον–
τος δραχμὴν μίαν, γυναικῶν
πασῶν ἀνὰ δραχμὰς τέσσαρας,
ὄνου ὀβολοὺς δύο, ἁμάξης ἐχού–
σης τετράγωνον δραχμὰς τέσσαρες,
ἱστοῦ δραχμὰς εἴκοσι, κέρατος δρα–
χμὰς τέσσαρες, ταφῆς ἀναφερομε–
νης καὶ καταφερομένης δραχμὴν μ[ι]–
αν τετρώβολον. Ἔτους θ΄ Αὐτοκράτορος
Καίσαρος [Δομιτιανοῦ] Σεβαστοῦ [Γερμανικοῦ], Παχὼν ιε΄.

From the precept of . . . how much is payable for the duties owing to the arabarch in Coptos, according to the judgment he has written on this stele by Lucius Antistius Asiaticus, prefect of Mount Berenike:
for a helmsman of the Red Sea, eight drachmas;
a ship's lookout, ten drachmas;
a guard, five drachmas;
a sailor, five drachmas;
a shipbuilder's servant, five drachmas;
an artisan, eight drachmas;
women for the purposes of prostitution, one hundred and eight drachmas;
women arriving by ship, twenty drachmas;
women of the soldiers, twenty drachmas;
a ticket for camels, one obol;

a seal for a ticket, two obols;
per outward journey for each ticket of a man going up, one drachma;
all women going up, four drachmas;
an ass, two obols;
a covered wagon, four drachmas;
a mast, twenty drachmas;
an animal horn, four drachmas;
a funeral procession going up and down, one drachma four obols.
Year 9 of the Emperor Caesar (Domitianus) Augustus (Germanicus), the 15th day of the month Pachys.[145]

Clearly we cannot pretend to understand all the references contained in this tariff. Nonetheless, it is quite apparent that a system was in place whereby all users of the roads between Coptos and the Red Sea were taxed, and that this tax was collected by the military and was probably used to defray the expenses of the garrisoning of the Eastern Desert. The *apostolion* mentioned in the inscription may represent a kind of pass or ticket of the sort that was required for travel in many parts of Egypt under the Romans.[146] The Coptos tariff may thus be seen both as a revenue-raising measure as well as a means of controlling traffic on an important internal route.

It certainly seems that Coptos was an important centre for the control and taxation of the Red Sea trade. However, when we are considering the extent to which the Roman government desired to control the trade, we should bear in mind the rigid control exercised over all aspects of travel in Egypt. Given the valuable nature of the cargoes being carried, and the considerable imperial income which would have been generated from customs dues as well as the wealth from quarries and mines in the area, we should indeed have been very surprised if there had been no such control over the Eastern Desert roads. Indeed, the centralisation of the routes from Berenike and Myos Hormos upon Coptos may very well have been designed to make this control and monitoring easier.

The role of Coptos, however, was not just a military and administrative one. As will be discussed in the next section, there appears to have been a considerable merchant community at Coptos. Indeed, the situation of Coptos as the roadhead for the major routes to the Red Sea would have made it the natural base for traders who were active in this commerce. The Red Sea ports would have been too remote to have acted in this role: Coptos, however, had all the facilities which would have been necessary for these merchants.

From this high level of mercantile activity, several dependent industries seem to have arisen at Coptos. The city appears to have been involved in the manufacture of textiles, some of which may well have been used for export in the Red Sea trade.[147] In addition, the city's market was involved in the purchase of silver bullion, which may well have been used in the commerce with India. A letter dating from AD 115 mentions the daily fluctuations of the price of silver at Coptos:

τό ἄσημο'ν νυν ἐστ. τξβ. ώς γὰρ οἶδας, ἐν Κόπτῳ καθ' ἡμέραν διάφοροι γείνονται τιμαί.

Uncoined (silver) is now 362 (drachmas). For, as you know, the best prices in Coptos change day by day.[148]

While this citation does not mention the eastern trade, it seems to single out Coptos particularly as a place at which the price of uncoined silver varied greatly, presumably as compared to other locations. This fluctuation may well have been a result of the demand from merchants about to sail to India or Africa, who would need large quantities of such bullion. Thus, the silver merchants may well have been able to ask higher prices whenever there happened to be a strong demand for bullion for the Red Sea trade, causing the price of silver to fluctuate.

Whether or not this is the case, we can nonetheless see that the important role of Coptos in the Red Sea trade is well established, both from the point of view of the activities of merchants and of the government. Its central position in the trade, both in touch with Alexandria and at the head of the routes through the Eastern Desert virtually assured it of a significant role. Accordingly, Coptos became an important centre of mercantile activity, and a vital link in the Red Sea trade. We should note, however, that this role came from the logistic requirements of the trade, such as bullion, goods for export, food supplies and so on. Whatever else it was, Coptos does not appear to have been a centre for the actual sale of the goods brought into Egypt via the Red Sea. As will be seen, the 25 per cent customs duty on imported goods had to be paid at Alexandria, so merchants were presumably not allowed to sell their goods at Coptos. Accordingly, the goods were next loaded onto one of the many freighters plying the Nile for the journey to Alexandria.

Alexandria and the journey to Rome

The great Mediterranean port of Alexandria was famed for its wealth and its active merchant community,[149] and it was to this port that the goods of the Red Sea trade were brought after their journey down the Nile from Coptos. Unfortunately, the continuous habitation of this site since its foundation has limited the possibilities of archaeological investigation, and it is difficult to learn a great deal about the merchant community of Alexandria other than from the information that is revealed in the literary sources. Fortunately, the wealth of the city and the commercial activity found therein were often commented upon in the ancient world,[150] and Strabo in particular mentions the important role of the merchant community of Alexandria in the eastern trade.[151] In view of this, and of the strategic location occupied by Alexandria upon the Mediterranean, yet in constant touch with the interior by the Nile valley, it is hardly surprising to find the city occupying a pivotal role in the Egyptian Red Sea commerce. This is noted by Dio Chrysostom:

τήν τε θάλατταν τὴν καθ' ὑμᾶς ἅπασαν ἐκδέχεσθε, κάλλει τε λιμένων καὶ μεγέθει στόλου καὶ τῶν πανταχοῦ γιγνομένων ἀφθονίᾳ καὶ διαθέσει, καὶ τὴν ἔξωθεν ὑπερκειμένην ἔχετε, τήν τε 'Ερυθρὰν καὶ τὴν 'Ινδικήν, ἧς πρότερον τοὔνομα ἀκοῦσαι χαλεπὸν ἦν· ὥστε τὰς ἐμπορίας, οὐ νήσων οὐδε λιμένων οὐδὲ πορθμῶν τινων καὶ ἰσθμῶν, ἀλλὰ σχεδὸν ἁπάσης τῆς οἰκουμένης γίγνεσθαι παρ' ὑμῖν.

and you also receive goods from the whole Mediterranean sea because of the beauty of your harbours, the greatness of your fleet and by the abundance and selling of the goods of every place; and you have also the power over the outer seas, both the Red Sea and the Indian, whose name was rarely to be heard formerly, so that the trade not only of islands or ports or some straits or isthmuses but virtually the whole world comes to you.[152]

Thus, it was to Alexandria that the goods of the Red Sea trade came after being conveyed downriver from Coptos. At the conclusion of the journey down the Nile, the goods were impounded in a public warehouse in order that the government might extract its 25 per cent tax, the so-called *tetarte*. This is recorded in *P. Vindob.* G 40822, in which the merchant guarantees to place the goods in the warehouse at Alexandria under the seal of his creditor:[153]

καὶ κατοίσω εἰς τὴν
[ἐν 'Αλεξ]ανδρείᾳ τῆς τετάρτης παραλημπτικὴν ἀποθήκην καὶ ὁ–
[μοίω]ς ποιήσω ὑπὸ τὴν σὴν ἢ τῶν σῶν ἐξουσίαν καὶ σφραγεῖδα.

and I will convey (them) to the customs-house for receiving the *tetarte* in Alexandria and I will likewise place (them) under the authority and seal of you or of your agents.[154]

This seems to be a reference to another impoundment of the goods as happened at Coptos. This time, however, it is explicitly stated which tax was to be taken out at this time: it is the *tetarte*. Thus, we perhaps have another explanation for the high level of security under which these goods seem to have travelled through Egypt besides their great value: it was also necessary to prevent the merchants from selling their goods before they reached Alexandria, and so evading the *tetarte*.

After this transaction, it would seem that the merchant was then free to do whatever he wanted with his goods. In many cases, merchants may have sold their goods in Alexandria: presumably this is what the merchant in *P. Vindob.* G 40822 had to do in order to pay off his loan.[155] On the other hand, merchants who were not so encumbered may have preferred to keep their goods and freight them to Rome or elsewhere. It seems likely, however, that the majority of the goods would have been sold as they emerged from the customs-house at Alexandria.

Alexandria had a reputation in the Roman world as a great manufacturing centre,[156] and it appears that many of the goods brought there from the Red Sea trade were used as a part of this manufacture. Pliny describes Alexandria as a centre for the reworking of Arabian incenses, and describes what appears to have been a substantial industry for the reprocressing of these goods, complete with extensive security measures designed to prevent the workers from purloining any of the valuable incense:

> at, Hercules, Alexandriae, ubi tura interpolantur, nulla satis custodit dilgentia officinas! subligaria signantur opifici, persona additur capiti densusue reticulus, nudi emittuntur.
>
> But at Alexandria, by Hercules, where the frankincense is prepared for sale, no diligence is enough for guarding the factories! A seal is put on the workmen, a dense mask or net is placed on their heads, and they are sent out naked.[157]

Pliny also mentions the production of textiles at Alexandria,[158] and it would seem at least possible that silk would have been reprocessed there also as part of this textile industry. Certainly there was a considerable textile industry throughout Egypt,[159] and it would therefore be surprising if such a manufacturing centre as Alexandria were not heavily involved in this industry.

In addition to the goods which were produced from the products of the eastern trade, it is also quite likely that various goods were manufactured at Alexandria and shipped to India and elsewhere on the outward leg of the Red Sea trade. Textiles have been already mentioned, and feature often in the lists of goods for which there was a market in India and Arabia in the *Periplus*.[160] Glass too was a product of Egypt,[161] and it likewise is a common export from Egypt to the East.[162] Thus, it appears that Alexandria was involved in manufacturing both of goods made from items imported from the East, as well as of goods which were made in Egypt and could be exported to India, Arabia and elsewhere.

Alexandria was thus an important centre in the conduct of the eastern luxury trade, both from the point of view of the government, who used it as the place at which they extracted the *tetarte*, and from that of the merchants, who bought, sold and reprocessed their goods there. While archaeological confirmation from the site has not yet been found, and may never be, enough testimony exists in our literary sources for us to be sure that Alexandria was a site of prime importance in the eastern trade.

From the foregoing it can be seen that the Egyptian Red Sea trade attained considerable significance during the early centuries of Roman rule in Egypt. In these earlier years, then, much of the pattern was set which was to remain throughout the period of Roman rule in Egypt. A few changes did occur in later years, and these are detailed further on in the chapter. First, however, it is proposed to examine what can be learned about the participants in the trade, and the manner in which it was conducted.

The conduct of the Egyptian Red Sea trade

There are a few sources which allow us to study the individuals who operated the trade routes, and those who were involved in the commerce in one way or another. Indeed, of all the areas of this study perhaps the one with the richest sources of information is Roman Egypt, due to the conditions which prevail in Egypt allowing the preservation of large quantities of papyri and ostraka. Thus we are able to learn at least a little about the people who were involved in the eastern commerce.

The merchants of the Egyptian Red Sea trade

As was discussed in the Introduction, the author of the *Periplus Maris Erythraei* was a Greek-speaking resident of Egypt, an experienced merchant who had been involved in the trade and possessed great first-hand experience of the voyages to India and Africa.[163] It would not be surprising, of course, for residents of Egypt to have dominated the trade, and indeed in one instance Strabo implies that the trade was to a great extent in the hands of the merchants of Alexandria:

> τῶν τε Ῥωμαίων καὶ εἰς τὴν Εὐδαίμονα Ἀραβίαν ἐμβαλόντων μετὰ στρατιᾶς νεωστί, ἧς ἡγεῖτο ἀνὴρ φίλος ἡμῖν καὶ ἑταῖρος Αἴλιος Γάλλος, καὶ τῶν ἐκ τῆς Ἀλεξανδρείας ἐμπόρων στόλοις ἤδη πλεόντων διὰ τοῦ Νείλου καὶ τοῦ Ἀραβίου κόλπου μέχρι τῆς Ἰνδικῆς, πολὺ μᾶλλον καὶ ταῦτα ἔγνωσται τοῖς νῦν ἤ τοῖς πρὸ ἡμῶν.
>
> And since the Romans recently invaded Arabia Felix with an army, which my friend and companion Aelius Gallus led, and the merchants of Alexandria are now sailing with fleets by the Nile and the Arabian Gulf as far as India, these places are better known to us than to those before us.[164]

Given the important position of Alexandria in the Red Sea trade as described in the previous section, the prominence of Alexandrine merchants is to be expected. Indeed, it may even be that many of the merchants whom we find resident at Coptos and other similar places in Egypt were in fact based at Alexandria, and simply moved further down the Nile when a shipment arrived.

Of course, such a lucrative trade would have also attracted many other merchants from the Mediterranean to become involved. One particularly interesting papyrus actually dates from the Ptolemaic period, but given the Roman reluctance to interfere with a working system it is probable that the situation in this papyrus can be applied to the Roman period also. The document in question is the text of a loan agreement, by which a consortium of five partners, all with Greek names, arranged a loan to finance an expedition to 'the spice-bearing lands'.[165] In this text we see what must have been a relatively common arrangement among merchants of limited means. Without the finance to support an expedition themselves, a group of merchants gather together and take out a loan which they would then use both to equip their expedition and pay for the transport costs, as well as to purchase the goods at the destination. The sale of these goods, once they had been brought into Egypt, should have provided sufficient funds to pay back the creditors and provide the partners with a reasonable profit.[166] Although a voyage to any of the sources of the luxury goods imported into Egypt must have been a massive undertaking, the possibility of creating a consortium such as this one in order to make a voyage and hire space on a cargo ship would allow those with insufficient finance to participate on their own the chance to become involved in the trade. Thus, Casson's contention that the India trade (due to the rougher and longer voyage requiring stronger and more expensive ships) would have been restricted to richer merchants may not necessarily be the case.[167] Partnerships such as this one may well have allowed small-scale traders to join in the lucrative India trade.

Of course, such people would still have been among the wealthier members of society, or they would never have been able to contract a loan in the first place; they do not, however, need to have been a part of society's elite. This is illustrated by the papyrus under discussion: of the five guarantors to the loan agreement, four are soldiers in the army. The actual partners to the contract are likely to have been roughly of the same social class as their guarantors (or lower). Thus, the trade seems to have been open to a fairly broad band of the members of society in the Mediterranean world.

Other merchants, on the other hand, seem to have participated in the trade on an individual basis. These merchants, when they were not able to finance the trip themselves, would obtain a loan and pledge the goods as security for the repayment of the loan. This situation is illustrated in the papyrus from the Vienna collection, *P. Vindob.* G 40822, to which reference has already been made.[168] The agreement contained on the recto of this document reads as follows:

> ο μένων σου ἑτέρων ἐπ[ι]τρόπων ἤ φροντιστῶν καὶ στήσας
> [δώσω τ]ῷ σῷ καμηλείτι ἄλλα (τάλαντα) ε[ἴ]κοσι πρός ἐπίθεσιν τῆν εἰς Κόπτον
> [ἀνόδο]υ καὶ ἀνοίσω διὰ τοῦ ὄρους μετὰ παραφυλακῆς καὶ ἀσφαλείας
> [εἰς τὰ]ς ἐπὶ Κόπτου δημοσίας παραλημπτικὰς ἀποθήκας καὶ ποι–
> [ήσω ὑ]πὸ τὴν σὴν ἤ τῶν σῶν ἐπιτρόπων ἤ τοῦ παρόντος αὐτῶν

[ἐξουσία]ν καὶ σφραγεῖδα μέχρι ποταμοῦ ἐμβολῆς καὶ ἐμβαλοῦμαι
[τῶι δέ]οντι καιρῶι εἰς ποταμὸν ἀσφαλὲς πλοῖον καὶ κατοίσω εἰς τὴν
[ἐν ᾿Αλεξ]ανδρείᾳ τῆς τετάρτης παραλημπτικὴν ἀποθήκην καὶ ὁ–
[μοίω]ς ποιήσω ὑπο τὴν σὴν ἤ τῶν σῶν ἐξουσίαν καὶ σφραγεῖδα, ταῖς
[τοῦ λοι]ποῦ ἀπὸ τοῦ νῦν μέχρι τεταρτολογίας δαπάναις πάσιας καὶ φο–
[ρέτρου] ὄρους καὶ ναύλων ποταμίταις καὶ τῶν ἄλλων κατὰ μέρος ἀνα–
[λωμά]των· πρὸς τὸ ἐνστάντος τοῦ ἐν ταῖς Μουζεῖριν τοῦ δα–
[νείου σ]υνγραφαῖς τῆς ἀποδόσεως ὡρισμένου χρόνου ἐὰν μὴ δικαί–
[ως τότ]ε χρεολυτῶ τὸ προκείμενον ἐν ἐμοῖ δάνειον τότε εἶναι
[πρὸς σ]ὲ καὶ τοὺς σοὺς ἐπιτρόπους ἤ φροντιστὰς τὴν ἐγλογὴν καὶ δλο–
[σχερῆ] ἐξουσίαν ὡς ἐὰν αἱρῆσθε ποιήσασθαι τὰ τῆς πράξεως χωρὶς
[διαστ]ολῆς καὶ προσκρίσεως, κρατεῖν τε καὶ κυριεύειν τὴν προκ[ει–]
[μένη]ν ὑποθήκην καὶ τεταρτολογεῖν καὶ τὰ λοιπὰ ἐσόμενα μέρη
[τρία μ]εταφέρειν οὗ ἐὰν αἱρῆσθε καὶ πωλεῖν καὶ μεθυποτίθεσθαι
[καὶ] ἑτ[έ]ρωι παραχωρεῖν ὡς ἐὰν αἱρῆσθε καὶ τὰ καθ’ ἑαυτὴν διοικονο–
[με]ῖσθαι καθ’ ὅν ἐὰν βούλησθε τρόπον καὶ ἑαυτῶι ὠνεῖσθαι τῆς ἐπὶ τοῦ
καιροῦ φανησομένης τιμῆς καὶ ἐκκρού[ει]ν καὶ ἐνλογεῖν τὰ πεσούμενα
[ὑπέρ τοῦ προκειμέν]ου δανείου τῆς πίστεως τῶν πεσουμένων
[οὔσης π]ερὶ σὲ καὶ τοὺς ἐπιτρόπους ἤ φροντιστὰς ὄντων ἡμῶν ἀσυκοφαν–
[τήτ]ων κατὰ πάντα τρόπον. τοῦ δὲ περὶ τὴν ἐνθήκην ἐνλείματος
[τ]ε καὶ πλεονάσματος πρὸς ἐμὲ τὸν δεδανεισμένον καὶ ὑποτεθει–
[μένον ὄντος . . .]

of your other agents or managers, and I will weigh and give to your camel-driver twenty other talents to be loaded for the road up to Coptos, and I will take (them) through the mountains under guard and security to the public customs-house at Coptos, and I will place (them) under the authority and seal of you or of your agents or of whoever of them is present until the loading on the river, and I will load (them) at an opportune time on the river on a safe boat, and I will convey (them) to the customs-house for receiving the *tetarte* in Alexandria and I will

> likewise place (them) under the authority and seal of you or of your agents, assuming all future expenses from now until the reckoning of the *tetarte*, both the passage of the mountains and the boatmen and other expenses according to (my) portion. If, at the appointed time for repayment in the loan agreement at Muziris, I do not then rightly pay off the loan in my own name, then there will be to you and to your agents or managers the option and full authority to exact the amount without notification or summons, to seize and control the aforementioned security and to pay the *tetarte* and to transfer the other three-quarters to wherever you wish and to sell, transfer the security or to give it to someone else, as you wish, and dispose of the goods themselves in whatever manner you wish, and to cause them to be bought at the price current at the time, and to remove and reckon expenses arising from the aforementioned loan, good faith for these expenses being to you and to your agents or managers, there being no legal action of any sort against us. Concerning your investment, shortfall or excess shall be to me, being the borrower and offerer of security.[169]

In this case, then, we can see that the merchant, this time an individual rather than a member of a consortium, has taken out a loan to purchase goods and has pledged the goods purchased as security for the loan. It is, of course, possible that this loan too was taken out by a consortium and the merchant in the papyrus is only a representative, but nowhere is this implied in the papyrus. The agreement in the text, as established by Casson, stipulates that the debtor transport the goods to Alexandria and place them under the creditor's name and seal there until the loan has been paid off.[170] The loan was contracted at Muziris in India with a financier who was wealthy enough to provide this kind of loan, as well as maintain agents in Egypt. This person was possibly a member of the Roman 'merchant colony' in Muziris, which was mentioned in the previous section. Without his own means of transport, the merchant paid the shipowner, and later the cameleers, in order to obtain cargo space. Indeed, the verso of the papyrus refers to six parcels which the merchant had loaded aboard the ship *Hermapollon*,[171] for which he presumably paid the master of the ship the cost of carriage. The *Hermapollon* was no doubt carrying several such consignments for various merchants, possibly in addition to the cargo of its owner or charterer.

In this way merchants of relatively limited means could participate in the trade with India, Arabia and Africa. Either in a consortium or as an individual they could take out a loan and purchase their stock, pledging the stock as security on the loan. They then arranged for the carriage of the goods to Egypt, where they were conveyed to Alexandria and placed in the public warehouse there, at which time the *tetarte* was levied and removed. By the terms of the loan in *P. Vindob.* G 40822 it appears that the merchant would then sell the goods in Alexandria rather than convey them to Rome and sell them there, as the loan provisions allow the creditor to seize the goods in Alexandria in the event of default. Presumably the way in which the debtor intended to pay off the debt was by sale of the goods, and so we conclude that in this case at least the goods must have been sold *in* Alexandria. This may well have been the usual practice, although it is difficult to tell as we do not have any parallel examples.

In addition to these smaller operators, we also possess evidence for merchants wealthy enough to maintain their own ships, or at least to charter them on a regular basis without the need to obtain loans in order to do so. Indeed, it was probably on the ships of these traders that the merchants discussed earlier hired space, and in some cases (such as in the case of the Vienna papyrus) it was to them that they turned in order to obtain their finance. Such wealthier merchants also seem to have maintained agents in various places involved in the trade. We might recall that the lender in the Vienna papyrus had representatives at both Coptos and Alexandria, as well as the representative with whom the papyrus was actually drawn up, presumably at one of the Red Sea ports. Here, we are clearly dealing with people of far greater means than those discussed earlier.

An example of this wealthier type of merchant is afforded by a dedicatory inscription from a temple at Medamoud in the Nile valley.[172] Aelia Isidora and Aelia Olympias were, as the inscription reveals, clearly women of considerable wealth who were able to set up a dedication in a temple, employ an agent and maintain their own ships, or at the very least regularly charter them. The inscription reads:

> Λητοῖ θεᾶ̣ μεγίστη̣
> Αἰλία 'Ισιδώρα καὶ Αἰλί[α]
> 'Ολυμπιὰς ματρῶναι
> στολᾶται ναύκληροι κα[ὶ]
> [ἔμπο]ροι ἐρυθραικαὶ ἅμ[α]
> [. . . 'Α]πολιναρίω̣
> ἐπάρχ[ω̣. . .]ς 'Ολυμ–
> πιάδος καὶ [. . .
> ἀμφοτέρων [. . .
> ἀνέθηκαν [. . .

> To the great goddess Leto, Aelia Isidora and Aelia Olympias, distinguished matrons, *naukleroi* and merchants of the Red Sea, together with Apollinarios the *eparch* of . . . of Olympias and (Isidora) both . . . dedicated (this).[173]

These two women are clearly merchants of more substance than the relatively small players discussed earlier. For one thing, the fact that they were able to make a dedication in a temple implies some wealth, as does their employment of an *eparch*. The most significant term, however, is the expression *naukleroi*, which indicates that they either owned or chartered merchant ships;[174] in this case, these were ships that were trading on the Red Sea. It is unclear exactly what role Apollinarios the *eparch* had: he may have been the captain of the women's ships,[175] or, as is probably more likely, their business manager.[176] In either case, he is clearly ranked below the two women in the inscription and should be considered their subordinate.[177]

Aelia Isidora and Aelia Olympias were clearly able to conduct their business on a much larger scale than would have been possible for those merchants who were forced to borrow funds to conduct an expedition to India. Very possibly they maintained agents in various places associated with the trade just as did the creditor in the Vienna papyrus. These agents would have purchased goods in India and shipped them to Egypt on ships either owned or chartered by the women, whereupon they would be conveyed to Alexandria. It is difficult to say exactly how involved the two women were in this trade, but it is probable due to their social standing and wealth that most of the work was done by their agents. However, their involvement seems to have been their primary occupation, as they call themselves merchants and shipowners on their dedicatory inscription – clearly the income generated by their trading activities was enough to sustain them in their social position.

Indeed, Aelia Isidora and Aelia Olympias seem to have been distinguished ladies of relatively high social status. Their possession of the *nomen* Aelia indicates that they or their ancestors had received the Roman citizenship under Hadrian, so this places them in the upper echelons of society. In addition, in their inscription they style themselves as *matronai stolatai*, a title of some distinction that implies they owned considerable property and could conduct their affairs without a guardian.[178]

The Archive of Nicanor also mentions agents of several different individuals who probably operated in the same manner as did the agents of Aelia Isidora and Aelia Olympias. Several individuals, or their agents, are mentioned in the archive as maintaining offices at either Myos Hormos or Berenike, and sometimes at both locations. One Parthenios son of Paminis is attested in the archive as having interests at both Myos Hormos and Berenike,[179] and is also mentioned as the dedicator of a temple inscription at Coptos.[180] Thus it would appear that this man was able to maintain agents at the two Red Sea ports and Coptos.[181] Others, including individuals who appear to be Roman citizens, are also mentioned in the Nicanor archive.[182] All these indicate a considerable merchant community operating in the Red Sea trade, many of whom were wealthy enough to maintain agents at several locations important in the trade.

There is also evidence of a still higher echelon of participants in the trade who appear to have operated entirely through agents, often their own freedmen. Such individuals, given the attitude to trade and merchants which was prevalent in the Roman world,[183] did not personally involve themselves in the commerce but, like the senators of Rome who conducted their business affairs through intermediaries, maintained some distance between themselves and their investments in the Red Sea trade.

One such individual who is attested in the Nicanor archive is Marcus Julius Alexander, who is mentioned as having business interests at Myos Hormos and Berenike between AD 37 and 44.[184] This individual was a member of an extremely rich and influential Jewish family in Alexandria, and was most probably the brother of Tiberius Julius Alexander, prefect of Egypt, and the nephew of the Jewish philosopher Philo.[185] Thus we see a prominent member of the *ordo equester* involved in the Red Sea trade. Presumably, of course, such a person would have conducted all his business activities by means of agents rather than personally, but it is nonetheless clear that it was not just relative nonentities in the Roman world who were engaged in the Red Sea trade.

Another individual of this type was Annius Plocamus, a *publicanus* who had farmed the Red Sea taxes from the Roman government.[186] In the account of Pliny which mentions this man, already quoted above in connection with the trade with Sri Lanka, it is stated that in the reign of Claudius a freedman of Annius Plocamus was blown off course while sailing around Arabia. Thus, this freedman was presumably engaged in commercial activities on the Red Sea on behalf of his master when he was blown off course.[187] Inscriptions mentioning freedmen of Annius Plocamus have also been found on the route between the Red Sea and the Nile, although these date from AD 6,[188] indicating the involvement of this family in the Red Sea trade many years before Claudius' reign. This family appears to have been of some importance, and a part of the local aristocracy of Puteoli, an Italian port heavily involved in the eastern commerce.[189]

A third example of a person of high rank being involved in this commerce comes from a later period, the third century. Firmus, who briefly seized Egypt as an imperial pretender after AD 272, is described in the *Historia Augusta* as having gained some of his wealth by sending merchant ships from Egypt to India.[190] Although much of the information contained in the *Historia Augusta* is unreliable, this account at least indicates that it would not have been unthinkable for Firmus to have gained his wealth in this way. In these three examples, therefore, we can see evidence of the involvement of individuals of quite high rank in the Red Sea commerce.

Of course, there would have been numerous opportunities for various persons with capital to have profited as a result of the trade without actually becoming involved, although regrettably there is no clear evidence which can tell us who they were. Some such may have become involved in the area of financing expeditions in the way the creditor of the Vienna papyrus did, or simply acting as the financial backer of a trip to India. It would appear from the evidence presented that the Red Sea commerce could be very profitable, so it would perhaps be surprising if some of the wealthy members of upper-class Roman society were not involved in the commerce in some way.

Direct imperial involvement in the trade

Some evidence has been put forward to suggest that the emperors themselves may have also been involved in the commerce in some way. Indeed, Sidebotham has suggested that all the imperial activity such as the construction of roads and ports and the provision of military stations in the Eastern Desert can be traced to direct imperial involvement in and profit from the trade.[191] Accordingly, we should examine the evidence Sidebotham offers, as it could both tell us the extent of imperial involvement and offer an explanation for the provisions the Roman government made for the trade. On the other hand, if there turns out to be no evidence of direct imperial involvement in the Egyptian Red Sea commerce, we will be forced to look elsewhere to find the reason for these major works provided by the government.

Sidebotham puts forward evidence from the Nicanor archive, as well as some amphora plugs from the excavation at Quseir al-Qadim, to show the involvement of imperial slaves or freedmen in the Red Sea commerce.[192] It is contended that these pieces of evidence, which mention the names of imperial freedmen or slaves, are proof that the emperors were engaged in the Red Sea commerce by means of their freedmen agents. However, it should be noted that these ostraka and plugs are similar to the remainder of the Nicanor archive, and simply mention the provision of various items of food or other staples to these imperial freedmen. Thus, as Casson has pointed out, the existence of freedmen of the emperor at these ports does not have to indicate that they were actually involved in the trade: they could well have been involved in some form of local government.[193] Areas of possible involvement which suggest themselves might be the collection of various taxes which were imposed at the Red Sea ports, or the administration of the system of passes which was in force on the Eastern Desert roads, as revealed in the Coptos tariff. While there is no concrete proof for these suggestions, we can equally say that there is no proof that these imperial freedmen were directly engaged in the Red Sea commerce on behalf of their imperial masters.

Accordingly, it would seem somewhat dangerous to construct a hypothesis of imperial encouragement of the trade based upon direct involvement from such questionable evidence. It may indeed be the case that the emperors were involved in the Red Sea commerce in some manner by means of their freedmen, but it has not been proved. Indeed, even if it was the case, it is still a long way from saying that this justified the expense of constructing facilities in the Eastern Desert and providing military garrisons in the area. The profit realised from some limited imperial investment in the commerce would surely not offset the expense of providing all these facilities. We must look for a reason for the construction of these facilities elsewhere than in the protection of direct imperial investment in the Red Sea commerce.

Non-residents of the empire involved in the trade

As well as the numerous members of Roman society involved in the trade, there is also evidence of merchants from outside the empire being involved in the eastern commerce of the empire. The presence of these individuals shows quite clearly that the trade was never a monopoly of any particular group: there is no evidence that the Romans ever tried to restrict participation in the trade in any way. Thus, many of the theories mentioned in the Introduction, which describe exclusive monopolies in the eastern trade being protected or broken by the Romans, are clearly unsupportable. The evidence for these individuals is certainly fairly incidental in nature and tells us very little about the persons concerned, but it is still significant, and attests to the involvement of various non-residents of the empire in the Red Sea commerce.

Indian merchants are attested at Alexandria in two literary references, showing that Indians visited Roman Egypt: in one case this presence is explicitly stated as being related to trade. Dio Chrysostom mentions that Indians and Arabs were to be seen in the audiences of shows at Alexandria,[194] and in another instance Xenophon of Ephesus mentions an Indian rajah who had come to Alexandria to sightsee and to trade.[195] Archaeological evidence from the Red Sea ports also suggests the involvement of Indians in the commerce. A Tamil-Brahmi graffito was found at Berenike naming a Chera chieftain, Korran, showing the presence at Berenike of Tamil-speaking individuals in the first century AD.[196] In addition, a Tamil family name has been found among the inscriptional evidence at the Quseir al-Qadim excavation,[197] and this same name has also been found at the excavation of the port of Arikamedu in India.[198] It would thus seem highly likely that Tamil merchants were involved in the Red Sea trade in Roman Egypt, although we are unclear exactly what it was that they were doing. Given the attestation already noted that Indian merchants came to Alexandria to trade, it would not be surprising if these Tamils were merchants also.

Similar evidence has come to light showing the participation of Arabs in the trade. Apart from the mention by Dio Chrysostom cited above, this evidence is epigraphic. The most significant of these inscriptions comes from a temple dedication at Coptos, in which a citizen of Aden in south Arabia who was involved in the Red Sea commerce made an offering to Isis and Hera.[199] This evidence is complemented by three Minaean graffiti found in the Wadi Hammamat on the road from Coptos to Quseir al-Qadim:[200] although the information given in the inscriptions is minimal, the location of the graffiti would suggest that the authors had some involvement in the Red Sea commerce.[201]

The apparent participation of these individuals in the trade is important, because many scholars have supposed that the Egyptian Red Sea trade was developed by the Romans at least in part to remove non-Roman 'middlemen' such as the Sabaeans and the Nabataeans from their involvement in the commerce.[202] The presence of these non-Romans as active participants in the trade in Egypt clearly shows that the exclusion of 'middlemen' was not a driving motive in the Roman policy toward the Egyptian Red Sea commerce. If the Romans intended by promoting the Egyptian commerce to exclude non-Roman elements in the trade, why then would they allow non-Romans to participate freely in the trade within Egypt? Obviously, the Romans did not exclude such individuals from Egypt, and this in turn makes it most unlikely that the Romans ever had any intention of excluding any non-Roman intermediaries in the trade, Arab or otherwise. As far as can be told, participation in the Red Sea trade was open to anyone who had the capital to be so involved, and who was willing to pay the duties that the Romans levied.

Ships and shipping of the Red Sea trade

In addition to the merchants who were involved in the Egyptian Red Sea trade, there were several other groups of people who gained their living from the trade in a more peripheral manner. Chief among these would have been those who manned the ships which made the voyages to India, Arabia and Africa. There is some evidence to suggest that there was an active community of sailors and shipwrights based in the Red Sea ports. The vessels used by the Romans were probably the same as those used in the Mediterranean, and were manned in a similar way.[203] This would appear to be confirmed by the discovery of a pictorial graffito at Berenike depicting a large square-rigged ocean-going merchantman similar to the types used on the Mediterranean at the time.[204]

The Coptos tariff provides a list of individuals involved in the manning of ships who needed to traverse the desert to the Red Sea. These include 'helmsmen of the Erythraean Sea', ship's lookouts, sailors, shipbuilder's servants and artisans.[205] This variety attests the existence of a substantial maritime community at the Red Sea ports, as well as shipbuilders who perhaps actually constructed ships for the trade, but at least were certainly involved in their maintenance.

The ships manned by these people were either owned or chartered by *naukleroi*, who have already been mentioned in this section. *Naukleroi* were more merchants than seafarers: often the inscriptions describe the same people as both *emporoi* (merchants) and *naukleroi*. The inscription recorded earlier in this chapter concerning Aelia Isidora and Aelia Olympias is one example of this: the two ladies were described as '*naukleroi* and merchants of the Red Sea',[206] showing that the two occupations were here filled by the same people. Similarly, another inscription from the second or third century describes a group of Palmyrene traders active in the Red Sea commerce in the same terms.[207]

There do not seem to have been any 'shipping firms' or similar arrangements involved in the Red Sea trade: as far as our meagre evidence allows us to investigate, it appears that those merchants who owned ships operated them as an (obviously) necessary part of their business of trading in the merchandise of the Red Sea, but not as a commercial venture in themselves. These individuals would presumably hire the crew members noted above in order to man their ships for the voyage: whether on a per-voyage basis or somewhat more permanently we cannot tell, although it is probable that the hiring was done as a combination of the two. Regardless of which is the case, however, it is apparent that the Red Sea commerce provided a living to many individuals who were involved in shipping the goods and maintaining the ships in a seaworthy condition.

Caravan transport within Egypt

Another group related to the conduct of the Egyptian spice trade was the camel and donkey drivers of the Eastern Desert, who were of course indispensable to the successful conduct of the commerce. The most important information in this regard comes from the Archive of Nicanor. We have already noted the value of this archive in supplying names of various individuals who were involved in the Red Sea commerce, but it also gives us the names of those who were actually partners or associates in Nicanor's transportation business. These ostraka indicate a business in supplying individuals at Myos Hormos and Berenike with assorted goods between 18 BC and AD 69. From the various ostraka, which with few exceptions consist of receipts for goods received at Myos Hormos or Berenike, we can identify the names of some of those who participated in the family business: it included Nicanor son of Panes, Philostratos and Apollos, his brothers, Miresis and Peteharpocrates his sons, and Isidora the daughter of Menodoros, whose affiliation with the family is not clear.[208]

The ostraka also provide evidence of the kinds of goods transported by this company. Interestingly, they do not seem to be trade goods according to the information we have, although some have suggested that this is the case.[209] Instead, the goods carried are food and drink, and other everyday items of low value such as mats, medicines, clothing and rope.[210] The business would thus appear to have been concerned with the provision of the necessities of life to the residents of the Red Sea ports of Myos Hormos and Berenike. Clearly these places were heavily, if not entirely, dependent upon the Nile valley for the provision of food, drink, and anything else necessary for the continued running of an office at one of the ports. Thus, the opportunity existed for enterprising transporters to gain a living by the supply of these necessities. The papyri and ostraka excavated at Quseir al-Qadim and Berenike also reflect this: many of them are also concerned with the supply to the port of goods similar to those mentioned in the Nicanor archive.[211]

There is no immediate reason apparent why the Nicanor business was not involved in the transport of the valuable trade goods. There are, however, a few possibilities that might be suggested, although there is no evidence for any of them. One may be that the archive which was found dealt only with one-way traffic from Coptos to the Red Sea, whereas the return traffic (which would of course include the trade goods) was recorded elsewhere and has not been found. If this, however, were the case then one might expect that the receipts found would include mention of goods destined for export (such as glass, textiles and silver), which they do not. Another possibility is that the government may have licensed certain transporters to carry the trade goods, and the Nicanor business was not included in that number. It may also be possible that the merchants of the Red Sea trade employed their own drivers and guards to carry the valuable goods, and employed independent firms such as Nicanor's only for the transport of staples which did not require any degree of security. However, these ideas must remain speculation in the absence of any evidence.

The existence of separate caravans for the expensive import goods may, however, be implied in the Vienna papyrus, where the writer refers to 'your' (i.e. the creditor's) camel driver, implying that the driver in question was either permanently employed by the creditor or at least had been exclusively engaged by him for this particular trip.[212] Thus, whereas businesses such as Nicanor's shuttled their goods up and down the desert roads all year,[213] the large caravans carrying the imported goods from the East were specially organised only when the boats returned from India and Arabia. As the boats from each destination would all arrive at approximately the same time, due to the fact that they were all dependent upon the monsoon for their return voyage,[214] the organisation of these caravans would have been limited to, at most, a few months of the year.

Several ostraka and inscriptions found at Quseir, along the desert roads and at the road station of el-Zarqa indicate that Nabataeans were involved in the commerce, chiefly as camel and/or donkey drivers. These inscriptions are generally dated in the second century AD, and consist for the most part of caravaneers' greetings or columns of figures.[215] It is possible that Nabataeans were brought into Egypt or came there of their own accord because of their knowledge of the desert and experience in conducting caravans in their own homeland.

We can identify a wide variety of people who were involved in the Egyptian Red Sea trade. These individuals vary widely in their relative wealth and social status, ranging from the freedmen agents and administrators as well as those listed in the Coptos tariff who also drew an income from the trade in some way or another, right up to perhaps the emperor himself. Unfortunately, we are unable to determine what effect this income from the trade might have had on the society of Egypt as a whole, or in what way it might have affected the economy of the province, due to the absence of any trade figures of real significance.

What does seem clear, however, is that the trade was of sufficient volume to provide many individuals, including some of considerable wealth, with a reliable source of income. This applies not only to those who were directly involved in the trade as merchants, but also to people who were involved in peripheral industries which nonetheless relied substantially on the eastern commerce, such as Nicanor's transport business and the shipbuilders and craftsmen who maintained the ships of the Red Sea trade. In all these areas, the trade was clearly significant enough to provide these individuals with a living. The possibility thus exists of the commerce exerting at least some influence on the political and economic makeup of the province of Egypt, if not on the Roman East as a whole.

Government involvement in the Red Sea trade

In addition to the participation of private individuals in the commerce, our evidence also attests to the involvement of the imperial government in various ways. One significant area of governmental involvement is the collection of customs duties by government officials, while another was the provision of roads, ports and fortifications on the Red Sea coast and on the desert journey from that coast to the Nile valley. By examining the evidence which exists dealing with these areas, it is hoped that some conclusions can be reached concerning the reason for the government involvement in the Egyptian Red Sea commerce.

Government officials and the collection of customs duties

In the course of the journey from the Red Sea ports to Alexandria, the merchants of the Red Sea trade would encounter several Roman government officials, both civilian and military. While some of these individuals were involved in the administration and monitoring of all traffic in Egypt, some of them appear to have performed tasks specific to the Red Sea trade. These dealings seem to have begun as soon as the ship landed at one of the Red Sea ports. When they docked, the ships entered the territory under the jurisdiction of the *praefectus montis Berenicidae*, but the official with whom the merchants had to deal immediately was a functionary known as the *arabarch*. This official is known to have fulfilled two functions with respect to the Red Sea trade, both to do with the collection of duties and tolls of various types.[216]

The first function of the arabarch is seen on the verso of *P. Vindob* G 40822, which gives a list of goods carried in the shipment in question and includes mention of some goods being removed by the *arabarch* at the time of the ship's arrival in Egypt. The document states that small proportions of ivory and fabric which had been imported were removed by the *arabarchs* at the Red Sea port of arrival: ivory tusks to the value of 1,175 drachmae out of a total value of the shipment of 76 talents 5,675 drachmae, or 0.25 per cent; and fabric to the value of 1,592 drachmae 3 obols out of a shipment to the total value of 8 talents 5,882 drachmae 3 obols, or 2.88 per cent.[217]

There are several points in this papyrus which warrant mention. First, the account mentions goods removed 'by the *arabarchs*' whereas elsewhere the office is always referred to in the singular.[218] It thus may be that there were in fact several of these officials, as the other citations do not actually require that there be only one *arabarch* at a time; alternatively, the office might have been made a multiple one for a short time and then later changed back to being a single office. In the absence of any other information it is difficult to tell, but the Vienna papyrus certainly indicates that at least at one time there was more than one person filling the post of *arabarch*. Another point of interest is the differing rates of duty levied on different goods. The shipment of 60 containers of Gangetic nard does not appear to have been levied at all; the ivory attracted a levy of 0.25 per cent whereas the cloth was taxed at 2.88 per cent. It may have something to do with the bulkiness of the items, as the tax is highest on the item with the least value per pound, the cloth. The cloth is valued at 70 drachmae per mina of weight, whereas the ivory was valued at 100 drachmae per mina. The weight of each of the 60 containers of nard is not stated, but as it is valued at 4,500 drachmae per container we can be sure it was worth considerably more on a value per mina basis than the other goods.[219] It is possible that we might view this duty as a kind of 'road use' tax by which the *arabarchs* penalised most heavily those goods which were less valuable on a cost-per-weight basis: the tolls may have been intended to defray the cost of the maintenance of the roads and *hydreumata* along the route, and so the goods which took more room in the caravans for less eventual return to the government when the *tetarte* was imposed were taxed the most heavily at the port of arrival.

Similarly, goods entering the port of Berenike from elsewhere in Egypt, either for local consumption or for export, were taxed. In the 1997 excavations of the site an archive of ostraka from the customs-house at the port was found, which consists for the most part of orders to let certain goods pass through the customs-house.[220] The official to whom these dues were paid is not mentioned, although it may well have been the *arabarch*. The only officials mentioned in the Berenike archive are 'those in charge of the customs-gate', and one Andouros, a *quintanensis*, a military post in charge of part of a camp.[221] This would appear to mean that the military were involved in the collection of these dues, but in what capacity is not clear.

Another toll levied on users of the Eastern Desert roads by the *arabarch* was, as has already been seen, the charges for road use described in the Coptos tariff.[222] Unlike the tax levied at the ports, these taxes were levied upon persons and beasts of burden using the road; the Coptos tariff is clearly not the same tax as that mentioned in the Vienna papyrus. Again, the occupation of the *arabarch* seems to be primarily associated with the collection of various taxes and levies, under the supervision of the *praefectus montis Berenicidae* who was himself responsible to the prefect of Egypt.[223]

The office of *arabarch* is very possibly identical to the post of *alabarch*, which is mentioned by Josephus as having been held by Alexander, brother of Philo and father of Tiberius Julius Alexander and Marcus Julius Alexander.[224] Several scholars have come to the conclusion that the offices were in fact the same, and referred to an officer in charge of revenues in the Eastern Desert.[225]

The Roman satirist Juvenal refers to an *Aegyptius Arabarches*,[226] which was most likely a disparaging reference to Tiberius Julius Alexander. Thus, even though Josephus does not actually state that Tiberius himself was *alabarch*, the family relationship combined with the similarity of the terms would seem to imply strongly that the terms *alabarch* and *arabarch* in fact refer to the same office.

One objection which might be raised to this, however, is that the references in Josephus all seem to refer to someone resident in Alexandria rather than in the Eastern Desert and subordinate to the *praefectus montis Berenicidae*. One possible explanation for this is that the officials who removed the taxes in the Red Sea ports were functionaries who simply acted upon the orders of the *arabarch* in distant Alexandria. Another possibility is that there were several people holding this post at one time, as indeed would seem to be implied in the Vienna papyrus's use of the plural to describe the office. Thus, one individual could have been *arabarch* in Alexandria, and responsible for some sources of revenue there, while another could have been *arabarch* in the prefecture of Berenike, and responsible for the collection of revenue in that area.

There also appears to have been another official who was involved with the collection of customs duties in the Red Sea ports. An inscription from the early Augustan or possibly the late Ptolemaic period from the Nubian temple of Dakka mentions someone holding the office of *paralemptes* (customs-collector) of the Red Sea:[227]

> [Ἀπολ]λώνιος Πτολεμαίου
> [ἀραβάρ]χου υἱός στρατηγὸς τοῦ
> [Ὀμβ]είτου καὶ τοῦ περὶ Ἐλεφαν–
> [τίνην] καὶ Φίλας καὶ παραλήμπτης
> [τῆς Ἐρ]υθρᾶς θαλάσσης . . .
>
> Apollonios, son of the *arabarch* Ptolemaios, *strategos* of Ombeitos and the region around Elephantine and Philae, and *paralemptes* of the Red Sea.[228]

While it is clear that the office is different from that of *arabarch*, the relationship between the two posts is unclear. It is possible that the position of *paralemptes* involved the collection of dues from merchants who had travelled across the Eastern Desert from the Red Sea into the region of Elephantine and Philae (modern Aswan). As has been noted earlier, the routes across the Eastern Desert do not appear to have been concentrated upon Coptos until the reign of Tiberius.[229] It is possible then that in these early years there was a customs-collector based at Syene who collected *portoria* in that region which were different from those collected by the *arabarch* for use of the Eastern Desert roads.

As we have already noted in the earlier discussion on the Red Sea trade in Egypt, the eastern merchandise reaching Coptos was impounded in a public customs-house there until the relevant dues were paid, as the Vienna papyrus revealed. It is possible that these taxes were the same as those collected by the *paralemptes* of the Red Sea in Syene in an earlier period, although the papyrus reveals nothing of the nature of these taxes or the amount that was exacted. Nonetheless, given the fact that taxes had already been paid to the *arabarch* at the Red Sea port of arrival (as is shown on the verso of the papyrus and discussed above), it would seem most likely that the taxes paid in Coptos were to a different authority; this authority might have been the *paralemptes* of the Red Sea. Alternatively, of course, since the only attestation we have for this post dates from the earliest period of Roman occupation, or perhaps even earlier, the position of *paralemptes* may have been abolished by the time of *P. Vindob.* G 40822. This certainly would explain the failure of the Vienna papyrus to mention this official, but again we cannot be sure. Regrettably, it would seem that the administrative structure of the Egyptian Eastern Desert in the early imperial period must remain unclear.

As has already been discussed in the subsection on Alexandria, the final and major tax exaction on a shipment of eastern goods passing through Egypt was the *tetarte*, which was paid in Alexandria. Unlike the previous lesser levies that were exacted on the Red Sea and in Coptos, and which appear to have been paid directly to a government official, the collection of the *tetarte* was farmed out to publicans. In Pliny's reference to the freedman of Annius Plocamus, to which reference has already been made on other occasions, he states that Annius Plocamus 'purchased the *uectigal* of the Red Sea from the treasury'.[230] Given the fact that the other taxes we have examined were paid directly to government officials, it would seem likely that the *uectigal* farmed by Annius Plocamus was the *tetarte*. However, it is also possible it is yet another levy on the Red Sea commerce collected by the Romans of which we have no other knowledge. Regardless, it is abundantly clear that the Roman government collected significant tolls from any eastern luxury merchandise passing through Egypt. With this fact in mind, then, it will be instructive also to take careful note of the provision of military protection in the Eastern Desert. What exactly was it that the Roman army was doing in the Eastern Desert?

The military presence in the Eastern Desert

The routes between the Red Sea ports and the Nile valley are equipped with forts, called *hydreumata*, which are distributed at fairly regular intervals along the roads. The features which these *hydreumata* typically exhibit are fairly uniform, including a substantial walled enclosure capable of housing troops and offering protection to passing travellers, and enclosing a well, whence the name *hydreuma*. Control of a string of fortified wells such as these along a route would effectively give control of that route, as well as the ability to offer effective protection and revictualling to anyone who was using the route.

Particularly informative is the siting of these fortifications. Almost without exception, the *hydreumata* are sited on the valley floor on the direct line of the road even when more defensible high ground is available. They are thus clearly not intended primarily as defensive installations, but are rather concerned with protecting and controlling the route.[231] These forts are clearly not designed to suppress desert tribes or any such general security measure, but are solely intended to house soldiers who were concerned with controlling the desert roads.

In addition to the *hydreumata*, which are found on most of the Roman roads of the Eastern Desert, a system of watchtowers is also present on the Coptos–Quseir road.[232] The towers on this road number approximately 65 and are found both close to the route and high in the hills surrounding it. The towers are much more common in the more mountainous eastern region of the route, where sighting and signalling distances are much shorter. In the flatter, more open territory closer to the Nile, there was clearly less need for whatever function it was that the towers filled.

Zitterkopf and Sidebotham established that the towers were intervisible and that their intervisibility existed independently of the *hydreumata*. It would thus be possible to signal from one end of the route to the other simply by waving a flag or flashing a polished shield from each tower in succession, with no need for any signalling from any of the forts. From this they concluded that the towers were primarily signal stations designed for signalling up and down the road, while also possibly filling route-marking and security functions. However, they noted that the use of these towers as watchtowers would have been hindered by the presence of some towers on the wadi floor, where they would presumably have been of little use in supervising the route and the approaches to it.[233]

While it would certainly seem clear that the towers were used for signalling along the route, their use as watchtowers should not be rejected altogether. There still remains the possibility that the towers existed for a dual purpose: that is, they could have been used for both security and signalling purposes. The security role is also indicated by the system that was used to man the towers. Several groups of ostraka and other inscriptions have survived, which appear to be a roster system for the manning of the towers.[234] These documents give the names (or numbers) of pairs of guards which alternated daily with another pair. On their day of duty, one guard of the pair is listed as *ano* (up) and the other as *kato* (down).While it has been suggested that these terms refer to patrols 'up' and 'down' the road,[235] this is unlikely because it would mean that there would have been one-man patrols travelling up and down the roads in the middle of the desert, which would seem a rather dangerous and unusual practice.[236] On the whole, Bagnall's suggestion that the terms refer to pairs of guards on the watchtowers, one on top of the tower and the other in the wadi on the road,[237] seems by far the most logical.

This rostering system has implications for the purpose of the towers. If the towers were used exclusively for signalling along the route, it is difficult to imagine what role the guard rostered as 'down' could have played. A linear signal route would have required only *one* signalman, who would remain in the tower awaiting signals. However, as Bagnall notes, the two-guard system would allow the tower guard to sight approaching bandits or some other trouble and signal to the 'down' guard in the valley to investigate.[238] In addition, he could signal along the line of towers to get additional help from the nearest *hydreuma* if that were necessary. The towers were therefore probably used for a variety of purposes, including signalling, security and possibly route-marking.

The existence of such a complex system of fortifications obviously implies a substantial investment by the Roman authorities in the Eastern Desert, in terms of both money and manpower. Generally speaking, it has been assumed that these facilities were provided in order to protect the caravans from the threat of banditry.[239] Indeed, there is considerable evidence which would suggest that there *were* substantial security threats in the Eastern Desert, making it at least likely that the fortifications were designed to protect the traffic on the road.

Certainly the nomads who lived in the Eastern Desert would have presented a problem to traffic passing through this area in Roman times, as indeed they had in Ptolemaic times. There were various peoples who inhabited these regions, generally grouped by the Romans under the broad heading of 'Trogodytes', and there is some evidence that these peoples raided traffic using the Eastern Desert roads from time to time. Several votive offerings from the *Paneion* at el-Kanais on the Berenike–Edfu road dating from the Ptolemaic era give thanks for the dedicator being 'saved from the Trogodytes',[240] indicating that these nomadic inhabitants could offer a threat to traffic traversing the road. No doubt the rich caravans carrying high value but portable items such as silks, spices, gems and precious metals would have provided a tempting target to nomads living in this area. It may be that, in the early period at least, these nomads were the primary threat against which the security measures in the Eastern Desert were built. Problems with nomads, however, were not confined to the earlier period. As will be described further on in this chapter, a group called the Blemmyes occupied the region and severely curtailed the trade from the later third century onward.[241]

Such rich targets as the spice caravans would prove tempting for others besides the desert nomads such as the Trogodytes and the Blemmyes. There is considerable papyrological evidence to indicate that after the second century AD in particular, there was a considerable banditry problem within Egypt, derived chiefly from displaced villagers who fled their lands to avoid crippling tax burdens.[242] In order to combat this problem, a large and complex security system was put in place throughout the whole province. By this system Egyptian villagers were grouped into small bands of about nine men under the leadership of an officer called a *dekanos*, and then used for various policing duties including acting as guards in the watchtowers.[243] Many of the names of the guards on the watchtower guard rosters mentioned above are Egyptian, indicating that the system of *dekanoi* was used in the Eastern Desert, and that villagers could be drafted for duty on the watchtowers in this region. However, the system of watchtowers is not only confined to the Eastern Desert but also attested in papyrological evidence within the Nile valley, even though no physical remains have survived.[244] It would thus seem clear that whatever security problem prompted the construction of these watchtowers was more widespread than just along the routes in the desert but rather spread throughout Egypt, although of course the valuable cargoes traversing the desert roads would have been especially in need of protection.

That this security situation was occasioned by a substantial rise in the level of banditry in the later second century, which itself was caused by a more severe tax regime, is well attested. Egypt was, by the second century, renowned for its high level of bandit activity,[245] and this is reflected in the documentary evidence. There is considerable evidence of displacement and rebellion in the villages of Egypt, especially after AD 160 or so, which leads to a very rapid decline in population in many villages of Egypt during this period.[246] Several papyri from this time refer to people leaving the land to evade taxes and taking up a life of banditry.[247]

Allowing this to continue not only would adversely affect law and order, but also would adversely affect the tax income gathered by the Roman officials due to the reduced number of people actually working the land and paying taxes. This then no doubt explains at least in part the interest the Romans had in protecting the caravans travelling from the Red Sea to the Nile valley. If these were not protected they would provide an extremely tempting and vulnerable target for bandits, and it is conceivable that the richness of the pickings might encourage more people to a life of banditry rather than one of obediently paying taxes to Rome. That these caravans were indeed an attraction to bandits is demonstrated by the Greek novelist Xenophon of Ephesus, who describes a bandit who settles in Egypt in order to live off the trade from India.[248] Obviously the spice and silk trade could provide a thief with a rich living, so the Romans were forced to make greater provision for the protection of this trade as tax-evasion, banditry and lawlessness increased in the later second and third centuries.

Thus we can clearly see that the Roman government took a strong interest in the Egyptian Red Sea trade, both from the perspective of collecting taxation and customs, and from the point of view of protecting the caravans militarily. However, both the Vienna papyrus and the Coptos tariff mention the use of private guards on the desert roads. We might then very well ask the question: if the Roman troops and their fortifications were there to provide protection for the caravans, why would it have been necessary to provide private guards?

One possible explanation is that the Roman troops were not, in fact, primarily interested in protecting the caravans. Sidebotham has suggested that at least part of the role of these troops could have been that of controlling and monitoring the traffic rather than simply protecting it.[249] Indeed, it may even be that the protective role of the Roman army in the Eastern Desert of Egypt has been greatly overstated, and that their main area of interest was in supervision of the traffic.

A reason for such control immediately presents itself: we have already seen that the government extracted several different taxes and dues from the Red Sea traffic, ranging from dues extracted at the ports to the *tetarte* which, according to the evidence we have, seems to have been imposed at Alexandria. Such taxes might well have been avoided, however, if a merchant were to land his goods at an uncontrolled port, or if he were to convey them inland on an unmonitored route so that he could dispose of them before any or all the taxes were paid. Therefore, in this hypothesis, the chief role of the Roman soldiers was not to *protect* the caravans, but rather to ensure that the goods passed along the approved routes and were impounded in the customs-houses at Coptos and at Alexandria until the appropriate duties had been paid. The Roman control of the major routes and watering points throughout the desert would have ensured that alternative routes were difficult if not impossible, and thus ensured that all the taxes found their way into the imperial purse as intended.[250]

Nonetheless, the protective role cannot be discarded entirely. An inscription from Antinöe (which will be given in full in the next section) describes the *Via Hadriana*, a road connecting Antinöe with the Red Sea. The road is described as passing through 'safe and even places' and being equipped with 'wells, stations and guardposts',[251] in terms which suggest that all these were benefits provided by the euergetism of the emperor. However, if the sole purpose of the Roman troops had been to control and monitor the traffic, one might be surprised to see their fortifications listed among the benefits provided by the emperor. In order for these installations to have been seen as a boon to the merchants of Antinöe, it would seem that at least some sort of protective role should be allowed for the Roman military presence in this area.

We should probably therefore understand the Roman troops in the Eastern Desert to be fulfilling both protective and monitoring roles. It is nonetheless possible that at times the protective role of these troops may have been over-emphasised, while conversely their control and monitoring function has been downplayed or ignored altogether. Their presence would undoubtedly have made it difficult or impossible for merchants to have evaded the payment of the *tetarte* and other taxes. Nonetheless, the *hydreumata* could have also been used as shelter by merchants, and the troops in these installations would have provided protection from bandits, at least in the close vicinity of a *hydreuma*. However, troops might have several kilometres to cover before they reached the scene of an attack, and so most merchants would also have engaged private guards to ensure their cargoes were kept safe.

In either case, then, we can see that the chief interest held by the Roman authorities in this traffic was the collection of taxes. We should see their protection and control of the Red Sea commerce in the same light as their protection of the quarries in the Eastern Desert: the soldiers were there to protect an important source of imperial income, and to ensure that this income was not diminished, either by theft or by evasion.

The primary motivation for the construction of military facilities in the Eastern Desert, and indeed for the presence of all the government officials in the region, was therefore the extensive tax revenues which accrued to the state as a result of the trade. As will be demonstrated below,[252] these tax revenues were considerable, and the protection of this important income is more than enough to account for the Roman interest in guarding and monitoring the caravans. We may also, therefore, expect to find similar interest in the protection of spice, silk and incense traffic in other places in which it was found, such as Arabia and Syria.

A point which must be emphasised is the essential *reactivity* of the Roman government's involvement in the trade. As other aspects of the international trade in the Roman East are studied, this principle will be noted again and again. In the Egyptian trade there is no trace of a deliberate Roman policy designed to encourage (or for that matter discourage) the commerce for the sake of boosting the empire's economy or for any political end. In this case as in others, the sole official Roman interest in the trade was to milk it for all it was worth, and to provide sufficient protection to ensure that this tax revenue continued to flow.

Egyptian trade in the Antonine period

The prosperity of the Egyptian Red Sea trade appears to have continued well past the initial period of development in the first century AD. Indeed, given the way in which the trade expanded as a result of the establishment of peace in the Mediterranean in the first century, it would be surprising if the pre-eminent peace and prosperity of the Antonine period had not brought similar prosperity to the eastern luxury trade.

There is, in addition to the evidence for the continuation of the trade along the lines used in the first century AD, some evidence which seems to indicate important initiatives to encourage trade in Egypt in the second century. If this is the case, this should be seen as a significant departure in the Roman attitude toward the commerce. As has already been shown, the Romans generally did not act to guide, promote or encourage the trade, instead confining their investment to the provision of port facilities and of military supervision and protection to ensure that the commerce continued to provide a source of revenue for the imperial purse. The actual development of new lines of trade is unprecedented, and if this proves to be the case in the second century then we should identify it as a major change in Roman policy toward the Red Sea trade. Before we examine these new developments, however, we will first examine the continued use of the trade routes used in the first century.

Red Sea commerce in the second century

The ports of Berenike and Myos Hormos continued to be used during the second century, although the archaeological evidence from the ports would seem to indicate that they declined from the peak of activity in the first century.[253] Graffiti from the reign of Hadrian have been found on the road from Coptos to Quseir al-Qadim,[254] showing that this road was in use at this period. It would seem therefore that the conduct of the Red Sea commerce in the second century AD continued along previously established lines, although on a somewhat reduced scale. This continued contact with the East is also probably reflected in the numerous contemporary literary references to India from this time. The *Geography* of Claudius Ptolemy in particular displays a great deal of accurate information on India, while less scientific but nonetheless significant allusions to India and places further afield abound in the literature of the period.[255] In one example, Dio Chrysostom commented about the vigour of the Red Sea trade in his description of Alexandria during Trajan's reign,[256] showing that the trade was in good health in his time. Aristides also, writing in the same period, makes similar comments.[257] Although the archaeological evidence would indicate that the trade had declined in this period, these literary allusions assure us that it had not disappeared.

One important difference during this period, however, is in the way in which the region of the Eastern Desert was administered. In the first century the Eastern Desert region was a military area under the command of the *praefectus montis Berenicidae*, who was directly responsible to the prefect of Egypt. In the second century, however, this situation appears to have changed and the Eastern Desert was brought under the normal civilian administration found in the rest of Egypt. *P.Hamburg* 7 of AD 132 states that the *arabarch*, who in the first century had been under the command of the *praefectus montis Berenicidae*, now took his orders from the civilian *epistrategos* of the Thebaid.[258] Accordingly, at some time prior to this the Red Sea coast must have been made part of the normal provincial administration of Egypt.

As well as this change, which may have been brought about by a reduced concern for the security of the Eastern Desert, there was also an expansion in the number of routes available to the merchants of the eastern trade in the Antonine period. These, regardless of their apparently limited success, may have been intended to promote the eastern trade.

Trajan's canal from the Nile to the Red Sea

The first of these initiatives was the construction of a canal along the Wadi Tumilat between the eastern branch of the Nile delta and the head of the gulf of Suez at Clysma. This canal had been constructed much earlier, and had subsequently been rebuilt on several occasions. Earlier work on a canal at or near this site was undertaken by Necho, Darius I and Ptolemy II Philadelphus, and was recorded by several historians of the Classical period.[259] It would appear that Trajan decided to rebuild and reopen the canal of Ptolemy II, which had long since silted up.[260] The construction of this canal and its attribution to Trajan are recorded by Ptolemy, who mentions the construction of the *Amnis*

Traianus at this site, passing from the Nile at Babylon near modern Cairo to the Red Sea at Clysma.[261] The course of this canal is still discernible in some places.[262]

Although the exact purpose of these canals is not explicitly stated, the connection of the Nile valley to the Red Sea would have been very convenient for the Red Sea trade, as it would obviate the need for the goods to be transported over the desert between the Red Sea ports and the Nile. Indeed, in approximately AD 170 Lucian refers to the connection of Clysma to the Nile and its use as a port to reach India:

> ἀναπλεύσας ὁ νεανίσκος εἰς Αἴγυπτον ἄχρι τοῦ Κλύσματος, πλοίου ἀναγομένου ἐπείσθη καὶ αὐτὸς εἰς Ἰνδίαν πλεῦσαι
>
> When the young man had sailed into Egypt as far as Clysma, and a ship was then departing, he was persuaded to sail to India.[263]

Since the young man in question had sailed from Alexandria, it was clearly possible to sail from there to Clysma, which could have been achieved only by means of the canal.[264] In addition, this citation testifies to the use of Clysma as a port involved in the Red Sea trade with India. It is thus clear that the canal was used in connection with the Red Sea trade, and it appears to have been in use fairly consistently over the rest of the Classical period, as several papyri of the third century and later make reference to the canal.[265] Indeed, the greatly reduced costs of water transport in the ancient world when compared with land transport would make it a very attractive alternative to the other Red Sea ports, which required the goods to be transported over the Eastern Desert.

It is a matter of some interest, then, that Clysma did not supplant Myos Hormos and Berenike entirely. As has already been noted, the use of these ports continued into the second century, despite the presumably greater cost of their use due to the need for land transport. The main reason, it would seem, for the continuation in use of these ports is that the prevailing wind in the northern Red Sea comes consistently from the north, making it very difficult for a sailing vessel to reach the tip of the Gulfs of Suez and ‘Aqaba.[266] Thus, especially when these winds were blowing hard, it may well have been easier for ships to put in at Berenike or Myos Hormos than to continue north to reach Clysma. However, despite this, the evidence we have for the use of Clysma, as well as for the use of the Nabataean port at Leuke Kome on the opposite side of the Red Sea,[267] demonstrates that ships were able to make the journey to the northern end of the Red Sea.

Sidebotham suggests that Clysma may have been used for bulkier cargoes such as grain and textiles, which could have been exported from the Arsinoite nome in the Fayyum oasis where they were produced.[268] These bulky goods would be far more suited to carriage by the canal than by the overland passage to the Red Sea ports, and so this may be the reason why both Clysma and the southern Red Sea ports continued in operation side-by-side. Bulkier cargoes, which could not easily be transported overland, would have used the canal, whereas the lighter and more expensive items of the Red Sea trade were more easily transported by land to or from Coptos. In addition, their higher values could more easily absorb the cost of overland transport.

The quantity of heavier cargoes such as grain and textiles being exported from Egypt to India and Arabia may have increased in the Antonine period, whereas trade in the previous century may have been more in coin, which is of course much more easily transported. This could be indicated by the fact that the issues of Roman *denarii* found in the coin hoards in India are almost exclusively Julio-Claudian:[269] perhaps by the second century more trade was being carried on in kind rather than for cash, and so the volume of goods leaving Egypt increased. If this is the case, it could have provided a need for the construction of the canal so the bulky goods could be exported efficiently.

In any case, despite the evidence which we have for the use of the Wadi Tumilat canal in the second and third centuries, it seems that it did not prosper greatly. Archaeological investigations of the port of Clysma have revealed that it flourished mainly in the Ptolemaic period and then in the fourth century and later, with relatively little use apparent in between.[270] Apparently, then, Clysma experienced only limited use in the second and third centuries. This situation appears to have continued until developments in the fourth century reduced the significance of Berenike and caused Clysma to flourish, as will be discussed in the next section. Nonetheless, the evidence we have already noted does indicate that the canal, and thus presumably Clysma too, was used at least to some extent in the second century AD.

As to whether Trajan intended the canal as an encouragement to the Red Sea trade, it is very difficult to say given the absence of any literary accounts of the construction of the canal. While it might initially be difficult to imagine what other use the canal might have had aside from its commercial function, it is still doubtful that we could with justification call it a deliberate attempt to foster the Red Sea trade. If the canal indeed was designed with a commercial motivation in mind, it is more likely to have been done as an act of euergetism by the emperor than as anything that could be dignified by the name of 'economic policy'. Also, it may be that the reconstruction of the canal was not considered a new development in the trade so much as the repair of an artery of trade from the Ptolemaic period. The canal was after all not a completely new initiative: given the existence of previous canals on the site it is quite likely that Trajan simply opened up a canal which was already in existence and merely needed dredging out and repairs. It is possible that we should see the repairs to the canal as analogous to the repairs to the Coptos–Red Sea roads noted earlier in the reign of Tiberius.

One possibility that probably should not be overlooked is that the canal may in fact have been built not for commercial reasons, but for military ones. Indeed, there is some reason to suppose that it, like the emperor's other major constructions, was built with a military purpose in mind.[271] It may have even been possible that Trajan was contemplating a circumnavigation of Arabia in emulation of Alexander the Great's intention, perhaps in association with his Parthian expedition. If this were the case, a canal connecting the Red Sea to the Nile might have been of use in allowing the circumnavigating fleet to reach the Mediterranean. While there is of course no proof for this, it perhaps should be considered as a possible alternative explanation for the construction of the canal.

The Via Hadriana

The canal of Trajan, however, was not the only work in Egypt in this period which may possibly have been designed to promote the Red Sea trade. In the following reign, the Emperor Hadrian also appears to have taken action to promote this trade by the construction of a new road through the Eastern Desert, the *Via Hadriana*. The course of the road is currently being surveyed for the first time. The survey has revealed that the road departs from the Nile city of Antinöe and heads straight to the Red Sea, reaching it well north of Myos Hormos, and then continues down the Red Sea coast, passing through all the ports of the eastern commerce until Berenike, the terminus of the road.[272] This road is mentioned in an inscription from Antinöe commemorating its construction. After Hadrian's titulature in the nominative, the inscription continues:

> ὁδὸν καινὴν Ἁδριανὴν ἀπὸ
> Βερενίκης εἰς Ἀντινόου διὰ
> τόπων ἀσφαλῶν καὶ ὁμαλῶν
> παρὰ τὴν Ἐρυθρὰν θάλασσαν
> ὑδρεύμασιν ἀφθόνοις καὶ
> σταθμοῖς καὶ φρουρίοις δι–
> ειλημμένην [ἀν]έτεμεν
>
> (Hadrian) built the new Via Hadriana from Berenike to Antinöe, through safe and even places by the Red Sea, and equipped at intervals with plentiful wells, stations and guardposts.[273]

The inscription seems to imply civilian use of the road: it is hard to imagine what this might be apart from the conveyance of the Red Sea traffic. Unlike Trajan's canal, however, there is no additional need such as the capacity to transport bulk cargoes which can be adduced to account for the construction of the *Via Hadriana*. As far as can be told, the new road simply duplicated the role already performed by the roads between Coptos and the Red Sea. Can this then be seen as an attempt to foster the growth of the Red Sea trade, or perhaps evidence of something a little more sophisticated than the simple desire to collect taxes?

Sidebotham and Zitterkopf suggest that the *Via Hadriana* may have been intended more as a military or administrative road than a commercial one.[274] This is perhaps supported by the apparent lack of fortified *hydreumata* on the section of the road crossing the desert, which might indicate the absence of traffic which needed to be protected or monitored.[275] However, given the wording of the commemorative inscription noted above, it appears that at least some commercial use of the road was envisaged by Hadrian.

A possible answer lies in the chosen Nile terminus of the road, Antinöe. This city was founded by Hadrian in AD 130 in the course of his visit to Egypt, at which time the road also was commenced. Although the city was founded to commemorate Hadrian's lover Antinous, who drowned in the Nile at this point, the foundation should be seen as a part of Hadrian's overall policy of founding urban centres, construction of various public works and other acts of euergetism throughout the empire in general.[276] The probable answer lies in Hadrian's desire to give his new foundation a source of income and wealth. It may be that Hadrian decided to attempt to divert some of the caravan traffic coming from the Red Sea to Antinöe by the new road. Accordingly, there is no need to see the *Via Hadriana* as an attempt deliberately to foster the Red Sea trade. Rather, it would seem more likely that it was an attempt to use the Red Sea trade to foster the growth of a newly founded Hellenistic city in Egypt.

In this way it can be seen that Hadrian did not depart from traditional Roman attitudes toward the Red Sea trade in the construction of his road. Far from being an attempt to expand the Red Sea trade itself, it is simply another Roman exploitation of the wealth generated by the trade, although in this case to a slightly different end. In so doing, of course, Hadrian's action testifies to the wealth which could be gained from the exploitation of this trade.

It would thus appear that in the second century AD the Egyptian Red Sea trade continued to operate, although perhaps on a more limited scale than in the first century. For the most part, this trade continued to flow along the same routes that it did in the previous century, that is, from the Red Sea ports of Berenike and Myos Hormos to Coptos via the roads through the Egyptian Eastern Desert. There were, however, two developments in the period, the *Amnis Traianus* and the *Via Hadriana*. The canal may have been necessary to move bulk cargoes upon which the trade had begun to depend more, or it may even have been built as a military enterprise without any commercial purpose. Hadrian's road, as we have seen, may have been built to provide a source of income to the new foundation of Antinöe. In neither case is there good cause for postulating a proactive Roman 'economic policy' aimed at encouraging and expanding the Red Sea trade. Rather, as ever, the Roman policy continued to be a reactive one of responding to needs, mainly with the objective of maximising the indirect tax income from the commerce.

Decline of the trade in the third century

The general decline in the volume of the Red Sea trade seems to have continued and intensified in the third century. In the early years of the third century, however, the trade was still active. Much of the evidence that comes from the end of the second century and the beginning of the third interestingly mentions the previously unattested activity of Palmyrenes, both traders and soldiers, in the Red Sea commerce. Before examining the downturn of the trade in the later third century, therefore, it is proposed to examine the evidence for the trade in the Severan period, especially that which refers to the activities of Palmyrenes.

Palmyrene participation in the Red Sea commerce and trade in the Severan period

The merchants of Palmyra were especially active in the second century AD in the commerce which reached from the head of the Arabian Gulf at Spasinou Charax into Roman Syria. However, toward the end of that century a series of wars in Mesopotamia adversely affected their commerce, which may have caused some traders to begin using different routes.[277] Accordingly, some Palmyrene merchants may have followed the trade upon which their livelihood depended into these new trade routes, which brought some of them to Egypt in the latter half of the second century AD.

The evidence for Palmyrene involvement in the Red Sea trade is indeed quite considerable. One particularly important inscription found at Coptos records a dedication by a group of Palmyrene merchants of the Red Sea, which reads as follows:

>]ιον Ζαβδάλα Σαλμά–
> νου καὶ 'Ανείνα 'Αδρια–
> νῶν Παλμυρηνῶν
> ναυκλήρων 'Ερυθραικῶν,
> ἀναστήσαντα ἀπὸ θεμελίου
> τὸ προπύλα[ι]ον καὶ τὰς στουὰς
> τρεῖς καὶ τὰ θυρώ[μ]ατα ἐκ και–
> νῆς, τὰ πάντα ἐκ τῶν ἰδίων
> αὐτοῦ, φιλοκαγαθίας χάριν
> ['Α]δριανοὶ Παλμυρηνοὶ συν–
> έμποροι τὸν φίλον.

> Zabdalas son of Salmanos, also (called ?) Aneinas, of the merchants of the Red Sea from Hadriane Palmyra, who has set up anew from the foundations the propylaea and the three stoas and the chambers, entirely from his own funds, his colleagues the merchants of Hadriane Palmyra (set this up) to their friend, for his friendship and distinction.[278]

This inscription appears to describe a distinct community of Palmyrene merchants and shipowners who were operating in the Egyptian Red Sea trade. Another fragmentary inscription from Denderah further downstream, generally dated between 160 and 212, also mentions Palmyrene merchants and *naukleroi*.[279]

Indeed, the building in which the inscription was found at Coptos has been interpreted as having been the headquarters of a Palmyrene trade guild or some similar organisation, based upon the evidence from the inscription and twelve *stelai* found at the site carved in the typical Palmyrene 'frontal' pose.[280] Although this interpretation has been challenged, as the *stelai* concerned are all of Egyptian workmanship,[281] the inscription found there would certainly seem to indicate the existence of at least a Palmyrene community and some sort of cultic organisation at Coptos. Whether or not we could categorise such an entity as a 'trade guild', we can have little doubt that the Palmyrene merchants of Coptos and Denderah formed a notable and distinct community in these cities, and may well have combined their resources for commercial enterprises as well as for religious ones.

The commerce in which these merchants were engaged was, no doubt, the same as that in which the other merchants of Coptos were involved: that is, the Red Sea trade with Arabia and India. Some, however, have suggested that they might have been involved in the transportation of goods from Palmyra itself, through Arabia and across the Red Sea, and then to the Nile valley.[282] There is in fact no evidence at all to suggest that such an extraordinarily circuitous route was ever in use, and no reason to suppose that the Palmyrene merchants of Egypt were not private individuals engaged in the same trade as their counterparts from Roman Egypt and further afield.

These merchants were not the only Palmyrenes to be found in the Egyptian Eastern Desert, however. An inscription from Coptos[283] shows that a unit of Palmyrene archers was based at that site at some time before AD 216.[284] In addition, a Greek dedication uncovered in the 1996 season of excavation at Berenike was made by a Palmyrene archer named Marcus Aurelius Mokimos to Caracalla and Julia Domna, and is dated to AD 215.[285] Another inscription from the 1997 season is probably a military inscription from the same period.[286] It seems clear that Palmyrene auxiliaries were present at Coptos and were also involved in the patrolling of the desert roads between Coptos and the Red Sea ports. It is most probable that they were brought there due to the similarity of terrain in the Eastern Desert and the desert fringe of Syria, and the extensive Palmyrene experience in desert patrolling gained by the protection of caravans in Palmyrene territory.[287] Their presence there indicates the continuing necessity of patrolling the Eastern Desert roads, which must show that the trade was still functioning in this period.

The Palmyrenes, of course, were not the only people using these trade routes at this time: the eclectic mix of merchants who had always used this area continued to do so throughout the Severan period. The Medamoud inscription describing the trading activities of Aelia Isidora and Aelia Olympias (which was described previously)[288] is generally dated to this period also, indicating the continuing participation of Egyptian Greeks in the commerce throughout this time.[289] In addition, archaeological investigations appear to show that the commercial traffic was still using the Red Sea roads and ports. Graffiti from the third century are present on the road between Coptos and Quseir al-Qadim,[290] and the Palmyrene inscriptions from Berenike indicate that the port was still in use in this period.

The Severan period thus appears to have been a time of continuing, though declining, activity at the Egyptian Red Sea ports. Sidebotham also contends that the Severan period was a time of declining contact with India, based on his reading of the late second and early third century written sources. These show a decreased awareness of places such as India and Arabia, and an apparently greater reliance on hearsay evidence than on observation.[291] This may, however, be more a commentary on the quality of the sources than on the vitality of the eastern trade.

Decline of the trade in the third century

There is considerable evidence to show that the Egyptian Red Sea trade suffered a marked downturn in the later third century. This is not to say that the trade ceased altogether: there is still evidence that the commerce through the Red Sea ports was active in the later third century, such as the mention of Firmus' trading activities at that time in the *Historia Augusta*.[292] Nonetheless (as will be seen), there is good reason to believe that the volume of commerce passing through the Egyptian Red Sea ports declined significantly at this time.

The archaeological evidence for such a decline is generally negative: that is, it consists for the most part of an *absence* of finds for the later third century as compared with the periods beforehand and afterward. There is evidence for trading activity on the Red Sea from the Severan era; similarly, it will soon be seen that there is comparable solid evidence for the conduct of the trade in the fourth century. In the later third century, however, there is a marked lack of finds of any sort in most locations associated with the trade. While the absence of finds from just one or two locations could not be taken to have any real significance, a solid pattern of such absences from a wide variety of sites associated with the Egyptian Red Sea trade can legitimately be taken as evidence for a decline of the trade during this period.

Perhaps the most noticeable decline in the amount of physical evidence comes from the Egyptian Red Sea ports. It appears that the port of Quseir al-Qadim, which we have elsewhere identified as Myos Hormos, ceased to be used by the end of the second century. Ceramic and numismatic evidence from the site ceases almost entirely by this time, with the exception of one billon tetradrachm of the last half of the fourth century, which cannot be taken by itself as evidence of the continued use of the port during that period.[293]

Similarly, the recent excavations at Berenike have uncovered a pattern of decline in the third century. Between the two periods of main use at the port, the first and second centuries AD and the fourth to fifth centuries, there is very little datable evidence.[294]

This decline in volume of traffic using the Egyptian Red Sea ports also appears to parallel developments in the coin evidence from India. After the decline in the use of Roman silver coinage in southern India after the Julio-Claudian period, the major Roman currency used in Indian trading was the *aureus*. Numerous examples of imperial *aurei* from the Antonine and Severan periods have been discovered in southern India.[295] However, there are no Roman coins at all from the later third century. While it is true that the *aurei* of this period were so heavily debased that they would have been in any case of extremely limited use in international trade,[296] the apparent coincidence of the disappearance of Roman coins from India with the decline of the Egyptian Red Sea ports would seem to indicate a general downturn in the Red Sea commerce in the later third century. It could be argued that trade could have continued in bullion and/or trade goods in this period despite the debasement of coinage at this time. However, as will be discussed shortly, the debasement of the coinage would most probably have reflected a significant bullion shortage, which would itself have made commerce more difficult.

Each taken by themselves, the decline of Myos Hormos, or Berenike, or the cessation of the use of Roman coins in southern India would not be conclusive evidence of a decline in the fortunes of the Red Sea trade. However, when taken together, they certainly do seem to indicate such a decline. Many scholars have taken the evidence from coinage, coupled with the evidence for severe unrest in Egypt and throughout the Roman East in this period,[297] as sufficient to establish a generalised decline in the eastern trade.[298] Coupled with the evidence from the excavations at Berenike and Quseir al-Qadim, to which these scholars did not have access, there is compelling reason to postulate a decline in the fortunes of the eastern long-distance trade in the third century AD.

There are several reasons why the civil wars and economic crisis of the third century might have had a damaging effect on the eastern long-distance trade.[299] The greater prevalence of warfare would, of course, impede the trade severely. It has already been seen that the trade began to prosper in a period of peace and Roman prosperity beginning in the later first century BC;[300] it should hardly surprise us that the resurgence of internal warfare in the third century would damage the trade. Similarly, the rampant inflation which gripped the Roman world throughout the third century would have harmed international commerce as the buying power of Roman currency collapsed. The scale of this inflation is illustrated in Tables 2.1 and 2.2, which show the decline in silver content of Roman *denarii* and *antoniniani* in the course of the third century.[301]

As the central government struggled to find bullion to pay the troops, it resorted to systematic debasement to obtain more coinage.[302] As this took place, however, the confidence of traders in the coinage eroded, and trade tended to

Table 2.1 Silver content of imperial *denarii* AD 193–241

Emperor	*Date*	*Silver (%)*	*Weight (g)*	*Silver weight*
Pertinax	193	87.11%	3.16	2.75
Didius Julianus	193	81.33	2.95	2.40
Severus	193–194	78.42	3.14	2.46
Severus	194–196	64.58	3.07	1.98
Severus	196–211	56.28	3.22	1.81
Caracalla	211	54.41	3.20	1.75
Caracalla	212–215	50.94	3.28	1.67
Caracalla	216	53.35	3.15	1.68
Caracalla	217	50.78	3.07	1.56
Macrinus	217–218	57.85	3.15	1.82
Elagabalus	218–219	45.30	3.15	1.43
Elagabalus	219–220	48.39	2.96	1.43
Elagabalus	221–222	45.48	3.05	1.38
Alexander	222–228	43.03	3.00	1.29
Alexander	229–230	45.11	3.24	1.46
Alexander	231–235	50.56	2.94	1.49
Maximinus	235–238	47.73	3.04	1.46
Gordianus I	238	62.80	2.77	1.71
Balbinus	238	55.00	2.80	1.55
Gordianus III	240–241	48.11	3.03	1.46

Table 2.2 Silver content of imperial *antoniniani* AD 215–253

Emperor	*Date*	*Silver (%)*	*Weight (g)*	*Silver weight*
Caracalla	215–217	51.18	5.09	2.60
Macrinus	217	60.38	4.87	2.94
Elagabalus	218–219	45.58	4.94	2.26
Balbinus	238	49.75	4.79	2.37
Gordianus III	238–239	47.77	4.51	2.16
Gordianus III	240	49.77	4.48	2.24
Gordianus III	241–243	44.68	4.43	1.98
Gordianus III	243–244	41.63	4.16	1.66
Philip	244–245	42.82	4.22	1.82
Philip	245–247	43.25	4.01	1.74
Philip	247–248	43.25	4.14	1.78
Philip	248–249	47.07	4.12	1.94
Decius	249	47.64	4.02	1.92
Decius	250–251	41.12	3.97	1.64
Gallus	251	36.54	3.42	1.26
Gallus	252	36.15	3.52	1.28
Gallus	253	35.12	3.45	1.22
Aemilian	253	35.50	3.53	1.36

be carried on in barter rather than monetary transactions.[303] Given the greater degree of difficulty of transporting bulk goods, long-distance trade must have been severely affected. In addition, the serious inflation would have greatly reduced the ability of citizens to purchase luxury goods.

The effects of an increase in unrest, an unreliable coinage, and a diminishing market combined to curtail severely the activities of the eastern long-distance trade. While such a reduction is impossible to quantify, we may gain some idea of the scale of the reduction by examining the effects of the crisis on internal trade within the empire, as reflected in the numbers of shipwrecks from given periods of time. The shipwrecks found in the Mediterranean from the late Hellenistic and Roman periods show that the greatest period of trading activity was from *c.* 200 BC to AD 200, with a significant dip in the third century, recovering somewhat in the fourth.[304] While these figures refer to trade in the Mediterranean basin, it would seem probable that the trade in the Red Sea will have followed the same pattern.

The later third century was also a time of rising unrest and banditry in Egypt, probably caused by the onerous tax burdens imposed by the government in an effort to increase the supply of money. Egypt seems to have suffered severe demographic disruption after the AD 160s, and this situation does not appear to have been corrected throughout the third century. Banditry had always been a problem in Egypt, but the problem seems to have intensified in the later second and third centuries as many villagers left their homes and often took up a life of banditry in order to avoid their increasingly burdensome tax obligations. As discussed by Alston, *P.Thmouis*, an account of taxation in a region of the Nile Delta, records a catastrophic decline in the population of several villages as well as severe unrest in the AD 160s.[305]

The situation became much worse in the last thirty years of the third century, however, as Egypt was racked by a series of invasions and rebellions which were not ended until after Diocletian regained control of Egypt at the end of the century. The Blemmyes, a nomadic tribe from the south, began to raid and occupy the southern parts of Egypt and the Eastern Desert in the later third century, and continued to do so throughout the fourth and fifth centuries.[306] They raided extensively in the latter part of the third century, seizing Coptos between 268 and 270 until they were finally driven off by the future Emperor Probus.[307] They continued to trouble southern Egypt for many years, resulting in a retraction of the frontier to Philae south of Syene by Diocletian,[308] and the creation of a special command against them, the *dux Aegypti et Thebaidos ultrarumque Libyarum*, which is attested from AD 308/309 at Luxor.[309] Nonetheless, they continued to occupy large areas of southern Egypt and the Eastern Desert at various times throughout the next two centuries. It is also possible that the Blemmyes' attack on Coptos in 268 may have been part of an alliance with the Palmyrenes who invaded Egypt in 270 and occupied the country until their defeat by Aurelian in 272.[310]

After the Palmyrene invasion, Egypt was racked by a long series of imperial usurpations, beginning with Firmus soon after the expulsion of the Palmyrenes, and culminating with those of Achilleus and Domitius Domitianus in the reign of Diocletian. In the suppression of the latter, Diocletian destroyed the city of Coptos in about 297, and besieged the city of Alexandria.[311] As has been discussed, both these cities were important centres in the eastern commerce, and their removal would have adversely affected what was left of the trade. The end of the third century therefore appears to have been a time when the Egyptian Red Sea trade was basically untenable: the market for its goods had declined due to the empire's financial crisis, the routes across the Eastern Desert were troubled by bandits and nomadic tribes, and finally Diocletian had taken two of the most important centres of the commerce out of action.

Recovery of the trade in the later period

However, the Red Sea trade did eventually recover from the poor state into which it had fallen in the later third century. Presumably this was because of the re-establishment of order in the empire by Diocletian and Constantine, and the restablilisation of the currency, especially Constantine's introduction of the gold *solidus* which became the pre-eminent trade coin of the whole East in the late Roman and Byzantine periods.[312]

There is considerable evidence to indicate that Trajan's canal between the Nile and the Red Sea and its associated port of Clysma was at its peak of trading activity in the fourth and fifth centuries AD. As has already been noted, the papyrological evidence dealing with the use of the canal dates almost entirely from this period;[313] literary evidence also points to the use of Clysma as a port for the Indian trade in the fourth century.[314] The archaeological record indicates that this was a period of high use of the port at Clysma: more than three thousand coins of the later Roman period were found in the French excavations of Clysma in the 1930s compared to only one coin of Hadrian from the preceding period.[315] As Raschke has suggested, it is likely that this surge in use of Trajan's canal and of the port at Clysma is due to Diocletian's destruction of Coptos, which would have rendered the more southerly ports of the Red Sea temporarily unusable.[316] Combined with the resurgence in the financial state of the empire at the close of the third century, this created a new demand for readily accessible ports in the northern end of the Red Sea. Clysma was one obvious choice; Aila ('Aqaba) in Arabia, which also experienced a surge in prosperity at this time, was another.[317]

Despite this, it would seem that the ports of the southern Red Sea soon recovered from the destruction of Coptos and were able to participate in the renewed period of prosperity in the fourth century. Evidence from the excavations at Berenike shows that the port recovered from the slump of the later third century and continued in use well into the Byzantine period. Indeed, the majority of trenches at the site contained substantial evidence of activity at the port from the early fourth century through to the early sixth century,[318] including apparent evidence of contact with south Arabia and/or Axum.[319] Interestingly, a great deal of the evidence from this period seems to indicate the presence of a distinct non-Egyptian ethnic group at the site: it is possible that these are in fact the Blemmyes, who perhaps controlled the port at this time.[320]

In addition to Berenike, another port of the Red Sea coast seems to have come into use at this time. The University of Delaware's excavations of the late Roman fort of 'Abu Sha'ar on the Red Sea coast have revealed use of this installation from the fourth century AD through to the seventh. This occupation is divided into a military occupation from the late third and early fourth centuries to some time later in the fourth century when the fort was abandoned, and a Christian settlement making use of the abandoned fort which existed there from perhaps the late fourth and early fifth centuries through to the early seventh century.[321] Epigraphic evidence found at the site seems to indicate that 'Abu Sha'ar was used as a port for the Indian trade, at least in the early period of its occupation. A Latin inscription found at the site read:

>]noua Maximi[
>]um mercator[[322]

The publishers suggest a reconstruction of *ad usum mercatorum*, 'for the use of merchants' or something similar, with *Noua Maximiana* being the designation of a military unit: this reading seems likely.[323] This would then indicate that the early fourth-century occupation of the site (based on the name of the military unit and a Tetrarchic dedication also found at the site)[324] was for the use of merchants. Essentially, the fort and military protection in the area was designed to protect the Red Sea trade, in the same way that the forts of the Coptos–Berenike and Coptos–Quseir al-Qadim roads were used in the first and second centuries. It seems clear, therefore, that the trade had recovered to some extent in the early fourth century, and there were once more merchants operating on the Red Sea coast whose potential tax contribution made them worth monitoring and protecting.

Further evidence for a resurgence of the trade with India in the fourth century AD is provided by the numismatic evidence from the subcontinent itself, especially that from Sri Lanka, which acquires a great deal of importance in this period. Indeed, the volume of Roman coins from Sri Lanka is quite considerable at this time, showing that the late Roman and Byzantine periods represent the time of greatest trading contact with Sri Lanka. The fourth and fifth centuries are particularly well represented in this numismatic record, the most common coin finds being issues of Constantine I, Constantius II, Valentinian I and Theodosius I.[325]

It seems, however, that when the Roman traders re-entered the Indian Ocean, they were faced with competition from Persian and Axumite traders, who had established themselves while the Romans were absent in the later third century. The discovery of Persian and Axumite coins from this period at various points concerned with the Indian Ocean trade indicates that these traders were certainly active at this time,[326] and there are literary references to competition between Roman and Persian traders in the Indian Ocean during this period as well.[327] Nonetheless it would be greatly overstating the case to contend that the trade was now entirely in the hands of the Persian and Axumite 'middlemen', as the aforementioned literary reference certainly describes Roman traders being present in Sri Lanka. While it is certain that Persian and Axumite traders were now also active in the Indian Ocean, there is no reason to suppose that Roman merchants were absent.

The Red Sea commerce thus experienced a significant recovery at the close of the period under study, when the fortunes of the Roman Empire, badly shaken in the later third century, were revived by the efforts of Diocletian and Constantine. This is demonstrated by the archaeological evidence from the Red Sea ports, which indicates a surge in activity at this time compared to the lull in the previous period, as well as the numismatic evidence, especially from Sri Lanka, which shows that a significant commerce was underway between that island and the Mediterranean world in the fourth and fifth centuries, and indeed throughout the Byzantine period. Nonetheless, the structure of the commerce had changed somewhat, with more emphasis now being placed on ports in the north of the Red Sea, Clysma and Aila.

The third century was thus a period of great variety in the fortunes of the Egyptian Red Sea trade. Indeed, we may well describe this time as the end of the 'Classical' period in the commerce, and the beginning of the 'Byzantine' period of trade patterns. During this time, the patterns which the eastern commerce followed throughout the Classical period were finally abandoned, and a new set of patterns, which characterised the trade until the coming of Islam, were set in place.

Conclusion: the significance of the trade in Egypt

In this chapter we have examined a large accumulation of evidence about the eastern long-distance commerce in Egypt, which has allowed us to learn a great deal about this trade. It has been possible to reconstruct with some accuracy the manner in which the trade was carried out. Regrettably, however, the relative economic significance which the trade had in Roman Egypt is impossible to discover, given the absence of any reliable or usable trade figures. We can, however, see that there were some groups of people who were able to make a living from the trade, not only the merchants directly involved in the commerce, but also those who benefited indirectly from the commerce, such as desert transporters, sailors, shipbuilders and others. The fact that numerous people were thus able to gain a living from the commerce would of course indicate that the trade was not insignificant. Inevitably, however, in a province with such a lively and diverse economy as was possessed by Egypt, the significance of the trade must have been watered down to some extent. Nonetheless, it cannot but have contributed to the overall prosperity of Roman Egypt: to what extent, however, it is very difficult to say.

The commerce does, however, appear to have been of some significance to the Roman government, especially considering the expense and effort that was put into the construction and maintenance of military facilities in the Eastern Desert. As far as can be told, this interest is related chiefly to the collection of the taxes which were imposed on the trade, and accordingly theories of Roman involvement for other reasons, such as to weaken other trade routes or stimulate the economy of the empire, should be rejected. In order to ensure that the merchants paid their taxes, it was necessary both to protect them from brigandage and to prevent them from disposing of their goods before the taxes were paid. The revenue from the taxes, especially the *tetarte*, must have been considerable,[328] and is more than enough to explain the Roman military presence in the Egyptian Eastern Desert.

The Roman interest in the Red Sea trade, then, should be seen as a reactive one. The Romans should not be understood as deliberately stimulating the Red Sea trade, but rather as reacting to the existence of a trade that was already there, and being interested in protecting the trade as a source of imperial income. This military supervision can thus be seen as analogous to that provided for the quarries in the Eastern Desert: both are to protect imperial income, although the income from the quarries was direct rather than indirect as was the case with the Red Sea trade.

Despite the limitations of the available evidence, we are nonetheless able to glean a significant understanding of the workings and the importance of the Egyptian Red Sea commerce. Indeed, this picture is far more detailed than that which we are able to gain from any other area where the trade was active, and the conclusions drawn here may in fact be applicable in other areas where our information is more limited.

3

THE ARABIAN INCENSE TRADE

Like the sea trade into Egypt, the overland trade in aromatics which reached Arabia already had a long history by the time of the Roman entry into the affairs of the East in the first century BC. The Arabian perfumes of frankincense and myrrh had long been prized among the peoples of the Near East, and were an important part of both Near Eastern and Mediterranean religious practices. Accordingly, a strong market already existed for these commodities in the Mediterranean world, and the inhabitants both of the incense-producing regions and of those regions on the trade routes were able to exploit this market to their advantage.

Many of the trade routes between southern Arabia and the Mediterranean crossed the Nabataean kingdom. By the time of the Romans' appearance in the East, the Nabataeans were heavily involved in this trade and had attained considerable wealth and power.[1] In this chapter, we shall examine the sources of the incense and the routes by which it was carried into and throughout the kingdom. From this, and from the other evidence of the trade which can be assembled, we shall attempt to determine what effect the trade had upon the societies of Nabataean and Roman Arabia, and upon political developments in those spheres.

The trade routes of the Nabataean kingdom

The Nabataeans, who may have originated in the Arabian peninsula,[2] occupied the area south and east of the Dead Sea by the fourth century BC. By the first century BC they had expanded to become a wealthy and powerful kingdom by their control and exploitation of caravan routes through their territory. In the first literary reference to the Nabataeans, Diodorus Siculus refers to their wealth and its source:

> οὐκ ὀλίγων δ' ὄντων 'Αραβικῶν ἐθνῶν τῶν τὴν ἔρημον ἐπινεμόντων οὗτοι πολὺ τῶν ἄλλων προέχουσι ταῖς εὐποριαῖς, τὸν ἀριθμὸν ὄντες οὐ πολὺ πλείους τῶν μυρίων· εἰώθασι γὰρ

> αὐτῶν οὐκ ὀλίγοι κατάγειν ἐπὶ θάλασσαν λιβανωτόν τε καὶ σμύρναν καὶ τὰ πολυτελέστατα τῶν ἀρωμάτων, διαδεχόμενοι παρὰ τῶν κομιζόντων ἐκ τῆς Εὐδαίμονος καλουμένης Ἀραβίας.

> Although there are not a few of the Arab tribes using the desert as pasture, these greatly exceed the others in wealth, being not much more than ten thousand in number. For not a few of them are accustomed to bring down to the sea frankincense, myrrh and the most valuable of the aromatics which they receive from those who carry them from Arabia called Eudaimon.[3]

It can be seen from this quotation that, in Diodorus' view at least, the wealth of the Nabataeans was based upon their trade in aromatics and was well established by 31 BC. As was noted earlier,[4] their trade was primarily in the South Arabian aromatics such as frankincense and myrrh rather than in the Indian spices and other eastern goods which made their way into the Red Sea by the sea passage from India. It remains possible, however, that some of these Indian spices could have found their way to Petra from Eudaimon Arabia (Aden), which is known to have received cargoes from India.[5] Nonetheless, all literary references to Petra's trade refer solely to South Arabian aromatics,[6] and it must therefore be assumed that these formed the basis of Nabataean wealth, at least in so far as that wealth was derived from trade.[7] This is a point which deserves some emphasis, as many scholars have mistakenly assumed that Petra grew wealthy on the proceeds of Chinese and Indian goods.[8] There is in fact no solid evidence for this at all, and consequently to speak of the Nabataean kingdom as a participant in a wider 'spice trade' in commodities from India and China is a mistake.

The overland trade routes of the Nabataean kingdom

The incense trade of the Nabataeans, according to Strabo, was supplied by two main sources: the Minaeans, living in south-western Arabia, and the Gerrhaeans, who lived near the Persian Gulf.[9] Of the routes from these two sources of supply, that from the Minaeans, known commonly as the 'Incense Road', is quite well attested. In describing the trade in frankincense, Pliny related how the incense had to be brought through the land of the Gebbanitae.[10] This southern Arabian tribe appears to have held a monopoly over the frankincense commerce on this route.

> euehi non potest nisi per Gebbanitas, itaque et horum regi penditur uectigal. caput eorum Thomna abest a Gaza nostri litoris in Iudaea oppido |$\overline{\text{XIV}}$| $\overline{\text{LXXXVII}}$ D p., quod diuiditur in mansiones camelorum LXV. sunt et quae sacerdotibus dantur portiones scribisque

> regum certae, sed praeter hos et custodes satellitesque et ostiarii et ministri populantur: iam quacue iter est aliubi pro aqua aliubi pro pabulo aut pro mansionibus uariisque portoriis pendunt, ut sumptus in singulas camelos ✱ DCLXXXVIII ad nostrum litus colligat, iterumque imperii nostri publicanis penditur.
>
> It cannot be carried except through the Gebbanitae, and thus a tax to their king is also paid. Their capital Thomna is 1487 1/2 miles from the town of Gaza in Judaea, on the Mediterranean Sea, which journey is divided into sixty-five stages for camels. There are also fixed portions which are given to the priests and royal scribes, but beside these the guards and their attendants, the gatekeepers and the servants plunder also: indeed wherever their journey goes they pay at one place for water, at another for food or lodging, and also the various taxes, so that for one camel 688 denarii are consumed in reaching the Mediterranean, and then taxes are paid to the publicans of our Empire.[11]

This account clearly shows the existence of this route, as well as the considerable expense involved in carrying the incense to the Mediterranean. There is indeed archaeological and epigraphic evidence for the existence of Nabataean contacts with southern Arabia at this time, which may well indicate that the Nabataeans engaged in commerce with the region.[12]

The other source of overland traffic came from the city of Gerrha on the Persian Gulf, mentioned by both Strabo and Pliny.[13] Strabo furthermore states that the Gerrhaean merchants dealt in Arabian aromatics which they obtained from South Arabia, travelling there in forty days as against the seventy days taken by those who came from Aila (modern 'Aqaba).[14] Given its geographical location, much of the trade of Gerrha would probably have been with the Parthian realm, as Strabo relates.[15] However, it would also seem that some of the incense was carried to Petra, because Strabo states that the Gerrhaeans and Minaeans carried their incense into the country of Palestine through Petra.[16] These then constitute the two major roads by which the incense was brought to Petra: along the more direct route from South Arabia to Aila and thence to Petra, and via Gerrha and then across the north of Arabia to Petra.

This latter traffic may have travelled by a route between Mesopotamia and Petra via Dumata (Jawf in Saudi Arabia) mentioned in a confused account by Pliny,[17] although the usefulness of this route is questioned by Potts, who prefers a route further south directly from Gerrha via Teima.[18] It may, of course, have been the case that both routes were in use: the Gerrhaeans may have sent their merchandise directly overland by the route through Teima, or alternatively by raft up the Euphrates through Babylon and thence overland through Dumata, and from there either to Teima or directly to Petra (see Map 3.1). Certainly Strabo was aware that both overland and riverine transport were used:

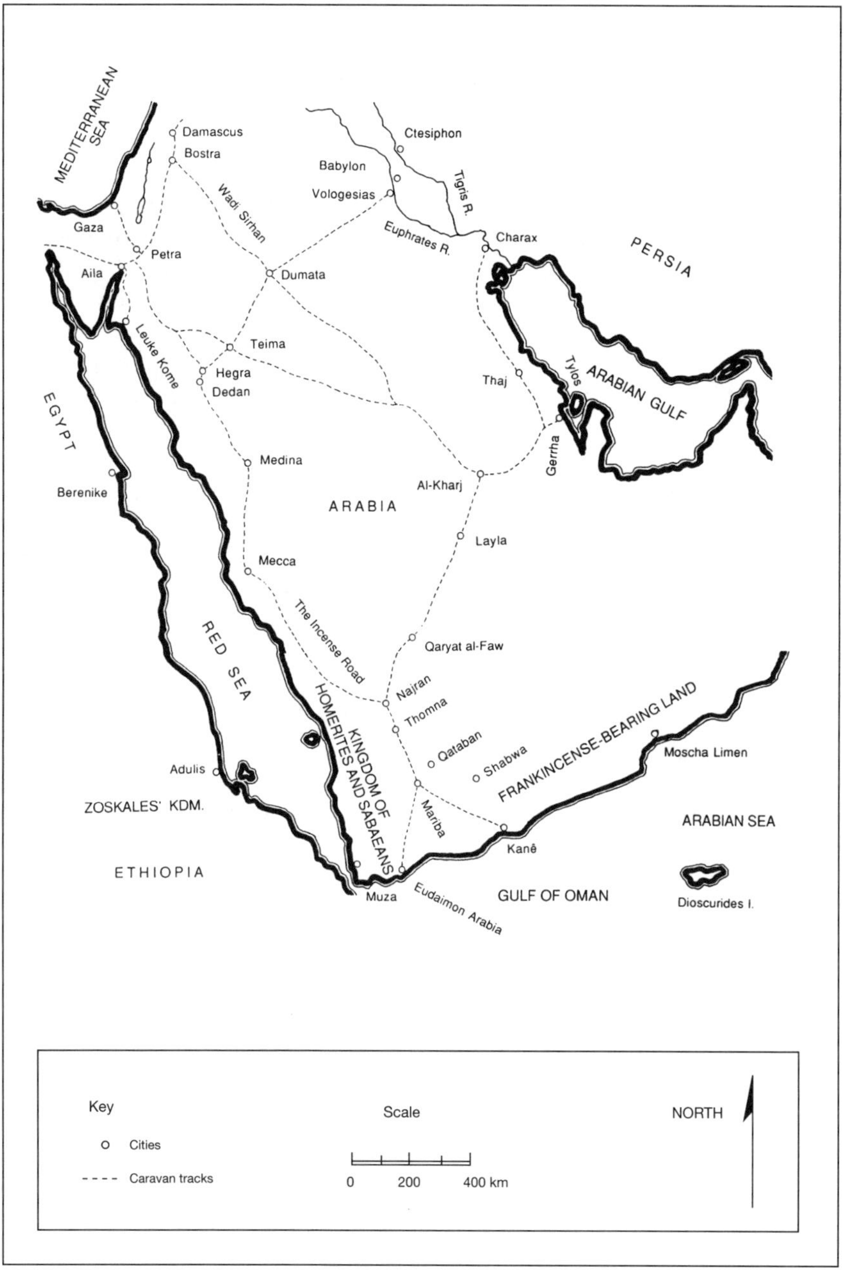

Map 3.1 Caravan tracks of the Arabian Peninsula – showing the major caravan tracks in use in the first centuries BC and AD which are discussed in the text. Titles of kingdoms are those used in the *Periplus*

> πεζέμποροι δ' εἰσὶν οἱ Γερραῖοι τὸ πλέον τῶν Ἀραβίων φορτίων καὶ ἀρωμάτων. Ἀριστόβουλος δὲ τοὐναντίον φησὶ τοὺς Γερραίους τὰ πολλὰ σχεδίαις εἰς τὴν Βαβυλωνίαν ἐμπορεύεσθαι, ἐκεῖθεν δὲ τῷ Εὐφράτῃ τὰ φορτία ἀναπλεῖν εἰς Θάψακον, εἶτα πεζῇ κομίζεσθαι πάντῃ.
>
> The Gerrhaeans for the greater part trade by land in Arabian goods and aromatics. Aristobulus, however, says that the Gerrhaeans carry most of their goods by rafts to Babylon, and from there they sail the goods up the Euphrates to Thapsacus, and then they carry it overland to all parts.[19]

The land-based route, following the most direct path from Gerrha to Petra, would certainly make more sense if it followed the route proposed by Potts. However, Potts ignores the riverine route described by Strabo and Pliny in his rejection of the possibility of Gerrhaean caravans passing through Dumata. While Strabo speaks of this riverine traffic going all the way up the river to Thapsacus, Pliny's mention of a route from Mesopotamia through Dumata makes it likely that some of this Euphrates traffic was sent through this route.

There is, indeed, evidence for Nabataean occupation which is to be found at both Teima and Dumata, which may be related to this commerce. In the case of Teima the presence of Nabataean inscriptions and pottery indicate that this oasis may well have been a part of the Nabataean kingdom.[20] One funerary inscription in particular carries the formulaic phrase 'for the life of . . .' which is usually followed by the name of a Nabataean king: if this is the case then it would seem to indicate that the Nabataean king ruled Teima.[21] Similarly, inscriptions at Dumata indicate that this site also was garrisoned by the Nabataeans. An inscription in Nabataean dating from AD 44 mentions one Ganimu, who was a military commander at Dumata, showing clearly that the Nabataeans maintained some kind of military presence there.[22] These facts indicate that both these sites were of importance to the Nabataeans, and the reason for that importance may well have been their significance as the points at which the Gerrhaean incense caravans entered the Nabataean realm.

Leuke Kome

Another route by which the incense came to Petra was through the port of Leuke Kome, which has not been located although it was probably at the mouth of the Gulf of 'Aqaba at 'Aynunah.[23] This port was probably constructed in order to gain some of the trade which was passing up the Red Sea even in pre-Roman times, perhaps as an alternative to the Egyptian ports, which were possibly already taking some of the Arabian incense trade and diverting it away from Petra.[24] Groom nevertheless suggests that the vast majority of the trade was carried overland and that the Nabataeans would have been unlikely to have built a port which would compete with the overland trade.[25] However, the *Periplus* states that considerable quantities of frankincense were traded by sea from the South Arabian ports of Kanê and Moscha Limen, as well as myrrh from Muza, and shipped to Egypt.[26] The most likely explanation for the development of Leuke Kome would be as a response to the appearance of this trade: Leuke Kome would redirect to the Nabataean kingdom trade which would otherwise have been lost to Egyptian ports. In any case, by the time of Aelius Gallus' expedition in 25 BC, Leuke Kome had become a busy centre of trade, a 'great emporium' according to Strabo, from which large caravans carried aromatics up to Petra:

> εἰς τὴν Λευκὴν κώμην, εἰς ἣν καὶ ἐξ ἧς οἱ καμηλέμποροι τοσούτῳ πλήθει ἀνδρῶν καὶ καμήλων ὁδεύουσιν ἀσφαλῶς καὶ εὐπόρως εἰς Πέτραν καὶ ἐκ Πέτρας, ὥστε μὴ διαφέρειν μηδὲν στρατοπέδου.
>
> to Leuke Kome, to which and from which the cameltraders travel in safety and ease to and from Petra in such great numbers of men and camels that they do not differ in anything from an army.[27]

It would appear from this that the Nabataeans' attempt to gain some of the seaborne traffic in the Red Sea for themselves was, at this early stage at least, largely successful.

The *Periplus* contains a well-known passage about Leuke Kome which deserves attention, as it has been the occasion of considerable scholarly debate. This debate centres on the identity of a centurion and an officer charged with collecting the import duty at Leuke Kome, and specifically as to whether they were Roman or Nabataean officers.[28] The passage describes Leuke Kome as a port of trade mainly for smaller Arab boats (presumably as opposed to the larger Greek vessels which would travel to the Egyptian ports),[29] but nonetheless it testifies to Leuke Kome's continued importance as a port of trade in the first century AD:

> ὃ λέγεται Λευκὴ κώμη, δι' ἧς ἐστὶν εἰς Πέτραν πρὸς Μαλίχαν, βασιλέα Ναβαταίων, ἀνάβασις. ἔχει δὲ ἐμπορίου τινὰ καὶ αὐτὴ τάξιν τοῖς ἀπὸ τῆς Ἀραβίας ἐξαρτιζομένοις εἰς αὐτὴν πλοίοις οὐ μεγάλοις. διὸ καὶ παραφυλακῆς χάριν καὶ εἰς αὐτὴν παραλήπτης τῆς τετάρτης τῶν εἰσφερομένων φορτίων καὶ ἑκατοντάρχης μετὰ στρατεύματος ἀποστελλεται.
>
> which is called Leuke Kome, from which there is a road to Petra, to Malchus the king of the Nabataeans. It acts as a market to the small ships which come to it loaded with freight from Arabia. Because of this as a guard a customs officer for the 25 per cent tax on incoming goods is despatched there, and also a centurion with a garrison.[30]

The term *paraleptes* or *paralemptes* ('customs-collector') is elsewhere attested of both Roman and Ptolemaic officials, and 'centurion' of course is a rank in the Roman army. However, it has been pointed out that centurion was also a rank in the Nabataean army,[31] as is attested by an epitaph on one of the tombs at Medain Saleh where the Latin title *centurio* is transliterated into the Nabataean QNṬRYN'.[32] Thus it is altogether possible that the officers mentioned in the *Periplus* could be Nabataean rather than Roman. However, Raschke suggests that the officers were Roman, tasked with collecting the 25 per cent import duty and thus ensuring that Roman vessels did not avoid the tax by going to Leuke Kome instead of Berenike or Myos Hormos.[33] This theory is attractive, and seems to accord well with the *Periplus*'s description of the customs-collector as a 'guard', which would otherwise seem a fairly unusual term. One might expect such a word to describe the centurion and his cohort, but in the text it seems to apply to the customs-collector. This then prompts the question what exactly it was that the customs-collector was guarding against. If Raschke's view is accepted, the answer is supplied: he was guarding against the evasion of the *tetarte* at the Roman ports of Berenike and Myos Hormos. If there had not been such a collector at Leuke Kome as well as in Egypt, ships might well have evaded this heavy impost by offloading their cargoes at Leuke Kome.

It should also be noted that it would appear very unsound for the Nabataean kingdom itself to have charged the *tetarte*. If they had, this would presumably mean that any goods being taken through the Nabataean kingdom and thence into the Roman Empire would have had to pay the duty twice: once at Leuke Kome to the Nabataeans and then again at the port of entry into Roman territory. It would thus have been suicidal for the Nabataeans to have charged this tax, as this would divert all of their trade very rapidly to Egypt, where the *tetarte* had to be paid only once.[34]

Whatever the answer to this particular question might be, these passages certainly show that Leuke Kome was an important port of trade and that international commerce used the port to the extent that it was necessary to send a tax-collector there. While there may be some questions remaining about the administration and ownership of the port, it is beyond doubt that the reason it was constructed and maintained was as an emporium for the aromatics trade. As such it represented an alternative to the overland route from South Arabia, and perhaps also an alternative for seaborne traffic to the Egyptian Red Sea ports.

These then were the sources of the incense which the Nabataeans then carried to the markets of the Roman world, and from which their wealth appears to have been largely derived. The relative proportions of traffic, or indeed the overall volume of the trade, are impossible to determine but the prominence afforded them by the ancient authors and the high value of the goods as described in the introduction clearly demonstrate that the trade was of considerable importance.

The routes to the Mediterranean

From Petra the incense was carried by road to Gaza and Rhinocolura on the Mediterranean. This road is attested by Pliny,[35] and has been excavated at several locations. It is equipped with stations and towers which were built by the Nabataeans and later improved by the Romans,[36] and maintained by them until at least the Severan period.[37] These Mediterranean ports were evidently considered to be of great significance by the Nabataeans, and the protection of traffic along the routes leading to them was of sufficient importance to warrant such military investment.

From these ports the aromatics may well have been shipped straight to Rome and to other parts of the empire, although it is possible that some went to the great port of Alexandria where, as has already been discussed, the incenses were worked up for sale.[38]

It certainly does seem that some of the trade through the Nabataean kingdom passed into Egypt (see Map 3.2). Recent research by Zayadine has shown that there were several routes which crossed the Sinai peninsula, and which could have been used to transport the incense from either ʻAqaba or Petra to Alexandria.[39] Several of these routes in fact show archaeological evidence of Nabataean traffic. Nabataean graffiti have been found in the Wadi Umm Sidreh and the Wadi Taba, both on the ancient road between ʻAqaba and Suez, showing that Nabataean traffic passed this way.[40] It is therefore entirely possible that in addition to the traffic which crossed the Negev direct to Gaza, there was also an appreciable amount of trade which was carried from the Nabataean kingdom into Egypt.

There is also evidence that traders from South Arabia used the path of the later *Via Nova Traiana* from Aila through Petra and then north toward Bostra and Damascus. In describing the territory around Damascus, Strabo relates an account of merchants from Arabia Felix being attacked by brigands in the Ituraean mountains:

> ἔπειτα πρὸς τα ’Αράβων μέρη καὶ τῶν ’Ιτουραίων ἀναμὶξ ὄρη δύσβατα, ἐν οἷς καὶ σπήλαια βαθύστομα, ὧν ἓν καὶ τετρακισκιλίους ἀνθρώπους δέδασθαι δυνάμενον ἐν καταδρομαῖς, αἳ τοῖς Δαμασκηνοῖς γίνονται πολλαχόθεν. τὸ μέντοι πλέον τοὺς ἀπὸ τῆς εὐδαίμονος ’Αραβίας ἐμπόρους λεηλατοῦσιν οἱ βάρβαροι.
>
> Then towards the parts inhabited by Arabs and Ituraeans mixed together there are difficult mountains, in which there are deep-mouthed caves, one of which is able to receive four thousand people in a raid, which are made against the Damascenes from many places. Indeed for the most part the barbarians were robbing the merchants from Arabia Felix.[41]

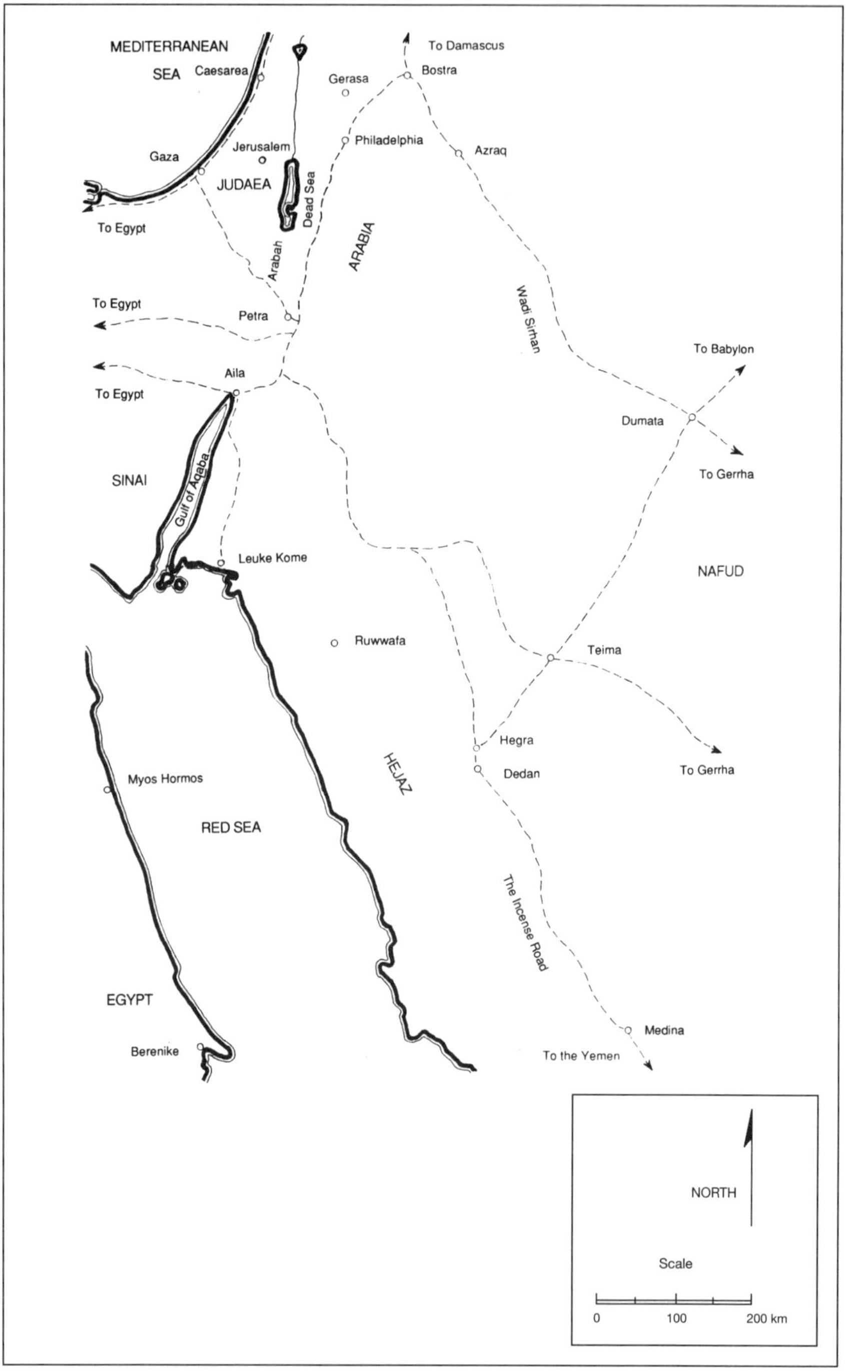

Map 3.2 The Nabataean kingdom – Showing major internal caravan tracks

Merchants from Arabia Felix who were in this area, that is in Ituraea south of Damascus, can have come through Petra only along the road which later came to be called the *Via Nova*. This provides evidence that this route was in use in the Nabataean period, well before the Romans took over in AD 106 and commenced the construction of their road. This is further confirmed by the fact that sites on the southern part of the route have been dated on the basis of pottery samples to the Nabataean period.[42] It is clear then that the *Via Nova* was no Roman innovation, but rather a Roman re-use of an existing Nabataean caravan track.[43] While much of the trade coming through Petra would probably have continued to use the path from Petra to Gaza, it is apparent that at least some traffic instead opted to travel north on this road toward Bostra. This would have given the traders access to the markets of northern Syria, although some incense could also be shipped to Rome from Tyre or Caesarea Maritima.

We can see that Petra was clearly a very significant place in terms of the trade in aromatics from the Arabian peninsula. As has been shown, frankincense and myrrh were brought there along many routes, ranging from the 'Incense Road' from southern Arabia and the trans-Arabian route from Gerrha to the road from the Red Sea port of Leuke Kome. The advantageous situation of Petra at the junction of these routes from Arabia with those that reached the Mediterranean gave the Nabataeans the opportunity to exploit the caravan trade and to grow rich.

However, these routes were not the only paths by which Arabian incense could reach the markets of the Roman Empire. The Ptolemies had already started to build up their trade through the Red Sea ports with India, which also offered the opportunity to reach the incense-producing region of Arabia by sea. As has been discussed in Chapter 2, the Romans provided ports, roads and protection to the merchants using the Red Sea route. In addition, they conducted some aggressive military campaigns in the area. How then did these changes affect the prosperity of the Nabataeans, or the commerce upon which much of that prosperity depended?

The Nabataean aromatics trade in the first century AD

The aromatics trade through Petra may have come under considerable pressure from the growth of the Egyptian Red Sea trade. Strabo states that the aromatics formerly brought to Leuke Kome (and thus through Petra) had by his time for the most part been redirected through Myos Hormos:

> ἐκ μὲν οὖν τῆς Λευκῆς κώμης εἰς Πέτραν, ἐντεῦθεν δ' εἰς Ῥινοκόλουρα τῆς πρὸς Αἰγύπτου Φοινίκης τὰ φορτία κομίζεται, κἀντεῦθεν εἰς τοὺς ἄλλους· νυνὶ δὲ τὸ πλέον εἰς τὴν Ἀλεξάνδρειαν τῷ Νείλῳ· κατάγεται δ' ἐκ τῆς Ἀραβίας καὶ τῆς Ἰνδικῆς εἰς Μυὸς ὅρμον·

> The loads then are carried from Leuke Kome to Petra, and from there to Rhinocolura in Phoenicia near to Egypt, and from there to other places. But now the majority is brought to Alexandria by the Nile, being brought down to Myos Hormos from Arabia and India.[44]

It would certainly seem that at least some trade was lost by the Nabataean kingdom to those shippers who were using the Egyptian Red Sea ports, and thus there is a *prima facie* case for a Nabataean decline in the first century AD. Avraham Negev and others have added to this piece of literary evidence some further archaeological and numismatic evidence for such a decline. This is attributed to both the cheaper cost of sea transport and the deliberate policy of the Roman administration.[45]

The archaeological evidence adduced in support of this consists chiefly of surface surveys of the roads between Petra and the Mediterranean ports and excavations at such towns in the Negev as Oboda and Mampsis. These surveys appeared to show a lack of activity on the road past the middle of the first century AD, as well as the destruction of the towns, presumably by nomadic tribes, at about the same time.[46] This was further supported by the evidence from Nabataean silver coinage, which shows a gradual decline in silver content during the first century AD, until it fell to approximately 20 per cent during the later years of Malchus II and the entire reign of Rabbel II.[47] This decline, Negev argues, was caused by a decline in prosperity, itself caused by the loss of the aromatics trade, combined with the effects of nomadic disturbances in the middle of the first century. Negev also states that this loss of revenue was partly redressed by the colonisation of the Hauran and the increasing importance of Bostra at the expense of Petra.[48] The actual cessation of the trade Negev places at AD 7, based upon a sharp decline in the silver content of Nabataean coins at that particular date.[49] Many scholars both before and after Negev have taken the view that this decline in trade was caused by a deliberate act of Roman policy, designed to alter the 'balance of trade' back to more favourable terms for Rome. This policy, it is argued, was accomplished by the systematic encouragement of the commerce in Egypt, as well as the destruction of the influence of the Sabaean and Nabataean 'middlemen' by military means.[50]

Roman military action and Nabataean trade

In view of this thesis, then, the possibility of Roman military intervention to destroy Arabian influence and participation in the spice and incense trades should be examined. Probably the best known of the Roman military adventures in Arabia is the expedition of Aelius Gallus, who was prefect of Egypt shortly after the accession of Augustus.

The actual expedition took the form of the construction of a massive armada at Cleopatris in Egypt, which then sailed to Leuke Kome under the direction of Gallus, guided by Syllaeus, the vizier of the Nabataean king. From Leuke

Kome the expedition marched southwards into Arabia Felix, where it assaulted several towns and captured all but one, the capital Marsaiba. Lack of water and the prevalence of disease forced the abandonment of the expedition at this point, upon which the remnants of the force returned to Egypt through Myos Hormos.[51] Strabo blamed the failure of the expedition on the treachery of Syllaeus, but in fact the likely cause of the failure was poor military intelligence, causing a failure to plan and prepare adequately for such an arduous campaign.[52]

Many scholars have suggested that the chief purpose of this expedition was to control the transit traffic from India which passed through Eudaimon Arabia, or to control the output of Arabian incense from the region.[53] These reconstructions envisage such motives as gaining control of the spice-trade routes in order to redirect them to Egypt, so weakening the southern Arabian 'middleman'; the weakening of the Nabataean kingdom which, as we have already seen, gained a great deal of its trade from Arabia Felix; and finally increasing the trade passing through the Red Sea ports of Egypt.

However, these conclusions are quite unjustified. Any transit trade that Eudaimon Arabia possessed had already ceased as soon as the ships of Greek and Roman Egypt began to make the direct sailing to India, obviating the need for a transfer of cargoes in Arabia.[54] Thus, we can safely discard any theory concerning the removal of southern Arabian 'middlemen' from the trade, for if the South Arabians had *ever* held an exploitative monopoly over the India trade, it was long gone by the time of Gallus. Similarly, there is no need to assume that the Romans were attempting to gain any 'control' over the incense trade from Arabia either. Strabo himself makes it perfectly clear that Augustus desired to conquer Arabia Felix simply to annex the territory and to seize its proverbial wealth.[55] Indeed, as Bowersock points out, it is probable that the association of Arabian incense with royal power and divinity was a potent motivation to Augustus.[56] Thus, we should view the expedition of Aelius Gallus as economically motivated only in the most basic sense: the intention was to seize the region in order to enrich the Roman treasury, and to maximise the prestige of the Romans and their emperor. As far as any intention to control the incense trade, or to direct it to Egypt rather than the Nabataean kingdom, is concerned, there is simply no evidence to justify such a conclusion.

There are other Roman incursions in Arabia in the first century AD which have also been put forward as possible attempts to influence the course of the trade by means of direct military intervention. Gaius Caesar seems to have campaigned in Arabia in the course of his expedition to the East in AD 1–3. Pliny mentions a brief campaign near the 'Arabian Gulf' (Gulf of 'Aqaba) prior to Gaius' better-attested expedition to Armenia. Pliny describes this in the following terms:

> in Arabicum sinum, in quo res gerente C. Caesare Augusti filio signa nauium ex Hispaniensibus naufragiis feruntur agnita.

> in the Arabian gulf, in which it is said that when Gaius Caesar, the son of Augustus, was campaigning there, the standards from Spanish shipwrecks were identified.[57]

The campaign here mentioned is sometimes suggested as having been an attempt to dominate or control the Arabian trade routes, specifically those by which incense was transported into the empire.[58] This view, however, lacks any support, particularly given the dearth of any evidence by which we might reconstruct the motives for the expedition. In his other mention of the expedition, Pliny tells us that Gaius did not actually penetrate into Arabia, but only remained near the Gulf of 'Aqaba:

> Romana arma solus in eam terram adhuc intulit Aelius Gallus ex equestri ordine; nam C. Caesar Augusti filius prospexit tantum Arabiam.
>
> Aelius Gallus of the equestrian order alone has brought Roman arms into this territory, for Gaius Caesar the son of Augustus only glimpsed Arabia.[59]

Thus, Gaius' campaign was only a brief one which did not penetrate into Arabia at all. It is impossible to attribute any commercial motives to it, even if it could be shown that the Romans would wage war for such reasons. By far the most likely possibility is that Gaius campaigned against nomadic tribes on the fringe of the Nabataean kingdom, perhaps because they were threatening the stability of the kingdom or otherwise raiding the settled area.[60] In any case, there is absolutely no valid reason to suppose that this expedition had anything to do with the control of the spice or incense routes.

Another event which has aroused interest in this respect is the apparent destruction by the Romans of the port of Eudaimon Arabia (Aden), on the southern coast of the Arabian peninsula. In describing this port, the author of the *Periplus Maris Erythraei* states that:

> νῦν δὲ οὐ πρὸ πολλοῦ τῶν ἡμετέρων χρόνων Καῖσαρ αὐτὴν κατεστρέψατο.
>
> But now, not long before our own time, Caesar destroyed it.[61]

This passage has aroused a great deal of controversy, as there is no known Roman campaign which would answer to this description. Several possible candidates have been suggested, including Aelius Gallus, Gaius Caesar, Claudius, Nero and even Septimius Severus, but none of these is without its problems and some are downright impossible.[62] Despite this, many have suggested that this passage is evidence that the Romans destroyed Aden in order to prevent Arabian 'middlemen' from dominating the trade through the Red Sea, and to allow their own ships sailing to Egypt to take over the spice and incense trade.[63]

This, however, overlooks the fact that the same passage of the *Periplus* indeed *does* mention the reason that Eudaimon Arabia had lost its trade, and that this reason had nothing to do with the attack by 'Caesar'. As has already been noted in connection with the expedition of Aelius Gallus, the *Periplus* states that trade had ceased to flow through Eudaimon Arabia because ships ceased to call there after they began to sail from Egypt to India directly.[64] It was the discovery of the use of the monsoon by the traders who used the Red Sea which spelt the end of Aden's significance as a port, and not any commercially motivated Roman attack.[65] If there was a Roman attack on Aden, it could not have been motivated by the desire to 'cut out the middleman' because if there indeed ever had been any middlemen in Aden, they had already been 'cut out' by the exploitation of the monsoon by Greek and Roman traders. Accordingly, the statement by the author of the *Periplus* that Caesar attacked Eudaimon Arabia is no proof of a commercially motivated Roman foreign policy.

The most likely explanation for this passage would be a garbled local memory of the expedition of Aelius Gallus, which entered the country (not the city) called Eudaimon Arabia, which was then later confused with the decline or destruction of the town by other hands.[66] Nonetheless, whatever the explanation for this passage, it is clear that it was not an attack caused by commercial considerations, and is no evidence for a Roman desire to eliminate Arabian participation in the spice or incense trades.

The effect of Egyptian trade on the commerce of the Nabataean kingdom

Despite the fact that the weakening of the Nabataean kingdom by deliberate Roman policy can safely be rejected, there still remains the statement of Strabo discussed earlier that the trade which formerly passed through Leuke Kome generally went through Myos Hormos at the time he was writing.[67] There thus remains the possibility that the rise in importance of the Egyptian Red Sea ports caused a corresponding decline in trade passing through the Nabataean kingdom.

With reference to Strabo's remark concerning Leuke Kome, however, it should first be noted that he was referring only to seaborne trade going through Leuke Kome itself, not to the whole aromatics trade including the overland routes. While ships may have been attracted to Berenike and Myos Hormos instead of Leuke Kome by the facilities available at the former ports, such considerations do not necessarily apply to the overland caravan trade. Strabo's statement that traffic using Leuke Kome had decreased cannot be turned into a proof of a general decline in Nabataean fortunes, as he says nothing about any corresponding decline in the overland trade coming up the 'incense road' or across the Arabian peninsula from Gerrha.

Indeed, we do know that trade *did* continue, at least to some extent, into Leuke Kome. The *Periplus*, as has already been noted, refers to smaller Arab vessels using the port and the fact that there was a garrison and a customs-collector there.[68] As the date of the *Periplus* is now generally agreed to be mid-first century AD,[69] and thus some fifty years after the time of Strabo, this reference shows that Leuke Kome did not pass out of use. It was still clearly being used enough to require the posting of a body of troops and a customs-collector at the location. While its significance may have declined from the first century BC, Leuke Kome was certainly no ghost town by the time of the writing of the *Periplus*.

The continued existence of land-based commerce in the first century

Even after the construction of Leuke Kome and the expansion of the sea trade into Egypt, there is considerable evidence that the land routes in the incense traffic continued to be of primary importance to the Nabataeans. Pliny speaks of both land-based commerce and of sea traffic, indicating that seaborne traffic through Egypt existed at the same time as overland traffic through the Nabataean kingdom.[70]

Crone, however, envisages a land-based monopoly in the time of Juba (Pliny's source) giving way to seaborne traffic by the time the *Periplus* was written in the mid-first century AD.[71] However, this view is not tenable. Pliny certainly does speak of a 'monopoly' by the king of the Gebbanitae,[72] as we have seen, but he also speaks of frankincense being exported by sea to Egypt. Similarly, the *Periplus* states that the king of the 'Frankincense-bearing Land' (Hadramaut) caused all frankincense grown in his territory to be shipped through the ports of Kanê and Moscha Limen to Egypt.[73] Evidently, these monopolies were not global, as Crone seems to envisage, but only limited to the incense grown in a particular area. In establishing her thesis that the trade on the 'Incense Road' completely disappeared in the first century AD, Crone has taken comments in primary sources which refer merely to local monopolies and attempted to apply them to the entire incense trade. However, as has been seen, the mutually contradictory nature of these primary references shows that they do not refer to universal monopolies but only to local areas. The land-based and seaborne commerce evidently existed side-by-side, and any monopolies which existed were only over a specific local area, and did not cover the whole trade in any given commodity.

In addition, the occupation of the site of Hegra in the Hejaz shows that the overland incense traffic did not disappear in the first century AD, but rather maintained its vitality for at least that period. This station, the modern site of Medain Saleh in Saudi Arabia, was established as a major Nabataean military post in the late first century BC.[74] This is attested by a series of impressive rock-cut tombs of Nabataean military officers and officials, many of which can be accurately dated by their inscriptions. The earliest tomb dates to AD 1 while the last bears a date of AD 75.[75] While various ideas have been suggested as to the purpose of this outpost, such as a fallback position in the event of Roman invasion of the kingdom,[76] or as a defensive frontier post,[77] it seems most probable that an outpost of such size so far from the centre of the kingdom must have been there to protect a valuable commodity indeed. This can have been none other than the incense trade.

The occupation of this site indicates that its commercial importance was maintained at least up until AD 75, the date of the last dated tomb inscription. Of course, this does not necessarily mean that Medain Saleh was abandoned at that time, only that tomb construction ceased there. Burial after that date may, for instance, have been in existing family tombs, or alternatively the garrison at the site may have been reduced or removed for some reason. F.V. Winnett, working from Nabataean inscriptions at Hegra and Safaitic inscriptions, has postulated that one Damasi, elder brother of the *strategos* of Hegra, Maliku, unsuccessfully rebelled shortly after the accession of the last Nabataean king Rabbel II in AD 71, involving some of the Safaitic tribes of the area in his attempt.[78] Although nothing is known of the course of the rebellion or the fate of Damasi other than that the rebellion was defeated,[79] it is possible that a military rebellion at Hegra might have subsequently caused the removal or downgrading of the force there, perhaps as a security measure to avert the possibility of another such revolt. It is also possible that the revolt was so serious that the garrison of Hegra was substantially destroyed and could not be replaced. Clearly, the importance of Medain Saleh due to its trade had continued at least until this time, and even the lack of tomb inscriptions after AD 75 does not necessarily mean that the site had lost its significance. The fact that its importance did continue after AD 75 is demonstrated by the Roman occupation of the site after they annexed the Nabataean kingdom in AD 106, which is known from the Roman military inscriptions at the site.[80]

Thus, we see that the traffic passing up the 'Incense Road' from southern Arabia continued to flow for at least the first three-quarters of the first century, and probably longer. The theory that the sea trade replaced the more expensive caravan traffic at the beginning of the first century is clearly wrong, because the Nabataean investment in the construction and garrisoning of Medain Saleh at the same time would have been completely pointless if the overland traffic had ceased. The presence of Nabataean and then Roman troops at this location is clear proof that the 'Incense Road' did not cease its operation during the first century, unless it did temporarily for the last quarter of that century. This traffic, moreover, must have still been of considerable value, for it was considered worthy of a sizeable protective force at Hegra and consequently of substantial military expenditure.

This continued existence of the trade along the 'Incense Road' when cheaper waterborne transport existed would seem to require some explanation. Groom has shown that this fact can be explained by the timing of the frankincense harvests in Arabia with regard to the optimum sailing times for the Red Sea, combined with the greatly increased demand for the aromatics which caused the growers to commence a second harvest.[81] The harvest times for the frankincense are noted by Pliny:

> meti semel anno solebat minore occasione uendendi; iam quaestus alteram uindemiam adfert. prior atque naturalis uindemia circa canis ortum flagrantissimo aestu,
>
> . . .
>
> autumno legitur ab aestiuo partu: hoc purissimum, candidum. secunda uindemia est uere, ad eam hieme corticibus incisis; rufum hoc exit, nec conparandum priori.
>
> When there was less opportunity to sell, it was the custom to gather it once; but now profit brings in another harvest. The earlier and natural harvest is around the rising of the dog-star
>
> . . .
>
> the Summer crop is collected in the Autumn: this is the most pure, and is white. The second harvest in in the Spring, the bark having been cut in the Winter for this purpose; red sap comes from this, not to be compared with the former.[82]

When the harvest times supplied by Pliny are compared with the sailing times mentioned in the *Periplus*, a discernible pattern of trade emerges which can account for the continued survival of the land-based caravan traffic even after the Red Sea trade became predominant.[83] The *Periplus* makes it clear that ships sailing to India could not participate in the better Autumn crop of frankincense, as they sailed from Egypt in July,[84] and did not return until the time of the Spring crop. They could collect some of this inferior crop at Moscha Limen on their return journey.[85] The journey to collect the Autumn crops of myrrh and frankincense had to be organised separately, commencing in September,[86] and returning with the north-east monsoon, which usually commenced in mid-October.[87] The incense caravans, which of course did not have to wait for the monsoon to commence, would be able to arrive at Gaza at about the same time that the ships were leaving South Arabia. Thus the ability of land-based traders to get their incense to market before the seaborne traders might provide a reason for the continued survival of the overland trade when the alternative of cheaper sea transport was available.[88] It is clear that, modern theories notwithstanding, the overland incense trade from South Arabia was *never* fully supplanted by the sea route and probably remained in use for as long as the demand for frankincense and myrrh continued.

The Petra–Gaza road

The apparent decline of sites and roads in the Negev region which has been adduced as evidence of Petra's decline in the first century has also been shown to be incorrect. Initial surface surveys of the region showed no evidence of use of the Petra–Gaza road past the middle of the first century AD, and it was concluded that the trade going through Petra had ceased by this time.[89] More recent excavations, however, have shown that the roads in fact continued in use throughout the whole of the first century and well into the Roman period after annexation. Cohen has excavated such sites as Moje ‘Awad and Horbat Qasra, military sites on the Petra–Gaza road.[90] The excavation of these sites showed that they were not abandoned in the first century but continued to be used until well into the Roman period. Moje ‘Awad, for example, contained coins from the reigns of Aretas II, Aretas IV, Rabbel II, Trajan, Commodus and Caracalla as well as pottery and other evidence, showing clearly that it continued in use until at least the Severan period.[91] Similar finds were reported at Horbat Qasra, which yielded a coin of Caracalla and pottery from the second–third century AD, and at the nearby site of Mesad Neqarot. Here, Cohen discovered Nabataean potsherds and coins of the first century AD, while another tower in the vicinity contained pottery and coins from the second and third centuries AD.[92]

This evidence makes it clear that the Petra–Gaza road continued in use throughout the first century AD and for some time after, and that both the Nabataean and Roman governments maintained their protection of the route, as evidenced by the continuing occupation of military sites. Accordingly, there is no support for the theory that Petra declined due to a loss of trade in the first century to be found in an examination of these roads. Although we can never be sure as to the exact purpose of any military installation or set of installations, it is certainly the case that some considerable traffic must have been using the road throughout this period. Since there is abundant literary evidence for the use of this road by the incense trade in the early part of the first century, there is no real reason to suppose that such trade did not continue to use the road well into the Roman period. Furthermore, Cohen’s investigations seem to show that Oboda was continually occupied through the period,[93] thus indicating that Negev’s thesis of a massive nomadic incursion in the mid-first century AD, which resulted in the destruction of Oboda and the abandonment of Medain Saleh,[94] is largely ephemeral. While it is certainly possible that there were disruptions in the course of the first century caused by nomadic incursions, their effects seem to have been quite limited and of no great duration. There does not seem to have been any disruption of the incense trade, or at least none that has left any tangible evidence. Thus, the evidence from the Petra–Gaza road does not provide any support for the contention that the trade of the Nabataean kingdom declined during the first century AD.

The silver content of Nabataean coins

It nonetheless remains true that there may have been some decline in Nabataean prosperity through this period, although any decline was nowhere near as catastrophic as has been postulated. Such a decline would, however, account for the reduction in the silver content of the Nabataean coinage throughout the period.[95] The decline can be seen clearly in the tables in Appendix B, showing the silver content of the Nabataean silver *drachma* throughout the first century AD, expressed as a percentage (i.e. the fineness of the coin). These tables show clearly that there was a serious decline in the silver content of Nabataean coins over this period, to the extent that they would have been substantially useless for foreign trade by the time of the reigns of Malchus II and Rabbel II. Negev used these data to construct his theory of an effective cessation of the incense trade through Petra in AD 7, the time of a particularly sharp decline in the silver content.[96]

Certainly in the later first century, the Nabataean coinage would have been useless for international transactions due to its debasement, and can have been used only within the kingdom itself.[97] Silver, however, is not the only medium of exchange suitable for the incense trade; one might well argue in fact that gold would have been more suitable for the trade in frankincense and myrrh due to the very high value of the goods. Thus, the strong possibility exists that the Nabataeans continued to trade using gold vessels and bullion. The likelihood of this is shown by the fact that the distinctive red-gloss Nabataean pottery appears to have been made in a limited number of sizes, probably made in imitation of gold vessels which were themselves manufactured only in a limited range of standardised weights.[98] Thus, while the silver content of Nabataean coinage had declined greatly, the presence of stamped gold vessels of fixed and uniform weights would have provided the Nabataean merchants with a perfectly adequate means of exchange.

The fact that the devaluation of the coinage was not an indicator of the relative prosperity of the kingdom is demonstrated by the physical remains of Petra today. These impressive monuments were built in the course of the first century, the very period of the alleged decline.[99] Negev, however, attempts to explain the construction of these monuments as the expenditure of savings rather than as an indicator of the continued viability of the incense trade.[100] While not without parallels, such extravagance seems extraordinary, particularly as it postulates that the Nabataeans built few monuments in the period of their greatest prosperity but then commenced building them after the source of that prosperity was lost. On the whole, it seems far more likely that the magnificent monuments of Petra are an eloquent witness to the continuing prosperity of the Nabataean realm in the first century AD. Indeed, it is possible that these buildings may provide some explanation for the drop in silver content of the coinage visible in AD 7, as the enormous expenditure which such a building programme would have made necessary might have caused some economic pressure and a resultant debasement of the coinage.

It should also be noted that in the period of the most severe debasement, the reigns of Malchus II and Rabbel II, there was in fact a similar, though nowhere near as severe drop in the silver content of Roman imperial coinage and other silver coins of the period.[101] When the silver content of the Nabataean coinage is compared to the silver content of Roman imperial issues over the same period, it quickly becomes apparent that the declines in the silver content of Nabataean coins are generally equivalent, though much more severe, to debasements of Roman coins of the same time periods. It is probable that the debasements of Nabataean coinage are responses to the same economic pressures as are the Roman declines, and thus not necessarily anything to do with the incense trade. While it is not proposed to go into the reasons for the Roman devaluation, it would seem that there was a general period of economic pressure throughout the whole Mediterranean area in the mid to late first century AD which caused it. The steeper decline in the values of Nabataean coins compared to Roman is accounted for by the fact that the Nabataean kingdom had no silver reserves of its own, whereas the Romans of course still had access to considerable supplies.[102] Thus, any pressure which caused a drop in the supply of silver at Rome would most probably cause a far steeper drop in supply at Petra. In this way, then, we can account for the decline in the silver content of Nabataean coins without the necessity of a corresponding decline in the Arabian aromatics trade.

The development of Nabataean agriculture and the importance of the Hauran

A further argument which has been suggested as proof of a trade decline in the Nabataean kingdom is the development of intensive agriculture in some areas of the realm, most notably in the Hauran. In his investigations Negev identified what he called the 'Late Nabataean period' from *c.* AD 70–106 in which he asserted that the Nabataeans' former dependence upon trade was replaced by intensive agriculture both in the Negev and in the Hauran.[103] While it is certainly true that such agricultural development did occur,[104] the conclusion that it was developed to *replace* trade is not justified. On the contrary, it has been pointed out that active commerce causes a large non-productive population, which then necessitates the development of more agriculture in order to feed the communities of merchants, caravaneers and others associated with the trade.[105] It is thus possible that the development of agricultural installations in the Negev and the Hauran was a response to increased trade, rather than to a decline.

Indeed, Zayadine has conducted investigations around the site of Petra itself at such places as al-Barid, Wadi Sleisel and Sabra which reveal agricultural installations in close association with caravanserais and situated on roadheads leaving the capital.[106] These 'satellite-stations' around Petra each consist of water-points, a fort-caravanserai, a roadhead and agricultural installations, in which caravans and those associated with them could be serviced (see Figure 3.1).[107] At Wadi Ras Sleisel, for example, there are remains of agricultural terraces used for both food production and water catchment, as well as a military structure, all situated on an important east–west route to the north of the main city of Petra. This, as Zayadine concludes, would seem to be a station designed for the provisioning of caravans, as well as their protection, control,

Figure 3.1 The el-Beidha area north of Petra, Jordan. This would have been a suitable area for the revictualling and organisation of caravans, and remains of such installations have been found there

and no doubt taxation.[108] These installations, including their agricultural areas, were clearly designed and built with the needs of the caravan trade in mind, as their siting on caravan routes leaving the city shows. They demonstrate clearly that the Nabataean development of agriculture cannot be divorced from the incense trade: rather there was a close association between the two.

There is, however, some evidence that would seem to indicate a shift in the northern trade route from the Arabian Gulf via Dumata, which might account for the development of agricultural installations in the Hauran in particular. Pliny speaks of this route passing from the Gulf to Petra via Dumata.[109] In the latter part of the first century AD this route seems to have shifted to travel from Dumata up the Wadi Sirhan to Azraq, a significant water source,[110] and then to the northern Nabataean city of Bostra. One of the main indicators of this is the fact that Rabbel II seems to have moved the royal residence to Bostra.[111] There is evidence of a considerably increased Nabataean investment in the north of the kingdom during the reigns of Malchus II and Rabbel II, indicated by the vast increase in the number of inscriptions in the Hauran area dating from those reigns compared to the earlier period.[112] The presence of a trading route here also seems to be indicated by the presence of a Nabataean garrison at Dumata, probably protecting trade travelling from there up the Wadi Sirhan to Azraq, which was noted earlier.[113] It would seem, then, that the trade which had been passing from the region of Gerrha across the Arabian peninsula to Petra via Dumata began in the mid-first century to be rerouted from Dumata up the Wadi Sirhan to Bostra.

It has been suggested that this shift was largely due to an attempted Roman 'redirection' of the trade routes, causing trade to travel via Bostra and Palmyra to the detriment of the traffic which passed through Petra.[114] The link with trade at Palmyra should be rejected, however, because, as has been noted, the commerce at Petra consisted mostly of incense brought from Arabia Felix, for which there is no practical route through Palmyra. As will be discussed later,[115] the trade at Palmyra consisted chiefly of items brought by sea from India to the Arabian Gulf. Accordingly, the prosperity and trade of Palmyra can have had little or no bearing on that of Petra as they were based upon different commodities. The deliberate Roman fostering of Bostra to replace Petra can also safely be rejected, as there is no reason to imagine why the Romans would prefer one over the other: both were part of the Nabataean kingdom, and in either case the Nabataeans would benefit from the trade.

The reason for this shift in the trade route can probably be found in the rising prosperity of the Decapolis region in this period. Indeed, it has been noted that the increasing wealth of the Decapolis at this time, exemplified by such cities as Gerasa, coincides with the increased Nabataean activity in the Hauran and the development of Bostra.[116] Much of this development is associated with the Syrian legateship of M. Ulpius Traianus, the father of the Emperor Trajan, during the reign of Vespasian.[117] This development was in turn made possible by the construction of roads linking the Decapolis to Caesarea on the Mediterranean during the Jewish war, which after that conflict would have dramatically improved communications across the Jordan to the Mediterranean.

It may then be that the reason for the shift of the route to Bostra rather than to Petra was as a result of the increased urbanisation of and prosperity of the Decapolis and the greater access to the sea afforded by the new roads. This easier access attracted merchants to use the Wadi Sirhan and to carry their goods either through the Decapolis to the sea, or to be consumed in those cities. The Nabataeans too involved themselves in this commerce, as is attested by the evidence of Nabataean commercial activity within the Decapolis. The excavations of Philadelphia and Gerasa have provided evidence of Nabataean activity and occupation,[118] and there is a memorial *nephesh* (cenotaph) from Petra which commemorates a Nabataean who resided in Gerasa and was buried there.[119] Thus, there is a great deal of evidence to suggest that Nabataeans lived and traded in the Decapolis at this time, and participated in the flourishing economic activity there in the late first century AD. In addition, the traffic which had formerly entered the kingdom by the 'Incense Road' could also use this route by travelling via the oasis and emporium of Teima and thence to Dumata.[120] However, this route would add quite some distance to the journey and there is no reason to suppose that the incense traffic would have abandoned Petra entirely. In any case, the commerce would have continued to pass through the Nabataean realm at some point, so even if Petra itself suffered some dimunition of its trade, this would seem to be compensated by the increase in traffic

Figure 3.2 Ed-Deir (the Monastery), Petra, Jordan. This structure is probably a temple, completed in the years before the Roman annexation of the Nabataean kingdom

via the Wadi Sirhan, which would still enrich the Nabataean kingdom now centred at Bostra.

There is no compelling evidence for a general collapse of the aromatics trade passing through the Nabataean kingdom in the first century AD. On the whole it would seem that the trade in Arabian aromatics remained reasonably steady throughout this time. This is not to say that there were not fluctuations in the trade: Leuke Kome for instance certainly seems to have lost some of the importance it had at the beginning of Augustus' reign. There also seems to have been some economic pressure and perhaps decline in the latter half of that century, but throughout all this the Arabian incense trade through the Nabataean kingdom appears to have survived. Moreover, as long as the trade survived it would have continued to bring prosperity to the Nabataean realm. The kingdom which the Romans took over in AD 106 still probably drew a substantial proportion of its wealth from the trade in Arabian incense.

The significance of the aromatics trade in the Nabataean kingdom

Unlike the situation in Roman Egypt, there is only a small amount of evidence which allows us to learn the nature of this trade and of those who were involved in it. Nevertheless, some literary and inscriptional sources do mention the

Figure 3.3 El-Khazneh (the Treasury), Petra, Jordan

activity of Nabataean merchants along the 'Incense Road', in the kingdom itself as well as throughout the Roman Empire, while other sources give an indication of the involvement of the Nabataean government in certain aspects of the trade.

The Nabataeans as traders

The earliest literary references describe the Nabataeans as a people who were nomads rather than the settled people we find in the Roman period.[121] In their early years the Nabataeans indulged in some brigandage, as Diodorus reports:

> τὰ μὲν οὖν πρὸς τὴν ἕω μέρη κατοικοῦσιν Ἄραβες οὓς ὀνομάζουσι Ναβαταίους, νεμόμενοι χώραν τὴν μὲν ἔρημον, τὴν δὲ ἄνυδρον, ὀλίγην δὲ καρποφόρον. ἔχουσι δὲ βίον λῃστρικόν, καὶ πολλὴν τῆς ὁμόρου χώρας κατατρέχοντες λῃστεύουσιν, ὄντες δύσμαχοι κατὰ τοὺς πολέμους.

> Toward the eastern parts there live the Arabs who are called Nabataeans, who inhabit a country that is partly deserted and partly

> waterless, with a small part which is fruitful. Leading a life of brigandage they overrun and pillage the greater part of the surrounding territory, and are difficult to defeat in battle.[122]

It would seem from these references that in the earlier Hellenistic period the Nabataeans were what we might consider 'typical' nomads. Thus, when they settled into a more sedentary lifestyle in later years, they may well have retained the skills of the desert and the knowledge of how to survive in it. These skills would certainly have placed them in an advantageous position to exploit the caravan trade coming up from southern Arabia, and this is what they seem to have done in the later Hellenistic period.

Whether or not the Nabataeans settled under the influence of the trade or simply began to be involved in the trade after they had settled is difficult to tell.[123] However, it would be reasonable to surmise that once they had become involved, the combination of their geographical location astride the trade routes and their skill in negotiating the desert paths through that territory would enable them to profit greatly from the southern Arabian incense commerce. The Nabataeans would thus seem to have been involved in the commerce chiefly as *transporters*. They did not grow the crops themselves, nor did they bring them from the incense fields of southern Arabia after they had been harvested. Their role seems to have been that of taking over the incense from the Minaean and Gerrhaean caravans when they arrived in Nabataean territory, and then conveying them to the sea at Gaza and Alexandria, or for consumption in the cities of Roman Syria itself. As discussed earlier in the chapter, Diodorus and Strabo both refer to the fact that the Minaeans and Gerrhaeans conveyed their aromatics to Petra,[124] while in another place Diodorus states that the Nabataeans conveyed to the Mediterranean goods which they had received from those who brought them from Arabia Felix.[125] There is, however, some evidence of a Nabataean presence in southern Arabia, so it seems that at least some Nabataean merchants traded this far afield.[126]

The medium of exchange for these transactions was most probably gold, as Strabo records that the merchants of Arabia Felix sold their wares for gold and silver.[127] As has been discussed, the silver content of Nabataean coinage dropped dramatically in the course of the first century AD to the point where it would have been useless for all except transactions within the kingdom itself.[128] However, Vickers has shown that the Nabataeans probably continued to trade using gold vessels, stamped with a fixed weight and functioning effectively as a large denomination coin.[129] Thus, even though the silver content of Nabataean coinage had declined greatly, the presence of these gold vessels would have provided the Nabataean merchants with a means of exchange to continue their trade.

As to the identity of the participants in the commerce, their social standing and the source of their wealth, we must accept that for the moment there is no evidence which would allow us to form any conclusions. Nonetheless, by the prominence which the caravan trade occupies in our literary sources, we might expect that the commerce and its practitioners would have held considerable significance in Nabataean society. Beyond that, however, our evidence will not allow further speculation.

The involvement of the Nabataean government in the trade

However, there are certainly indications that the Nabataean government took an active interest in the trade. Mention has already been made of the complex of 'suburbs' with agricultural installations and caravanserais which surround Petra.[130] Due to the fact that these stations appear to have been provided with military protection as well as watering and revictualling points, it would seem that they were constructed by the Nabataean government to meet the needs of the caravan trade. Zayadine suggests that they were built to enable caravans to be resupplied, controlled and taxed,[131] as well as allowing the central area of Petra to be kept relatively free of the caravan traffic so that the city could concentrate on its important roles as a royal capital and religious centre.[132]

Such stations also exist in more outlying areas. Archaeological evidence exists of a complex of stations in the Hisma area of southern Jordan, as well as the forts along the Petra–Gaza road which have already been discussed in this chapter.[133] The stations in the Hisma are sited so as to cover virtually any approach route that a caravan might take from Arabia into the Nabataean kingdom.[134] Many of these stations were abandoned by the Romans on their annexation of the kingdom,[135] but those on the route of the *Via Nova* from 'Aqaba to Petra and those on the Petra–Gaza road were retained at this time. In the deeper desert, too, we find evidence of the Nabataean government's involvement in the protection and monitoring of the caravan traffic. There is evidence of a station of some sort manned by Nabataean military personnel at Dumata, at the entrance to the Wadi Sirhan, which presumably existed to protect the traffic entering the Nabataean realm from the trans-Arabian route from Gerrha and the Arabian Gulf.[136] Similarly, at Medain Saleh, the point at which the 'Incense Road' from southern Arabia entered the Nabataean kingdom, there was a military station of particular importance, as has already been noted.

This evidence would appear to testify to the importance of the caravan trade to the Nabataean economy. As with the Romans in Egypt, it is difficult to say what the motivations for the construction of these posts were, but it is likely that the collection of taxes and customs duties was of primary importance. Nonetheless, the construction of these installations testifies to the fact that the incense traffic was seen as a lucrative source of income to the government, and was thus probably an important factor in the economy of the Nabataeans.

The economic significance of the trade in the Nabataean kingdom

According to the ancient writers, the Nabataean kingdom appears to have derived its income from a number of sources. These sources included pastoralism,[137] obtaining bitumen from the Dead Sea,[138] and dry farming.[139] Despite these other sources of revenue, however, Diodorus explicitly states that the Nabataeans became much wealthier than the other Arab tribes because of their involvement in the trade in frankincense and myrrh.[140] Thus, although he considers and mentions the other sources of income which the Nabataeans enjoyed, it is clear that in his view the pre-eminent wealth that they enjoyed over the other Arabs was due to the trade which they carried on in carrying the frankincense and myrrh over their territory.

Strabo too indicates that the Nabataeans obtained at least a great part of their wealth from their trading activites. Although he does not say this specifically, he gives great prominence to the fact that the Nabataeans were involved in the commerce in aromatics, occasionally stressing the large volume of traffic which passed through Petra.[141] In addition, he mentions that the Sabaeans and Gerrhaeans had become extremely wealthy due to their involvement in the frankincense trade:[142] it is not unreasonable to assume that the Nabataeans too, heavily involved in the same trade, would have grown wealthy in the same way. Pliny mentions the lucrative nature of the incense trade, and the amount expended in taxes and charges in getting a load of incense from Arabia Felix to the sea.[143] Many of these taxes would no doubt have been paid into the coffers of the Nabataean kingdom.

Indeed, we can still see the evidence of the Nabataeans' wealth. While we have no real way of determining the incomes of the kingdom or the expenditures to which it was committed, the spectacular monuments of Petra which the visitor can still view provide convincing testimony to the wealth of the Nabataeans. The construction of such imposing edifices must have involved the Nabataeans in considerable expense, and it would seem that only in a period of great prosperity would they have been able to complete such an undertaking as they did. This point is particularly important when it is borne in mind that most of the monuments appear to have been constructed in the course of the first century AD,[144] testifying to this period as one of great wealth in the Nabataean kingdom.

It is difficult to identify what could have caused this prosperity other than the incense trade. Certainly such things as agriculture, livestock raising and the bitumen of the Dead Sea must have contributed, but these by themselves are insufficient to explain the evident prosperity of the Nabataeans, particularly given the insistence of the ancient writers that this prosperity was a result of their trade. It would appear that, at least to a great extent, the prosperity of the Nabataean kingdom as evidenced in their monuments and as described by the literary sources must be ascribed to the caravan trade.

There would thus seem to be ample reason for considering that the Arabian incense trade was of great economic significance in the Nabataean kingdom.

Certainly, such military posts as Medain Saleh can show us that the Nabataean military played a significant role in the protection of the caravan traffic. The evidence of the caravan stations around Petra also shows that government involvement was not purely military, but also extended to the provision (no doubt at some cost) of watering and revictualling facilities for the caravans at Petra, and possibly at other sites as well. Thus, although we have no details of the system of taxation by which the government may have exploited the caravan traffic passing through its realm, we can take the involvement and interest of the Nabataean government in the Arabian incense trade as a very strong possibility.

Thus, despite the overall lack of evidence, we may legitimately conclude that the Arabian incense trade probably held considerable significance for the economy of the area. When the Romans annexed the kingdom in AD 106, they acquired a territory in which the incense trade had some considerable significance, as well as considerable potential for revenue to be gained by the taxation of this trade.

Trade in *Provincia Arabia* in the Antonine period

The Nabataean kingdom came to an end and became the new Roman province of Arabia in AD 106. Although the exact circumstances are unknown, the annexation appears to have been at least relatively peaceful and may have taken place upon the death of the reigning king, Rabbel II, who had reigned since AD 71. The epitomator of Cassius Dio briefly records the event in the following words:

> κατὰ δὲ τὸν αὐτὸν τοῦτον χρόνον καὶ Πάλμας τῆς Συρίας ἄρχων τὴν Ἀραβίαν τὴν πρὸς τῇ Πέτρᾳ ἐχειρώσατο καὶ Ῥωμαίων ὑπήκοον ἐποιήσατο.
>
> And at around the same time Palma, the governor of Syria, subdued Arabia about Petra and made it subject to the Romans.[145]

Upon or soon after this invasion, the kingdom appears to have been organised as a province governed by a senatorial legate with a garrison of a single legion. In keeping with the greater importance of the northern part of the kingdom during the later first century AD, the governor appears to have been based at Bostra,[146] and the remains of a legionary camp indicate that the legion was based there too.[147]

The annexation of the Nabataean kingdom

The reason for the annexation is never explicitly stated, but the possibility of commercial motives has been suggested.[148] This, however, is quite unlikely. If the Romans had desired to remove the 'Arabian middleman' they could have done it long before; indeed military expeditions had previously been started against the Nabataeans, although not for commercial motives.[149]

Roman client kingdoms existed in the East because they fulfilled some role which the Romans either could not or did not wish to. By the end of the first century AD most of these kingdoms had been incorporated into the provincial system.[150] The persistence of the Nabataean kingdom in these circumstances shows clearly that it was not viewed as an economic rival by Rome, but as a useful vassal. However, toward the end of the first century and into the second, it seems that the Romans wished to incorporate the remaining client states, and so (presumably) upon the deaths of their respective kings the kingdoms of Herod Agrippa II and of Rabbel II were annexed by Rome.

Whether or not the decision to annex Petra was planned in advance to take place on the death of Rabbel, or, as has been suggested, took place in response to disturbances in the kingdom at that time,[151] we cannot tell. It is clear, however, that the decision to invade would have been occasioned by political or military considerations of some sort, not by any commercial motive. Under Trajan, Rome pursued an expansionist policy: Dacia and Parthia were attacked in major campaigns, while (as has been noted) client states, such as the Nabataean kingdom and the kingdom of Herod Agrippa II,[152] were incorporated into provinces. There is certainly no need to look for any special commercial consideration in the annexation of Petra: rather, we should have expressed surprise had the kingdom *not* been annexed at that time in the light of Roman policy elsewhere. The annexation of the Nabataean realm may well have been thought militarily expedient in the light of the upcoming campaign against Parthia, as Graf suggests,[153] or the internal situation in the Nabataean kingdom could have decayed to the extent that Cornelius Palma thought that Roman intervention was necessary to restore order.[154] Certainly the unusual timing of the annexation, while Trajan was still engaged in Dacia, together with the apparently *ad hoc* nature of the invasion force, composed of detachments of troops from surrounding provinces rather than a specially prepared invasion army, would suggest that the intervention was not planned and occurred in response to some crisis within the Nabataean kingdom.[155]

Another consideration which could have affected the decision to annex the Nabataean kingdom is the possible lack of an heir to take over the kingdom on the death of Rabbel II. While there is evidence that Rabbel had a son, Obodas,[156] it may be that he had either predeceased Rabbel or was not of age, or otherwise considered unable to govern by the Romans.[157] Indeed, the lack of an heir or some succession crisis coupled with an ageing king may have been sufficient to provoke the kind of unrest suggested by Freeman as the trigger for the Roman invasion.[158] There are certainly examples of client kingdoms reverting to provinces when no suitable heir was available: for example, Judaea was made a province after the death of Herod Agrippa I because Agrippa II was not yet of age.[159] Thus it is altogether possible that the Romans may have decided that the time was right to annex the Nabataean kingdom after Rabbel's death if there was no strong heir capable of taking over the kingdom, particularly if there were severe disturbances over the succession. Regardless of the exact reason for the Roman action, we can be assured that it would have been military or political reasons which motivated them. There is no coherent case to be made for a mercantile motive.

Trade in the Roman province of Arabia

Whatever the reason for the Roman annexation of the Nabataean kingdom was, it seems that the takeover in no way affected the continuance of the incense trade. In fact, it appears that the Romans changed as little as possible when they took over the kingdom. Many developments which have been put forward as evidence of Roman 'provincialisation' can now be shown to have occurred either before or after the annexation, while other developments such as the replacement of Aramaic by Greek in legal documents of the province would have been made necessary simply by the fact that the Roman governor could not read Aramaic.[160] Indeed, it may well be argued that little changed in Arabia in AD 106–114 apart from the replacement of the king with a representative of the emperor and the disbandment of the Nabataean army.[161] In this climate, it would be difficult to imagine the Romans deliberately taking any action which would disrupt the patterns of long-distance trade in the province, particularly when that trade would no doubt bring significant funds to the treasury by the imposition of taxes and duties.

Perhaps the most significant act undertaken by the Romans on their annexation of the kingdom was the construction of the *Via Nova Traiana*, a new road which ran from Bostra to Aila. As has been noted, this route was not an innovation but followed the path of a pre-existing caravan route which had long been used by the Nabataeans.[162] Milestone inscriptions make it clear that this construction went hand in hand with the creation of the province; indeed, by the time coins commemorating the annexation appear, the road was largely finished.[163] The milestones state that the road was constructed and Arabia was converted to a province at the same time, under the governorship of Claudius Severus who presumably took over command when Cornelius Palma had returned to Syria, or at least when a separate Arabian command was created distinct from the province of Syria:[164]

> Imp. Caesar
> Diui Neruae f. Nerua
> Traianus Aug. Germ.
> Dacicus Pont. Max.
> Trib. Pot. XV Imp. VI Cos. V
> P. P. redacta in formam
> prouinciae Arabia uiam
> nouam a finibus Syriae

> usque ad Mare Rubrum
> aperuit et strauit per
> C. Claudium Seuerum
> leg. Au[g. pr. pr.]
>
> The Emperor Caesar . . . Traianus Augustus . . . , when Arabia had been transformed into a province, opened up and paved a new road from the borders of Syria as far as the Red Sea by C. Claudius Severus, governor.[165]

The view that trade had declined or disappeared in the Nabataean kingdom before the annexation also implies that Petra, the major centre for trade in the kingdom, had lost its importance by that time. Following this viewpoint, there has been a prevailing view that the *Via Nova* bypassed Petra, connecting it to the main route only by a side road.[166] Graf, however, has shown that Petra was most probably on the main route of the *Via Nova*, and this testifies to its continued importance at this time.[167] First, Petra is shown on the main north–south route through Arabia on the *Tabula Peutingeriana*.[168] In addition, Petra's continuing importance in this period is shown by its receiving the title *metropolis* before Bostra,[169] and its use as the seat of the Roman assizes.[170] Graf also demonstrated the existence of Roman road remains immediately to the north of Petra which are of the same width and arrangement as the *Via Nova* between Amman and Bostra.[171] To this can be added the fact that there is inscriptional evidence of military personnel stationed at Petra itself in the Roman period, which attests to the continuing importance of the site and the necessity of protecting and monitoring traffic passing through the city.[172]

Indeed, it would seem that as soon as the road was put into place, merchants were quick to exploit it and the opportunities presented by the integration of the Nabataean kingdom into the Roman provincial system. As was mentioned earlier, there is both physical and literary evidence that merchants had used this route well before the arrival of the Romans, and it is difficult to believe that merchants would not take advantage of the new road once it was finished. Indeed, a preserved papyrus letter from one Julius Apollinarius, a legionary stationed at Bostra, mentions that soon after the Roman annexation, merchants were arriving at Bostra from Pelusium in Egypt every day.[173] It seems clear that these merchants saw considerable new opportunities in the province of Arabia at this time. Although we are not told what type of merchants these were, nor what it was they were interested in, it is nonetheless true that their presence implies that trade in the Nabataean kingdom had not come to a standstill either before or upon the Roman annexation.

Indeed, the opening of the *Via Nova* may well have had some important effects upon the patterns of long-distance trade in the province. The construction of a road along an already used caravan route, and its provision with guard posts and caravanserais,[174] would no doubt have attracted merchants, and this may have affected the use of such alternative routes as the Petra–Gaza road. Traffic coming up the incense road which until the construction of the *Via Nova* would have generally used the roads across the Negev might after that time have chosen to come up the *Via Nova* into the Decapolis and thence to the Mediterranean.[175] Thus we may view this trade also as possibly contributing to the rising prosperity of the Decapolis cities at this time,[176] along with the trade from the Wadi Sirhan discussed earlier. It would seem then that the trade which had existed under the rule of the Nabataean kings continued to be active under Roman rule: indeed, it is very possible that integration into the Roman provincial system brought commercial advantages and stimulated trade. Certainly it seems that the merchants from Pelusium thought that this would be the case.

The Roman occupation of Medain Saleh

The continuing importance of trade in the new province is further demonstrated by the Roman garrisoning of the outpost at Medain Saleh (Hegra). While some have doubted the assertion that this region was actually a part of the Roman province,[177] it is undoubtedly the case that Roman troops were stationed in the region, as their presence is attested by numerous inscriptions in the area. Whether or not one wishes to adduce this as evidence of the area's constituting part of the province, it unquestionably signals Roman control of at least Hegra and the route to it from the province.[178]

These inscriptions attest the presence of at least two Roman *alae* and possibly elements of the province's legion, the *III Cyrenaica*. The graffiti were initially recorded by Jaussen and Savignac and have since been recorded and commented upon by several others.[179] Seyrig dated these inscriptions to the later second century,[180] but Speidel has pointed out that one of the units attested, the *ala ueterana Gaetulorum*, was in Arabia by the time of Marcus Aurelius.[181] Indeed, the fact that this unit was in Judaea prior to the annexation of Arabia (as is shown by a diploma of AD 86)[182] makes it quite likely that it was transferred to Arabia either at the time of annexation or very soon afterward.[183] The military occupation of the site seems to have continued until perhaps a little before the time of Caracalla, as the lack of the *nomen* Aurelius among the inscriptions indicates that the series stopped before then.[184] For most of the second century AD there was a considerable Roman garrison based at this remote outpost. The inscriptions are grouped together rather than widely scattered,[185] which makes it more likely that the units were based there rather than simply passing through the site.

The presence of these units is clear evidence of the continued importance of the trade coming along the old 'Incense Road'. Just as in the Nabataean period discussed earlier, it is very difficult to see the point of stationing troops at this remote locality unless it was related to the caravan traffic. We know of no other Roman interest in the area other than the caravan traffic, and there is no concrete evidence that this region was the approach route of any nomadic invasions or raids.[186] We do, however, know that the route passing through Medain Saleh was important because of the trade in frankincense and myrrh, and it is in this light we must attempt to understand the Roman garrisoning of this post. The military remains from the Eastern Desert of Egypt show clearly that the Romans were willing to expend considerable effort in protecting the routes which this valuable commerce used,[187] and it would appear that the Roman station at Medain Saleh is another case in point.

Regardless of the actual Roman motivation for the annexation of the Nabataean kingdom and the construction of the *Via Nova Traiana*, merchants made use of the opportunities presented by these events to further their commerce. There is no support to be found for the notion that Petra was in decline at this time, either before or after the Roman takeover, nor that the trade upon which it had relied for its livelihood had moved or been moved elsewhere. The presence of merchants at Bostra, the continuing importance of Petra and the continued garrisoning of Medain Saleh and the Petra–Gaza road show clearly that the Arabian incense trade remained a significant factor in the economy of the Roman province of Arabia for some considerable time after the annexation.

Arabian trade in the third and fourth centuries

While the incense traffic thus appears to have continued in the first century of Roman occupation, there is evidence that the trade underwent some changes in the course of the third century AD. In particular, we shall see that there is the possibility that for the first time some trade from India and further afield began to come through the province. In addition, paralleling the experience in Egypt discussed in Chapter 2, it appears that the Arabian traffic was affected by the economic and political crisis of the later third century.

Trade in the Severan period

Herodian makes one brief and very confused reference to the continuation of the incense trade in the earlier part of the third century. However, this reference tells us only that incense was still being exported from Arabia Felix to the Roman Empire in the later period,[188] not whether the incense was being carried overland through Arabia or by sea through Egypt. We can however learn that the demand for these aromatics was still present in the empire and thus merchants would have continued to find a market for their goods. Indeed, given the religious significance of these incenses in the ancient world, it is hardly surprising that the demand did continue. Of course, if all the trade by this time passed through the Egyptian Red Sea ports then the trade would no longer have been of any significance to Roman Arabia. There are reasons, however, for concluding that this was not the case.

The occupation of the site of Medain Saleh by the Romans has already been noted, and the continued use of this site in the Severan period would indicate that the aromatics trade was still passing through this site. There is also evidence of Severan garrisoning of the deep desert in the Wadi Sirhan, which has already been noted as a route whereby trade may have entered the province of Arabia. Archaeological and inscriptional evidence from the Wadi suggests that there was considerable activity there in this period, especially at the Azraq oasis. Severan milestones dating from AD 208–10 have been found on a road leading north from the oasis,[189] and Latin building inscriptions of 200 and 201 give evidence of Severan occupation in the small fort at Qasr el-Uweinid near the Azraq oasis.[190] In addition, aerial photographs of Azraq itself show the remains of an older, larger fort beside the Tetrarchic building standing today at the site.[191] It is quite possible that this fort would have also dated from the Severan period, as the small fort at Qasr el-Uweinid would have been completely untenable without a garrison at Azraq also.[192]

However, this attention does not seem to have been confined to the Azraq oasis and the roads leading to it. There is also evidence that at various times, most probably in the Severan and also later in the Tetrarchic period, the Romans patrolled in some way the entire length of the Wadi Sirhan as far as Jawf. An inscription, found at Jawf itself, was set up by a centurion of the *legio III Cyrenaica* as a dedication for the well-being of two *Augusti*.[193] Although the emperors are not named, the formula used in the inscription is characteristic of the second century, so the most likely candidates would be Lucius Verus and Marcus Aurelius (AD 161–169), or Septimius Severus and Caracalla (AD 197–211). In view of the Severan date of the fortifications at the northern end of the wadi at Azraq, we might consider the second date to be more likely. In either case, this inscription provides evidence of Roman activity far into the Arabian desert at this time.

That this activity most probably took the form of patrols along the length of the Wadi Sirhan is made probable by another inscription found at Azraq which seems to describe the entire route of the road:

> [D.n. Diocletiano . . .
> . . .
> per mil. fortiss. suos
> legg. XI Kl. et VII Kl.
> et I Ital. et IIII Fl. et
> I Ill., praetensione
> coligata mil. suis ex
> leg. III Kyr. A Bostra
> Basianis m. p. LXVI et
> a Basienis Amat. LXX
> et ab Amata Dumata
> m. p. CCVIII.
>
> Diocletian . . . by his brave soldiers of the legions XI Claudia, VII Claudia, I Italica, IIII Flavia and I Illyricorum, linked by outposts to

> his soldiers from the legion III Cyrenaica, from Bostra to Basianis 66 miles, from Basianis to Amata 70 miles, and from Amata to Dumata 208 miles.[194]

This inscription appears to describe a patrol area or series of outposts linked along the road passing down the Wadi Sirhan from Bostra to Dumata, the ancient name for Jawf. Speidel's interpretation is that the posts are to be understood as linked in a chain,[195] whereas Kennedy and MacAdam believed the inscription gave distances from a fixed point, Dasianis, which they equated with Azraq.[196] Speidel's interpretation is to be preferred simply because the earlier interpretation called for the route to end at an unattested place called Bamata Dumata, located at the end of the Wadi Sirhan but still some 70 Roman miles short of the known site of Jawf. Speidel's interpretation, by contrast, correctly gives the distance between Azraq and Jawf and ends the route at the oasis of Jawf instead of in mid-desert, as logic would dictate.

Nonetheless, either interpretation shows clearly that the Romans were maintaining outposts and/or patrols, presumably the meaning of the obscure term *praetensio*,[197] along the road during this period. Although this inscription dates from the Tetrarchy,[198] the presence of a Roman centurion at Jawf in the Severan period as noted above, coupled with the known Severan activity in the Azraq area, makes it more than likely that some similar patrolling arrangement must have existed then also. This would seem to indicate that the Romans had some interest in the deep desert in the Severan period. What then *was* that interest, and was it at all associated with the caravan trade?

Some scholars have suggested that the patrols into the desert areas which were instituted in the reign of Severus were purely military in character, and had nothing to do with any trade using the routes in the area. These have generally suggested that the Wadi Sirhan was blocked by the Severan fortifications because of the use of the wadi as an invasion route by tribes living in the interior.[199] Indeed, it is pointed out that the wadi has been a popular route for raiding parties even up until this century.[200] It has also been pointed out that these Severan posts in the desert are parallel to similar posts in Africa,[201] which might indicate that they were part of a general programme of advanced patrols in desert regions of the empire rather than specifically related to the Arabian caravan traffic.

It would be foolish indeed to deny any association of the forts in the Wadi Sirhan with the general security of the area. No doubt one of the purposes of these forts was to deny the use of the oasis and consequently the route which passed through the oasis to any desert raiders who might desire to use the route as a thoroughfare into the settled area of the province. Although the problem of Saracen raiders was not as severe as some would make out, it still unquestionably existed.[202] It would seem more than likely that the placing of these posts was in part at least to promote the security of the region and to suppress banditry and raiding in the settled area of the province.

This is reflected also in the posts in the desert of North Africa which date from this time.[203] These too are placed at oases in the desert on approach routes to the settled area of the province, and can rightly be seen as parallels to the Severan occupation of the oasis at Azraq and blocking of the north-western end of the Wadi Sirhan. It would seem from this that Septimius Severus instituted a general policy of denying these routes and oases to tribes who might use them to attack both Roman troops in the area and the sedentary inhabitants of the respective provinces.

Nonetheless there are several reasons for thinking that, beside these general considerations, there were factors at play in Arabia which were specific to that area. The north African posts are indeed deep in the desert and remote from the settled area of the province, but they are nowhere near as remote as Jawf or Medain Saleh. For example, the post at Castellum Dimidi in Mauretania Caesarensis is approximately 250 km from the coast, whereas Jawf is over 400 km from Azraq, which is itself only a fort, and nearly 500 km from Bostra, the nearest significant city. It might be argued that the posts in the Wadi Sirhan were advance posts for the troops at Azraq, but it is difficult to imagine that they needed to be quite so far in advance! Indeed, if the sole intention of the Romans was to prevent the use of the Wadi Sirhan by invading raiders, then the fortification of the Azraq oasis would have sufficed for this admirably, as it would deny the use of the oasis to the raiders and block off the Wadi as an access to the province. If there was nothing in the Wadi itself that the Romans were interested in, then it would seem pointless to patrol the entire length of the road when the nomads could be effectively blocked by the forts at Azraq. Rather, the patrolling of the whole road suggests that there was something of value using the road, and that the Romans wished to protect it.

The previous history of the wadi as a trade route, shown by the Nabataean garrisoning of Jawf,[204] makes it perfectly clear what this interest would have been: the incense traffic from Arabia Felix.[205] The posts at such places as Jawf and Medain Saleh cannot be considered as parallels to the Severan desert posts in Africa, as in Arabia there was an already well-established history of usage at these oases which is absent at the posts in Africa. This history must be taken into account when these places are examined and an explanation for their garrisoning sought.

There is also the possibility that as well as the traditional incense trade there also arose in the Severan period a new trade in the Wadi Sirhan which may have increased the value of this route still further to the Romans. As will be discussed in Chapter 4, the trade of Palmyra in spices and silks from India rose to great prominence in the second century AD. However, in the periods when Rome and Parthia were at war, this trade may have suffered some disruption,[206] and accordingly the merchants would have been obliged to seek another route by which their wares could be transported to the Mediterranean. The direct overland route between the Gulf and Arabia which passed through the oasis of Dumata (and consequently well clear of Parthian lands and the theatre of war between Rome and Parthia) would have been an ideal alternative to the Mesopotamian route. Thus it may be that during the Severan wars against Parthia, the disrupted caravan traffic began to use this route and enter the Roman Empire by means of the Wadi Sirhan, prompting the Romans to increase their protection of the wadi.[207]

There is therefore a reasonable case to be made for the continuing importance of the eastern commerce in Arabia, and the involvement of the Roman military in its monitoring and protection. Of course, this does not have to be attributed to any far-sighted economic policy but simply to the desire of the imperial government to collect the taxes which accrued to it from the traffic. We should continue to distinguish carefully between Roman *direction* of caravan traffic (which has not been convincingly demonstrated in any area) and Roman *reaction* to new developments in the traffic. In the absence of any clear indication that the Romans attempted to divert or direct the caravan traffic at any other time, we should assume that the redirection of the incense trade to the Wadi Sirhan was done by the merchants themselves seeking a less vulnerable route to bring their merchandise into the empire.

From this it would seem that the incense traffic was still alive and well in Arabia during the Severan period, and may indeed have been supplemented by caravans carrying Indian and Chinese goods arriving from the head of the Arabian Gulf. However, after the close of the Severan period, the third century brought a severe political crisis in many areas of the Roman Empire which appears to have had very serious economic repercussions.

Arabian trade in the later third century

As has already been discussed, it appears that the political crisis of the third century had grave economic results throughout the Roman Empire. In many areas of the empire there is evidence that the economy stagnated and money in particular lost its importance as a means of exchange, due to severe devaluation by the government.[208] In these circumstances, it would be hardly surprising if such a capital-dependent activity as the long-distance trade were badly affected.

There is indeed some evidence from Arabia which would seem to confirm this, and to show that the overland incense traffic succumbed at least in a large part to the increasing costs and decreasing market of the trade in the third century. The first piece of evidence is the apparent abandonment of the post at Medain Saleh at the beginning of the third century. The Greek and Latin graffiti at the site referring to Roman military occupation have all been dated no later than the early third century, while the absence of the imperial *nomen* Aurelius in any of the inscriptions would seem to indicate that occupation had ceased by the time of Caracalla.[209] Certainly there are no later inscriptions, and the site is not mentioned in the *Notitia Dignitatum* and so was presumably abandoned by the fourth century. Thereafter, it was probably left to the supervision of local Arab *phylarchs* with very limited imperial control.[210]

It would seem most likely that the military post at Hegra ceased to be of sufficient value to maintain the garrison there by the end of the Severan period, and that the Romans never again considered it worthwhile to send troops there. It has already been argued that the only plausible reason for the existence of this remote post (900 km from the legionary base at Bostra) was the protection of the incense caravans travelling up from Arabia Felix and the collection of their tolls. Accordingly, it is very likely that the removal of the garrison there reflects a significant decline in the incense traffic passing through the station.

The economic difficulties of this period, coupled perhaps with the decline in income from the incense traffic, may also have caused some decline in the city of Petra itself at this time. There is some evidence that the inhabited area of Petra was reduced somewhat in this period, particularly on the north side of the city.[211] It is certainly possible that such a decline may have been caused by the economic factors which were causing difficulty throughout the empire at this time. It is even possible that in the case of Petra, this problem was exacerbated by the fact that a higher proportion than normal of the city's finances was derived from the incense trade rather than agriculture. Thus, any decline in the incense trade, as seems likely from the evidence at Medain Saleh, might have had a more severe economic effect on Petra than on other cities less involved with the trade.

Given the evidence for a similar decline in the Egyptian Red Sea commerce as discussed in Chapter 2, it would not be surprising that the Arabian incense traffic suffered some dimunition at the same time. Thus, in the third century we see evidence of a reduction in the volume of the eastern trade as well as in the interest of the Roman authorities in protecting the reduced traffic.

Recovery under the Tetrarchy

The situation does not seem to have remained so grim for long, however. After the political crisis of the third century had been ended, there is considerable evidence for the recovery of Roman Arabia in both agriculture and trade. In particular, there are several indications that trade began once more to flow along the caravan routes of Arabia. At the same time, the cultivated and populated area of the province was dramatically increased during the Tetrarchic era.[212]

In the area of trade, in particular, two important locations stand out. One is the Wadi Sirhan, which has already been described in connection with the Severan activity in the region. As noted in the discussion of that topic, an inscription from the reign of Diocletian attests to the existence of a Roman patrol along the wadi as far as Jawf, some 400 km from Bostra. This is a clear indication that the wadi was being used as a communication route of some sort, and moreover as one that the Romans sought to protect. As was the case in the Severan period, this would most probably indicate that the Wadi Sirhan was in use as a means of bringing both Arabian incense into the province as well as goods from India and further afield. Such traffic in this period may have formerly passed through Palmyra until the destruction of that city in AD 272.

Another locality which seems to have risen in importance during the Tetrarchic period is the port of Aila, now known as ʻAqaba. At the beginning of the fourth century, Eusebius recorded that Aila was in use as a port for the Indian trade, and had been allotted a substantial garrison, consisting of the *Legio X Fretensis*, which was transferred there from Jerusalem.[213] Whether or not this posting was due to the increasing port activity or as part of the increase in the garrison of Arabia as a whole which occurred during this period is difficult to say, but recent archaeological investigations at the site have shown the large scale of both commercial and military activity at Aila in the later Classical period.[214] Although there is evidence at the site for occupation and commercial traffic from the first through to the fourth centuries,[215] the bulk of the datable physical remains at Aila are from the fourth century, pointing to this period as the peak of commercial activity there.[216]

This increase in the importance of Aila seems to be roughly synchronous with the rise in significance of the port of Clysma in Egypt as detailed in Chapter 2. This may well have been related to the destruction of Coptos by Diocletian in the late third century, which would have effectively ended, at least temporarily, the commercial importance of Berenike.[217] Clysma and Aila would have been able to exploit the eclipse of the older Red Sea ports and receive the cargoes that were being brought by sea from both India and Arabia. Thus, despite the difficulty of navigating the northern reaches of the Red Sea, the removal of the Nile emporium of Coptos made the former trade route to the Nile from Berenike untenable, and so the merchants were forced to sail further up the Gulf to use the ports of Clysma and Aila.

The third century would thus appear to be a significant time in the history of the incense trade in Arabia. During the political and economic crisis of that century the nature of the trade changed dramatically: prior to that time the incense route from South Arabia seems to have continued to function. Much of this trade seems to have been brought to a standstill by the poor economic conditions of the third century, however, when the economic situation improved again under the Tetrarchy many things had changed. By this time the two main routes in use seem to have been the Wadi Sirhan, now carrying trade which formerly would have passed through Palmyra, and Aila, receiving goods from India and Arabia which before had gone to the Egyptian Red Sea ports.

The Limes Arabicus

A particular area of the Roman presence in Arabia in the later period which has aroused considerable controversy is the system of fortifications and roads known as the *Limes Arabicus*. There are significant remains in the Jordanian desert of a complex system of roads, forts and watchtowers,[218] generally following the line of the *Via Nova Traiana*. The great majority of datable remains in the fortification system are from the later Roman and Byzantine periods, during which time there appears to have been a substantial garrison in this area consisting of perhaps three legions.[219] Nonetheless there are some remains which date from the earlier period of the Roman province.

It has been argued that these fortifications were built as a response to the depredations of nomadic tribes living in the desert to the east of the *Via Nova*.[220] This we might regard as the 'traditional' viewpoint, strongly favoured by Parker and also by many others, which accords with Luttwak's view of an imperial grand strategy of defensive frontiers (in the later period), aimed at excluding the enemies of the empire and preventing their attacks.[221] Accordingly, whether or not the *Limes Arabicus* actually conforms to this view has some implications for the current debate over the existence of an imperial grand strategy and the nature of the Roman frontier.[222]

The 'traditional' viewpoint then sees the Arabian *Limes* as essentially a *latitudinal* barrier: it is chiefly designed to control and monitor the movements of nomads *across* the line of fortifications and to prevent raids by the desert dwellers into the area inhabited by sedentary farmers within the province. It follows from this that the *Via Nova* was primarily intended as an artery of communication between these fortifications, allowing quick communication between the forts and rapid deployment of troops to any area in which they might be needed along the frontier.[223] The nomads are seen as essentially hostile, and presenting a constant threat to the sedentary inhabitants of the province; their raiding is kept in check only by the watchful Roman troops in their fortifications.

However, there are several reasons why this interpretation must be called into question. The first area which will be examined is the role and nature of the *Via Nova Traiana* and the fortifications along it and to the east of it. These fortifications are distributed along two roads: in the south, between Udruh and the Red Sea, there is only the line of the *Via Nova* which has a series of road stations that were occupied by the Romans upon the annexation of the province in AD 106.[224] Further north, there is another road to the east of the *Via Nova* which branches off the main route south of Udruh and continues north at least as far as the Wadi el-Hasa, and very possibly further into the central region of the province.[225] The *Via Nova* itself is generally unfortified in this region, with the exception of a few widely spaced road stations which appear to have been garrisoned by the Romans soon after the annexation.[226] The eastern route, however, has many forts. The forts on this route mostly date from the later third century, but there is evidence that traffic used this road as early as the second century.[227]

It would thus seem most unlikely that the *Via Nova* was intended to be a defensive frontier when it was first built, regardless of what it may have become later. As has been noted, the road was built soon after the province was annexed. The forts, however, apart from a few exceptions, were not built until much later. The theory that the Romans built this road as a defensive frontier is not tenable given the fact that on substantial stretches of the road there were no fortifications for a great many years. It is indeed obvious that the

Romans wished to use this road not as a latitudinal barrier but as a longitudinal route.

The uses for such a route would have been considerable. As a military road it could provide access to the legionary base at Bostra for any troops in the south of the province, while as an administrative route it could provide rapid communication from one end of the province to the other. Besides these uses, it is also possible that the Romans were interested in the control and protection of the valuable caravan traffic which was using this route. It is noteworthy that of the small number of forts which were garrisoned immediately upon the Roman takeover (see Map 3.3), several of them are those on the line of the *Via Nova* south of Petra, such as Khirbet el-Khalde, Quweira and Humeima. These sites have pottery evidence of occupation by Roman troops from soon after annexation until well into the Byzantine period.[228] Much of the road north of Petra, however, was left unfortified until at least the Severan period. It is interesting to note that the section of road south of Petra, which was equipped with Roman posts immediately upon annexation,[229] was precisely that section which would have carried the incense caravans to Petra. As was discussed earlier, the Petra–Gaza road was also in use and fortified immediately upon the Roman takeover.[230]

In this way, the route taken by the incense caravans from ‘Aqaba to Petra and thence to Gaza was provided with road stations upon the Roman annexation, whereas the remainder of the *Via Nova* was left largely unfortified. It may be that the initial Roman military deployments along the southern *Via Nova* were related to the incense caravans as they made their way north toward Petra and from there to the Mediterranean. This system of fortifications is thus probably similar to the fortifications in the Eastern Desert of Egypt. As we have seen, these forts were clearly designed to monitor and protect the caravan traffic passing from the Red Sea to the Nile.[231] Given the incense traffic which we have seen was using this route, it is quite likely that the forts between Aila and Gaza were designed for the same purpose as those in Egypt: for the monitoring of the caravan traffic.

The forts built in the later period, however, do not have an immediately apparent commercial purpose, even though we have seen that commerce was probably still present in the province at this time. It is thus possible that *these* forts, if not the earlier ones, were related to the need to defend the province from nomadic incursions. There is certainly some evidence from Classical literary sources and inscriptions which refer to trouble with ‘Saracens’.[232] Even though the accounts themselves do not specifically refer to widespread and severe ‘nomadic menace’, they have nonetheless on some occasions been taken to be symptomatic of a wider threat than brigandage.[233] That there were *some* troubles cannot be disputed, as indeed there were some troubles in virtually every border province of the Roman Empire. Thus, for example, we have the Nabataean–Greek bilingual inscription from the Hisma, which seems to refer to a Roman cohort defeating some enemy in the second century,

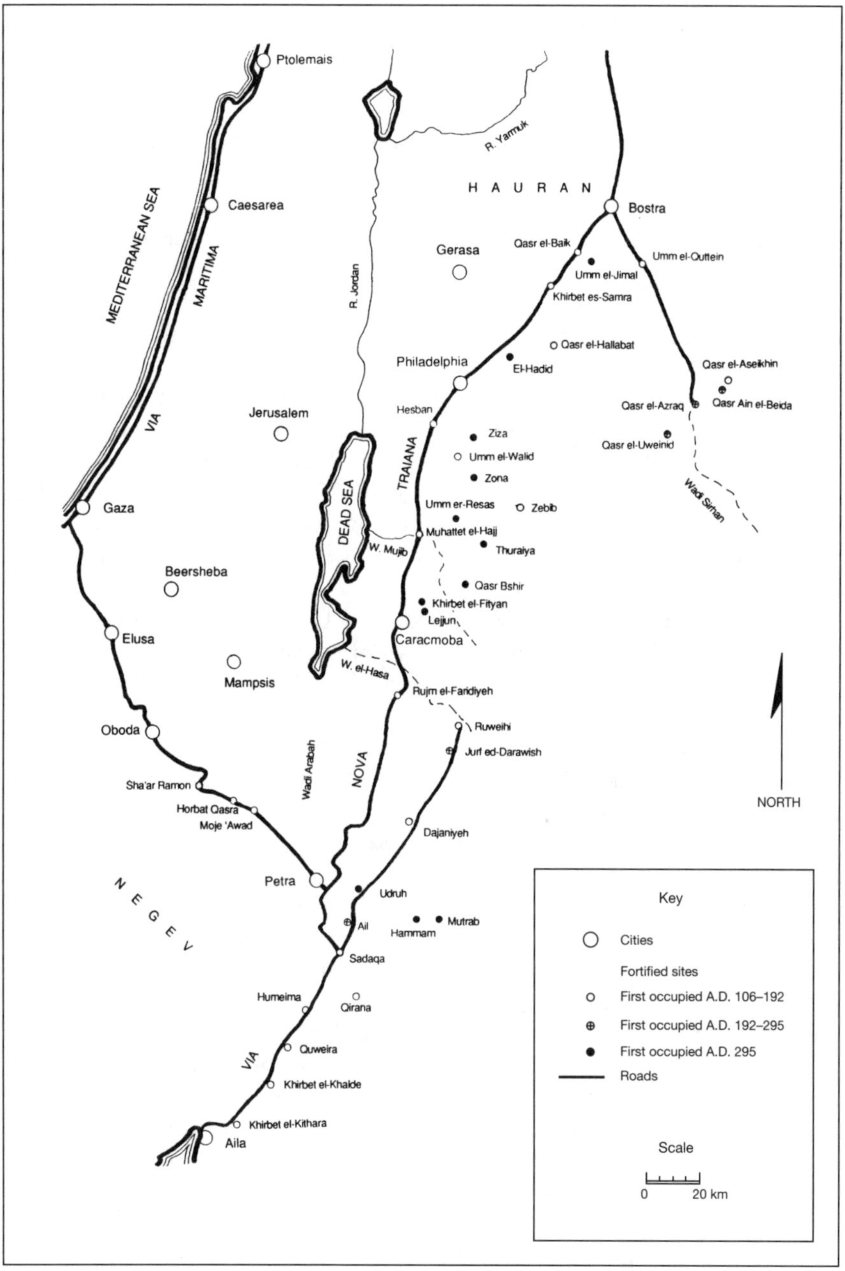

Map 3.3 Roman fortifications in Arabia and the Negev – Please note that the date assigned to each site is not the date of the current construction at the site but the date of the earliest Roman occupation of the site based on pottery or inscriptional evidence

presumably tribesmen from the region.[234] Also, we might note the role of several Severan outposts in the Wadi Sirhan which seem, in part at least, to be designed to prevent the use of the wadi as a route for raids. Such incidents as this, however, are not uncommon throughout the whole area of Roman rule and are probably more to be thought of as troublesome banditry than a sizeable military threat from outside the empire.

Indeed, if there were a significant nomadic threat to the inhabitants of the province, it would be reasonable to expect many other fortifications than just the military ones along the *Limes Arabicus*. One would expect the worried inhabitants of Arabia to have erected strong walls around their towns, and to have concentrated their activities on towns and areas near the forts for the sake of security. This, however, does not appear to be the case. From the results of a survey of a part of the Wadi el-Hasa, E.B. Banning suggests that a model of co-operative mutualism between nomad pastoralists and sedentary agriculturalists explains the evidence far better than does the hypothesis of hostility between these groups.[235] In this study, it was found that in the survey area there were widely scattered remains of camps, farmsteads, small hamlets and villages as well as the more substantial towns.[236] Furthermore, it was noted that there was no evidence throughout the area surveyed of any significant attempt at circumvallation at any of the sites.[237] This is far more consistent with the model of mutualism than it is with that of hostility.

Nonetheless, there seems to have been conflict as well, although not necessarily of the sort that Parker envisages. This is revealed in Graf's study of the Safaitic and Thamudic inscriptions of the Arabian and Syrian deserts.[238] These texts demonstrate that these people who wrote them were considered in many cases as residents of the province, not as outsiders. For example, the tribe of the 'Ubaishat appear not only in Safaitic inscriptions from the desert, but also in another inscription as the *demos* (people) of the village of Si' in the southern Hauran, within the province of Arabia.[239] It is clear from these inscriptions that these transhumant pastoralists who travelled far into the desert were nonetheless regarded as the inhabitants of a town within the Roman province. In this case at least, the townspeople and the nomads who 'threaten' them turn out to be the same people! Similarly, members of the tribe of the 'Awidh, attested in several Safaitic inscriptions from northern Jordan,[240] are mentioned as priests of a local temple at Deir el-Laban 40 km north of Bostra and as commanders of a local military contingent at Rama to the south-east: both, again, within the borders of the province.[241] This pattern is repeated throughout the tribes found in the Safaitic corpus;[242] it demonstrates that the view of the Safaitic tribes, and indeed of the 'Saracens' in general, as wandering, pillaging nomads is untenable.

Indeed, the evidence suggests that the threat against which the forts of the *Limes* was built was possibly not an external one at all. A further examination of the Safaitic inscriptions reveals that the threat the forts were designed to face was one of restive provincials, among whom were certainly the nomads who grazed their flocks in the desert part of the year, but also very likely the agriculturalists who spent all their lives within the boundaries of the province. A great many of these inscriptions mention 'rebellion' or 'flight' from Roman authority: words which seem unusual for enemies of Rome, but certainly those that we might expect from a rebellious population. In one example, a member of the tribe of 'Ubaishat mentioned above is recorded as having 'rebelled against the people of Rome',[243] while many other inscriptions mention 'flight' and 'escape' from Roman authority.[244] While these texts contain few clues to allow them to be dated with any accuracy, the preponderance of Roman fortifications in the region dating from the third century and later would seem to indicate that this is the period in which most of this unrest took place. Thus, we see that the sedentary inhabitants of the province probably had a varied relationship with the pastoralists: raiding and conflict on the one hand, but also the possibility of peaceful relationships in some areas.[245]

The forts of the *Limes Arabicus*, then, appear to have served as a protection in an area of considerable unrest. This unrest, as well as the internal nature of the problem, is illustrated by a Severan inscription from the road between Damascus and Emesa:

> hoc proesidium construxit in securitatem publicam et Scaenitarum Arabum terrorem.
>
> This fort was built for the public safety and as a terror to the tent-dwelling Arabs.[246]

This fort is located many miles from the edge of the desert, well within the province, showing clearly that the *Scenitae* whom the Romans intended to intimidate were nomadic pastoralist inhabitants of the province, not raiders from outside. The problem being addressed here is clearly brigandage within the province, not an external threat. It would thus seem most likely that the other forts of Roman Arabia were built with this type of threat in mind. Rather than being a barrier, they were intended to protect the communications of the Roman forces and the wealthy inhabitants of the province from the depredations of restive provincials who had begun to prey upon vulnerable travellers.

Along with the vital military and administrative communications of the Roman army, there were also the incense caravans and the wealthier provincials that needed to be protected, providing a compelling reason for the construction of the system of forts in Arabia. By their presence, then, the forts of the *Limes Arabicus* could help the Romans in a number of ways. First of all, they could prevent interference by bandits and restive provincials with the apparatus of Roman government. Second, by making banditry more difficult they would help to preserve the Roman tax-base, which, as discussed in Chapter 2, was being eroded in the second and third centuries by increasingly large numbers of people turning to brigandage as a way of avoiding their onerous tax burdens. Third, by protecting the incense caravans they would remove from the brigands some of the richest prizes that would have been available to them, as well as maintaining the inflow of customs payments payable by the caravans. Naturally, the communications along the more remote areas and on the fringe of the cultivated area were the most vulnerable, and it is in these areas that we find the most forts, particularly in the later period when the unrest seems to have been at its most severe.

Thus, in an overview of the fortification system in Arabia we can discern an initial interest in protecting the caravan traffic coming from Arabia Felix giving way, in deteriorating economic and political circumstances, to a general concern about provincial unrest threatening Roman communication, tax collection and administration. As the parallel from Egypt shows, there is a link to be made between the protection of caravans and the suppression of banditry and tax evasion generally, and thus we do not have to divorce one from the other. Rather, the more dire the economic circumstances became, the more attractive a prospect for brigandage the caravans would become, making a life of 'flight from Rome', as many of the Safaitic inscriptions call it, more enticing than it might otherwise have been. In these circumstances the protection of caravans was a continuing priority, demonstrably so in Egypt and thus quite possibly in Arabia also.

Conclusion: the incense trade in Nabataean and Roman Arabia

From the available evidence, the incense trade appears to have been a quite significant factor in the Nabataean kingdom and in the Roman province of Arabia which succeeded it. Despite the fact that in many ways our research is hampered by a lack of evidence, particularly with respect to the organisation of the trade and its participants, it is still possible to reach certain conclusions about the Arabian incense trade in the Roman and Nabataean periods.

The Nabataean kingdom in particular, at least in the period that it still existed as an independent state, seems to have derived a relatively high proportion of its income from the incense traffic. It certainly seems that the ancient writers thought that this was the case: Diodorus, for instance, explicitly ascribed the pre-eminent wealth of the Nabataeans to their participation in the incense trade, and although other writers mentioned other sources of income, none of them contradict Diodorus' view. The coming of the Romans must inevitably have caused some disruption to this trade, but we have seen that the frequently stated idea of deliberate Roman action, whether military or economic, to destroy the trade of the Nabataean kingdom must be rejected. There may well have been some reduction in the amount of trade which was passing through Leuke Kome, but this should be attributed to the greater convenience of the journey through the Egyptian Red Sea ports, not to any direct government interference.

After the Roman takeover, the distribution of revenues gleaned from the trade by the state would have been more widely dispersed, leading to a reduced impact on the province itself. Nonetheless the customs duties and taxes imposed by the state meant that the trade represented a significant source of income for the Roman treasury, and the Romans took steps, just as they did in Egypt, to ensure that this source of wealth was kept safe from banditry and other disturbances. Such protection, however, appears to have been as far as the Romans were prepared to go in their involvement in the trade. There is no evidence that the annexation itself, or any of the other Roman military activities in the area, were ever occasioned by the incense trade. The Romans' relationship with the incense trade was strictly reactive: they acted only to secure and protect a source of direct income to the state, never to enrich the merchants themselves or to influence directly the course of the trade.

By the third and fourth centuries the significance of the trade was eroded still further by the dire economic position of the empire, but nonetheless it continued at least to some extent. However, the reduced significance of the trade and the larger area of the province devoted to farming activities in the fourth century and later can only have meant that the overall significance of the trade was considerably reduced by that time.

In conclusion, then, the Arabian incense trade can be seen to have had a steadily decreasing significance throughout the period under discussion. Even at the height of its importance under Roman rule, however, there is no evidence that its existence ever concerned the Romans enough to modify their foreign policy or any other aspect of their administration. Although there is no direct evidence pertaining to Arabia, parallels from other areas would indicate that when other policy imperatives (such as aggression against a foreign enemy) came into play, the caravan trade held a very low priority indeed.[247] There is no convincing case to be made that Arabia was any different.

4

THE TRADE OF PALMYRA

One of the most famous of the sites associated with the caravan trade is the city of Palmyra. Indeed, there can be very little doubt of the significance of the caravan trade at Palmyra, as well as the fact that Palmyra on at least one occasion in the third century rose, albeit briefly, to the forefront of affairs in the Roman world. There is considerable question, however, as to what extent the trade may have influenced the growth of Palmyra, the evident prosperity of the city, and the political developments which occurred there.

The rise of Palmyra

The beginning of Palmyra's ascendancy in the long-distance eastern commerce is difficult to reconstruct from the available evidence. Neither Strabo nor Isidore of Charax even mentioned Palmyra in their descriptions of the region,[1] although Pliny and Appian do mention its existence.[2] Neither, however, gives the impression that the city had any of its later importance, even though Appian does mention that the city was a centre of long-distance trade between the Parthian and Roman realms. In these early years it appears that the inhabitants of the oasis were still semi-nomadic, as Appian states that they were able to remove all their material wealth across the Euphrates when Antony attacked them in 42 BC.

The origins of Palmyrene trade

The oasis of Tadmor, which came later to be called Palmyra by the Greeks, already had a long history of habitation, but the urban development that characterised the city in the Roman period does not appear to have commenced until the first century AD. There are traces of the beginning of urbanisation and the establishment of the 'national' cult of Bel from the late first century BC to the early first century AD, revealing that the city began to coalesce from the surrounding tribes around the oasis at about this time.[3] The city was incorporated into the Roman Empire at a relatively early date. The Palmyrene tax law of AD 137 mentions the involvement of Germanicus in the affairs of the city in AD 18–19,[4] and a boundary-marker states that the boundaries of the territory of Palmyra were fixed by the governor of Syria, Creticus Silanus, between AD 11 and 17.[5] It has even been suggested that the Temple of Bel, dedicated in AD 32, was erected to celebrate the inclusion of the city into the empire.[6] Whatever the exact date and circumstances of the inclusion, it was relatively early and the city should accordingly be understood as a tributary city of the province of Syria for the majority of its existence under Roman control.

The oasis itself, and the important area of farming territory to the north-west of the city,[7] would have provided a significant area for development once the surrounding tribes began to co-operate in the establishment of the city. The new urban centre was thus provided with a perennial source of water as well as a wide area which could be exploited for the purposes of raising livestock, qualities that would prove to be of immense importance in the eastern commerce of the city. In his account of Palmyra, Pliny described the town as blessed by good lands and springs of water, despite its desert location:

> Palmyra urbs nobilis situ, diuitiis soli et aquis amoenis, uasto undique ambitu harenis includit agros.
>
> Palmyra is a city famous for its location, for the richness of its soil and for its pleasant springs, and its fields are surrounded by a vast sea of sand.[8]

Thus, the landowning aristocracy of the oasis and its surrounding territory were well placed to exploit the opportunities that the commerce presented when they arose.[9] Exactly how those opportunities came about, however, is a topic which deserves some consideration. Was Palmyra merely fortunate in its location, which allowed it to profit from trade that would have passed through the oasis or nearby anyway, or did the Palmyrenes themselves take action to ensure that the trade *did* come through Palmyra?

It has been thought that Palmyra's commercial success was completely fortuitous, based entirely upon the location of the oasis upon the trade route from Mesopotamia into the Roman Empire which was then exploited by the inhabitants of the city.[10] However, the track across the desert from the Euphrates via the oasis of Palmyra is assuredly *not* a 'natural' one for caravans passing from Mesopotamia to the Roman East. This route is not mentioned by either Strabo or Isidore, both of whom describe routes which we might consider as far more logical, following the Euphrates river where possible. Such a route would provide the traveller with both a ready-made means of communication and water supply, as well as frequent settlements which would ensure a good supply of food and shelter. None of these things are found in the desert around Palmyra. For Palmyra to become a commercial success required the Palmyrenes to *create* a trade route which passed through their city. Routes across the desert such as the one through Palmyra cannot be maintained except where the caravans can be protected from the depredations of desert tribesmen, as well as provided with points for water and shelter.[11] In the absence of such provisions, the only practical route is the one that crosses the Euphrates at Zeugma and passes through Mesopotamia to the head of the Gulf.[12]

Indeed, this route seems to be the one that most non-Palmyrene merchants continued to take in the Roman period. In the corpus of commemorative caravan inscriptions from Palmyra which make up our chief primary source for the trade, we find no reference to non-Palmyrene merchants using the route through Palmyra or participating in Palmyrene caravans. On one occasion Greek merchants are referred to, but these are described only as being resident in Seleucia, not necessarily involved in commerce passing through Palmyra.[13] The picture that we thus have of the development of Palmyrene commerce is not that of the city benefiting due to its fortuitous location on the trade route. Rather, we see the merchants of this oasis city, in concert with the landowning aristocracy of the town, deliberately utilising the city's qualities and contacts with the surrounding tribes to *develop* a trade route which enabled them to prosper. We should not think in terms of the city coming into existence due to the trade route, but of the trade route coming into existence due to the enterprise of the inhabitants of the city. Of course, once the trade was exploited the city was able to grow wealthy in ways it could not otherwise have done, but this should not obscure the fact that the commercial vocation of Palmyra was the result of an initiative of its citizens, not the chance location of its oasis. The lengths to which the Palmyrenes would go, both diplomatically and militarily, to preserve and enhance this commerce will become apparent as we continue to study the trade which came through the city.

Another mistaken impression is that the opportunity which enabled Palmyra to expand its trade was the decline of the Nabataean kingdom and its annexation by Rome in AD 106.[14] While it is certainly true that Palmyrene trade does appear from the caravan inscriptions to have increased in intensity soon after the Roman annexation of the Nabataean kingdom, it does not necessarily follow that the trade which came to Palmyra had formerly passed through Petra. First, as discussed earlier, such evidence as there is suggests that the trade through Arabia continued well into the Roman period.[15] We must also bear in mind the actual lines of trade and the articles being traded, for the literary sources always state that the trade of the Nabataean kingdom was in incenses such as frankincense and myrrh from southern Arabia. The trade of Palmyra, by contrast, was not in these commodities. Appian informs us that Palmyrene trade was conducted in 'Indian and Arabian goods from Persia',[16] so it is clear that the trade of the Nabataean kingdom and that of Palmyra were not related. Thus, events or influences on one line of trade would not necessarily influence the other, and the Roman annexation of the Nabataean kingdom can have had little or no effect on the developing trade passing through Palmyra.

Palmyrene commerce in the Gulf

The bilingual caravan inscriptions found at Palmyra, commemorating individuals who assisted the caravans in some way, confirm Appian's statement that Palmyrene trade was conducted chiefly with Persia. These inscriptions are in both Greek and, uniquely in a subject city of the Roman East, the Palmyrene dialect of Aramaic.[17] Although they do not mention the actual items in the trade, they frequently mention the individual who commanded the caravan, the *synodiarch*. They also frequently feature the destination of the caravan and other details as well as the name of the honorand, usually a Palmyrene official who has helped the caravan in some way.[18] These provide the chief primary source for the student of Palmyrene trade, and by an examination of them we can build up a reasonably coherent picture of this trade, the routes by which it was conveyed and, at least to some extent, the significance which the trade had to the city as a whole (see Figures 4.1 and 4.2).

Many inscriptions describe expeditions which departed Palmyra and travelled to one of the cities of Mesopotamia and then returned. Others mention colonies of Palmyrene merchants in various places, while still others describe sea voyages from the Gulf to 'Scythia', which is northern India. Throughout all of them, a clear pattern of Palmyrene trade emerges: the caravans were trading with cities in southern Mesopotamia which appear to have obtained their goods by sea from India (see Map 4.1).

Figure 4.1 The Grand Colonnade, Palmyra, Syria. Note the brackets here and in the Agora (4.2) which held statues of caravan leaders and other honoured citizens

Figure 4.2 The Agora, Palmyra, Syria

The earliest caravan inscriptions describe groups of Palmyrene merchants who appear to be resident in the cities of Seleucia and Babylon.[19] These, however, are the only occasions on which these cities are mentioned, and as they are very early (AD 19 and 24 respectively) it is probable that they represent an early stage in the development of Palmyrene commerce. Soon, however, the pattern emerges which the trade continues to follow for the remainder of its existence: the caravans travel chiefly to Spasinou Charax, the capital of the kingdom of Mesene on the Gulf. After AD 140 they also travelled to the city of Vologesias, further up the Euphrates but still on the route between Palmyra and the Gulf.[20] Of the inscriptions mentioning caravans or merchants involved in the caravan trade listed by Gawlikowski,[21] one each of them mention as their destination Seleucia or Babylon, one mentions Phorath (a site on the Gulf near Charax), eight mention Vologesias and sixteen mention Charax.

Charax thus appears to be the main port with which this trade was conducted. A typical example from AD 81 reads as follows in the Greek text:

> [Ζ]αβδιβωλον 'Ο[γ]ηλου το[ῦ 'Αμ]–
> μαθου τοῦ 'Ααχει Παλμυρην[ον]
> οἱ ἀπὸ Σπασίνου Χάρακος ἀν[αβ]–
> άντες Παλμυρηνοὶ ἔμπορο[ι]
> τειμῆς χάριν.
>
> To Zabdibol son of Ogeilu son of Ammat son of A'aqi the Palmyrene, the Palmyrene merchants who have ascended from Spasinou Charax (dedicated this) in his honour.[22]

Judging by the appearance of these inscriptions at this time, it would seem likely that Palmyrene trade with the Gulf was established at some time during the course of the first century AD. The frequency of the mention in the inscriptions of the port of Spasinou Charax, capital of the Parthian vassal state of Mesene, shows that this emporium played a central role in the trade of Palmyra. Charax

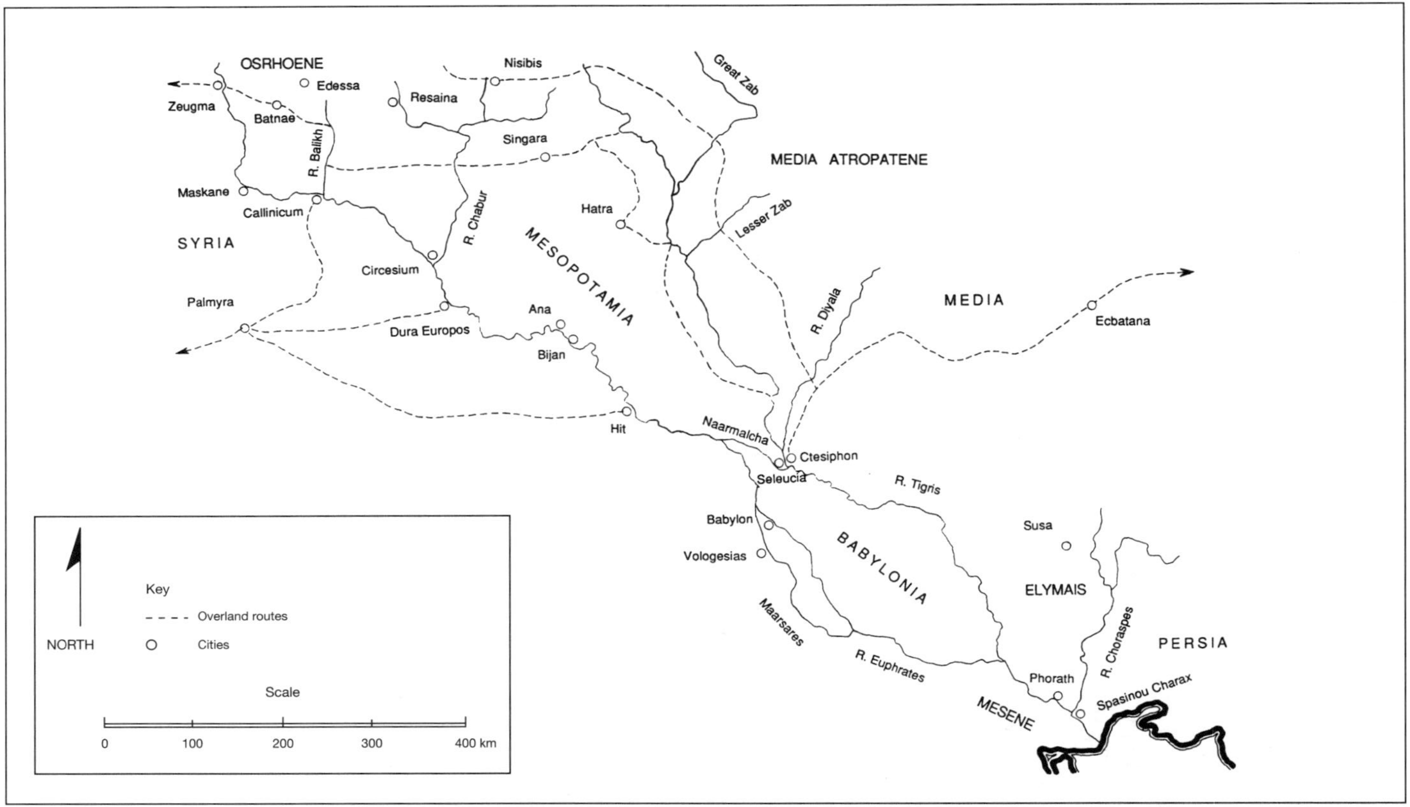

Map 4.1 Trade routes of Syria and Mesopotamia – trade routes of Roman Syria and Mesopotamia in the second and third centuries AD. Please note that only overland routes are shown: routes using or following rivers are not marked

obtained most of the goods which subsequently found their way to Palmyra by the sea route from India, and it appears that Palmyrene shipowners were also involved in this area of the trade. The participation of Palmyrenes in this part of the commerce is demonstrated by another honorific inscription from Palmyra, which reads:

> Μᾶρκον Οὔλπ[ιο]ν Ἰαραιον Αἱρα[νου]
> τοῦ Ἀβγαρου υ[ἱὸν] τὸν φιλόπατριν·
> [ἔ]μποροι οἱ ἀν[αχ]θέντες ἀπὸ Σκυθ[ίας]
> [ἐν] πλύῳ Ὁνα[ιν]ου Ἁδδουδανου τοῦ
> [. . .], πάσῃ προ]θυμίᾳ βοηθήσαντα
> αὐτοῖς καὶ συνλαζόμενον, τειμῆς
> χάριν, Δύστῳ τοῦ ηξύ ἔτους.

> To Marcus Ulpius Iarhai son of Hairan, son of Abgar, the patriot, the merchants who have returned from Scythia on the ship of Honainu son of Haddudan son of . . . , having helped and assisted them with great willingness, (dedicated this) in his honour, in the month Dystos in the year 468 (AD 157).[23]

This inscription demonstrates that Palmyrenes participated in the furthest stages of the trade with India, as well as in the caravan trade to the Gulf. The images of ships in Palmyrene funerary sculpture also attest to the fact that many Palmyrene merchants were shipowners who were involved in the trade between India and Spasinou Charax.[24]

The existence of this sea trade enables us to gain some insight into the kinds of goods that the Palmyrenes obtained from northern India. The ports at which the ships from Charax docked in 'Scythia' were almost certainly the same ports at which ships from Egypt docked, Barygaza and Barbarikon.[25] If this is so then the detailed accounts of the goods and transactions contained in the *Periplus Maris Erythraei* in its account of the trade between India and Egypt should apply also to the trade between India and the Gulf.[26] Certainly we know that silk was a part of the Palmyrene commerce, as Chinese silks have been recovered in the archaeological investigations of the tomb-towers of Palmyra.[27] We thus have evidence for the use of silk at Palmyra, and it is therefore highly probable that silk was an important part of the transit traffic passing through the oasis also.

Despite the fact that the routes from Egypt and Charax reached the same terminus, it would seem that there was no relationship between the two lines of trade, and they continued to be operated separately. There is no evidence of a classical circumnavigation of Arabia, and the author of the *Periplus* seems quite uninformed about the Gulf itself, in contrast to his extensive first-hand knowledge about the remainder of the Arabian peninsula.[28] Salles' suggestion, however, that this was because the Gulf was closed to Roman shipping and restricted to 'Arab' (i.e. Palmyrene and Characene) control,[29] is without support. Salles notes that the knowledge of the Gulf in Roman sources such as the *Periplus* is dramatically less than that which was known to the Hellenistic sources.[30] That this is certainly true no one can deny, but it still does not justify Salles' conclusion. It is more likely that the greater knowledge of the Hellenistic geographers stems more from the easier *land* access available to them: before the rise of the Parthian state the Seleucids dominated this area and land access would have been relatively easy. In the Roman period, however, access, though not necessarily cut off, would still have been more difficult, and in any case the merchants of Alexandria who financed the ships from Egypt would simply have had no reason to send their ships to the head of the Gulf. This, not the enforcement of any ban on Roman shipping in the Gulf, is what caused the relative ignorance of Roman writers with regard to this area. In view of this, Casson's statement, that the writer of the *Periplus* ignores the region of the Gulf because it was of no interest to Roman shippers,[31] appears to be sound.

Salles' theory is also difficult to reconcile with the status of Palmyra and Mesene at the time. Palmyra was a subject city of the Roman Empire, and it is not likely that Rome would have taken kindly to such a city participating in a blockade of Roman interests. It is equally unlikely that the Parthians and Characenes would have considered the Palmyrenes, inhabitants of a city in the Roman Empire, as anything other than Romans themselves. Thus, the idea of a ban on Roman ships in the Gulf would appear to be unsupportable. 'Roman' ships *were* in the Gulf, for that is what the Palmyrene ships would have been considered; other Roman ships traded out of Egypt and would have had no reason to enter the Gulf.

The kingdom of Mesene

The political situation of Mesene, and the extent of Palmyrene and Roman influence within that kingdom, is a subject of vital importance in understanding the rise of the trade between Palmyra and the East. Palmyra has sometimes been understood as an 'intermediary' between the Parthian and the Roman realms, and it has been assumed that Palmyra strove to steer some sort of 'middle course' between the two powers. This view is derived from a statement of Pliny, who declared:

> priuata sorte inter duo imperia summa Romanorum Parthorumque, et prima in discordia semper utrimque cura.
>
> It has its own fate between two great empires, of the Romans and of the Parthians, and at the first discord is always the concern of both sides.[32]

This, however, was certainly not the case in Pliny's time and it may be that he is quoting an earlier source.[33] As we have seen, Palmyra had already been incorporated into the Roman Empire by Pliny's day, and (as will be discussed below) in later years Palmyrenes often held high Roman status, both equestrian and senatorial. These facts alone make it perfectly clear that Palmyra was by no means a neutral state between the two empires but rather an integral part of the Roman realm.

Indeed, it is interesting to note that there seems to be no evidence of any Palmyrene interests with the Parthian court itself. Rather, we find instead evidence of Palmyrenes active in the government and maintaining interests within the kingdom of Mesene, while seemingly all but ignoring the court of the Great King. Palmyrene interests in Mesene are evident from a very early stage. An inscription from the Temple of Bel at Palmyra, dated to about AD 18/19, states that a Palmyrene named Alexandros assumed embassies on behalf of Germanicus to the kings of Mesene and Elymais.[34] The appointment of this Palmyrene to such embassies would make no sense were it not already the case that Palmyra had extensive interests in these kingdoms. It is clear that from the very beginning of Palmyrene commerce in the area in the first century AD, relations were maintained with the kingdom of Mesene and other states in the area. It is also no doubt more than a coincidence that these interests were within an area of commercial contact: unquestionably these interests in Mesene arose from, or were designed to encourage, the commerce with the Gulf cities.

However, in the Antonine period the interests of Palmyra in the kingdom of Mesene, as well as the frequency of inscriptions describing caravans in the area, appear to have taken a quantum leap. There are, for example, a total of six caravan inscriptions from the period AD 19–131, whereas there are at least nineteen from the period AD 131–161. In addition, during this period there are inscriptions which attest to Palmyrenes holding positions of high authority under the kings of Mesene. Some of them are described variously as the satrap of Tylos (Bahrain), the archon of Phorath, and the archon of Maisan (i.e. Mesene).[35] Still more intriguing is the example of So'adu son of Bolyada, who appears to have been resident at Vologesias, held some power described as *dynasteia* either there or at Palmyra (or possibly both), and was able to erect a temple of the Augusti in the city![36]

The exact role or position held by So'adu and others like him, for example Marcus Ulpius Iarhai, who seems to have filled a similar role at Charax, is quite unclear. We do not in fact know *who* placed them in these positions, nor indeed what the real nature of their position was. It may for instance be that they were placed there by the Palmyrene government. Certainly they were honoured by the government, as in the inscription honouring So'adu cited above, but this is not proof that it was the government that placed them in their positions in the first place. Teixidor, on the other hand, considers that these individuals were the heads of tribal associations, not city appointments, based on the greater instance of tribal gods in their dedications as opposed to the city's chief divinity, Bel.[37] While this may be the case, the evidence is still tenuous and cannot be regarded as conclusive. There is certainly little or no reason to describe men such as So'adu as a kind of 'resident consul' of Palmyra, whose chief role was to support and protect their own countrymen. They may very well have, and obviously did, take upon themselves such tasks, but this is a long way from saying that they were specifically placed there by the Palmyrene authorities in order to undertake such a role. A far more likely explanation for the role of such people is that they were simply the head of the community of Palmyrene merchants in the city, presumably appointed to that position by the merchants themselves. Another possibility is that they held some local authority given to them by the kings of Mesene. As we have seen, such positions were reasonably common. It is at least possible that individuals such as So'adu or Iarhai were in fact Palmyrenes who held some local post of authority in Vologesias or Spasinou Charax, and were thus in a position to help their fellow-countrymen when they were in need. Whatever the case, it is certain that these people were able to wield an extraordinary amount of influence in the cities of Mesene.

It is clear that a political situation existed in Mesene which enabled Palmyrenes to hold high office in the kingdom, and even to honour the emperor of Rome there; both highly unusual in what has been thought to have been a vassal kingdom of the Parthian Empire.[38] Furthermore, either this political situation or the Palmyrene influence which it made possible appears to have been very conducive to Palmyrene commerce, as the increased number of caravan inscriptions from this time attests.

A recently published inscription from Seleucia appears to shed some light on this question, allowing us to explain this seemingly extensive influence of a Roman city within a kingdom which has been regarded as a Parthian vassal. This inscription was engraved upon a bronze statue of Herakles in Seleucia, and reveals that the statue was taken from Mesene by the Parthian King Vologeses III when he invaded Mesene:

> Ἔτους τοῦ
> καθ' Ἕλληνας
> ΒΞΥ βασιλεὺς
> βασιλέων 'Αρ–
> σάκης 'Ολογάσος,
> υἱὸς Μιραδάτου βα–
> σιλέως, ἐπεστρα–
> τεύσατο Μεσσήνῃ
> κατὰ Μιραδάτου βασι–
> λέως υἱοῦ Πακόρου τοῦ
> προβασιλεύσαντος, καὶ
> τὸν Μιραδάτην βασιλέ–
> α ἐγδιώξας τῆς Μεσσήνης
> ἐγένετο ἐνκρατὴς ὅλης
> τῆς Μεσσήνης, καὶ εἰκόνα
> ταύτην χαλκῆν 'Ηρακλέ–

ους θεοῦ, τὴν μετενεχθει-
σαν ὑπ' αὐτοῦ ἀπο τῆς Μεσσή-
νης, ἀνέθηκεν ἐν ἱερῷ τοῦ-
δε θεοῦ 'Απόλλονος τοῦ
χαλκῆς πύλης προκατα-
θεμένου.

> In the year 462 by the Greek reckoning (AD 150/151) the King of Kings Arsaces Vologeses, son of Meredates (i.e. Mithradates) the king, campaigned in Mesene against Meredates the king, the son of Pacorus who was king before, and having pursued Meredates the king from Mesene he became the ruler of all Mesene, and when this bronze statue of Herakles the god had been brought by him from Mesene, he set it up in the temple of the god Apollo with the bronze gates in front.[39]

This inscription, together with the apparently anomalous Palmyrene influence which seems to have existed in Mesene in the second century, allows us to reinterpret the history of the region at this time, and explain the sudden rise in significance of the Palmyrene caravan traffic in the same period.

Bowersock and Bernard have both suggested that the Herakles inscription, together with the evidence for Palmyrene involvement in the kingdom, implies that Mesene was in fact a Roman client kingdom for some time in the second century AD.[40] This would explain the influence that Palmyrenes were able to wield within Mesene, particularly the ability of So'adu to erect a temple of the Augusti at Vologesias, which is otherwise difficult to explain, and it would explain why Vologeses of Parthia attacked Mesene and removed its king from his throne in AD 150/151. Vologeses' attack in this year is perhaps best understood as the beginning of an aggressive stance against Rome by a newly crowned king. Unwilling to attack Rome directly, he desired instead to remove a source of Roman influence in, as it were, his 'own back yard', and so attacked Mesene.[41]

The influence of Palmyrenes is far more readily explained by the hypothesis of Mesene being a Roman client kingdom. Under the rule of a king friendly to Rome, it is hardly surprising that notable and influential people from Palmyra who already held commercial interests in the area might be elevated to high rank in the local government of parts of the kingdom, particularly those parts closely associated with the caravan trade such as Vologesias. Such influence would then also afford many opportunities to help and expand the caravan traffic. The son of A'abi, for example, who was a Palmyrene but was archon of Maisan (Mesene), was honoured for having 'favoured his native city and its merchants'.[42]

The most likely time for this Roman influence to have commenced was during Trajan's Parthian campaign. Dio Cassius records that Trajan was received hospitably at Spasinou Charax by Athambelus, the dynast of Mesene, and that he 'remained loyal' to Trajan even when compelled to pay tribute.[43] Even though Hadrian formally renounced Trajan's conquests, it is possible that he retained some influence in Mesopotamia, and the continuing clientship of the king of Mesene could quite conceivably be just such an area of influence.[44]

Although such Roman influence is far more likely to have been to ensure that the Parthian king was surrounded by Roman clients rather than to secure trade concessions,[45] the effect of Roman influence in Mesene was a rapid flourishing of Palmyrene commerce with the area. As we have seen, Palmyrenes, who probably already had trade interests in this region, were able to establish themselves in high political office in Mesene and so place themselves in a better position to offer help and encouragement to caravans. These circumstances no doubt greatly encouraged the Palmyrene traders, and so the frequency of the caravans intensified in the second century AD. It seems that it was not AD 106, the Roman annexation of Petra, which was the crucial date in the expansion of Palmyrene commerce, but rather AD 114–117, the years of Trajan's campaigning in the East. Though the political gains to Rome from these campaigns were little, they were perhaps not as slight as has been thought. Certainly, they provided the Palmyrene merchants with a valuable commercial opportunity which they did not let slip.

Nonetheless, the capture of Mesene by the Parthian king in AD 150/151 does not appear to have halted the trade. The series of eight caravan inscriptions honouring Marcus Ulpius Iarhai all date from the period AD 156–159, so it is clear that the caravan trade continued throughout this period. However, it should be remembered that caravan inscriptions were usually made in honour of someone who had helped the caravan in some difficulty that it might have encountered. Accordingly, the inscriptions honouring Iarhai may not necessarily be an indication of greater *frequency* of caravans but of greater *difficulty* encountered by them at this time. Iarhai appears to have successfully met the challenges created by the change of regime at Charax and enabled the Palmyrene commerce to continue.[46] It may be that in the confused conditions following the Parthian takeover, Iarhai was able to exercise whatever influence he had in Mesene to ensure that Palmyrene caravans were once more allowed to enter the kingdom. By the dates of the inscriptions, however, this may not have been possible until AD 156. We should, however, take note that it seems to have been a Palmyrene who strove to get the commerce going again: neither Roman nor Parthian government seem to have taken any action to restart the commerce.

This is further borne out by the fact that, when war broke out between Rome and Parthia under Lucius Verus in AD 162, the series of caravan inscriptions cease and only recommence after the death of Vologeses in 192. Indeed, the corpus of dated caravan inscriptions has gaps in all the years where Rome and Parthia were at war. This may well indicate that the commerce ceased whenever war between the two powers broke out.[47] If this is the case, it would indicate that the caravan traffic was not a great priority in setting either Roman or Parthian foreign policy.

All the evidence in our possession indicates that the merchants of Palmyra were not wide-ranging in search of their merchandise. On the contrary they seem to have confined their attentions almost exclusively to the one trade route which ran from Palmyra, across the desert in the manner described below, down the Euphrates to Charax, and thence to India by sea. The continuation of Palmyra's prosperity thus hinged upon their diplomacy, which was able to keep the Indian and Gulf end of their trade route open, and on their control of the desert, which was able to keep the trade flowing through the oasis of Palmyra itself and on to the markets of the Roman Empire.

The overland traffic to the Mediterranean

At the opposite end of this trade route which ran from Palmyra to India, we have the problem of exactly how the caravans came and went between Mesopotamia, Palmyra and the Mediterranean. Gawlikowski has suggested that the Palmyrene traders made use of the Euphrates river whenever possible, traversing the desert only as far as was necessary, then taking to boats once the river was reached.[48] This is supported by the fact that there were garrisons of Palmyrene archers at various points along the river, notably at 'Ana and Bijan, both islands in the Euphrates.[49]

There are several possibilities for the point at which caravans leaving Palmyra for Charax could have reached the river and commenced the riverine part of their journey. These no doubt varied according to whether the caravan was heading downstream on its way to Charax or upstream on its return, and also according to the degree of navigability of the river at different times of the year. One of the best attested routes is that between Palmyra and Hit on the Euphrates, which was furnished with a formed road and several caravanserais for protection and shelter.[50] The Palmyrene posts further upstream, however, demonstrate that Hit was not the only point at which Palmyrene traffic reached the Euphrates. Possibly Hit was the point at which riverine traffic disembarked on the upstream leg of the journey, whereas caravans heading downstream would proceed from Palmyra to a closer point on the river before taking ship. The pack animals could then be grazed and slowly moved to Hit (or to whatever point ships travelling upstream could reach) while they awaited the return of the caravan.[51] Whatever the exact location of the embarkation and disembarkation points, the far cheaper costs of waterborne transport in the ancient world would make it much more probable that Palmyrene traffic used the route via the Euphrates wherever possible.

Thus it can be seen that Palmyrene commerce generally followed one route (at least as far as we can tell by the available evidence). Caravans would depart Palmyra, traverse the desert to the nearest point at which the Euphrates was navigable at that time, and then take ship for the journey down the river. The river could be followed all the way to Vologesias or to Charax, where goods which had been transported there from India could be purchased. After these transactions were complete, the caravan would once again take ship and return up the Euphrates to the furthest point upstream at which it was navigable, where the pack animals would be waiting for the return journey to Palmyra. As to what happened to the goods once they reached Palmyra, we have little or no evidence, but one might presume that they were conveyed to the Mediterranean ports for shipment to Rome, or else consumed in the cities of Roman Syria. One inscription may indicate that the goods were transported to Antioch, where the *tetarte* was levied. This inscription mentions an individual who was councillor at Antioch as well as a collector of the *tetarte*,[52] which seems to indicate that Antioch was a place for the collection of this customs duty. Of course, other ports on the Mediterranean seaboard may have been used for this purpose also.

It is evident that Palmyra was deeply involved in the caravan commerce with the East, particularly in the second century AD. As we have seen, however, this commerce did not enrich the oasis city merely because Palmyra happened to be situated upon an international trade route. Instead, the flourishing of the commerce through Palmyra and the wealth which it brought to the city can be attributed directly to the enterprise and initiative of the Palmyrenes themselves. The trade routes, the caravanserais, the caravan guards and many other factors were each either the initiatives of the Palmyrene government or of Palmyrene individuals, and the evidence for either Roman or Parthian action to develop or encourage this trade route is non-existent.

The organisation of the caravan trade

A question which has caused some considerable interest has been the internal organisation of the caravans which travelled from Palmyra to the Gulf, and the types of Palmyrene citizens who could be found involved in the caravan trade. This is an important issue because (as will be examined further on in this chapter) the participation of various elements of Palmyrene society in the caravan trade can give us some insight into that society and into some important differences between the Palmyrene societal structure and that of other ancient cities.

Views of Palmyrene society and the caravan trade

The Palmyrene inscriptions relevant to the caravan trade have been frequently studied, and have most recently been listed and summarised by Gawlikowski.[53] A particularly noteworthy aspect of this list is the recurring official and/or semi-official positions which are mentioned within the inscriptions. We can distinguish several different roles, notably that of the *synodiarch* and the *archemporos*, as well as numerous other individuals who usually appear as the honorand of the inscription, and who have been usually grouped under the general appellation of the 'patron' or 'protector' of the caravan. Such individuals as M. Ulpius Iarhai and So'adu son of Bolyada who are described as 'helping' the caravans or assisting in some more specific way are important examples of the latter group. From these inscriptions, then, it ought to be possible to build up some sort of picture of the organisation of the caravan trade, and then use this information to come to some understanding of Palmyrene society.

This methodology has, indeed, been used on previous occasions. Rostovtzeff was perhaps the first to do so, and he came to the conclusion that these patrons as well as the *synodiarchs* and the others mentioned in the inscriptions were evidence for a class of 'merchant-princes', whom he described as the true rulers of Palmyra.[54] In what has been probably the most important and influential contribution to this study, however, Ernest Will substantially revised this understanding,[55] and it has been his viewpoint which has generally held the field since.[56]

In his study, Will established a difference between the caravan leader, the *synodiarch* or in some later inscriptions the *archemporos*, and the patron or protector of the caravan, who was usually the honorand of the commemorative inscription. This fact is demonstrated by several inscriptions which make a clear distinction between the caravan leader and the patron who has fulfilled some other role (often unspecified) which has helped the caravan. The *synodiarch* was seen by Will as a professional, a specialist who was hired by a group of merchants to organise the caravan and convey its goods to its destination and back.[57] The patron, by contrast, Will sees as usually filling the role of financial backer, someone who provided both money and beasts of burden, as well as in some cases armed retainers, to enable the caravan to reach its destination safely.[58] In this view, the caravan leader is sometimes seen as a sort of subordinate of the patron: indeed, in some cases the leader is the son of the patron. Will, however, sees this as a somewhat unusual arrangement, and draws a distinction between these caravan leaders and an 'ordinary' caravan leader.[59]

In describing the financial and support role of the caravan's patron, Will emphasised that these people could not have been merchants themselves, but must have possessed considerable estates and wealth from which they could provide both the necessary financial backing and particularly the beasts of burden which would have been required for such an expedition.[60] The evidence for such estates has been excavated in the area to the north-west of Palmyra, where there are considerable remains of substantial estates which would have been able to provide the necessary animals and other support which caravan expeditions would require.[61] Thus, Will described a system whereby the rich herding magnates of the city involved themselves in the trade by providing the financial backing and logistical support which made the expeditions possible, and the gratitude of the merchants for this involvement is reflected in the caravan inscriptions.

The dependence of the Palmyrene caravans on these herding estates to the north-west of the city is undoubtedly sound. The trade must have been dependent on the involvement of the magnates who owned these estates, as only they would have been in a position to finance these expeditions and to provide them with the logistical support that they needed. Indeed, the fact that those involved in the support of the caravan trade may have derived at least a proportion of their wealth from these estates is possibly shown by an inscription from Palmyra. This inscription appears to mention pastoral holdings which were owned by Marcus Ulpius Abgar, who is elsewhere attested in caravan inscriptions.[62] If this is indeed the case, then it seems that Abgar was involved in both pastoral activities and the caravan trade: he would thus appear to fit Will's model of a wealthy pastoralist who became involved in directing caravans. What relationship, then, exists between these men and the *synodiarchs* and *archemporoi*?

The organisation of the caravan trade

The first thing which needs to be noted is that, upon a close examination of the caravan inscriptions, the class of 'patron' or 'protector' of the caravan does not really appear to exist. What we find instead among those honorands in the inscriptions who are not the actual leaders of the caravans in question are a variety of individuals who appear to have performed a wide range of services for the caravan, some of which are specified and some of which are not. Thus, if these people are being honoured for some *specific* help which they provided for the caravan rather than any generalised regular role, there is in fact no need at all to postulate the regular role of the 'patron' of the caravan.

Indeed, when the corpus of caravan inscriptions is examined it is apparent that many of these people are being honoured for some *specific* act of assistance. There is no evidence that these individuals had any other role or involvement with the caravan in question beside that for which they are being honoured. Perhaps the most obvious examples of this type are those inscriptions where some military assistance is being commemorated. One inscription from the Temple of Baalshamin describes an event of this sort: it would appear that a caravan under Hagegu and Taimarsu came into some difficulty, most probably a nomad attack, and was saved by a military force led by So'adu the son of Bolyada.[63] While the exact nature and purpose of such Palmyrene military forces will be discussed in the next section, for now it is enough to note that So'adu does not appear to have had any other involvement in this caravan other than that of providing military help. As far as the inscription informs us, So'adu's involvement with the caravan under Hagegu and Taimarsu began and ended with his military intervention to save it, and we have no compelling reason to suppose that he had any other interest in it.

Similarly, we find occasions when an official of a foreign power, often a Palmyrene himself, has helped a caravan or a group of merchants and is honoured by them. In one case, a caravan which had come from Charax and Vologesias recognised the help given them by the archon of Phorath, a port in the territory of Charax:

> τοῦ 'Α]λεξάνδ[ρου, ἄρχοντα
> Φορ]αθων τῆς περ[ὶ Σπασινου
> Χα]ρακα· ἡ μετὰ Μαλχο[υ τοῦ
> 'Αζ]ειζου παραγενομένη
> ἀπ[ὸ τ]οῦ Χαρακος εἰς Παλμυρα
> (καὶ) 'Ολογαισίαν συνοδία, τειμῆς
> ἕνεκεν, ἔτ[ο]υς ανυ',
> μηνὸς Γορπιαίου.
>
> To . . . son of Alexandros, archon (?) of Phorath near Spasinou Charax, the caravan with Malku son of Azizu which has come from Charax to Palmyra and Vologesias (dedicated this) in his honour, in the year 451, in the month Gorpiaios (AD 140).[64]

In this instance it would seem that the archon of Phorath has been of some assistance to the caravan. It is not hard to imagine some way in which such an official might have extended his patronage to the caravan to help it along its way, but there is no reason given in the inscription to suppose that this man had any association with or interest in the caravan prior to its arrival at Charax. Indeed, it would be difficult to imagine how a man in Phorath could have been associated with the preparations for a caravan in far-off Palmyra. Again, we cannot find any evidence for the regular role of caravan 'patron' in this inscription. Instead we see the members of a caravan honouring a person who has helped them at some point along their journey, in this case no doubt in assisting them during their stay within his own dominions. Once more, the inscription gives no indication of any particular interest or involvement held by the archon in the caravan except for the help which he gave it while it was at Phorath.

Another type of inscription which appears to confirm this general pattern is that which honours Roman authorities. In one case, dated at AD 135, a caravan which has returned from Charax with its leader honours a Roman centurion, Julius Maximus, although the reason for this honour is not specified.[65] In another inscription from AD 161, a caravan returned from Charax under Nesa son of Bolyada honoured Marcus Aemilius Marcianus Asclepiades, a councillor of Antioch and a collector of the *tetarte*.[66] Again, the specific reason for this honour is not mentioned. In both these cases there is no good reason to suppose that these individuals had any direct involvement, financial or otherwise, in the caravan. Given the parallels above, it would seem far more likely that they assisted the caravan in some way in the course of their duties, most probably involving the collection of customs dues or something similar.

With the examples of these types of inscriptions in mind, it would be pertinent to re-examine those inscriptions more usually cited as examples of the 'caravan patron' to see if they do indeed justify the conclusion that there was such a thing. These inscriptions are those mentioning Marcus Ulpius Iarhai and some which honour the So'adu mentioned earlier in regard to military intervention.[67] In the case of So'adu, the inscriptions seem to imply that he was resident in Vologesias and provided help to the caravans passing through that location. In the inscription concerning him mentioned above, after the report of his 'saving' the caravan comes a general statement that he helped citizens, caravans and merchants in Vologesias. As has been discussed earlier,[68] he appears to have done this while he was resident in some official capacity in Vologesias, either as the head of the Palmyrene community there or in some official capacity under the kings of Mesene.

Whatever help So'adu gave to the caravans was done while he was living in Vologesias, and should be separated from the military assistance which would most probably have been within Palmyrene territory. Thus, the help which So'adu gave to his fellow-countrymen in Vologesias is probably similar to that given to Palmyrene caravans by the archon of Phorath mentioned earlier, and by other Palmyrenes in official positions within the kingdom of Mesene who are also honoured in inscriptions.[69] Again, there is no need to imagine So'adu as having any pecuniary interest in the caravan, let alone being its organiser and prime financier. Rather, we should envisage him as an important and powerful resident of Vologesias who was able to use his power and influence in that city to assist Palmyrene merchants, and who was honoured for this both by the merchants and by the council of Palmyra.

With this in mind, it is easy to see parallels with the inscriptions mentioning M. Ulpius Iarhai, perhaps the most commonly cited of the 'caravan protectors'. In some cases he is mentioned as a caravan leader, but on several other occasions Iarhai is honoured for helping either a caravan or merchants on a ship from India. In one example, dated AD 157, he is honoured for 'helping in every way' a caravan from Charax which was led by his own son, Abgar:

> [Μᾶρκον Οὔλπιον 'Ιαραιον] 'Αιρα[νου τ]οῦ 'Αβγαρο[υ
> [ἡ] ἀναβᾶσα ἀπο Σπασινου Χαρακο[ς]
> συνοδία ἧς ἡγήσατο 'Αβγαρος υἱὸ[ς]
> αὐτοῦ, βοηθήσαντα αὐτῇ παντὶ
> τρόπῳ, τειμῆς χάριν, ἔτους ου'
> μηνὸς 'Αρτεμισίου.

> To Marcus Ulpius Iarhai son of Hairan Abgar, the caravan under his son Abgar which has come from Spasinou Charax (dedicated this) for helping it in every way, in his honour, in the year 470 in the month Artemision (AD 159).[70]

It is clearly very difficult to separate the roles of *synodiarch* and 'patron' when such a close relationship appears between leader and honorand, and when in at least one case Iarhai actually acted in the capacity of leader himself. In other cases where merchants have dedicated a statue to Iarhai, it seems that the services performed by him were carried out at Charax itself; at least one cites help *in* Charax and the others all state that the caravans came back from that place. Therefore it is at least possible that Iarhai was fulfilling the same sort of role at Charax as So'adu had performed in Vologesias a few years earlier: either head of the local Palmyrene community or some official capacity under the kings of Mesene. In either case, he would have been in a position to help the caravans, especially in the unsettled conditions that must have prevailed after the Parthian king recaptured Mesene in AD 150/151. It is certainly the case that he had some interests in some caravans, especially the one of which he was the leader, and most likely the one led by his son. However, this is still not evidence for the existence of a regular, separate role of 'caravan patron', and clearly not for the separation of such a role from that of *synodiarch*.

It would seem that there is no solid evidence for the existence of a 'patron' or 'protector' of the caravan in the way Will proposed. Rather, each of those honoured in the caravan inscriptions at Palmyra helped the caravan in some specific way, but without necessarily being involved in the caravan itself or having any financial interest in it. Certainly there may have been occasions on which the honorand *did* have some interest in the caravan, but this is not evidence that such a role existed on a regular basis.

The synodiarch

Having eliminated the role of 'patron' in this way, we are left with the problem of explaining who it was that organised the caravan, provided the necessary beasts of burden and other logistical requirements, and financed the expedition. Fortunately, however, we do not have to look far, for the example of Marcus Ulpius Iarhai provides a possible answer. Iarhai was a rich and influential man, as the caravan inscriptions in his honour certainly attest. The wealth of this family would seem to be based originally not on the caravan commerce but on agricultural and/or pastoral holdings near Palmyra, as was discussed earlier in this section. Thus, Iarhai seems to fall into that category of men identified by Will as the originators of the caravan commerce, the possessors of estates, beasts and money: in other words, the 'caravan patron'. However (as we have already found), an examination of the corpus dealing with Iarhai reveals one inscription in which Iarhai is the *synodiarch* himself and another in which his son acted in that capacity. Will considered that this arrangement would be unusual, and stand in contrast to the more common arrangement where the caravan leader was an employee of the patron. But are we really justified in making such a conclusion? Could it not be that the one who provided the financial backing, the logistical support *and* led the caravan was none other than the *synodiarch* himself? This would certainly explain Iarhai's appearance as a caravan leader as well as apparent 'patron': for in this reconstruction there is in fact no difference between the two offices. The situation which Will saw as unusual, with a magnate such as Iarhai acting as leader, would thus in this reconstruction be a regular occurrence, and we would not be surprised to see a caravan financed by this family being led by Abgar, the son of the great Iarhai.

This view is given some support by a later inscription which appears to describe a caravan leader giving heavy financial support to a caravan at his own expense:

> ἡ βουλ[ὴ καὶ ὁ δῆμος Ἰ]ούλιον
> Αὐρήλιο[ν Σαλαμά]λλαθον
> Μαλῆ τοῦ [Ἀβδαίου ἀ]ρχέμπορον,
> ἀνακομίσα[ντα τὴν] συνοδίαν
> προῖκα ἐξ ἰδίων, τειμῆς χάριν,
> ἔτους θξφ΄.

> The Council and the People to Julius Aurelius Salamallat, son of Male son of Abdai, chief merchant, who has brought back a caravan at his own expense, (dedicated this) in his honour, in the year 569 (AD 257/258).[71]

Although the fact that this act is honoured would indicate that the merchants themselves would normally have borne these costs, this inscription shows that the *archemporos* (apparently a later term for *synodiarch*)[72] was a man of considerable means. He evidently possessed sufficient wealth to bear an expenditure normally (presumably) split up among all the members of the expedition. This act would seem to be, as Will recognised, one of the acts of euergetism common to the ancient world in which the rich contributed to the public good out of their own pocket.[73] This, however, should give us an insight into the kind of person who acted as a caravan leader. This is no employee or technician: Julius Aurelius Salamallat is clearly a rich, influential man who wishes to increase his political influence and power, and such an act of euergetism is one way he could do this. A similar case is that of 'Ogielu ben Maqqai, an influential military leader honoured with statues by order of the Council yet described as one who had led caravans on many occasions.[74] Again, it would seem that the situation of a rich, aristocratic magnate acting as caravan leader is not an unusual one.

Indeed, given these examples we might consider that this was in fact the regular situation: merchants wishing to go to Charax would approach one of the wealthy magnates of Palmyra, who had the wealth and the materials to support such an expedition. This man would both organise and lead the caravan, and on some occasions he would perform such services that the merchants would honour him with a commemorative inscription. In the course of its journey, however, the caravan might encounter any number of other difficulties, from hostile nomads to unhelpful customs officials, and in these circumstances the caravan might be assisted by a Palmyrene or Roman in the area with sufficient power to help. This could especially be likely within the borders of the kingdom of Mesene, where many Palmyrenes had risen to positions of great power and influence. Such a person was on many occasions honoured with a statue and inscription by the grateful merchants and their leader, but such honorands cannot be grouped together as a general class of 'patron'. Rather we should recognise them as individuals without any necessary interest in the caravan who helped it in various specific ways. To find the true 'patron' of the caravan; its financier, backer and protector, we need look no further than the *synodiarch* himself.

Of course, such patronage would not come without its price, and there is no doubt that the caravan leader expected to make a handsome profit from the venture. He could perhaps participate in the actual purchase of goods, and thus to an extent act as a merchant himself, or he could simply be paid by the participants in the caravan a fixed sum or percentage of the profit for his organisation and help. The opportunities for profit for both the merchants and the caravan leader were no doubt great, and the caravans would have come to be a significant part of the wealth of both Palmyra and of its leading citizens.

Perhaps a more important motivation than wealth, however, was the honour which was associated with leading the caravans. As we have seen, participation in the protection and leadership of the caravans was thought worthy of commemorative inscriptions and statues. Thus, personal prestige in Palmyrene society may have been a significant motivation for the *synodiarch* class. This idea will be explored more completely in the section on Palmyrene society.

Finances

We have already discussed how the caravan received much financial backing from the caravan leader, but there would of course still be considerable expenses for each individual merchant. Although on some occasions (as we have seen) some of the caravan's expenses might be paid for by the leader or by some high official,[75] in an act of public munificence designed to increase his prestige and influence, the very fact that such acts are commemorated would seem to indicate that normally the merchants themselves would have expected to bear these costs. Such costs might include customs tolls, the finance necessary to purchase the goods in Charax, transportation expenses, tolls paid to various local chieftains to ensure safe passage, and many others.

While there are no surviving inscriptions or papyri to indicate these costs as there are, for example, in Egypt, we might reasonably expect that the financial organisation of the trade in Palmyra was not dissimilar to that for the Egyptian Red Sea trade. Indeed, there is a possibility that this might be indicated by an inscription from a funerary tower in Palmyra which describes a financial arrangement in the terms of a maritime loan, and thus may indicate that this type of loan was made to merchants travelling to Charax.[76] It is likely that such loans would have been similar to that recorded in *P. Vindob.* G 40822 and studied in Chapter 2, whereby the goods purchased were pledged as a security for the loan.[77] In all probability, this was the arrangement which would have been entered into by merchants with insufficient capital to purchase their goods outright, and would accordingly represent another area in which the wealthy magnates of the town could profit from the caravan trade.

From the available evidence, we have been able to build up some idea of the organisation of the caravan trade which passed through Palmyra. On the whole, it would seem better to reject the existence of a separate class of 'caravan patron', responsible for the financing and organisation of the expedition and its provision with sufficient beasts of burden for the journey. These duties for the most part can be assigned to the *synodiarch*, and the class of 'patron' can instead be thought of as comprising various individuals with no necessary link to the caravan who have helped it in some way and were honoured by the caravan for this reason.

Thus, the caravan trade seems to have been a privately initiated, organised and funded affair, in which groups of merchants would attach themselves to a wealthy Palmyrene aristocrat who could provide them with the means to make the journey. These magnates would act, either personally or by a representative, as the caravan leader for the journey. While they almost certainly gained financial reward for their help, perhaps more importantly they gained in personal prestige and power in Palmyrene society. However, this is not to say that the Palmyrene state, probably administered by these same nobles, did not appreciate the significance of this trade nor assist it in any way. On the contrary, we shall see that the Palmyrenes were prepared to go to quite extraordinary lengths to ensure that the trade upon which so much of their wealth depended could continue unmolested.

The Palmyrene caravan guards

Palmyra, by virtue of its distinctive role and location, was never an ordinary city of the empire. Perhaps no feature of Palmyra, however, is as unusual as the fact that the city appears to have maintained its own army. There are several inscriptions in existence which appear to describe some sort of military organisation operating out of Palmyra[78] that seems to have patrolled a wide area of the desert around the city, often at locations which are associated with the caravan trade.

The inscriptional evidence

Several inscriptions attest to the existence of some sort of Palmyrene military force, showing a variety of military activities that were undertaken by these forces. The first type of apparent military involvement is found in the commemorative inscriptions which have already been studied. In these, the honorand is often mentioned as having 'helped the caravan in every way', which is sometimes taken to mean that they offered the caravan military protection.[79] However, this phrase cannot necessarily always be taken to refer to military assistance. Some (as discussed in the previous section) may be referring to diplomatic and/or commercial assistance which the honorand offered the caravan; in other cases if military assistance *was* involved, this does not necessarily have to have come from an organised militia. As has been seen in Chapter 2 on the Red Sea trade in Egypt, caravans which passed over the desert roads between the Red Sea and the Nile valley employed private guards to protect them.[80] Given the high values of the goods being carried, it would be very surprising if such guards were not also employed by Palmyrene caravans traversing the route between Charax and Palmyra. So, if it is indeed military help that is being referred to in the caravan inscriptions, we might possibly understand such help to have been from private guards, perhaps employed by the *synodiarch*, rather than from an organised militia.

It may therefore be profitable to make a distinction between caravan guards, who were probably employed by the *synodiarch*, and the 'caravan police' or Palmyrene militia which (as we shall see), appears to have been organised and controlled by the city itself. Rostovtzeff did not make this distinction; he envisaged an organised militia which was, by some sort of 'trade agreement', allowed to operate within Parthian territory.[81] If this is the case, such a militia must have been able to operate outside the Roman Empire and within areas of Parthian influence, as the caravan inscriptions often refer to help received on the journey between Charax and Palmyra, the bulk of which was well outside the area of direct Roman rule. Will, however, rightly recognised that any such militia would have been regarded by the Parthians as a Roman military organisation, and would never have been allowed on Parthian territory.[82] However, while Will recognised that any actual escort which the caravans received, especially outside Roman territory, was likely to have been from private guards, he did not distinguish between these and the other military organisations which are attested by the inscriptional evidence. Instead, he regarded all these references as speaking of private guards and/or extraordinary commands authorised by the city.[83] However, as will be seen, some evidence points to a more permanent arrangement which appears to have existed side-by-side with the private guards employed by the *synodiarchs*, much as Roman soldiers and private guards appear to have worked side-by-side in the Eastern Desert of Egypt.

One of the indications that the Palmyrene military was a permanent body is the evidence for the maintenance of garrisons at various strategic points, most of which appear to have been associated with the caravan routes. One such garrison appears to have been maintained on the island of 'Ana, or 'Anatha, in the Euphrates river. The earliest evidence for a Palmyrene military presence there is found in an inscription of AD 132 set up by a Nabataean horseman at Palmyra, who stated that he was 'a horseman at Hirta and in the camp of 'Ana'.[84] Similarly, a dedication from the temple of Baalshamin in Palmyra dated at some time after AD 188 was set up by cavalrymen 'of the detachment of 'Ana and Gamla',[85] while another inscription from Umm es-Selabikh on the desert road from Palmyra to Hit records an individual who was '*strategos* at 'Ana and Gamla' in AD 225.[86] There is also archaeological evidence of the presence of Palmyrene soldiers at the island of Bijan, 27 km downstream from 'Ana, in the second and early third centuries: very possibly these soldiers might have been also under the command of the *strategos* of 'Ana and Gamla.[87] It is thus clear that a military presence was maintained by Palmyra in this area of the Euphrates, well downstream from direct Roman occupation before AD 164, marking this area as a very important one for Palmyra.[88] The significance of the Euphrates in the trade of Palmyra makes it probable that these military postings were dictated by commercial interest, and were intended to protect Palmyrene commerce travelling up and down the river.

Another important place which seems to have held Palmyrene troops is the city of Dura Europos, again on the Euphrates river (see Figures 4.3 and 4.4). Three inscriptions were set up in the Mithraeum of the city by Palmyrene archers; two of them, dating from AD 169 and 170, name *strategoi* of the archers at Dura.[89] It has been claimed that the Palmyrene garrison was already in Dura while the city was still in Parthian hands,[90] and was perhaps allowed to operate there by some sort of trade agreement with the Parthian government. It is certainly true that there were Palmyrenes in the city prior to this time, as there was considerable evidence of a Palmyrene community uncovered in the excavation of the city.[91] These, however, would appear to have been merchants, whom we would not be surprised to find in Dura at this time given the city's

Figure 4.3 The Euphrates river and the city fortifications, Dura Europos, Syria. Photo by Frank Strk

Figure 4.4 The Main Gate, Dura Europos, Syria. Photo by Frank Strk

position on the Euphrates route. The only evidence for a military presence prior to the capture of Dura by the Romans in AD 164, however, consists of an undated Palmyrene inscription which the excavators dated to *c.* AD 150.[92] It is far more likely, as Gawlikowski points out, that these soldiers did not arrive until after the capture of Dura by the Romans in AD 164.[93]

That these units are not Roman seems to be clear from the lack of any Roman unit designations, the total absence of Roman names or titles among the officers or men cited in the inscriptions, and the description of the commanders of these units as *strategoi* rather than any more conventional Roman term. Indeed, these *strategoi* are not the only ones found in the Palmyrene inscriptional corpus: the evidence in fact demonstrates that *strategos* was the title of an office at Palmyra which could have either military or non-military applications. In some cases it is clearly civil. One such inscription, dating from AD 242/243, mentions one Julius Aurelius Zabdilah. While the Greek merely calls him *strategos*, the Palmyrene goes further and calls him a *strategos* of the colony.[94] It would seem clear that this inscription is referring to a civil office, that of one of the *duumuiri* who were the chief magistrates of a Roman colony, which Palmyra had been since the early third century.

In other instances, however, the term *strategos* seems to be used to mean a military post. We have already noted the use of the term to mean the commander of a garrison at some point in the city's territory (or perhaps beyond it, as was certainly the case at Dura Europos).[95] There are also inscriptions from Palmyra which seem to indicate that the term *strategos* was also used as term for special military commands, or perhaps even regular ones. One of these, dated AD 198, refers to Aelius Boras, who held the title '*strategos* of the peace'. The missing fragments of the Greek text are supplied by the fragmentary parallel text in Palmyrene:

> [προστάγματι βουλῆς καὶ δήμου
> Αἴλιον Βώραν Τίτου Αἰλίου Ὀγείλου
> τὸν στρατηγὸν τὸν ἐπὶ τῆς]
> εἰρήνης κατασταθέντα ὑπό τε
> Μανειλίου Φούσκου καὶ Οὐενιδίου
> Ῥούφου ὑπατικῶν καὶ ὑπὸ τῆς πα–
> τρίδος, καὶ πολλὴν σπουδὴν καὶ ἀνδρεί–
> αν ἐνδειξάμενον καὶ στρατηγήσαντα
> πλειστάκις.

> By the decree of the Council and the People, (in honour of) Aelius Boras, son of Titus Aelius Ogeilu, *strategos* of the peace (Palm.: who established peace in the territories of the city), having been appointed by both Manilius Fuscus and Venidius Rufus, governors, and by his own country, and having displayed great enthusiasm and courage, and acting as *strategos* on many occasions.[96]

This office appears to have been a military one, judging by the Palmyrene statement that he established peace in the city's territory, and by the statement that he did so bravely: hardly an adverb that one would normally use for the holding of civic office. It is also noteworthy that he was appointed both by the Roman governor of Coele Syria, and by the city of Palmyra itself. Presumably therefore, the city was obliged to seek the permission of the Roman authorities before it could employ its own troops in any significant operation.[97] This, of course, would hardly be surprising.

What, however, was the exact nature of this office of *strategos* of the peace? The possible nature of such a post is made rather more clear by another inscription of the following year, AD 199:

> προστάγματι βουλῆς καὶ δήμου.
> αἱ τέσσαρες φυλαὶ Ὄγηλον Μακκαίου τοῦ Ὀγήλου Ἁγεγοῦ
> τοῦ Σεουήρα δι' ἀρετὴν πᾶσαν καὶ διὰ τὰς συνεχεῖς τὰς
> κατὰ τῶν νομάδων στρατηγίας συναράμενον καὶ τοῖς ἐνπό–

> ροις καὶ ταῖς συνοδίαις ἀεὶ τὴν ἀσφάλιαν παρασχόντα ἐν πάσαις συνοδιαρχίαις.
>
> By the decree of the Council and the People. The four tribes (honour) Ogeilu son of Maqqai, son of Ogeilu Hagegu, son of Sewira, for all his virtue and courage and for continually raising commands against the nomads, and for always providing safety to the merchants and the caravans in all his caravan commands.[98]

This man appears to have been given some sort of command against the nomads; this time unquestionably a military post and very probably a similar or identical post to that held by Aelius Boras in the previous inscription. Some have stated that these posts were not regular, and were probably created by the city especially to meet a specific circumstance, presumably some serious difficulties with the nomads.[99] However, both men are specifically cited as having held their posts more than once; Ogeilu 'continually' raised his expeditions against the nomads, while Aelius Boras held his commands under two successive governors of Syria. Indeed, it is quite probable that it was just such a command which was being exercised by So'adu son of Bolyada when he 'saved' caravans which were under attack by nomads.[100] Thus, even if such commands as these were not regular, they would seem to have been frequently bestowed, at least in this particular time period.

We should be careful also to note a distinction between these units under direct Palmyrene command and the numerous Palmyrene auxiliary units in the Roman army. The presence of these troops in the Eastern Desert of Egypt has already been noted, as has the likelihood that these troops were chosen for that role because of their experience of the desert.[101] Such units, however, were also used in many other parts of the empire, as well as in the vicinity of Palmyra itself. Palmyrene units and individual soldiers are attested by epigraphic evidence in Syria, Dacia, Numidia and even Britain, as well as Egypt.[102] Usually, these soldiers appear to have been either archers or *dromedarii*, especially in Egypt and Syria where their desert experience would have been useful.

One Palmyrene unit in the Roman army is particularly worthy of note, as it may help explain a link between these units and the Palmyrene caravan guards. The extensive records of the *Cohors* XX *Palmyrenorum* have been excavated at Dura Europos, testifying to the existence of this unit at Dura from AD 208 until 256, when the city was taken by the Persians.[103] It has previously been noted that a unit of Palmyrene archers was present at Dura in the years immediately following the conquest of the city by Lucius Verus in AD 164. It is altogether possible that the *Cohors* XX *Palmyrenorum* is in fact the same unit, except it has been 'regularised', given Roman officers, and incorporated into the Roman army as an auxiliary cohort.[104] Indeed, it may be possible that there was a general trend of 'regularising' the units of the Palmyrene caravan guards into Roman units, although this example is the closest we can come to a specific occurrence of this process.[105] Even so, we should note that after their incorporation into the Roman army (if that is indeed what took place) the priorities of these units were now Roman, not Palmyrene: they were there to defend Dura from Persian attack, not to protect the caravan traffic. As the inscription from Umm es-Selabikh cited earlier tells us, the Palmyrenes were still carrying out that role by means of their own archers well into the third century.

Nonetheless, it is quite likely that there is a relationship between the units of the Palmyrene caravan guards and the Palmyrene auxiliary units in the Roman army. The experience of desert warfare gained by the units of Palmyrene archers may well have made them attractive prospects for recruitment as Roman auxiliaries: as well as individual soldiers, whole units may have been transferred from Palmyrene to Roman military authority. In either case, the presence of the long-distance trade at Palmyra will have had a significant impact on the experience in desert warfare gained by the Palmyrenes, and thus on their recruitment by the Roman authorities.

There is therefore solid evidence for the existence of an independent Palmyrene military, which had permanent garrisons, commanders appointed by the city who were called *strategoi* and who could be placed over garrisons in certain areas or who could be given a more general command against the nomads within the city's territory. Many of these troop postings appear to have been related to the caravan commerce, based on the preponderance of evidence in the Euphrates valley region, an area of prime importance to the Palmyrene caravan commerce but which was not garrisoned by the Roman army.

The nature of the Palmyrene military forces

While the full organisation of the Palmyrene military forces is not recoverable, there are nonetheless some conclusions which can be safely drawn. Archers and *dromedarii* (archers mounted on camels) are the only troop types mentioned in the inscriptions. The archers were probably mounted on horses, as infantry would have been of very limited use in the desert. We know little about the command structure of these troops. As we have seen, their commanders were called *strategoi*, which appears to have also been the title of a city magistracy. This may indicate that the command of these troops was a civic office in Palmyra, held by the same type of people who made up the city's ruling aristocracy.

The location of these troops indicates that their purpose was to protect the caravan traffic from the Gulf from bandit attacks. Their priority does not seem to have been the physical defence of the city of Palmyra from an enemy such as the Persians; this was presumably the responsibility of the Roman auxiliary garrison in Palmyra itself.[106] Similarly, the sole area of Palmyrene military activity seems to be to the east of the city, between Palmyra and the Euphrates valley. Regular Roman troops were stationed to the west of Palmyra, and the caravans could presumably have gained protection from them in this area.[107]

How then did such a military force come to exist in a provincial city of the Roman Empire? The first thing that should be noted is that the presence of a local militia such as the Palmyrene troops may not have been as exceptional as it might seem. There is considerable evidence for the existence of city and provincial militias in the Roman Empire which were distinct from the regular Roman army, and which could be called out by provincial governors (in the case of provincial militias) or by city officials (in the case of city militias). These militias are attested as being used for emergency defence, police duties and even on military construction tasks.[108] It would thus appear probable that the Palmyrene troops were some sort of city militia, under the control of the officials of the city.

Nonetheless, this should not be allowed to obscure the fact that Palmyra had an unusually large and active militia. None of the other examples cited has anything near the same volume of evidence to attest its existence as the Palmyrene militia. The Palmyrene forces by contrast, as we have seen, appear to have been very active over a prolonged period of time and a wide expanse of territory. The reason for this must, of course, have been the peculiar demands of the caravan trade, as it has already been noted that the disposition of the Palmyrene troops as well as the surviving inscriptional evidence strongly suggest that these troops were primarily intended to guard the caravan routes.

A force such as this in the hands of a provincial city must inevitably have excited some unease among the Romans. It is certainly the case that a force such as the Palmyrene one, scattered in an assortment of encampments and caravanserais in order to oppose banditry, cannot have provided a realistic threat to the larger and more concentrated Roman forces. Nonetheless, it is unlikely that the Romans would have tolerated such an arrangement without some supervisory capability for themselves. Indeed, we should note that Palmyra had an auxiliary garrison throughout at least the third century,[109] which would have enabled the governor of Syria to supervise the activities of the Palmyrene militia. In addition (as we have already seen) the inscription concerning Aelius Boras the *strategos* of the peace mentions the fact that he sought permission for his military activities from the Roman governor, an arrangement which was no doubt regular. By these means, then, it would seem that the Romans maintained a close watch on the activities of the Palmyrene militia and ensured that the Palmyrenes did not take any action which did not have the full approval of the Roman government.

Nonetheless, we are still left with the question of why the Romans allowed such a militia in any case. The reason would seem to be the same as the reason for the presence of Roman troops in the Eastern Desert of Egypt: the tax revenue which was paid by the merchants into the imperial coffers. One of the Palmyrene inscriptions refers to a collector of the *tetarte* on incoming goods at Antioch,[110] so it would seem that goods coming into the empire by the route through Palmyra paid this levy just as those coming through Egypt did. For this reason, then, it would seem that the Romans permitted the Palmyrenes to operate a militia and to protect their caravan trade, for every caravan that successfully made the journey paid a significant sum into the imperial treasury. As with the trade in Egypt, there is no need or evidence to posit any more elaborate economic motive than this: the Romans, having in their possession a sizeable source of income, were keen to ensure that they extracted the maximum possible wealth from it. If this meant allowing the Palmyrenes to operate their own militia, then so be it.

The development of the Palmyrene militia in the second and third centuries

Throughout the time in which the Palmyrene military organisation operated, there seem to have been several changes, leading finally to a more substantial organisation which may have formed the backbone of the Palmyrene army in the later third century. In the early years of the Palmyrene commerce, we do not have any evidence for the existence of any military forces at Palmyra, although we of course may presume that the city maintained some forces of its own prior to its incorporation in the Roman Empire. In addition, it would be most likely that the caravans which made the journey to Spasinou Charax in this period were also accompanied by irregular guards, but, as we have seen, such guards should be distinguished from the Palmyrene militia.

It is from the second century AD that the first evidence for the existence of a Palmyrene militia comes, the inscription of the Nabataean cavalryman from the camp of 'Ana. The political status of 'Ana at this time is in some doubt: Dura Europos became Parthian again after a brief Roman occupation during Trajan's war, and it has generally been thought that 'Ana did not fall into Roman hands until the war of Lucius Verus in AD 164.[111] This has resulted in the belief that the Palmyrenes were permitted to place their troops at 'Ana under the same arrangement that is often postulated for Dura: that is, that the Palmyrene troops were permitted in Parthian territory due to their importance for the caravan trade.[112] However, as we have seen, it is most unlikely that there were any Palmyrene troops in Dura until that site was taken over by the Romans in 164, and it is accordingly unlikely that any agreement existed whereby the troops were permitted at 'Ana.

Far more probable is Gawlikowski's suggestion that the Palmyrenes retained control of 'Ana and other posts in its immediate area, such as Gamla and Bijan, after Trajan's Parthian expedition.[113] Thus, while the Parthians certainly reoccupied Dura after the Roman withdrawal from Mesopotamia in AD 117, this theory would suggest that 'Ana and its area remained Roman territory either by agreement or simply by the Parthians' failure to reoccupy it. The use of Palmyrene troops to occupy 'Ana at this time may thus be compared to the situation at Dura, whereby Palmyrene troops appear to have initially occupied the city in 164, only to be complemented by regular Roman troops later.[114] It would thus appear likely that the Palmyrene occupation of the sites in the Euphrates valley such as 'Ana, Gamla and Bijan may date from this period.

The presence of *strategoi* at these sites is not attested in the AD 132 inscription, but it is likely that these officers were simply the commanders of the garrison. During and after the Severan period, however, the use of the term changed. In the inscriptions of AD 198 and 199 which were discussed above, the existence of *strategoi* with apparently more wide-ranging commissions has been noted. These may reflect the more unsettled circumstances occasioned by the wars between the Romans and the Parthians under Lucius Verus, Septimius Severus and Caracalla. As has been noted, the series of caravan inscriptions ceases in AD 161 and resumes only in AD 193, followed then by another gap until 211. These dates generally correspond with periods of warfare between Rome and Parthia. While the effects of these wars will be noted further on in this chapter,[115] the coincidence of these disturbances and the appearance of terms at Palmyra such as '*strategos* against the nomads' may indicate that more unsettled conditions existed and a greater degree of military activity against the nomads was required.

As has been noted, another inscription indicates that there was still a garrison and a *strategos* at 'Ana and Gamla in AD 225. The Palmyrene occupation of these sites does not appear to have lasted much longer than this, however. The attacks of the Sassanid Persian dynasty which replaced the Parthians in 226 soon drove the Palmyrene troops from their posts on the Euphrates river. Bijan does not have evidence of Palmyrene occupation after the reign of Alexander Severus,[116] while 'Ana appears (as 'Anatha) in the list of Roman posts along the Euphrates conquered by Shapur I in his first invasion of Syria, which is usually dated to AD 256.[117] Dura, too, was destroyed by the Persians at this time and was never reoccupied. The evidence of the caravan inscriptions indicates that the commerce still continued after these events, as there are inscriptions commemorating caravans from AD 257/258 and 260.[118] It would appear, however, that the activities of the Palmyrene militia in the Euphrates valley must have ceased by the middle of the third century AD.

Nonetheless, it does not appear likely that the activities of the Palmyrene militia ceased altogether at this point. The ability of Palmyra to collect a substantial military force in connection with the activities of Septimius Odaenathus in the third quarter of the third century would rather indicate that this military capacity had been continued and perhaps even expanded. This is perhaps related to the existence of strong Persian forces and the possibility of greater trouble from the nomads, perhaps egged on by the Persians. While the expansion of the Palmyrene military in these circumstances will be noted further on in this chapter, it is enough now to note the uniqueness of this militia, especially in respect to its reliance on the caravan commerce for its existence. It would appear that it was the importance of the long-distance caravan commerce that caused the citizens of Palmyra to organise this protective force, and the importance of the commerce to imperial income in the form of taxes that caused the Romans to tolerate it.

The effect of the trade on Palmyrene society

Palmyra was for many reasons a highly distinctive city in the empire, and one in which the eastern commerce played a far larger role than elsewhere. The existence of such institutions as a city militia designed mainly to protect the caravan routes shows clearly that the caravan trade figured highly in the life of the city. Accordingly, in this section it is intended to study what can be gleaned about the relative importance of the caravan trade at Palmyra compared to the other sources of income which the city possessed, and to determine what social effects the existence of the caravan trade might have had.

The relative significance of the caravan trade at Palmyra

Regrettably, as with so many other areas of the eastern long-distance trade, there is no evidence which would enable us to quantify the volume of the eastern trade passing through Palmyra. The caravan trade was not the only source of income which Palmyra had. It has already been noted that there is evidence for substantial herding activities as well as agricultural development in the area to the north-west of Palmyra: indeed, these herding establishments especially were seen to have had a significant role in the development of the caravan commerce.[119] As well as contributing to the rise of the caravan commerce, these farming activities would also have made their own direct contribution to the economic life of the city.

This fact is reflected in the so-called *Portoria Palmyrenorum* or the Tariff of Palmyra. This document, an inscription from the agora in Palmyra, gives the dues which were to be paid on various items of merchandise in the market at Palmyra. The document is therefore not directly related to the transit caravan trade, but deals instead with goods consumed at Palmyra itself.[120] The information it reveals shows that Palmyra was a market for the produce of the desert and the pastoral region around the city, including such goods as wheat, wine, animal skins and other staples. While the produce of the territory of Palmyra itself was not taxed, that which was brought in from outside the city's territory was.[121] It is indeed interesting that some goods clearly were imported from outside the city's territory, for one effect of the city's apparent commercial vocation would have been a substantial non-productive population, which would then have necessitated food imports.[122] Thus, the presence of the caravan trade in the city might well have contributed to the market for the staple items listed in the tariff. Nonetheless, the existence of the tariff makes it clear that Palmyra enjoyed other sources of income beside the caravan commerce, as indeed we might expect.

Such sources of income, however, cannot explain the wealth which is so evident in the ruins of this desert city. The opulence of the city, its colonnades and temples demonstrate that it had some source of income which went beyond its local resources, which given the surrounding terrain must have been meagre indeed. This source of income can have been none other than the caravan trade.

Without this trade, Palmyra would have been a small, struggling community on the fringe of the desert. It can have been only the wealth generated by the caravan commerce that raised Palmyra to the splendour that is still visible today.

The significance of the commerce to the city is clearly expressed by the location of the commemorative caravan inscriptions. They have clearly been placed in positions of great prominence so that the greatest number of people could see the statues and their inscriptions, and admire the deeds of the benefactors of the caravans. Some are placed in the agora like the tariff inscription, but here the caravan trade has little to do with the market of Palmyra itself: as far as we know, the caravans would simply have passed through the city. The selection of the agora for these inscriptions would seem to have been chiefly dictated by the desire to have them prominently located in a public place. This is even more the case with those inscriptions which are found in the great colonnade in the centre of the city, and from various temples. In each case, the site has clearly been chosen for maximum prominence (see Figures 4.5 and 4.6).

Significantly, many of the caravan inscriptions were voted by the 'council and people of the Palmyrenes'.[123] Thus, even the government of the city was involved in the honouring of merchants and caravan leaders. No other place in the Roman East ever honoured merchants and those who helped them so prominently. It is evident that the authorities at Palmyra thought the protection and encouragement of the caravans was a matter of great importance to the continuing welfare of the city.

Figure 4.5 The Temple of Bel, Palmyra, Syria

Figure 4.6 The Temple of Baalshamin, Palmyra, Syria

This special significance of the caravan trade to the city, and especially the great wealth that it brought, may also perhaps account for some of the uniquely independent nature which we see manifested at Palmyra. We have already seen the way in which Palmyra maintained its own forces with Roman permission, but there are other indications also that Palmyra held an unusual status within the empire. One of the most striking things is the self-conscious 'easternness' of the city, compared to the almost complete adoption of Hellenism by other cities of the Roman East.[124] The religious activities of the Palmyrenes and their public inscriptions all present a curious mix of Hellenistic and Palmyrene precedents. The inscriptions in particular are usually Greek and Palmyrene bilinguals, or in the case of private inscriptions in Palmyrene only. The use of a local language in inscriptions in this way is unparalleled in Roman Syria.[125]

Whether or not this can be attributed to influences brought along the trade routes is problematical. There has been a tendency to label the style of art found at Palmyra as 'Parthian' and attribute its presence at Palmyra to contact with the Parthian realm, no doubt through the avenue of the caravan trade.[126] However, as Millar has pointed out, this style of art is found over a substantial area of Mesopotamia and the Hauran, and is difficult to ascribe to any particular point of origin; it is therefore no proof of the importance of the caravan trade in shaping Palmyrene culture.[127] We might, however, raise the possibility that this apparent independence and distinctiveness may have arisen from the wealth and power generated by the caravan trade, allowing the Palmyrenes to maintain their self-conscious 'easternness' more than other cities which were more directly dependent upon Rome. This is, of course, entirely hypothetical, and it may simply be that the isolation of the city from Roman centres and its contact with other Syrian and Mesopotamian cities was the reason this phenomenon arose. If indeed it was the case that the use of Aramaic was an index of Palmyrene independence, it is unusual that the Romans do not appear to have stopped the use of Palmyrene in public inscriptions after the suppression of the Palmyrene revolt in AD 272.[128] Perhaps the best that can be said in this regard is that there may have been a relationship between the caravan trade and the retention of Palmyrene in the public inscriptions of the city.

The place of the caravan traders in Palmyrene society

This notable significance of the caravan trade at Palmyra may also tell us something of the role the trade's practitioners had in Palmyrene society. Elsewhere in the Roman world (as has already been noted), merchants, although they could become wealthy indeed, were excluded from the highest orders of society.[129] In Palmyra, however, this does not appear to have been the case. It has already been noted that the commemorative inscriptions and statues which were put up both by and for caravan leaders and others involved in the commerce occupied positions of extraordinary prominence in the centre of the city. This would appear to reflect a high degree of civic pride in the achievements of these people, as well as a high level of prominence of these individuals.

Indeed, it would seem that caravan leaders were members of the city's elite, and that, far from trying to hide their involvement in trade they were very keen, as the commemorative inscriptions attest, to have their involvement with the caravan trade well known and publicised. One particularly important individual who also appears to have had a significant involvement in the caravan trade was Septimius Worod. One of the six surviving inscriptions that were erected in his honour sets out the offices he held in the city as well as his involvement with the caravan commerce:

ἡ βου[λὴ καὶ ὁ δῆ]μος
Σεπτίμ[ιον Οὐορώδην] τὸν κρά–
τιστον ἐ[πίτροπον] Σεβαστοῦ
δουκην[άριον, δι]κεοδότην
τῆς μητ[ροκολω]νείας καὶ ἀ–
νακομίσαν[τα τ]ὰς συνοδίας
ἐξ ἰδίων καὶ μαρτυρηθέντα
ὑπὸ τῶν ἀρχεμπόρων καὶ
λαμπρῶς στρατηγήσαντα και
ἀγορανομήσαντα τῆς αὐτῆς
μητροκολωνείας καὶ πλεῖστα
οἴκοθεν ἀναλώσαντα καὶ ἀρέσαν–

τα τῇ τε αὐτῇ βουλῇ καὶ τῷ δήμῳ
καὶ νυνεὶ λαμπρῶς συμποσίαρ–
χον τῶν το[ῦ θεοῦ] Διὸς Βήλου ἱε–
ρέων, ἁ[γνείας καὶ] τειμῆς ἕνε–
κεν, ἔτ[ους ζοφ´ μηνεὶ Ξανδικῷ.

> The Council and the People to Septimius Worod, the eminent *procurator ducenarius* of Augustus, *iuridicus* of the *metrocolonia* who has brought back caravans at his own expense and been given testimony by the chief merchants, who has brilliantly acted as *strategos* and *agoranomos* of the same *metrocolonia* and spent greatly of his own resources and been pleasing to the Council and the People, and who now brilliantly acts as *symposiarch* of the priests of the god Zeus Bel, as evidence of his integrity and honour, in the year 577, in the month Xandikos (AD 266).[130]

Septimius Worod was clearly an extremely important individual: he was at the very top (with the exception only of Odaenathus and his family at this particular time in Palmyrene history) of the Palmyrene political ladder. In other inscriptions he also is called the *argapet*, a Persian term meaning 'governor of the city'.[131] What is interesting from the viewpoint of this study is that his involvement in the caravan commerce is thought worthy of inclusion in what is in effect the man's *cursus honorum*. Roman equestrians and even Senators may have been involved in the eastern commerce and may even have drawn great profit from it, but none of them would have dreamed of including such a reference in a commemorative inscription. Not so at Palmyra: there, participation in the caravan commerce, especially benefactions to the caravans, was thought a matter of pride and great civic honour.[132]

Moreover, Septimius Worod was not the only individual at Palmyra who sought honour by recognition of his services to the caravan trade. The case of Julius Aurelius Salamallat, a caravan leader who brought back a caravan at his own expense, has already been noted; similarly, another inscription commemorates one Taimarsu ben Taime and his sons Iaddai and Zabdibol for saving a caravan an expense of 300 gold *denarii*.[133] It is clear that these people are engaging in the practice of euergetism which is common in the Hellenistic and Roman world:[134] they are paying for public benefits out of their own pockets to gain influence and prestige. In the context of this study, however, two things are worthy of note: first, that caravan leaders were the type of people who would be seeking such public honour and recognition, and obviously could aspire to an important role in the political life of the city. Second, that one way in which their public-spirited munificence could be displayed was by the provision of services to caravans. Clearly, the caravan trade was of great significance at Palmyra, and the caravan leaders were of a class of people who could rightly describe themselves as Palmyra's elite. Moreover, they wore their involvement with the caravan commerce with pride, and clearly regarded the caravan trade as a suitable area in which to display their talents and to build their prestige.

This is not to say, of course, that such people reached the elite *because* of their involvement in the caravan trade, or that any merchant involved in the trade could aspire to become a member of this elite. On the contrary, the bulk of the merchants involved in the commerce no doubt made a tidy profit, but are highly unlikely to have ever been able to reach the ranks of their city's political elite. This possibility, however, does appear to have been attainable for the class from which the *synodiarchs* came. Not only was participation in the caravan trade not an impediment to high civic office at Palmyra, but also it would seem that it could even be of assistance to one wishing to climb the Palmyrene political ladder.

Palmyra's equestrian officers

Another way in which the caravan traffic may have affected Palmyrene society is in the large number of individuals from the city who seem to have held equestrian rank, especially in the third century. In addition to the inscriptions from the Palmyrene corpus which mention members of the *ordo equester*, there are also several inscriptions from elsewhere in the empire which mention equestrian military officers who claim Palmyra as their origin.[135] Most of these were serving with Palmyrene auxiliary units, but some were attached to other eastern units which do not appear to have been Palmyrene in origin.[136] Indeed, there is a disproportionately large number of equestrian officers coming from Palmyra, particularly from the third century, when compared to other towns and provinces of the Roman East. For example, there are nine attested equestrian military officers from Palmyra operating with Roman auxiliary units in the first three centuries AD, compared to two each from Antioch, Heliopolis and Emesa, and one each from Tyre, Samosata and Seleucia.[137]

The large number of Palmyrene auxiliary units has already been noted, together with the likely association of these units with the Palmyrene caravan guards and their experience with the desert environment. It is likely that the large number of military equestrian appointments arose for the same reasons, together with the wealth which was characteristic of the city's economic prosperity in the second and third centuries. Indeed, Devijver notes that the economic flowering of the city in that period would have provided a fertile breeding-ground for the equestrian order.[138] In addition, the need for officers experienced with desert warfare and familiar with eastern types of units such as *dromedarii* and horse archers would have made Palmyrene officers, who had perhaps already gained such experience as a part of Palmyra's own armed forces, ideal for such service in the Roman army.[139]

Thus there seems to have been a number of ways, both direct and indirect, by which the caravan commerce affected the political and social makeup of Palmyrene society. Despite the fact that there are no statistics by which we might quantify these effects, it is nonetheless clear from much of the related evidence that the caravan commerce held a position of great significance in Palmyrene society. Having no better explanation ourselves, it would seem prudent to accept the Palmyrenes' opinion of the importance of the caravan trade and recognise that Palmyra, even more than other areas where the trade was active, was indeed an exception to the prevailing economic model of agrarian subsistence in the remainder of the empire. In the sense that a significant proportion of the city's wealth and influence is directly attributable to the caravan trade and its effects, it is not inappropriate to call Palmyra a 'caravan city'.

Palmyra in the third century: crisis, revolt and aftermath

After the civil wars which brought Septimius Severus to the imperial throne, the East began to loom large in the affairs of the Roman Empire. Severus' reign brought about a new series of wars with Parthia and its successor, Sassanid Persia, which could not but have affected Palmyra's trade. These effects were further compounded by the political crisis which racked the empire in the third century. These circumstances made the third century a time of far greater uncertainty and instability for Palmyra and its trade than the previous century.

Palmyrene commerce in the third century

The probable halt in caravan traffic which was occasioned by the wars of Lucius Verus, Septimius Severus and Caracalla against Parthia has already been noted. It is clear that, when the Romans wished to undertake a war of aggression, the needs of such things as the caravan trade were of little moment. Given the importance of the traffic to Palmyra, these cessations of the commerce must have had an adverse affect upon the economy of the city, and thus may be regarded as possible explanations for Palmyrene actions of the later third century. Of course, such disturbances as we see affecting Palmyra through this period may have adversely influenced other areas of the city's interests beside the caravan trade, and we should be careful before we ascribe to the caravan trade actions which may be equally well explained by other motives. Nonetheless, in a city as dependent on the long-distance trade as Palmyra apparently was, the caravan trade was probably a significant consideration in the determination of policy.

While the wars of the later second and early third centuries do appear to have adversely affected Palmyra's trade, this situation appears to have become worse only in the course of the third century. In AD 224 the Persian Ardashir overthrew the last Parthian king, Artabanus, and established the Sassanid monarchy which would prove to be a much more vigorous opponent of Rome than the Parthians had been.[140] Almost immediately the actions of Ardashir and his successors began to affect the Roman East, as well as the eastern caravan trade. The great increase in the number of military campaigns, as well as the frequent invasion of Roman territory during the third century, would certainly have had extremely disruptive effects on the eastern commerce.

It is noteworthy that after this time the Palmyrene caravan inscriptions cease to mention expeditions to Spasinou Charax. While caravans travelling as far as Vologesias are still attested,[141] it would seem that transit to Charax may not have been possible. Ardashir took possession of Mesene in AD 226,[142] which may have curtailed the Palmyrene commerce there. Some traffic must have continued through Charax, however, as the caravans reaching Vologesias would presumably pick up goods that had been brought there from Charax. The influence of Palmyrenes there, however, is likely to have been substantially reduced or eliminated altogether.

Worse still was to follow. In the middle of the third century, Ardashir's successor Shapur I launched a series of invasions of Roman territory, in the course of which he temporarily occupied Antioch and sacked several cities. These invasions culminated in the defeat and capture of the Emperor Valerian by Shapur in AD 260.[143] Such violent irruptions must inevitably have caused great disruption to the Palmyrene commerce, not to mention grave concern about the future of the city itself. In the course of these invasions, Dura Europos was captured by the Persians and destroyed, and the Palmyrene garrisons further down the Euphrates, such as 'Ana, were presumably lost at the same time or earlier.[144] In all this, the apparent inability of the Roman authorities to help the East against these invasions and their consequent disruption must have caused concern, and increased the perception that if Palmyra was to survive, it must take action on its own account.

The increase in military activity which no doubt had a disruptive effect upon the caravan traffic may have also been accompanied by a rise in the hostile activities of nomads. This is possibly reflected in the increasing activities of the Palmyrene militia in this period, as has already been noted. The appearance of the terms '*strategos* against the nomads' and '*strategos* of the peace' in AD 198 and 199 may indicate some rise in difficulties with the nomads, as may the appearance of the title *Ras Tadmor* in the middle of the third century.[145] Although this evidence is certainly far from conclusive, it may indicate that the nomads were threatening and disrupting the caravan traffic rather more frequently during the third century.

There is indeed some evidence which may throw light on the relations between Palmyra and the nomads at this time, and may indicate rising tensions in these relations during the third century.[146] The Arab historian al-Tabari mentions the existence of a tribal coalition called the Tanukh in his account of the destruction of Palmyra. Unfortunately the Arab accounts of Palmyra's fall are of limited historical value, as they present the destruction of Palmyra as exclusively a war between the Tanukh and Palmyra, without the involvement of the Romans.[147] Nonethless, the existence of the Tanukh and their King Jadhima, also mentioned by al-Tabari, has been confirmed by the discovery of an inscription at Umm al-Jimal commemorating a Nabataean tutor of Jadhima,[148] and another inscription from Namara which names Imru'l-qais, the son of Jadhima's nephew.[149] Thus, while the historical details of the struggle may have been lost in the Arab accounts, the enmity between Palmyra and the Tanukh to which they refer is likely to be based on fact. There thus is evidence which may well indicate the existence of a powerful coalition of nomadic tribes which was an enemy of Palmyra in the later third century AD.

The increasing disruption of the Palmyrene trade route may also be reflected in the rise in activity on alternative trade routes in Egypt and Arabia. It has already been noted that in the Severan period there seems to have been a rise in trading activity in the Egyptian Red Sea trade, as well as along the Wadi Sirhan in Arabia.[150] Given the increase in difficulties on the Palmyrene trading route at this time, it may well have been that merchants chose to send their wares through these alternative routes rather than through Palmyra.

The economic difficulties which would no doubt have come about due to this loss of trade would no doubt have been worsened still more by the general economic crisis of the middle and later third century AD. Palmyra is not likely to have escaped the adverse effects of this downturn: in all probability the Palmyrenes found that the markets for their wares were not as strong as they had been, either in the Roman East itself or elsewhere in the empire.

In such circumstances, the apparent decision of Palmyra's rulers to take an active hand in their own destiny is perhaps unsurprising. This combination of factors which appears to have affected Palmyra's trade in the third century would have made the rulers of the city more likely to take active steps to redress the situation should the opportunity present itself. Of course, in the circumstances of such events as the Persian invasions there may have been deeper concerns still: with the apparent inability of the Romans to protect the East, the Palmyrenes may well have felt that their very survival lay in their own hands. Indeed, in a city such as Palmyra where trade appears to have held a very prominent place in society, the subjects of survival and continuing commercial prosperity may have been regarded as closely related if not identical.

The rise of Palmyra as an independent power

The appearance of Palmyra as an independent military power is inextricably linked to the rise of Septimius Odaenathus, whose titles and career are dealt with in Appendix D. For now, however, it will be sufficient to note the appearance of Odaenathus on the historical record at this time, and his command of a substantial Palmyrene military force which was capable of inflicting defeats upon the Persians. He first appears in the confused aftermath of the defeat and capture of the Roman Emperor Valerian by the Persians in AD 260. Leading a considerable force of soldiers, Odaenathus restored the stability of the Roman East by defeating the imperial pretenders Macrianus and Quietus at Emesa in 261. After this, he avenged the defeat of Valerian by defeating the Persian forces and driving them out of Roman territory.[151] Thus, in short order Odaenathus restored a deteriorating situation in the East, and preserved Roman rule there.

The appearance of Odaenathus leading a force of Palmyrene military certainly does require some explanation. Formerly, it was held that Odaenathus inherited his position and titles from one Septimius Hairan, either his father or elder brother, who in turn inherited them from an Odaenathus the elder who is envisaged as living in the first half of the third century.[152] It now appears that this position should be rejected: the recent discovery of an inscription makes it most likely that there never was an Odaenathus the elder, and that the title of *Ras Tadmor*, the first of the series of titles held by Septimius Odaenathus, was invented for Septimius Odaenathus himself.[153] Thus, the appearance of Odaenathus at the head of substantial military forces to restore the situation after Shapur's defeat of Valerian in 260 was both sudden and wholly unprecedented. In recognition of his victories, and of his status as the only significant pro-Roman military power left in the East, Odaenathus was honoured by the Emperor Gallienus with the title *Corrector Totius Orientis* or something similar. Whether or not this was an 'official' Roman title, it was undoubtedly recognition of Odaenathus' military supremacy in the East. In addition, he had at some time prior to this been given the title *hypatikos*, which may mean that he was made governor of Syria Coele but probably was merely intended to honour him with consular rank.[154] In the years following, Odaenathus is attested as leading his troops to several victories over the Persians, perhaps even advancing as far as Ctesiphon.[155] Thus, from 261 until he and his son Septimius Hairan were murdered in 267, he continued to campaign against the Persians and against Roman pretenders, maintaining loyalty to Gallienus throughout.

From where then did Odaenathus obtain the troops with which he defeated the Persians in 261, and were they Palmyrene or Roman? It is, in fact, impossible to tell, but it should be noted that many historical writers speaking of this era refer to Odaenathus gathering his forces from the countryside rather than collecting the remaining Roman forces in the area.[156] In addition, Zosimus (admittedly a very late source) specifically states that Odaenathus used 'his own troops' combined with the remaining Roman forces in the area.[157] Given Odaenathus' apparent headship of Palmyra in the years preceding 261 it is more than likely that his troops in the first instance were Palmyrenes. Of course, as his influence and prestige increased during the 260s, and as he was awarded Roman military titles such as *Corrector*, regular Roman troops in the area would have come under his command also. The most probable origin of his forces, however, is the Palmyrene caravan police. While the military organisation of a small militia may well have been insufficient for the campaigns of Odaenathus, it would have provided him with a nucleus of experienced troops which could have been rapidly expanded to meet the emergency.

This independent military role also raises questions about the status of Palmyra itself during the 260s, which will also be discussed in Appendix D. In effect, Palmyra appears to have become in fact if not in law an allied state instead of a provincial city.[158] The Roman titles of Odaenathus do not disguise the Palmyrene base of his power nor the Palmyrene origin of his forces. It is clear that, rather than waiting upon Gallienus to rescue them in the aftermath of the defeat of Valerian, the Palmyrenes instead acted upon their own initiative (or that of Odaenathus himself) to restore the situation. To what extent, then, did the needs of the caravan trade or the effects of that trade help make this sequence of events come about?

While it is impossible to prove trade motives in Palmyra's actions in the 260s, the difficulties which the trade appears to have encountered in the third century, coupled with the significant place which trade held in Palmyrene society, would make it quite likely that the needs of the caravan trade lay behind at least some Palmyrene actions in this period. There is no doubt that the trade would have been adversely affected by the circumstances of the third century which were outlined above. Accordingly, it is quite possible that Palmyra was interested in defending and protecting its trade routes, and this may account for Odaenathus acting to defeat the invading Persians who were disrupting the trade and thus affecting the prosperity of the city.

However, the Persian invasions were disrupting a great deal more than just the caravan trade, and it is altogether possible that the Palmyrenes felt their city itself, not just its trade, was in danger of destruction. When Shapur defeated and captured Valerian, it must have seemed to the inhabitants of the East that Rome was now unable to protect them: Palmyra thus took matters into its own hands, and Odaenathus, leading the military forces of Palmyra, opposed the Persians and crushed Roman usurpers in the region. Thus, as the representative of the legitimate emperor at Rome (formalised after 261 by his appointment as *Corrector*), Odaenathus restored the situation in the East. Nevertheless, we should not discard trade motives altogether: it may well have been thought that by seizing the effective reins of power in the East, Palmyra would be able to halt the drift of the trade away from war-ravaged Mesopotamia and Syria to northern Arabia and Egypt.[159]

There is, however, one way in which it can be said that the caravan trade certainly did influence the appearance of Palmyra as an independent power, and that is by the existence of a military capacity at Palmyra. Such a force would never have been available if Palmyra had not depended so much upon its caravan traffic. However, the existence of such forces, combined with their experience in desert warfare, made Palmyra capable of resisting the Persians in a way that was not available to any of the other communities of Roman Syria. In addition, the wealth which had come to Palmyra by the conduct of its trade may well have contributed to its ability to raise military forces in these circumstances. In this way, then, it can be said that the caravan trade may have influenced the course of events in Roman Syria during the AD 260s.

Zenobia and the break with Rome

Upon the death of Odaenathus and his son in AD 267, the reins of power at Palmyra were taken by Odaenathus' widow Zenobia, ruling in the name of her son Vaballathus (Wahballat) who was still a minor. Initially, it would seem that Vaballathus simply claimed the titles of *Corrector* and King or 'King of Kings', all of which were probably titles inherited from Odaenathus.[160] While the milestones from which Vaballathus' titulature is obtained are undated, it would seem logical that the ones explicitly claiming imperial power would come from later in the revolt, whereas those using similar titles to those Odaenathus is known to have used would have come from soon after 267. These titles are seen on a milestone from the *Via Nova Traiana*, which bears a fragmentary Greek inscription with a more complete Palmyrene version:

> 'LH [YWH] WZKWTH DY SPTYMWS
> WHBLT 'ṬNDR[WS NHY]R' MLK MLK'
> W'PNRTṬ' DY MDNḤ' KLH BR
> SPT[YMY]WS ['DYNṬ MLK] MLK' W'L
> ḤYH DY SPTYMY' BṬZBY NHYRT'
> MLKṬ' 'MH DY MLK MLK'
> BT 'NTYWKWS
>
> For the safety and victory of Septimius Vaballathus Athenodorus, illustrious King of Kings, *Corrector* of the whole East, son of Septimius Odenathus King of Kings, and also for Septimia Bath-Zabbai (i.e. Zenobia), illustrious Queen, mother of the King of Kings, daughter of Antiochus.[161]

In this titulature there is no explicit claim for imperial power, only for the role and titles which Odaenathus had borne. Whether or not Vaballathus actually was entitled to these positions in the eyes of the emperor or of the provincial officials of the area is another question which may have some significance for the outbreak of the revolt. Regardless, the placing of this milestone on the *Via Nova* would indicate *de facto* power in the area after 267. Thus it appears that Zenobia was successful in the first instance in transferring the power held by Odaenathus to herself and her young son.

In about 270, however, the first indications of trouble begin. In that year, Zenobia sent Zabda, a Palmyrene general, to invade Egypt. Prior to this, however, or perhaps in the course of the same campaign, there seems to have been an attack on the headquarters of the *Legio III Cyrenaica* at Bostra by Palmyrene forces. An inscription from the temple of Jupiter Hammon at Bostra stated that the temple had been destroyed a *Palmyrenis hostibus* ('by Palmyrene enemies')[162] and the Byzantine chronicler Malalas recorded that the Palmyrenes invaded Arabia and killed the *dux* Trassus during the reign of Claudius Gothicus (AD 268–270).[163] After this, Palmyrene troops invaded Egypt, overcoming the resistance of the Roman forces there commanded by Tenagino Probus.[164] In addition, Zosimus records that Zenobia invaded Asia Minor as well, capturing territory as far as Ancyra.[165]

Despite these campaigns, the evidence would seem to indicate that full separation from Rome was still not envisaged. Coins issued at Antioch from the early period bear the portraits of both Aurelian and Vaballathus; Aurelian is styled as Augustus while Vaballathus is called variously *Rex*, *Imperator* and *Dux Romanorum*, but never Augustus.[166] This is also seen in papyri from Egypt during this period, which are dated by the regnal years of both Aurelian and Vaballathus, with Vaballathus in a subordinate position. These style Aurelian as 'Imperator Caesar Lucius Domitius Aurelianus Pius Felix Augustus' and Vaballathus, in second place, as 'Julius Aurelius Septimius Vaballathus, illustrious king, consul, Imperator, Strategos of the Romans'.[167] A similar range of titles is seen in the Palmyrene coinage from Antioch which was discussed earlier. In these examples, Vaballathus' titulature has evidently advanced from the titles he inherited from Odaenathus (i.e. King and *Corrector*), but he is still placed as subordinate to Aurelian. It would seem that even after the invasion of Egypt the Palmyrenes were hoping for imperial recognition of their conquests, with Vaballathus occupying a position of authority over the East subordinate to Aurelian, the sole Augustus. It was Aurelian's reaction that made the Palmyrene invasion a 'revolt': clearly he thought that Zenobia had gone too far, or he simply decided that it was time to rein in such independent powers as Palmyra and Tetricus in Gaul.

Thus, in the course of AD 271, Aurelian's portrait no longer appears on coins from Antioch, and is replaced with coins issued in the name of Vaballathus Augustus and Zenobia Augusta. From the same period also comes another milestone, claiming full imperial titulature for Vaballathus, including the title of Augustus:

> Im[p]. Caesari L. Iulio
> Aurelio Septimio
> Vaballatho
> Athenodoro Per-
> sico Maximo Ara-
> bico Maximo Adia-
> benico Maximo Pio
> Felici Inuicto Au[g].
>
> To the Emperor Caesar L. Julius Aurelius Septimius Vaballathus Athenodorus Persicus Maximus Arabicus Maximus Adiabenicus Maximus Pius Felix Invictus Augustus.[168]

It is most likely that these coins and inscriptions date from a time when the breach with Aurelian was seen as irreversible, perhaps even after he had commenced military operations to bring Palmyra to heel. The course of Aurelian's campaign of AD 272 is given in Zosimus and the *Historia Augusta*: after recapturing Ancyra and Tyana, he defeated the Palmyrene forces at Antioch and Emesa and then invested Palmyra itself. Zenobia attempted to flee to the Persians and was captured, whereupon Palmyra surrendered. After initially sparing the city, Aurelian sacked it after another uprising, probably in 273.[169]

Commercial motivations in the Palmyrene revolt

Why then did Zenobia embark upon such a revolt which must inevitably have brought the retribution of Rome upon her city? Several differing explanations have been put forward, including the possibility that the revolt was occasioned by trade motives. Schwartz has suggested that Palmyra's revolt arose out of a need to protect the interests of Palmyrene merchants in the unsettled circumstances of the third century.[170] Similarly, he sees the invasion of Egypt as motivated by the need to secure the interests of Palmyrene merchants there, who were suffering the effects of the disturbances which racked Egypt during the period.[171] It may also be possible that such motives could explain the attack on Bostra mentioned earlier, as the trade route which reached Bostra by the Wadi Sirhan may have been receiving trade which once would have passed through Palmyra.

Nevertheless, although the commercial vocation of Palmyra may well have had some bearing on the course of events, it is not likely to have been the only consideration. Indeed, it would seem difficult to justify such acts as the invasion of southern Asia Minor if Palmyra's motives were purely commercial, as there is no evidence that Palmyrene merchants ever operated in this area.[172] While it is certainly possible that the caravan trade may have been a consideration in the decision to attack Egypt and/or Bostra, it is not likely to have been the only determining factor behind the policy of Zenobia and Vaballathus.

Another possibility that might be considered is that Zenobia's rebellion should be seen as an Arab 'nationalist' revolt against the power of Rome. Such notions, however, should be rejected: for one thing, the adoption by Vaballathus of 'Arabicus' as one of his victory titles indicates that the Palmyrenes did not consider themselves Arabs.[173] Similarly, the claim of imperial titles, especially at the close of the revolt, would seem to indicate that what was being sought was some sort of accommodation *within* the Roman system: when there finally seemed no likelihood of accommodation with Aurelian, Vaballathus at last claimed the title of Augustus which he does not seem to have taken in the early stages of the revolt. Thus, his claims seem to move away from peculiarly Palmyrene titles toward more universalist Roman ones as the revolt progressed. This is hardly what would be expected of a separatist nationalistic movement. Equally, however, the revolt cannot be seen as a simple imperial usurpation as was common throughout the empire in the third century, and reasonably frequent in the East.[174] The presence of titles such as 'King' in Vaballathus' titulature,[175] coupled with the absence of a full imperial claim until near the end of the revolt, indicate that Vaballathus was not originally intending to claim the empire as Macrianus and Quietus had done in 261.

The true answer to the origin of Palmyra's revolt against Rome probably lies in the political situation of the later third century. It is quite possible that the revolt may have been occasioned by the same perceived needs which caused Odaenathus to lift Palmyra to the status of an independent power in the previous decade, and the perceived necessity to maintain that status after the death of Odaenathus. Some of the factors which created this necessity in the minds of Zenobia and her advisers may well have been associated with the caravan traffic; others, as in the time of Odaenathus, will have been more to do with the continued survival of Palmyra itself. At the accession of Vaballathus, Palmyra already possessed a great deal of power and influence. Whatever the formal status of the city, it was in effect the premier power in the East. It is possible, however, that with the death of Odaenathus and the defeat of the Persians, the provincial authorities of the East refused to recognise Vaballathus' inheritance of his father's titles. Thus, the Palmyrene forces attacked the regular Roman forces in Bostra, Egypt and Asia Minor in order to compel their allegiance to Vaballathus, and to maintain rather than to expand the dominant position of Palmyra.[176]

The absence of an effective imperial force in the East since 260 may have contributed to the feeling at Palmyra that the city's leadership of the East should be maintained in order to retain the stability won by Odaenathus. Just as other parts of the empire such as Britain and Gaul were separating off at this time due to the perceived failure of the central administration to protect them, it seems that Zenobia felt that only the continued domination of Palmyra could guarantee the stability of the East.[177] In any case, given the dominant position of Palmyra at the time, it is perhaps understandable that she was reluctant to let anyone else try.

Nevertheless, trade motives are likely to have figured in the thinking of Zenobia and her court at this time, even if such motives would have been secondary in nature to the desire for peace and stability. The series of wars with both Parthia and Sassanid Persia will have convinced the Palmyrenes that neither these powers nor Rome were especially interested in preserving the caravan trade. With Palmyra in its new position of power, however, the opportunity now existed for the city to exercise its strength to protect this traffic. Of course, the maintenance of peace and security in the East would also have a beneficial effect on Palmyra's long-distance trade, and so we might see Palmyra's trade interests as part of a broader picture which encouraged the Palmyrenes to try to retain their dominant position. Trade motives and political motives certainly do not have to be seen as mutually exclusive, especially in a city with such a dominant commercial vocation as Palmyra.

The presence of such trade motivations may also explain some of the points of resistance to Palmyrene leadership. As has already been seen, during the third century Bostra (by means of the Wadi Sirhan) and Egypt were receiving trade which might otherwise have passed through Palmyra. While it is unlikely that Zenobia directly attacked these places to remove trade competition and thus incur the vengeance of Rome, it is possible that Egypt and Arabia were foremost among the areas which resisted Palmyrene rule due to conflicting trade interests with Palmyra. Indeed, Schwartz identified the merchants of Alexandria as a likely source of opposition to the Palmyrene presence in Egypt due to their conflicting commercial interests.[178] It is also possible that the Tanukh tribal coalition which is known to have been active at Umm el-Jimal in this period may have been responsible for resistance to Palmyra in the area of Bostra.[179] This may in turn indicate that the Tanukh were profiting from trade passing throught the Wadi Sirhan and Bostra. Thus, the beginning of the Palmyrene revolt in 270 may have come about as an attempt by interests in Arabia and Egypt to break free of Palmyrene domination, which was then crushed by direct military intervention by Palmyra. This refusal to accept Palmyrene hegemony may itself have been partly motivated by trade considerations.

The sources are really far too fragmentary to insist on any single explanation to the extraordinary series of events in the Roman East in the period between 267 and 272. It would seem, however, that the revolt should be distinguished from other imperial usurpations of the era, as it should be distinguished from a nationalist uprising. Instead, the model which has been presented here, of the Palmyrenes attempting to cling to the position they had gained in the previous decade, would seem to explain the evidence in a satisfactory manner. In this view, the caravan trade assumes some importance, especially in explaining the reluctance of the authorities in Egypt and Arabia to submit to Palmyrene rule. The Palmyrenes would have felt that they alone could guarantee the peace and security that the East needed: moreover, such circumstances obviously favoured their caravan trade. Other authorities in the East, however, did not share this view: part of what motivated this may have been the reluctance to part with commerce which the Palmyrenes would have been keen to see passing through Palmyra again. When these two conflicting views came into conflict, it was Aurelian's decision to back the provincial authorities in Arabia, Egypt and Asia Minor that sealed the fate of Palmyra.

The effects of Palmyra's fall

The destruction of Palmyra by Aurelian seems to have brought the caravan trade of Palmyra to a close. There are no more caravan inscriptions after 272, and no evidence to indicate that the trade survived the destruction of the city. There is evidence of continuing trade elsewhere in Roman Syria and Mesopotamia, although there is no reason to believe that this trade appeared only after the fall of Palmyra. It is far more likely that it had coexisted all throughout the period of Palmyrene ascendancy.[180] In addition, the 'trade fair', which Ammianus mentions existing at Batnae in the fourth century,[181] is not likely to have emerged as a replacement for such an event at Palmyra, as Stoneman suggests: rather, Batnae is likely to have been a trade centre throughout the entire period.[182]

Instead of imagining the trade routes being 'relocated' elsewhere after the fall of Palmyra, we should perhaps view the fall as representing the removal of one of a number of coexisting trade routes in Syria and Mesopotamia. As has already been noted, it would seem that it was mainly the Palmyrenes themselves who used the route through Palmyra. The Greek, Jewish and Syrian merchants active in Mesopotamia had probably continued to use the Euphrates route all along, and no doubt continued to do so after the fall of Palmyra. The absence of competition from Palmyrene merchants may have enabled these merchants to obtain higher prices for a while, but the volume or price of the goods at Rome and in the empire is not likely to have been substantially affected. Indeed, the 'normalisation' of the Roman East by Aurelian, plus the conclusion of peace with the Persians after his death,[183] are more likely to have improved trading conditions.

Thus, the only people dramatically affected by the fall of Palmyra were the Palmyrenes themselves. The events of 272–273 left them without the infrastructure and ability to continue to participate in the trade. Despite this the city was not completely destroyed, and we have evidence that some institutions of Palmyrene life continued for some time after 273. Bilingual Greek–Palmyrene texts in the traditional style have been found in the Great Colonnade dating from AD 279/280,[184] which shows that the city was neither completely destroyed nor deserted, and the Palmyrenes were not dispossessed or massacred completely when Aurelian took their city for the second time. Indeed, it would seem that some of the Palmyrene aristocracy had co-operated with the Romans and retained their position of influence after the fall of the city. An inscription of 273 or later records that Haddudan son of Ogeilu, who was of Roman senatorial rank, had helped the troops of Aurelian and had been president of a religious banqueting association.[185] It would also seem that the cults of the city continued to function: the Temples of Bel, Baalshamin and Arsu continued to function while the Temple of Allat was incorporated into the camp of the Roman garrison.[186]

From these pieces of evidence it would certainly appear that many of the institutions of Palmyra continued for a period after 273, including the cults of the city, at least a part of the old aristocracy of the town, and the use of Palmyrene in commemorative inscriptions. Nonetheless, these institutions do appear to have gradually died out over the succeeding years: we hear no more of the Palmyrene aristocracy, and the inscriptions of 279/280 are the last that we know of in the Palmyrene language. This would appear to have been a natural process of assimilation into the Roman world, however, rather than a deliberate suppression of Palmyrene 'uniqueness' by the Romans, as has been suggested.[187] Rather, it would seem that, with the caravan trade removed, the consequent lack of wealth in the city, and the close proximity of a large garrison of Roman troops, the things that had made Palmyra distinctive gradually disappeared, and Palmyra became a normal garrison town of Roman Syria.

The cessation of the long-distance trade through Palmyra should thus probably be viewed as the result of the loss of the infrastructure which had made this commerce possible in the first place. One of the primary factors would have been the removal of the caravan guards, who had been used by Palmyra to keep the caravan routes safe. Given that these troops had probably been used to form the nucleus of the Palmyrene army in the 260s and 270s, it is hardly surprising that the Romans would not allow this organisation to continue. In addition, the sack of the city and the probable destruction of much of the old aristocracy of the town would have significantly reduced or removed altogether the capability of organising and financing the expensive caravan expeditions. Thus, despite the fact that the Romans do not appear to have suppressed all the institutions of Palmyrene life, it would seem that the sack of the city in AD 273 dealt the Palmyrene long-distance trade a blow from which it could not recover.

Conclusion: the trade of Palmyra

Palmyra was clearly no ordinary city of the Roman East. For a number of reasons, prominent among which must be the role of the city's commerce, it stands apart from all the other centres of this region. While the notion that the city was ruled by a class of 'merchant princes', as Rostovtzeff suggested, should be rejected, we can nonetheless identify many ways in which the caravan trade at Palmyra influenced the social and political setup of the city, and also contributed to the city's final clash with Rome which ended in its destruction and the end of its caravan trade.

This trade arose by the initiative of the pastoral Palmyrene nobility, who used their resources and knowledge of the desert environment to create a trade route on which Palmyra could prosper. These men organised and equipped caravan expeditions which were composed of merchants of whom we know little. They appear, however, to have usually been Palmyrenes themselves, and may well have often financed their participation in the caravan by a loan from the caravan leader or another of Palmyra's magnates. In the course of these expeditions, difficulties of various sorts often needed to be overcome, ranging from nomad attacks to recalcitrant customs officials. In many cases, upon the successful completion of the expedition, the actions of various individuals to help the caravan were commemorated by prominent public inscriptions in such places as the Agora or the main street of the city.

The high prominence given these inscriptions seems to reflect the significant role that the caravan trade had in the city. Despite the fact that the rulers of Palmyra were not, in the first instance at least, 'merchant princes', it is evident that they appreciated the important role that the trade had in the city and for their own prosperity. The very prominence of the commemorative inscriptions, and the evident pride with which the magnates of the city described their participation in and support of the caravan trade, clearly attest the high regard in which the caravan trade and its practitioners were held at Palmyra. Perhaps the most striking example of this is the recording of services to caravans as a part of a prominent citizen's *cursus honorum*: such a commemoration would be unheard of in Rome or indeed throughout much of the empire, but it was considered appropriate at Palmyra. It is quite evident that the caravan trade at Palmyra occupied a position of extraordinary prominence.

The reason for this prominence is not hard to find. The wealth of this city, which is so readily discernible even today in the physical remains of the town, can hardly be ascribed to agriculture or the other normal sources of wealth in the Roman Empire. Sited as it is on the margins of the desert, the wealth that Palmyra commanded and which allowed it to construct such magnificent buildings and for a brief time rise to great prominence in the affairs of the Roman East can have come only from the caravan trade. Thus, it is hardly surprising to find the commerce occupying a position of great importance at Palmyra.

In addition, the caravan trade has been shown to have affected other areas of Palmyrene life. The existence of an independent Palmyrene military organisation, whatever its exact structure might have been, was the result of the need to protect the caravan trade from the depredations of bandits in the desert region between Palmyra and the Euphrates. The military experience which was gained from this patrolling probably influenced the substantial use of Palmyrene recruits in the Roman army, as well as the considerable number of equestrian military officers who appear to have come from Palmyra. Indeed, the wealth generated by the caravan trade would possibly also have contributed to the large number of equestrian officers from Palmyra.

The significance of the trade in the tumultuous events of the third century, however, is rather more obscure. Given the deteriorating political situation at the time, it is perhaps more likely that motives of simple survival caused the Palmyrenes under Odaenathus to take an independent military and political role. Nonetheless, the existence of the Palmyrene caravan militia and the considerable experience gained in patrolling the desert no doubt contributed to Odaenathus' ability to raise his forces and defeat the Persians, and so the caravan trade can be seen as contributing indirectly to the rise of Palmyra at this time. Similarly, the trade does not appear to have had a direct influence upon Palmyrene relations with Rome in the period leading to the destruction of Palmyra by Aurelian in 273. However, it is possible that the reluctance of some Roman provincial authorities to submit to Palmyrene authority after the death of Odaenathus may have caused the Palmyrene breach with Rome, and this in turn may have been caused by trade influences. Despite this, it would appear that in general the interests of the long-distance caravan trade were of a secondary nature in determining Palmyrene policy in the third century.

It would thus seem clear that the caravan trade with the head of the Persian Gulf had a significant effect on the city of Palmyra, both economically, politically and socially. Indeed, these effects would appear to have been more pronounced at Palmyra than at any other site in the Roman East. Nonetheless, these effects appear to have been confined to Palmyra itself. Palmyra was allowed to chart the course it took due to the lucrative tax revenue that the trade brought to the Roman treasury, but in no case can it be seen that the needs of Palmyra or the trade which was centred there was allowed to influence Roman policy in the region. The trade route through Palmyra, and the attendant prosperity of the city, came about through the initiative of the Palmyrenes themselves. The lack of interest which the Romans showed in the trade is in no way better attested than by the lack of compunction they showed in destroying Palmyra when it stood in the way of their political ambitions. Clearly, the economic needs of the trade and of Palmyra were of no importance compared to Roman imperial glory.

5

TRADE IN SYRIA AND THE NORTH

The routes to the north of Palmyra are not as well attested as those through Palmyra, Petra and Egypt. Nonetheless, there is some evidence to show that merchants made use of the routes which departed Antioch and crossed the Euphrates at Zeugma. Among these was the famous 'Silk Road', as well as the route along the Euphrates described by Isidore which gave access to Mesopotamia and the Gulf.

These routes crossed an area that was often disputed by the Roman Empire and its Iranian opponents, the Parthian and then the Sassanid Persian kingdoms. Thus, in this area the eastern long-distance trade had the potential at least to be of some political significance, and perhaps even a factor in the determination of foreign policy by either of the two powers. Indeed, if the spice trade was ever going to be a political factor as far as the imperial government was concerned, it would have been in this area. Accordingly, it is proposed in this chapter to study the routes of the trade in the region of Mesopotamia and Syria, as well as to study evidence for either Roman or Parthian political interest in the trade.

The northern routes and the 'Silk Road'

The trade routes of Syria and northern Mesopotamia were used throughout the period of study by a variety of Greek, Syrian and Jewish merchants, and may well have contributed a greater share of the trade than the surviving evidence would suggest. As with many areas of history, our knowledge of the eastern commerce must be a function of the evidence which we are able to study. The mere fact that more evidence has survived from Palmyra or Egypt is no proof that in ancient times these trade routes were of greater significance. Indeed, the routes of northern Syria are of particular significance given that they traverse one of the main areas of conflict between Rome and both Parthia and Sassanid Persia, the Euphrates valley. It is possible that the trade routes in this area could have had some bearing on the strategies and policy of these powers in the course of their many conflicts. Even though in the course of this study we have found no evidence to suggest that the eastern long-distance trade was ever of significance in the determination of Roman policy, it may be that the northern routes were an exception.

The Euphrates route

There is some literary evidence to suggest that traders made use of the route which leaves Antioch and then crosses the Euphrates at Zeugma and proceeds down the Euphrates valley in order to reach the trading centres of the Gulf. Regrettably, this evidence consists for the most part of scattered references which do not give any clear picture. However, this is not to say that the evidence is without value: there is (as will be seen) enough evidence to attest the existence and use of the Euphrates route throughout the period under study. Certainly the use of these northern routes is attested after the destruction of Palmyra in AD 272; for example, Ammianus Marcellinus refers to the town of Batnae near the Euphrates not far from Zeugma as the site of a trade fair in the fourth century:

> Batnae municipium in Anthemusia conditum Macedonum manu priscorum, ab Euphrate flumine breui spatio disparatur, refertum mercatoribus opulentis, ubi annua sollemnitate prope Septembris initium mensis, ad nundinas magna promiscuae fortunae conuenit multitudo, ad commercanda quae Indi mittunt et Seres, aliaque plurima uehi terra marique consueta.
>
> Batnae is a town in Anthemusia founded by the ancient Macedonians, separated by a short distance from the Euphrates, which is filled with rich merchants when, during the annual festival held near the beginning of September, a great crowd of mixed fortune comes together for the fair, to buy and sell the things which the Indians and Chinese send, and many other things which are accustomed to be brought there by land and sea.[1]

Although it has been suggested that this trade fair took place only after Palmyra's destruction,[2] this is neither explicitly stated nor implied in the text, and it may very well be that Batnae had been an important centre for trade throughout the entire period. It would seem unlikely that Zeugma, long recognised as a site of great strategic importance due to the bridge crossing the Euphrates between it and Apamea on the opposite bank,[3] would gain commercial significance only at this late stage. It is far more likely that these routes had always been in use, and were used by Antiochene merchants, be they Greek, Syrian or Jewish, to reach the markets of Mesopotamia where silk and spices could be obtained for later resale within the Roman Empire. Indeed, as was noted in the Introduction, Strabo mentioned merchants crossing the Euphrates (presumably at or near

Figure 5.1 The Euphrates river from the Roman villa, Zeugma, Turkey. Photo by Frank Strk

Zeugma) and then travelling toward Babylon through the area between the Tigris and the Euphrates (see Figure 5.1).[4] Thus, at the beginning and the end of the period under consideration, there was commercial traffic using this route; there is no compelling reason to believe that it ceased in the intervening time.

Certainly, there were merchants active in Spasinou Charax, the terminus of the Palmyrene route, besides those who came there from Palmyra. Pliny, for example, refers to *nostri negotiatores* ('our merchants') who were active at Charax:[5] he is not likely to have used such an expression to describe Palmyrenes, but it is quite possible that these could have been Greek or Italian merchants from within the empire. There is also evidence of Jewish merchants active in this area; indeed, some of these merchants reached positions of power and influence in the kingdom of Mesene comparable to those held there by Palmyrenes.[6] Josephus, for example, mentions a Jewish merchant named Ananias who had access to the palace at Spasinou Charax and was able to teach his religion to some of the palace women and to a prince of Adiabene resident at that time in Charax.[7] Clearly, in order to have such influence he must have been highly regarded; although there is no evidence that he held a post comparable to the Palmyrene satraps of Tylos and Phorath, he was still obviously a man of influence. Evidently it was not just the Palmyrene merchants who were powerful and influential in Mesene, but others also. In the absence of any evidence for such merchants participating in the Palmyrene caravans, it would seem reasonable to assume that Ananias and those like him traded with Mesene by means of the Euphrates route.

The 'Silk Road'

While indeed many merchants may have used the Zeugma route to gain access to Mesopotamia and the Gulf, the Euphrates crossing could also have been used to gain access to the overland silk routes into Central Asia. The major termini of these overland routes seem to have been the cities of Nisibis, where the activity of silk merchants is attested, and Ctesiphon/Seleucia on the Tigris, from which the Persian royal road, utilised also by the Parthians, ascended to the summer capital of Ecbatana and thence into Central Asia.[8]

Seleucia on the Tigris is mentioned as the site of a community of both Greek and Palmyrene merchants in a Palmyrene inscription from AD 19, which honours a benefactor of the Temple of Bel at Palmyra.[9] Seleucia is not on the route of the normal Palmyrene commerce between Palmyra and Charax on the Gulf, and so presumably at this stage the Palmyrenes and the Greeks with them in Seleucia were interested in overland traffic coming along the Persian royal road from Central Asia. While Palmyrene interest soon shifted exclusively to the maritime route via the Gulf,[10] this inscription does demonstrate that there were trade opportunities of some sort in Seleucia on the Tigris. It may even be that, after the Palmyrenes had moved on, the Greek merchants in this city continued to trade there with caravans coming along the road from Ecbatana and Central Asia. Certainly these Greeks are not mentioned in connection with the Palmyrenes again in any of the Palmyrene caravan inscriptions. In any case, the existence of Seleucia as a place of trade can be considered proven, and with it the existence of overland trade entering Mesopotamia from Asia.

Similarly, Talmudic literature attests the presence at Nisibis of Jewish silk merchants,[11] although no accurate date can be given for this mention. It is clear, however, that in a later period, when Nisibis lay near the boundary between the Roman and Sassanid realms, it was an important centre for international trade. In the treaty which was dictated to the Persians by the Romans in AD 299, it was specified that Nisibis, within Roman territory, would be the sole point of trade.[12] It would seem reasonable that if Nisibis was an important trade centre at that time that it could also have been one in the preceding period. We can thus postulate the existence of an overland trade route from Central Asia entering Mesopotamia, as Nisibis by its location cannot possibly have been involved in any other silk trade than one based upon an overland route.

There is certainly one account of a merchant using the overland route into China during the Roman imperial period, well before the fall of Palmyra. Ptolemy records that the agents of one Maes Titianus, probably a Syrian merchant, made a long journey through Parthia and travelled as far as the 'Stone Tower', which must have been well into Central Asia. The case of

Maes Titianus shows clearly that, despite the predominance of the Palmyrene maritime trade in our sources, there nonetheless existed opportunities to obtain silk from the overland route through Central Asia. The optimal time for this trade to have commenced is probably after the Chinese general P'an Chao established control over what the Chinese called the 'Western Regions', that is the Tarim basin, in AD 74. This would have increased the opportunities for the free flow of silk along these routes,[13] and it is to this period that the expedition of Maes Titianus is probably to be allocated.

Maes himself seems to have been a Syrian by his Semitic name; he is described by Ptolemy as a Macedonian and so it is most likely that he was a Syrian who held citizenship of one of the Greek cities of Syria.[14] Ptolemy provides a brief account of the expedition, stating that he sent some of his agents toward China and that they went as far as a place called the 'Stone Tower', which lay on the border of China:

> Μάην γάρ φησί τινα, τὸν καὶ Τιτιανὸν, ἄνδρα Μακεδόνα καὶ ἐκ πατρὸς ἔμπορον, συγγράψασθαι τὴν ἀναμέτρησιν, οὐδ' αὐτὸν ἐπελθόντα, διαπεμψάμενον δέ τινας πρὸς τοὺς Σῆρας.
>
> For it is said that a certain Maes, who is also called Titianus, a Macedonian and a merchant like his father, had recorded the distance (i.e. to the Stone Tower), not having gone himself, but having sent certain men to China.[15]

It is evident from this account that, while most merchants would not have gone so far as Maes' agents did, the overland route to Central Asia was known and used during the period under consideration. Moreover, it is clear (as will be discussed in the next section) that there was mostly free access for Romans on this route: there is nothing to indicate that the Parthians or any other jealous 'middleman' tried to stop Maes' expedition.

Despite the feeling of some scholars that it was of only limited importance during this time,[16] the overland route seems to have existed as an important alternative supply of silk during the predominance of Palmyra. Indeed, the prominence which the Palmyrene trade appears to have in our period need be nothing more than an accident of our sources. There is really no way of knowing which, if either, of the two 'silk routes', the overland or the maritime, was the most used and prosperous one, as our sources reveal absolutely nothing about the real volume of trade on these or any other routes. Both were in use in the imperial period, and it is likely that the demand for silk at Rome was more than enough to sustain several routes of commerce.

Hatra

The Parthian vassal kingdom of Hatra flourished in the second and third centuries AD, as is attested by an impressive corpus of over three hundred Aramaic inscriptions found at the site. Situated in the desert between the Tigris and Euphrates rivers at a perennial source of water, Hatra would have been on or near the Mesopotamian trade route described by Strabo,[17] and so may have benefited by trade using this route. There is, however, no evidence of urban development at Hatra until the beginning of the second century, so if Strabo's route did affect Hatra's development, it did so slowly. The inscriptions reveal that Hatra grew in importance in the interval between the expeditions of Trajan, when it was a relatively unimportant oasis town, and the expedition of Severus, by which time it was a major city.[18] Thus, even if the trade passing between the rivers had an effect on the eventual development of Hatra, this trade continued for some time before causing any such development, and thus cannot be adduced as the major reason for the city's rise.

Indeed, despite the fact that Hatra has been called a 'caravan city',[19] the evidence does not support this. On the contrary, it shows that Hatra derived its wealth not from the caravan trade but from its position as a religious centre, the regional centre for the worship of the Sun god. The vast majority of the inscriptions from Hatra are religious in nature, referring to dedications made to the gods of the city,[20] and in his account of the Severan sieges of the city Dio Cassius states that its wealth was derived from great numbers of rich offerings to the Sun god.[21] The common ascription of Hatra's prosperity to the caravan trade would thus appear not to be justified by the evidence; it would seem that the city's role as a religious centre was far more significant in its rise to wealth.

Nonetheless, there remains at least the possibility that Hatra had some role in the caravan trade. There exist some inscriptions from the city which mention relations with far-flung sites in the Tigris-Euphrates region. Although they do not mention trade specifically, they indicate that the kingdom of Hatra maintained communications with some centres of trade and there thus may have been trade passing through Hatra. One such inscription mentions two locations, QRQBS and ḤSPS, identified as Qarqabes and Haspisa, two towns in the vicinity of Nisibis.[22] This would indicate that there was communication between Hatra and the area of Nisibis, where (as we have seen) the caravan trade with the East was active. It is thus at least possible that Hatra derived some trade from the overland silk route from central Asia, although clear evidence is lacking. If such trade did exist, it would presumably have been forwarded by Hatrene merchants along the track which linked Hatra with the Euphrates region in the area of Maskane, a route attested in another Hatrene inscription, although again without any specific reference to trade.[23]

Thus, we can admit only the possibility that Hatra was involved in the caravan trade, as there is no concrete evidence which unequivocally associates it with this commerce. Whatever commercial role Hatra may have had, it was undoubtedly disrupted by the rise of the Sassanid Empire, just as the commerce of Palmyra experienced similar difficulties for the same reason. Hatra's reaction to the Persian threat was to seek an alliance with Rome, as is attested by three Latin inscriptions mentioning the names of Roman auxiliary cohorts at Hatra.[24] In the end, however, this proved of no avail and Hatra fell to the Persians in about AD 240. Apparently, the city was destroyed and never again inhabited.

From the Euphrates to the Mediterranean: the trade in Roman Syria

Whatever the nature of Hatra's participation in the caravan trade with the East, it is clear that there were other trade routes in use in Mesopotamia besides the Palmyrene route from the Gulf up the Euphrates and then across the desert to Palmyra. However, the way in which the goods were brought from the Euphrates crossing through Syria and thence to the markets of the empire is not at all obvious. In areas such as the desert where there would have been little traffic beside the caravan trade present the commercial traffic is easier to trace. When we get to the more inhabited parts of Roman Syria, however, the sheer volume of evidence of everyday life which exists for these areas tends to obscure evidence for the caravan traffic. Nonetheless, there are a few indications which allow us to surmise at least what happened to the goods after they had reached the heart of the Syrian province.

Goods passing from both the Euphrates route and from the Palmyrene one may well have been brought through the city of Emesa, as several routes converge on this important city in the Orontes valley. Rostovtzeff thought that Emesa may have been another 'caravan city':[25] while such a conclusion is probably excessive it remains possible that Emesa may have been involved in the forwarding of goods to the markets of the empire. However it was that they crossed Roman Syria, many of the goods were probably eventually forwarded on to the great city of Antioch on the Orontes. In this place, the goods which had been brought there from both the Euphrates route and from Palmyra seem to have been subjected to the Roman 25 per cent import duty imposed upon eastern imports, the *tetarte*. An inscription in the Palmyrene corpus, which has already been noted, mentions one Marcus Aemilius Asclepiades, a councillor of Antioch and a collector of the 25 per cent tax (*tetartones*).[26] Presumably, therefore, Antioch was a collection point for this tax, and the goods were collected in a public warehouse there just as they were in Alexandria and the government's share was removed. Here also, presumably, the goods were sold either by the merchants who had brought them or by the government to further merchants who would then forward them by ship to Rome or to other points where such wares might be sold.[27] Of course, there may well have been other sites in Syria where the *tetarte* was extracted in addition to Antioch.

It is probable that this process took place before any reprocessing was done, as it would seem foolish to spend time and effort respinning the raw silk only to have the government remove a significant proportion of it. Far more likely is that the raw silk was brought directly to the place where the duty was extracted, and then sold to silk merchants who reprocessed it either in the east or further afield. Such reprocessing is attested in various cities of Roman Syria. One city that may have been involved in this trade is Edessa, which was possibly involved in the reprocessing of various goods, especially silk.[28] Certainly, from the literary references it would seem that the Phoenician city of Tyre continued to enjoy its ancient reputation as a place of cloth dyeing and manufacture.[29] It would be most surprising if this trade did not make use of the supply of silk being brought through both Palmyra and the Euphrates route.

Thus, it is quite clear that the eastern long-distance trade was present in Roman Syria, and may have had some effect on the local economy there, although such effect may have been limited and is in any case difficult to quantify. Nonetheless, the long-distance trade is attested at Nisibis, Seleucia, Batnae and far into Central Asia, showing that there was an overland route which reached Mesopotamia from Central Asia. This route thus provided an alternative to the route dominated by the Palmyrenes. Simply because we lack spectacular ruins or an impressive corpus of evidence should not mean that we should discount the importance of the overland route. In the absence of any information from the ancient world about the volume of the eastern long-distance trade, we can have no way of knowing which route was in fact more important. Similarly, the common assumption that such places as Batnae and Nisibis gained prominence only after the destruction of Palmyra is unwarranted, and unsupported by the evidence. Ptolemy's account of the expedition of Maes Titianus shows that the northern routes were indeed active in the period prior to the fall of Palmyra.

There is thus an important opportunity for the investigation of the political effects of this trade which should not be overlooked. When Rome made war upon its eastern neighbours, Parthia and then Sassanid Persia, the opposing armies often clashed in the area of northern Mesopotamia and the Euphrates valley, the very area through which this trade passed. Accordingly, many scholars have postulated that the trade routes were an important strategic consideration between the two powers, and may have even been the motive behind some of the military expeditions mounted by the warring parties.

Trade motives and Roman relations with Parthia

We have seen in the preceding section that there is sufficient evidence to show the existence of an overland trade crossing the Parthian Empire by which silk and other goods could be brought into Roman territory. The viability of these northern routes is, of course, entirely dependent upon sufficiently peaceful conditions which would allow the passage of goods along the trade routes.

In this respect, the northern routes suffered from a serious liability: they crossed the territory of Rome's main rivals, Parthia and the Persian Sassanid state which succeeded it. In time of war, then, it is quite possible that the trade could be severely curtailed. It is also at least possible that the exploitation of this trade could be used by the Parthians as some kind of economic lever against Rome, and that the Romans might consequently have the control of the trade routes and the trade thereon as one of their war aims in any campaign against the Parthians.

Among these military conflicts between Rome and its eastern neighbours, perhaps the most important, and indeed the one to which trade is most commonly attributed as a primary motivation, is Trajan's expedition against Parthia in AD 114–117. Even more than with other episodes in the relationship between Rome and Parthia, many scholars have tried to place commercial motives at the forefront of the reasons for this campaign.[30] These scholars assume that Trajan acted to destroy a Parthian trade monopoly on silk or other goods, or at least to remove any Parthian interference in the trade. While it is not proposed to provide a causation of Trajan's campaigns in the East in this work, the relevance, or lack of it, of the eastern luxury trade to his motivation must be examined. It should also be noted that the arguments raised in discussing Trajan's expedition will be pertinent to the other expeditions too, and so allow us to decide whether or not any of them might have been trade-related.

Parthian participation in the overland trade

The assumption is often made that, because luxury goods, and particularly silk, were transported across Parthian territory in order to reach the Mediterranean markets, the Parthians therefore exploited this opportunity and monopolised the trade. This view then gives rise to the idea of the 'Parthian intermediary' ruthlessly exploiting the trade and fixing prices, which in turn provides the cause for Roman attacks on Parthia.[31] There is, however, very little evidence to support the idea of the Parthians monopolising the silk trade or exploiting it in any way other than the exaction of normal and expected municipal tolls and levies. The only literary references to an attempted Parthian monopoly are found in Chinese records. The *Hou Han-Shou*, or Annals of the Later Han Dynasty, record an incident in which Chinese ambassadors were dissuaded from travelling to Rome by the Parthians because they wished to monopolise the silk trade.[32] In this account it is related that while in the Arabian Gulf region in AD 97, the Chinese ambassador Kan Ying was told that the *sea* voyage to the Roman realm was too far, and was thus persuaded to abandon his attempt to reach Roman lands. It has been assumed that the Parthians avoided mentioning the much shorter land route instead of the otherwise unattested sea route (which presumably would be around the Arabian peninsula) in order to keep the Chinese and Romans from coming into direct contact for the purposes of trade.[33]

In another reference, it is related that the Romans wished to send embassies to the Chinese but they were prevented from doing so by the Parthians, who wished to keep the trade in Chinese silks to themselves.[34] While this may well reflect Chinese perceptions of the situation, it will become apparent that there could in fact have been no real monopoly of the silk trade by the Parthians, certainly not of the exploitative type postulated by many. It must be remembered that there were many more difficulties on the road to China than the Parthians alone, and it may be that these, as much as any Parthian desire to exploit the silk trade, were the reasons that there was no direct contact between the Chinese and Roman governments. Even if the Romans had been able to send an embassy to the Chinese court, it is not likely, based on Roman dealings with other states, that trade would be high on the agenda. While the Chinese may well have thought in terms of trade, as their records seem to indicate, military matters would much more probably have been of interest to the Romans. It is hardly surprising that the Parthians wished to prevent any contact of *that* nature.

In any case, we *do* have an account of someone who was able to traverse Parthian lands along the overland route toward China, which indicates that there was no attempt by the Parthians to prevent contact between Roman subjects and the Chinese. In the previous section, the case of Maes Titianus was discussed. This Syrian merchant was able to travel, apparently unmolested by the Parthians, deep into Central Asia as far as a place known as the 'Stone Tower', unknown but certainly well past Parthian territory and approaching the area of Chinese influence.[35] It is quite clear from this that, whatever the Chinese perception of the situation may have been, the Parthians in fact made no attempt to prevent Maes from contacting the Chinese or other traders along the overland route.[36] If the Parthians had wished to prevent the Romans from obtaining direct access to Chinese silks, it is inconceivable that they would have allowed a Roman merchant such as Maes to pass directly through the middle of their realm. Evidently, there was free access for Roman merchants through the Parthian realm (at least in time of peace), and the idea of a Parthian monopoly on the trade in Chinese silk through their realm should be rejected.

Thus it is clear that if one wishes to assert the existence of a Parthian trade monopoly, one must both explain the episode of Maes Titianus, which has not been done, and be sure of the accuracy of the Chinese records and the identification of the place names contained therein.[37] Even if the accuracy of the Chinese records is generally accepted, however, the identification of Western place names and realms in these annals is still highly disputed, and it may well be that the whole episode concerning Kan Ying has been completely misinterpreted. Certainly the reference to a sea passage rather than the more normal overland journey raises many questions which should be answered before this reference could even be considered as evidence of Parthian trade policy. Could, for instance, the officials to whom Kan Ying spoke, whoever they might have been, have reasonably expected to keep the existence of the land route secret in an area where Palmyrene merchants were active? In fact, the most likely place on the Gulf for Kan Ying to have been told this information would be in the kingdom of Mesene, where Palmyrene merchants were very prominent and seem to have served in many official capacities under the kings of Mesene.[38] These Palmyrenes would have been most eager to make commercial contacts with the Chinese, and so it would seem most unlikely that Kan Ying would have been misdirected in this way. Further, if indeed there was no other way of bringing in the silk except through Parthian territory, what difference could it have made if the Romans and Chinese *did* come into contact with one another? Why indeed, if the Parthians had sought to prevent Roman–Chinese contact, would they have taken Kan Ying as far as the Gulf before turning him back, rather than just block his passage as soon as he entered Parthian territory? All these points raise serious questions about the usefulness of these Chinese records with regard to Parthian trade policy. Even if, as Graf concludes, the Chinese annals provide a generally accurate picture of the political situation of the first century, there are enough inconsistencies and difficulties to make the possibility of a Parthian trade monopoly extremely problematical. When Ptolemy's account of Maes Titianus is taken into account, it would seem clear that any such monopoly was ephemeral, if indeed it ever existed at all.

The impossibility of a Parthian silk monopoly

There is in fact a great deal of evidence to show that there could have been no Parthian monopoly on silk, and consequently no coherent trade-based motive for Roman campaigns against Parthia. First, there could have been no monopoly at all because silk was available by sea from India, to which it had presumably come from China. The *Periplus Maris Erythraei* clearly refers to silk being available in Indian ports.[39] Accordingly, there can have been no Parthian monopoly as long as there were other routes to import silk which did not cross Parthian territory at any point.[40] It would have been quite impossible for the Parthians to have fixed prices and controlled the trade as long as the silk could be obtained from elsewhere. Clearly the alleged Parthian monopoly on the silk trade can never in fact have existed, and if we reject the existence of such a monopoly, the supposed commercial motive for Trajan's expedition and other Roman wars against Parthia evaporates with it.

Indeed, if there had been any consistent attempt by the Parthians to exploit the caravan trade, let alone to monopolise it, it would be reasonable to expect that there would be extensive remains of such things as roads, bridges and caravanserais to channel and protect the caravan traffic. There is, however, very little archaeological evidence for the construction of such installations. There are, indeed, many remains of such constructions from the Sassanid period and later, reflecting the concern of those regimes with exploiting the caravan trade to the fullest possible extent, but none from the period under consideration.[41]

It is true that Isidore of Charax in his *Parthian Stations* does refer on two occasions to a 'royal station',[42] but there is nothing to show that these are in fact government-built caravanserais. On the contrary, the adjective *basilikos* ('royal') indicates that these stations were originally built for royal communications rather than for the use of merchants. The two stations, Alagma and Thillada Mirada, are situated on the Euphrates and the absence of other stations described as *basilikos* seems to show that these had once been stations on the Achaemenid royal road which Isidore included in his itinerary.[43] While merchants may certainly have made use of them, there is no evidence to show, and no reason to believe, that they were constructed by the Parthian government to encourage commerce.

One reason that gives good basis to doubt even the possibility of such exploitation is the fragmented nature of the Parthian state during most of the Roman imperial period. During the first century the Parthians experienced bitter dynastic strife which was exacerbated and encouraged by the Roman support of pretenders.[44] In addition to, or perhaps because of, this strife, many dependent kingdoms and regions which formed part of the Parthian realm, such as Mesene, Elymais and Susa, were able to achieve a considerable measure of independence in this period.[45] As was discussed earlier, Mesene in particular, and to a lesser extent other realms, seem to have conducted their own relations with Rome independently of Parthian authority. Once again, these facts demonstrate the great difficulty the Parthians would have experienced if they had tried to establish a monopoly over the trade coming through their borders.

The notion of an exploitative monopoly by the Parthians over the trade passing through their territory is entirely speculative and is essentially devoid of supporting evidence. Even if the Parthians had the inclination and the capability to exclude the Romans from the trade and thus to raise the price of the commodities artificially, it would not have been possible to do so. There could have been no monopoly, as the *Periplus* makes it clear that silk could be obtained from Indian ports and shipped directly to Egypt, avoiding Parthian territory altogether. Thus, if the Parthians had attempted to raise the price of silk, Roman merchants would simply have sought their silk in Alexandria. If the possibility of a Parthian trade monopoly is removed, as it clearly must be, then the possibility of a commercial motivation for Rome's Parthian wars must also be removed. Even if Roman foreign policy was ever affected by mercantile interests, there is no apparent motive of this type in the case of Roman relations with the Parthian Empire.

The significance of the trade in northern Syria and Mesopotamia

Despite the clear lack of evidence for any significant Parthian participation in the trade, we may still legitimately conclude that there was a certain amount of trade which passed over the overland routes from Central Asia into Roman

Syria, and also some trade which came up the length of the Euphrates from the Arabian Gulf and thence to Antioch or its region. The evidence for the existence of these routes, although scattered and limited, is nonetheless reasonably solid. We can have no way of knowing the volumes of trade which passed upon these routes. As has been seen in cities such as Petra and Palmyra, however, there is enough evidence to surmise that the trade acquired a certain significance in those places, and thus it may also have done in Roman Syria. As there was a proportion of the eastern 'luxury' trade which passed this way, the Roman cities of Syria and Palestine would presumably have seen a good deal of the merchandise of the eastern commerce passing through.

Nonetheless, the routes of northern Syria and Mespotamia would not have been without their difficulties as far as commercial traffic is concerned. We might reasonably suppose, however, that the existence of such an obvious and ancient route such as that along the Euphrates would not have been overlooked by merchants, and that consequently this route would have received extensive use. However, this route would have become untenable during any of the frequent wars in the area. Even this may not always have unduly affected the use of the route compared to other trade routes: after all, we have already noted that Palmyrene commerce also probably ground to a halt in time of war between Rome and Parthia or Persia. Although we are forced to a large extent to rely upon supposition, it would seem most likely that the eastern trade involved traffic coming from the Gulf or from the overland 'Silk Road' and then up the valley of the Euphrates to Syria throughout the Classical period of its existence.

One area of this trade that is clear, and reflects the conclusions drawn in other areas of this study, is that the Romans (or for that matter the Parthians) were never sufficiently interested in the eastern long-distance trade to allow it to dictate their foreign policy in any major way. No doubt, just as in Egypt and probably in the other areas that were traversed by this commerce, the Romans were happy to collect the *tetarte* and other duties, and might have even taken steps to protect them, but as a foreign policy imperative the trade was not a consideration. As has been shown, all the evidence which is from time to time put forward to show that Romans or Parthians were motivated by the interests of the trade in the formulation of their foreign policy in fact teaches nothing of the sort. There is no compelling evidence whatever to believe that Trajan's Parthian war, or indeed any of the other Roman or Parthian military adventures in the area, were ever motivated by the interests of the eastern long-distance commerce.

While it is difficult to draw conclusions about the nature or the significance of the trade in Syria to the extent that is possible elsewhere, this may be accounted for by the fact that it is more submerged in other activity in these northern regions than it is elsewhere. This fact, however, may also mean that the economic significance of the trade in this area was rather less than in an area such as Palmyra where the trade stood out more because of the lack of other activity. Such conclusions, however, must remain only conjecture. In an area of study where the waters are often muddy and the evidence often scattered and inconclusive, we must concede that in the study of the trade in Roman Syria and Mesopotamia this is particularly true.

6

THE LONG-DISTANCE TRADE AND THE IMPERIAL GOVERNMENT

In the course of this study, it has repeatedly been found that the Roman government did not allow its foreign policy imperatives to be deflected by the needs of the eastern long-distance trade. Indeed, the only policy which the government can consistently be found to have held with respect to this commerce was one of extracting as much tax money as possible from it. No act of Roman policy in the East need necessarily be assigned to the requirements of the trade, and none of the public works which were constructed for the trade can be attributed to any other policy motive than the desire to collect taxes.

Despite this, there are some indications in Roman literature that concern was expressed about the amount of money that was being 'wasted' on eastern goods, or about the way in which the trade enriched potential enemies of the empire even as it impoverished the empire itself. These concerns would appear to stand in opposition to the general argument of this book, that the Romans (by their actions at least) had no real concern about the eastern long-distance trade, and were interested in it only as a potential source of tax revenue. Indeed, these very concerns have from time to time been used as a basis to support views of an active Roman interest in the trade. Several scholars have argued that a Roman desire to reduce the outflow of coin expended in trade lay behind their alleged 'economic policies' by which they strove to remove 'middlemen' from the commerce and attempted to concentrate the trade in Roman hands.[1] Although we have seen that no such policies were ever put into practice, it will still be necessary to explain these apparent concerns expressed by Roman writers. Was there a real concern about an outflow of coin to lands beyond the empire, and was such a concern justified? If such a concern did exist, why did the Roman government not act to stop or reduce the eastern commerce?

The balance of payments

It has often been noted that the eastern trade must have cost a significant amount of money, and it has been suggested that the outflow of coin to pay for these 'luxuries' was, or should have been, an area of grave concern for the imperial government. In the Introduction, it was noted that the goods imported in this commerce were indeed expensive, and presumably at least a proportion of the costs of these items must have gone to the lands beyond the empire from which the goods came. There certainly would have been, at least to some extent, an outflow of coin involved in the trade, as the Indian coin hoards already discussed demonstrate. It is equally certain that the Romans were aware of this and occasionally complained about it. Were these complaints therefore justified, and what *was* in fact the damage being done, if any, to the empire by the loss of coin to Persia, Arabia and India?

Roman complaints about the cost of the trade

The Roman writers Pliny and Tacitus provide us with our best and most commonly cited examples of Roman concern about the amount of money being lost in the eastern commerce. Tacitus, for example, described a letter from Tiberius on the prevalence of luxurious living in his day, in which he mentioned

> illa feminarum propria, quis lapidum causa pecuniae nostrae ad externas aut hostilis gentis transferuntur?
>
> that particular (luxury) of women, for which for the sake of jewels our wealth is transferred to foreign or hostile countries?[2]

This statement (as will be seen) has been often taken along with other similar references as proof of an imperial concern over the amount of money that was being lost in foreign trade. Similarly, Pliny mentioned on two occasions the volume of money which was being expended in the eastern trade, and this too has been taken to be proof of opposition to the trade from within the Roman government due to concern about the drain of money. In the first instance, Pliny noted that India absorbed more than 50 million *sestertii* per year paid for trade goods:

> digna res, nullo anno minus HS $|\overline{\mathrm{D}}|$ imperii nostri exhauriente India et merces remittente quae apud nos centiplicato ueneant.
>
> It is an important matter, since India in no year drains less than 50 million *sestertii* from our empire and returns goods which are sold among us at one hundred times the cost.[3]

In the other reference, Pliny gives a different figure, this time totalling the amount spent on trade goods in all of Rome's eastern commerce as opposed to only that which was sent to India:

> minimaque computatione miliens centena milia sestertium annis omnibus India et Seres et paeninsula illa imperio nostro adimunt – tanti nobis deliciae et feminae constant.

> And by the smallest computation India, China and that peninsula (i.e. Arabia) take 100 million *sestertii* from our empire every year – so much do our luxuries and our women cost us.[4]

As has already been noted, the figures which Pliny actually quotes do not give us any real basis for calculating the volume of the eastern trade in this period, as they probably represent more Stoic moralising than usable trade statistics. However, for the purposes which we have at the moment, these quotations are useful, for they *do* reveal at least a professed concern among the Roman upper classes about the volume of silver coin which was being sent to India and other places.

Thus, despite the imprecision of Pliny's figures, there would still seem to be reasonable evidence that some elements in Rome, perhaps even the emperor himself, were seriously concerned about the drain of finance caused by the eastern trade. If such concerns *were* apparent in Roman thought of the imperial period, why do we not then find these concerns acted upon in the field of policy? If the emperors really were concerned about the outflow of coin to India and elsewhere, why do they appear to have done nothing about it?

Was there an 'adverse balance of trade' in the eastern commerce?

When the evidence is examined, it will in fact be found that the Romans do not appear to have had much to worry about concerning any outflow of coin arising from the eastern trade. First, we should note that by no means all of the commerce was conducted in coin. In fact, according to the *Periplus Maris Erythraei* a substantial proportion of the eastern commerce was conducted on an exchange system, either by direct barter or by the sale of export goods from Egypt.[5] Judging by the account of the trade as given in the *Periplus*, the 'balance of trade' problem does not appear to have been as serious as has been suggested. While it is certainly true that some areas, especially southern India, expected payment in cash or bullion, a large proportion of the trade would nonetheless have been paid for by the export of goods from Egypt, as well as wines, metals and other items from various areas of the empire.

It also must be borne in mind that a large proportion of the funds expended on the items of the eastern trade would have remained inside the empire, in the hands of merchants, manufacturers, reprocessors and indeed the government itself. In the Introduction, the importance of the reprocessing trade was emphasised, and it was shown that the value of items offered for final sale to the public was often much greater than that of the raw goods imported from the East.[6] This is very important, for it means that the bulk of the money expended on the purchase of luxury goods in Rome and in other markets did *not* go to 'middlemen' and merchants outside the empire: instead, it remained in the hands of Roman subjects. Added to the proportion of the price kept by reprocessors, the merchants and shipmasters themselves who conveyed the goods to the empire would have absorbed a significant portion of the final sale price. In addition (as will be seen in the next section) the revenue accruing to the government from each sale was also likely to be substantial.

Thus, it would appear that the vast bulk of the amount actually paid in cash at Rome and elsewhere in the empire for the items of the eastern trade in fact never left the Roman Empire. As has already been pointed out, the vast majority of 'middlemen' in the trade were in fact Romans,[7] so therefore the money which Tiberius complained Rome's women were wasting on jewellery for the most part remained in Roman hands. Indeed, a good part of it probably ended up as imperial revenue in one form or another. Accordingly, we can find little real support for the apparent concern about currency drain found in Pliny and Tacitus here, as much of the amount which they said was being spent on foreign luxuries must have remained within the empire.

Nonetheless, there was at least some drain of coinage, as the *Periplus* is clear that the major commodity required to purchase the pepper of Muziris and Nelkynda in southern India was coin, and this is amply confirmed by the presence of Roman coin hoards in the area. However, even in this case some perspective is in order: the coin hoards which have been found in Dacia and Germany are considerably larger than any found in India, so it would seem reasonable that the money which was being sent to the tribes of these areas in subsidies was at least as much a drain on finance as was the eastern trade.[8]

Another factor which must be taken into consideration is that many of the coins which were removed from the empire in the course of trade would have eventually found their way back in. This effect would have occurred due to the superior fineness and recognition which Roman coins enjoyed. Thus, anyone from outside the empire who wished to do business within it would have first to obtain Roman coins. In this way, there would have been a steady return flow of coins along the arteries of trade leading from the East into the empire.[9] Thus, while we must acknowledge that some coin was lost in the course of the eastern trade, we must also recognise that such loss was not as severe as might have been thought. Indeed, even if it had been a serious problem, it would seem that the Romans did not understand the fact, or at least did not care to do anything about it. On the contrary, as we have already seen throughout this study, the Romans built roads, caravan stations and ports in the Eastern Desert of Egypt and provided military protection for the caravans: actions which, it would seem, were designed to encourage the commerce with the East, not discourage it.

Thus, there would appear to be something of a contradiction between professed Roman concerns about the trade, the actual situation regarding the loss of coinage, and the actions which the Romans took with regard to the commerce. The question then must now be asked: if the Romans were not really concerned about the loss of gold and silver bullion to areas outside the empire, and indeed had no real reason to be concerned, why then were such pronouncements of concern about the loss of currency made?

Roman moralism and the eastern commerce

One notable fact about the pronouncements made by Tiberius (in Tacitus) and Pliny is that the remarks appear in the general context of complaining about luxurious living, and that women in particular are singled out as particularly culpable in this regard. In the Tacitus reference, for instance, Tiberius had been remarking upon a contemporary taste for all things luxurious, not just the goods of the eastern trade. Thus, the context of his comment is not that of fiscal concern but of condemning *luxuria*, and it is in this context that the statement must be understood. Similarly the remarks of Pliny can be understood in the same light: he was not complaining about financial problems of the empire; rather, he was moralising about the great cost to the empire of the *luxuria* of many of its citizens.

Similar sentiments are found in other areas of Roman literature. While it is difficult to draw firm conclusions from such source material, it is nonetheless among the works of the Latin elegists like Propertius and Ovid that references to eastern luxury goods are particularly common, and it is among these poets that the link between these goods and *luxuria* is most clearly established. A dominant strain in these references is that luxury-loving women are especially fond of these items, although this strain is not confined to the elegists, as has already been seen in the Pliny and Tacitus references quoted above. This association of *luxuria* and the desire for jewels and other such goods with women in particular is seen in the following lines from the *Ars Amatoria* of Ovid:

> Vos quoque non caris aures onerate lapillis,
> Quos legit in uiridi decolor Indus aqua
>
> You also do not burden your ears with stones
> Which the dark Indian gathers from the green water[10]

In this particular instance, Ovid's *praeceptor amoris* describes the supposed taste of women for such gemstones and claims to eschew it. Thus he adopts a pose of opposition to the excessive use of luxury goods, but at the same time is implying that women were very attached to such things. Of course, the stance Ovid takes on any given subject in his poems will depend entirely upon the particular 'pose' he has taken as narrator in that poem. Thus, we are not surprised to find a different attitude to expensive eastern items taken in other references. In one such case, for example, Ovid advises women to use a makeup which had frankincense and myrrh as important ingredients.[11] However, despite this, it would appear that the dominant strain in Roman literature, from both historians and elegists, is that the vice of *luxuria*, and the eastern goods which catered to that vice, were especially associated with women and, by implication, effeminacy in men.

Throughout virtually the entirety of Roman literature of the republic and principate, the exaltation of the *mos maiorum* and the severe, self-controlled heroes of Rome's mythical past was paramount. We see this reflected in Roman poetry, in speeches in the courts and in the succession of sumptuary laws which were enacted at various times through the years. In all these cases, the effeminate, adulterous and luxurious behaviour of the 'current generation' is contrasted with the upright behaviour of the heroes of older times.[12] The association of the vice of *luxuria* with women, and therefore by implication with *mollitia*, or effeminacy, should be seen in the same light as other Roman moralistic writings which exalt 'traditional' Roman values over the behaviour of contemporary Romans. Accusations of *mollitia* in various Roman sources are often characterised by associations of the victim with the use of items of the eastern trade, such as silk or perfumes.[13] For this reason, the complaints of Pliny and Tacitus about the eastern trade should be understood in the same way: they are far more typical laments about the contemporary taste for *luxuria*, associated here as elsewhere with the use of eastern goods, than they are complaints about a financial problem.

Thus, it is clear that those statements in Roman literature which have sometimes been taken as indicative of a concern about currency drain are in fact no such thing. Instead, these comments are concerned with opposition to the 'vice' of *luxuria*, which was seen as effeminate and 'un-Roman'. There was accordingly no attempt to stop the drain of currency to the East because (as we have seen) such a currency drain was far less serious than has been thought. Moreover, the Roman statements which have often been taken as proof of such concern have been shown to be something entirely different. We are, however, still left with a question: why did the Romans still do nothing to try to affect the incoming trade, given that they appear to have associated its goods with *luxuria*, a vice which they felt was destructive to their empire?

The reason appears to lie in the difference between Roman public pronouncements and actual policy. The pronouncements of Pliny and Tacitus should be understood as a reflection of typical Roman morality; as the rejection of 'luxurious' contemporary behaviour in favour of the *mos maiorum*. Similar concerns are expressed in the long series of sumptuary laws which were enacted throughout the republic and the empire. It is noteworthy, however, that these laws were enacted again and again, yet invariably seem to have been passed over and openly ignored within a very short time of their enactment. It would seem that the emperors, in their enactment of sumptuary laws and such like, were striving more for the *appearance* of opposing *luxuria* and other vices than they were striving actually to put a stop to it. The very fact that the emperors allowed the eastern commerce to continue unimpaired throughout all this period would seem to be adequate proof that these sumptuary laws, not to mention the pronouncements of Tiberius as recorded by Tacitus and the complaints of Pliny, should be seen as designed only for consumption by the public and the upper classes in Rome. They reflect the desire of the emperor, and of upper-class Romans in general, to conform to what was expected of Roman morality and behaviour; they cannot be taken as any guide to the Roman government's attitude to the long-distance eastern commerce.

It thus seems that the Roman government had little reason to be concerned about the eastern long-distance trade, and indeed there does not seem to be any real evidence of such a concern. Those concerns which we do find expressed in Roman literature of one sort or another do not in fact show a desire to reduce the amount of precious metal leaving the state, as has sometimes been claimed. Instead, these statements are primarily of a moralistic nature: they profess to be concerned about the vices of *luxuria* and *mollitia*, closely associated in the Roman mind. Moreover, it would appear that even this was more for the sake of appearance rather than it actually indicating anything the Roman government intended to act upon. Statements like this, like sumptuary laws, were primarily for public consumption: they reflected what the Roman emperor was expected to do, and the values that a true Roman was expected to have. There is absolutely no indication that such sentiments would have been carried any further than this, or that any attempt would have been made to stop the eastern commerce.

Against these statements, of course, is the evidence of the facilities built for the trade in Egypt and elsewhere. If one wished to take the complaints about the trade voiced by Tacitus and Pliny seriously this would seem to present an inexplicable contradiction: why would the Roman government oppose the conduct of the trade on the one hand but then provide merchants with roads, facilities and protection on the other? However, when we understand these complaints in the way that has been outlined above, the contradiction becomes more understandable. Having provided the Roman public with the pronouncements on morality that were expected of an emperor, the government could then turn with a will to the collection of the lucrative taxes which were collected from the eastern commerce.

The extent of state revenues from the trade

We have already seen in the discussion of the trade in Egypt that the tax revenue accruing to the government from the trade was the only significant reason to account for the construction of facilities and the provision of protection to the traders involved in the commerce. However, to account for such interest and expenditure the amount of income that the government gleaned from the commerce must have been considerable. Can we therefore gain any insight into the importance that this tax income represented to the imperial government? It will be the purpose of this section to attempt to enumerate the sources of income which the eastern commerce provided to the imperial government, and then to gain some idea of the relative place of this income in the overall tax base upon which the government drew.

Sources of imperial income in the eastern trade

In this survey of the Romans' eastern trade, several instances have been noted in which traders were compelled to pay duties of one sort or another to government officials. Although the bulk of the evidence for these sources of income comes from Egypt, this is in all probability a matter of survival of sources, and it is not unreasonable to assume that similar charges applied in other areas of the commerce.

The most significant source of tax income from the eastern trade would have been the *tetarte*, the 25 per cent tax which was levied on goods being brought into the empire. As has already been noted, this tax was levied at Alexandria and (probably) Antioch, as well as at the Nabataean port of Leuke Kome. This last case, however, may have been an exceptional one designed to ensure that no Red Sea shipmasters circumvented the payment of the *tetarte* by landing their goods in Leuke Kome instead of at Berenike or Myos Hormos.[14] Given the parallel of Alexandria, other important Mediterranean seaports such as Tyre may also have been collection points for the tax. The positioning of the main collection points at such places as Alexandria and Antioch implies that all commerce coming through the East was expected to pass through such places and pay its duty there. Indeed, as has been pointed out in Chapter 2 on the Egyptian Red Sea trade, part of the purpose of the soldiers guarding the trade routes in the desert may have been to ensure that the merchants did not attempt to sell their goods before the *tetarte* was paid in Alexandria.

The sources which we have on the *tetarte* nowhere reveal the exact commodities that were taxed. It has been generally assumed that all the goods of the eastern long-distance trade were subject to this impost, but this may not in fact be the case. As was noted in the Introduction, the general category of 'luxury goods' should not necessarily be applied to all the goods of the eastern trade. Such items as myrrh and frankincense were chiefly used for religious and funerary purposes, and would not have been considered as luxury goods by the Romans.[15] It is possible that such goods as these, for example, would not have been subject to the *tetarte*.

This may be supported by the presence of the customs-collector of the *tetarte* at Leuke Kome. Pliny mentions the collection of Roman tolls at Gaza from caravans which were bringing frankincense from southern Arabia,[16] and any goods being brought from Leuke Kome into the Roman Empire would probably have passed over the Petra–Gaza road. One would have presumed that the collector of taxes and duties at Gaza would then have charged the *tetarte*, both for the land-based traffic as well as the seaborne trade from Leuke Kome. Why then would there need to have been a collector of the *tetarte* at Leuke Kome as well?

A possible answer is that the customs-collectors at Gaza mentioned by Pliny may not have been collecting the *tetarte* at all. In fact, Pliny does not specify which tax it was that they were collecting: it may very well have been some other form of *portorium*. If this is the case, and this would appear to be the only reason that it would have been necessary to place a customs-collector at Leuke Kome, then it means that the Arabian incenses which had been brought by land from southern Arabia into the empire in fact never paid the *tetarte*. It would then seem at least possible that only goods which were imported into the empire from India and further afield might have been subject to this tax. It might also be added that a rescript of Marcus Aurelius and Commodus preserved in Justinian's *Digest*, the so-called 'Alexandrian Tariff', lists those goods which were subject to *uectigal*, probably at Alexandria: myrrh is listed, but frankincense is not.[17] We should, of course, realise that nowhere is it stated in the rescript that the *tetarte*, or indeed the *uectigal Maris Rubri* mentioned by Pliny in his account of the Roman discovery of Taprobanê, is meant; the tariff could be yet another tax levied on these imported goods. The rate of taxation is not given, so it is impossible to tell.

Nonetheless, the *tetarte* must have represented a significant source of income for the imperial government. It was, however, certainly not the only way in which the eastern trade was made to contribute to the imperial coffers. For example, as has been seen in the examination of the Egyptian Red Sea trade in Chapter 2, there were several different taxes which had to be paid to convey goods from the Red Sea ports to Alexandria.[18] *P. Vindob.* G 40822 mentions some of these: upon arrival at one of the Red Sea ports, the *arabarchs* removed some goods; the rate of taxation here seems to have varied from nil to about 3 per cent, although higher rates may of course have been charged for goods not mentioned in the papyrus. Similary, duties were extracted for trade goods and supplies passing into and out of Berenike, as revealed by the ostraka recently excavated there. These ostraka appear to be the receipts and orders for the local customs-house.[19] After transportation across the Eastern Desert, the goods were then impounded in the public customs-house at Coptos until some other taxes which are not specified were paid. These taxes may or may not have been the same as the so-called Coptos tariff, which was paid to the *arabarch* to purchase passes to travel the roads of the Eastern Desert. In this case, the taxes seem to have been paid for each person and pack animal in the group, regardless of what was being carried. After this, the goods could be conveyed to Alexandria where the *tetarte* was imposed. On the way down the Nile, however, the goods would presumably have been subject to the normal *portoria* imposed on all goods making this journey, whether from inside Egypt or from outside.[20] Added to this would then have been market duties at the point of sale and *portoria* at other ports through which the goods passed prior to their final sale. Although the evidence from other areas of the commerce is nowhere near as comprehensive as that coming from Egypt, we may confidently expect that the taxes extracted from the eastern trade in those areas were of the same order as those extracted from Egypt.

Thus, it would seem that there was a wide variety of taxes and duties which were extracted from the eastern commerce. While some of these, such as local market duties, may have gone into the treasuries of local officials, it would seem that the bulk of them, especially the lucrative *tetarte*, was paid into the imperial coffers. It is, of course, quite impossible to calculate what this income would actually have been, given that we do not know what the actual volume of the trade was. However, it may be possible to gain some idea of the order of this income compared to other sources, and so determine something of the possible significance of the trade to the imperial government.

The significance of the tax income to the imperial government

It is clear that there was a variety of ways by which the Roman government obtained income from the eastern commerce. In any attempt to determine how significant this income was to the government, however, we are affected by the same factors that prevent any accurate assessment of the volume of the trade itself. There are no actual records, and any figures we possess are of very limited value. The best we can hope to achieve is to gain some insight into the relative place of these duties in the tax base of the Roman Empire.

The only way, however, by which we might hope to gain some insight into the income generated by the *tetarte* is by the use of Pliny's trade figures. As has already been discussed, this is an endeavour which is filled with peril. If, however, we assume that Pliny used imperial customs receipts or something similar to arrive at his total trade figure of 100 million *sestertii*, there could be some basis for a calculation. This would, assuming that all the goods of which Pliny spoke were subject to the *tetarte*, yield a figure of 25 million *sestertii* per year in the Flavian period. We must, however, admit the possibility that this figure could be completely misleading. If, for example, Pliny did not use the value of the goods when the *tetarte* was calculated but the actual retail value at Rome after the goods had been reprocessed, the amount gleaned by the *tetarte* would be significantly less. On the other hand, if Pliny was describing only the amount of cash that was being spent and not taking into account those goods which had been purchased in barter transactions, the figure for the *tetarte* would be considerably larger. Thus, the figure could be anything from 10 million *sestertii* to perhaps 50 million, and that is only if we assume that Pliny's figures were approximately accurate, which is by no means certain.

Nonetheless, we now have a figure which we might compare with what we know of the tax income of the empire in the early principate. Suetonius, for example, stated that the tribute paid by all three Gallic provinces after Caesar's conquest of Gaul was 40 million *sestertii*.[21] Thus, an income from the *tetarte* in the Flavian period of between 10 million and 50 million is clearly not an inconsiderable sum: we might reasonably expect that the Roman government would take steps to ensure that this income continued to flow. Thus, even though we should rightly be extremely cautious of any totals derived from Pliny's trade figures, we can probably say that we can know something of the order of imperial income gleaned from the eastern trade, and that that order was not insignificant.[22]

Conclusion: the imperial government's attitude toward the trade

Throughout the course of this book we have noted the factors which may have influenced the attitude of the Roman government to the eastern long-distance trade, as well as other evidence which may allow us to reconstruct the imperial attitude towards this commerce. Numerous factors could be, and indeed have been, put forward by various scholars from time to time as possible influences on the Roman attitude to the trade. On the one hand, there is the possible drain of financial resources coupled with the moralistic concern about the effect of these luxury goods on the Roman state; on the other, the possibility of real financial gain, possibly to the emperor himself as a result of the activities of his agents, and certainly to the state through the collection of taxes and other dues. Assuming all these influences are valid, it would certainly seem to be a legitimate question to ask whether or not we can detect a coherent attitude to the trade from the imperial government through the period under consideration.

When all of these possible factors are examined, however, many of them do not appear to have really been as important as has often been suggested. The supposed drain of Roman finance to the East has been shown to be largely ephemeral; even if it was significant the Romans do not appear to have been unduly concerned by it. Even a moralistic interest in the bad effects of *luxuria* upon the empire's citizenry, which is a far more plausible reason for the Roman complaints about loss of money to the East than is any worry about the 'balance of trade', has been seen to be merely a form of posturing. There is simply no evidence at all to show that the Romans had any real concern about the effects of the eastern trade: certainly they had none upon which they wished to act.

Similarly, in the field of foreign policy, we have seen throughout the course of this book that the Romans undertook no policy moves which can be convincingly assigned to economic motives. Indeed, it is quite apparent that the needs of the trade were not a concern either positively or negatively when it came to Roman policy in the East, as will be summarised in Chapter 7. What then *does* remain that would enable us to determine the attitude of the imperial government to the eastern trade?

The only evidence for an 'imperial attitude to the trade' which can in any way be considered is the expense to which the government was prepared to go to protect (and perhaps monitor) the commerce in Egypt and Syria, and the taxes which they collected from it. In the course of this investigation it has been shown that the public works constructed by the Romans, especially in Egypt but also in other places, were designed purely to protect a lucrative source of tax revenue. Indeed, as is the case with Palmyra, when local authorities were willing and able to take on the burden of protecting the commerce, the Romans were quite willing to let them do so. The Romans guarded the caravans because the caravans were a substantial source of tax income for the empire; there is no other reason which has any basis in fact by which we might explain their interest in the protection of the caravan routes in the Eastern Desert of Egypt and elsewhere.

Thus, the only 'attitude' which the Roman imperial government can be realistically said to have had towards the eastern commerce was that it was a lucrative source of revenue. All the theories about Roman interest in removing 'middlemen', or reducing the outflow of coinage, or indeed of entertaining any kind of proactive policy toward the commerce have been found wanting for a lack of hard evidence. They must, therefore, be discarded. Instead, we must replace these theories with a picture in which the Romans allowed the trade itself to develop in whatever way it would, and did not trouble themselves to attempt to modify the trade in any way. The only thing that the Romans were concerned about with regard to the trade was that it could be a source of considerable income: even this idea they probably got from the Ptolemies, who had been levying taxes on the Red Sea commerce long before the Romans ever arrived in Egypt.[23] When all the evidence is examined, it seems that the only view the Roman imperial administration took of the eastern trade was as a source of revenue. This is as close as we can come to anything which can be termed an imperial 'policy' toward the eastern long-distance trade.

7

CONCLUSION

Throughout this book, it has repeatedly been found that the proactive economic policies which have been put forward by many historians of the spice trade cannot be substantiated, and that the Romans seem to have adopted a *laissez-faire* attitude to the eastern commerce. In addition, many of the ideas which have held sway about the nature of the trade have been found to be false. While many of these notions have already been rejected, some of them still make regular appearances when the eastern trade is being discussed.

Accordingly, it will be profitable to review in this section the observations which have been made in the preceding pages concerning the trade. It will be seen that, while we should rightly reject some of the views which have been held about the eastern long-distance trade of the Roman Empire, the commerce can still nonetheless be identified as a significant influence in the Roman East.

The nature of the trade

In general, it has been found that the eastern commerce of the Roman Empire was able to operate with relatively little government interference. While modern governments may attempt to foster their own economies by various interventionist means, it would appear that the Roman government did not do so. In no case has there been found concrete evidence, be it literary, archaeological or otherwise, that the Romans ever tried to influence or control the commerce to any substantial degree.

The documents which we have examined do not show that the government itself was directly involved in the commerce. Instead, on each occasion private individuals or associations of individuals are described who are in business for themselves and striving to make profit on their own behalf. While some individuals associated with the trade may have also held some government post,[1] there is no reason to assume that they are trading on behalf of the government. Rather they are far more likely to be simply both involved in commercial interests as well as working for the Roman government.

One of the most instructive documents for learning about the individuals involved in the commerce and the conduct of that commerce is the Vienna papyrus, *P.Vindob.* G 40822. In the text of this papyrus, several individuals are encountered, both private traders and government officials.[2] The private traders include the merchant, the creditor of the loan, and a camel-driver, each of whom is apparently either in business in the Red Sea trade or an employee of such a person. There are indeed several government officials encountered in the papyrus too, but without exception the sole interest they display is the collection of taxes: the *arabarch* at the Red Sea port, the customs-collector at Coptos and the collector of the *tetarte* at Alexandria. The entirety of the Roman military and government presence in the Eastern Desert of Egypt (and therefore most probably in other areas associated with the trade also) can be explained from this desire to collect the extensive taxes which accrued from the trade.[3]

Just as there is no evidence for government involvement in the commerce, so there is also no evidence that the Romans ever directed the trade or attempted to encourage some trade routes over others. Many works on the eastern trade, even in some quite recent writing, state that the Romans 'developed' or 'preferred' certain trade routes either for commercial motives, for example to allow the trade to bypass the war zone between Rome and Parthia;[4] or for political ends, such as to weaken the Nabataean kingdom and eliminate Arab 'middlemen', so bringing the commerce into 'Roman' hands.[5] In either case, as has been seen throughout this work, the evidence does not support such theories. Instead, it would appear that the merchants themselves sought out new routes when the old ones became unstable or unusable for some reason, and the Romans *reacted* to this by the construction of roads and the provision of military protection where necessary, in order to secure the tax income which the trade provided. For example, in Roman Egypt Strabo records that the number of merchants using the Red Sea ports jumped dramatically in the first few years of Roman administration.[6] These traders would have been using the pre-existing facilities from the Ptolemaic period, which the Romans then expanded and developed. Clearly the merchants were already using this route, responding to the increased stability of Egypt under Roman rule and the new prosperity brought about by the Augustan peace.[7] It was only after this, and in reaction to it, that the Romans developed the route by the construction of facilities and the provision of military protection.

This pattern is repeated throughout the whole area of the eastern trade. The Nabataeans were bringing frankincense and myrrh from Arabia Felix long before the Romans took over the region, and the Palmyrenes developed their own trade route to the head of the Persian Gulf without Roman assistance. In each case it is the merchants themselves who appear to have developed the trade routes, and the Roman authorities who responded to these developments by the provision of facilities to protect their tax income.

Indeed, it was the tax income that constituted the main area of interest in the eastern trade as far as the Roman government was concerned. This income (as has been seen) would have been quite considerable and possibly equivalent to the direct tax income of some provinces.[8] It is hardly surprising, therefore, that the Romans would have taken steps to ensure that this revenue was safeguarded and maximised. This would account for the military presence in areas where the eastern traffic operated, yet the lack of any apparent intent to guide or influence the trade, which we might expect if the Roman government had taken an actively interventionist stance toward the commerce. Since they were interested only in securing the tax income from the trade, however, they did not take any interest in guiding it toward certain routes; only in ensuring that where it did come the merchants were protected from brigandage and prevented from disposing of their goods before the proper taxes had been paid. In addition, it was probably felt that in the interests of order and the suppression of banditry the valuable caravans should be protected, as they would otherwise have provided an attractive target for bandits. Nonetheless, the customs revenues seem to have remained by far the most significant consideration in the involvement of the Roman government with the eastern commerce.

Another area which has been noted is the apparent independence of the various trade routes, and the general absence of restrictive monopolies in the commerce, which again contradicts much that has been written about the trade. For example, the overland incense trade through Petra seems to have existed at the same time as the seaborne incense trade through Egypt, despite the fact that they both depended on the same sources of incense. As would presumably be confirmed by the high prices which these goods continued to command in Rome right throughout our period of study, the market was sufficiently buoyant to support both trade routes at the time. That these high prices were not the result of restrictive monopolies has also been demonstrated: the monopolies which are often suggested for Parthia and South Arabia have been shown never to have existed.[9]

Thus, the character of the long-distance eastern trade of the Roman Empire in the period under consideration appears to have been basically an unrestricted and unregulated one, with very little government involvement in the actual trade itself. While the Roman government was keen to ensure that the money from customs duties levied on the trade continued to come into the imperial treasury, and took appropriate steps to ensure this was the case, the actual conduct of the commerce seems to have been exclusively in the hands of private entrepreneurs. As far as can be told from the evidence, the creation and abandonment of trading routes, the equipment of ships and caravans for the conveyance of the goods, the financing, reprocessing and sale of the goods were all done at the initiative of the private individuals involved in the trade, with an absolute minimum of government interference and regulation. The views of the eastern trade which postulate an active role for the government in the conduct of the commerce are without support from the evidence, and should accordingly be rejected in the absence of convincing proof. By contrast, it is felt that the model of the trade as presented here is in closer accord with our surviving evidence.

The effect of the trade on Roman foreign policy

In line with this general lack of government interference in the trade except for the purposes of tax gathering, it has also been found that the Roman government did not allow its foreign policy to be influenced by the needs of the eastern trade. Several acts of the Roman government in the East have been on various occasions been put forward as having been influenced by the 'need' to 'cut out the middleman' or something similar. In fact, the motives suggested are usually the same as those given for the direct involvement of the government in the trade as outlined in the previous section. As was outlined in the body of this work, such expeditions as Aelius Gallus' Arabian expedition, the annexation of the Nabataean kingdom in AD 106, and Trajan's Parthian war, among others, have been attributed to trade motivations.[10]

In each of these cases, however, it has been seen that there are other motives which far more readily explain Roman actions, and no convincing case can be put forward to sustain a mercantile motivation for these expeditions. Indeed, this is what we would expect given the conclusions reached in the previous section. Recent work has shown that in most cases a far less sophisticated motive lay at the root of Roman policy in the East in the Classical period. Isaac's recent reappraisal of the role played by Roman troops in the East has shown that they were generally there to perform police duties or poised for aggressive war against powers outside the empire.[11] While some have disputed his conclusions,[12] it would certainly seem that the case for the use of Roman military power to promote the interests of the long-distance trade is no longer defensible. The lack of any evidence in favour of such foreign policy moves on the part of Rome certainly supports Isaac's thesis, at least as far as commercial motivations for Roman military actions are concerned.

Indeed, throughout this work it has been noted that the one overriding factor which exerted a favourable influence upon the eastern trade was peace. Far from acting in the favour of the traders involved in the commerce, the frequent outbreaks of hostilities in the East, especially with the Parthians and later the Sassanians, seem to have brought the commerce to a halt, or at least adversely affected it.[13] These military expeditions were not in the interests of the eastern commerce or of its practitioners, be they Roman or non-Roman. Rather, the frequent outbreaks of hostilities in the East (almost always at the initiative of Rome until the mid-third century)[14] vividly show the *lack* of regard with which the Romans treated the needs of the eastern trade in the formulation of their foreign policy. If the Romans had been interested in promoting the trade, the best policy they could have followed in the East would have been a pacifist, non-interventionist one. This, they clearly did not do.

It is also interesting to note that, even though the Romans *were* clearly interested in collecting the tax income from the eastern trade, this interest seems to have had little influence on the formulation of foreign policy. When war stopped the trade, it also of course stopped the tax income from that trade: yet the Romans continued to make war on the Parthians. This would seem to indicate that a grave mistake is being made if we search for 'modern' reasons for war (i.e. economic motives) in explaining Roman actions in the East. The fact is, most of the Roman wars in the East, and very likely elsewhere as well, made no economic sense at all: the motivations for Roman aggression lie far more in Roman ideology than they do in the Roman economy.

There is no justification for the commonly held views that the needs of the long-distance trade lay at the root of Roman policy in the East. On the contrary, as has been seen, it would appear that the often highly aggressive Roman policy toward Parthia and in the East in general was very much *against* the interests of the eastern commerce. Even the tax income from the trade, which must have been considerable, appears to have been of no account in the formulation of Roman foreign policy. Evidently, the Romans had other priorities in mind when they formulated their policy toward the powers of the East.

The effect of the trade on the communities of the Roman East

Despite the absence of any evidence that the commerce affected Roman policy to any real extent, the same cannot be said of the political formations of the Roman East itself, nor of the economies of many of the communities in the region. In some cases it would appear that the eastern commerce had a very significant effect on communities of the Roman East, although this is by no means universally the case.

The community upon which the eastern trade appears to have had the most profound effect is Palmyra. As has been seen, the social and political structure of this city, and indeed perhaps some of the peculiarly independent status which it seems to have enjoyed, was deeply influenced both directly and indirectly by the city's commerce with the head of the Persian Gulf.[15] Such phenomena as the recording of services to the caravan trade in public honorific inscriptions, and even in the *cursus honorum* of one of the city's leading citizens, would indicate the high regard in which the trade was held by the city's administration and the high social position of the caravan leaders. While these caravan leaders do not appear to have been merchants themselves, they nonetheless were deeply involved in the caravan traffic and this reflects the high importance with which the trade was regarded at Palmyra. It seems therefore that the economic importance of the caravan traffic at Palmyra was significantly higher than the economic position of commerce generally in the Roman Empire,[16] and the social position of its practitioners was much higher than that of merchants throughout the bulk of the Roman world.[17]

Similarly, in the Nabataean kingdom there seems to have been some effect of the incense trade on elements of the kingdom's makeup. Although in this case there is virtually no evidence whereby we might learn of the social position of the merchants involved in this commerce, it does seem that the prosperity brought by the incense traffic contributed significantly to the wealth of the kingdom. In addition, many of the policy decisions of the Nabataean kings, such as the construction of posts at Medain Saleh, Leuke Kome and Jawf, were motivated by the needs of the incense trade.[18]

In other communities of the Roman East, however, the trade exerted a less profound, or at least not so readily discernible, influence. The bulk of Roman Egypt and Syria seem to have been unaffected by the passage of the goods of the eastern trade through their territory, at least as far as is indicated by the information which we have available today. It is perhaps possible that in these communities there was a wider variety of potential sources of income, which may have tended to 'dilute' the economic impact of the eastern trade. Certainly there is nothing to suggest the deep social influence of the commerce as at Palmyra in any of these communities, nor any indication that it was an important factor in the determination of policy as may have been the case in the Nabataean kingdom. It is possible, therefore, that only in the case of communities which were on the fringe of the inhabited Mediterranean world, such as Palmyra and Petra, could the eastern trade acquire great significance. In such places, the economic input from agriculture and herding and other such activities must necessarily have been limited due to the nature of the places concerned, and so the not inconsiderable wealth possible from the caravan trade became the easiest road to prosperity for these communities. In such circumstances, it is hardly surprising that the social position of merchants and the importance of the caravan trade in the determination of policy were far in advance of that which was current in 'normal' Roman provincial society.

It would therefore seem that the impact of the eastern trade on Roman communities in the East depended greatly on the presence or absence of alternative sources of income. In the bulk of the Roman East where the economy was not significantly different from the rest of the empire, the eastern trade may have had some regional impact but this has been lost to us. The commerce does not appear to have profoundly affected these places at all. In a few cases, however, the trade seems to have exerted more influence. These occasions seem to be those where the trade is the only or the major source of prosperity for the community. In these cases, something akin to Rostovtzeff's idea of a 'Caravan City' may have emerged, where, even if the caravan commerce was not the only reason for the city's existence, it was at least a significant factor in the life of the community.

Summary of conclusions

Thus, the picture which we have established concerning the eastern trade of the Roman Empire is a very different one to that which has often been presented. The ideas of trade monopolies being broken, maintained and redirected by a Roman government which was interested in the promotion of commerce and/or the retention of the commerce in Roman hands have been shown to be essentially without foundation. By contrast, a picture of the trade has emerged which shows a much less regulated environment in which nearly all of the initiative for the development and continuance of the trade belongs to private individuals, or perhaps some of the local governments of the Roman East. This is especially the case when such governments enjoyed a certain degree of independence, as appears to have been the case at Palmyra.

Perhaps the most noticeable poliitcal effects of the trade were those upon the local political formations of the region, especially at such locations as Palmyra and Petra where the trade was of great significance to the local economy. In these places, the eastern commerce became a significant factor in the prosperity of the city, and so it became a dominant factor in the social and political makeup and the pursuit of policy in some cases. Generally speaking, however, the more provincial societies were integrated into the Roman Empire and the more the financial significance of the trade was diluted by the presence of other sources of revenue, the less influence the eastern commerce seems to have had on the society in question.

This is especially the case when dealing with the empire itself as a political unit. The imperial government of Rome had many other priorities beside the eastern trade when it came to the formation of policy, and consequently there is not one major policy initiative of the Roman government in the period under consideration which can be primarily attributed to the needs of this commerce. While it is true that the Roman government seems to have regarded the eastern commerce as a source of considerable revenue, and taken steps to ensure that this revenue was secure, it becomes obvious that their interest in the commerce went no further than the collection of taxes. When the imperatives of Roman foreign policy and ideology intervened the needs of the eastern commerce and its practitioners were of little or no account.

The trade between Rome and the East in the classical period should be seen in a very different way from the manner in which it has often been understood. The evidence which we have in our possession clearly requires that we abandon ideas of an imperially directed commercial policy, the use of commerce as a tool of imperial foreign policy and an economically interventionist imperial government. Instead, we have a picture of a trade which was run largely at the initiative of the enterprising men and women who were actively engaged in it. It was these individuals who pioneered the trade routes, who chose the routes to be taken at any particular time, who organised protection and who drove the deals which ensured them a profit.

This pattern of trade remained substantially unchanged throughout the bulk of the period under study. Only at the end of this time was the trade temporarily crippled by the political and financial crisis of the third century AD. When the empire regained stability at the beginning of the fourth century, the trade regained some of its earlier vigour as well. However, it was now established upon different patterns and in many cases different routes to those that had been used in the first three centuries of the current era. For this reason, then, it is appropriate to end this study at the beginning of the fourth century, although some reference has been made to the trade in the fourth century to show the way in which the patterns of commerce had altered. The trade throughout the Byzantine period up until the Arab conquest forms a separate portion of the history of the Roman eastern trade which is deserving of its own study.

APPENDIX A

PRICES OF GOODS OF THE EASTERN TRADE AT ROME IN THE FIRST CENTURY AD

Information concerning the prices of various items of the eastern trade at Rome would be a useful tool in determining the relative accessibility of these goods in the Classical period. There is evidence of considerable knowledge of these goods in Roman society, especially in the upper echelons. This would seem to indicate that the eastern trade did not consist of a few traders trafficking merchandise of extreme rarity and astronomical price only to the very rich, but a commerce which could be carried on in some volume.

While the impression gained from the study of the trade appears to confirm that this was the case, a study of prices is necessary to indicate whether or not the goods were in fact accessible to those of medium income at Rome. Such accessibility would, presumably, be a necessary precondition for the apparently large volume of the commerce in the first three centuries AD. Fortunately, one source from this period does give prices for items of the eastern trade, giving some basis for attempting to reconstruct the accessibility of these goods to various social strata at Rome.

Prices according to Pliny

Pliny the Elder gives a list of prices of many plant items in the eastern trade.[1] These appear to have been the approximate retail prices of these items at Rome in Pliny's time although, as Pliny himself notes, the prices of goods could be dramatically affected by various outside influences such as a fire in the areas where the particular commodity was grown.[2] These are of course by no means all of the items of the eastern trade: these prices form a part of Pliny's discussion of plants in Books XII–XIII of his *Historia Naturalis*, and therefore they deal only with plant products in the trade. Nonetheless, they do provide us with a good insight into the approximate value of several of the commodities of the eastern trade at Rome in the first century AD (Table A.1).

Table A.1 Prices per Roman pound for commodities of the eastern trade in Pliny *NH*

Commodity	*Type*	*Reference*	*Price in* denarii
Ammoniacum		XII. 49	2
Amomum	In cluster	XII. 28	60
	Broken	XII. 28	48
Bdellium		XII. 19	3
Cardamom		XII. 29	12
Cassia		XII. 43	50
Cinnamon		XII. 42	10
	Daphnitis	XII. 43	300
Costus		XII. 25	5.5
Frankincense	1st quality	XII. 32	6
	2nd quality	XII. 32	5
	3rd quality	XII. 32	3
Ginger		XII. 28	6
Ladanum		XII. 37	2.5
Malabathron	Oil	XII. 54	100–300
	Large leaf	XII. 26	40
	Medium leaf	XII. 26	60
	Small leaf	XII. 26	75
Myrrh	Trogodytic	XII. 35	16.5
	Erythraean	XII. 35	16
	Perfumier's	XII. 35	12
Nard	Large leaf	XII. 26	40
	Medium leaf	XII. 26	60
	Small leaf	XII. 26	75
	Spikenard oil	XII. 26	100
Pepper	Long	XII. 28	15
	White	XII. 28	7
	Black	XII. 28	4
Styrax		XII. 55	17
Sweet Flag		XII. 48	1
Sweet Rush		XII. 48	5

The accessibility of the goods

To gain some idea of the relative value of these goods, it will be instructive to compare what is known from this era of the prices of wheat and some other items, as well as wages in this period. For example, the basic distribution of grain given to the *plebs* at Rome in the first century was 5 *modii* per month, and other evidence suggests that this was seen as an acceptable subsistence level.[3] The price of this wheat in the first century was approximately HS 3–4 (*sestertii*) per *modius* in most of the empire, varying up to about HS 8–10 at Rome itself, where prices were often much higher than in the provinces.[4] Thus, the goods of the eastern trade would have been well out of the reach of a person existing at a bare subsistence level.[5] However, it does indicate that they were not out of the reach of a person of fairly moderate means: even a soldier receiving HS 100 per month in the first century AD might not find some of the cheaper items beyond his reach, should he so desire. In addition, we should consider the fact that most of the goods would be used only in very small quantities, which would make their use accessible even to those of quite limited means on some occasions. Certainly, for the wealthy members of Roman society such items could have been purchased on a grand scale, and a person such as a merchant or artisan of adequate means could purchase them as well.

The items of the eastern trade, while certainly costly in the first century, were nonetheless not prohibitively so: a relatively extensive cross-section of Roman society would have been able to purchase them. Indeed, the seemingly widespread knowledge of the existence and uses of these commodities at Rome recorded by the literature of the day indicates that a relatively broad cross-section of Roman society indeed *did* buy them.[6] Though impossible to quantify, we can be sure that there was a buoyant market for the goods of the eastern trade at Rome in the first century AD.

Thus, the prices of these goods in Pliny's time placed them within the reach of a relatively large proportion of Roman society, although it would be impossible to try to determine exact figures. Nonetheless, the evidence from the prices of the goods of the eastern commerce seems to support the assertion that the Roman trade in the East fed a considerable consumer market: the idea of a 'luxury trade' in items of eastern provenance is somewhat misleading and should be rejected, or at least modified. Many of the items of the eastern trade were probably considered, if not necessities, then certainly relatively everyday consumer goods.

APPENDIX B

SILVER CONTENT OF NABATAEAN AND ROMAN COINS IN THE FIRST CENTURY AD

In Chapter 3, the silver content of the Nabataean coinage was discussed. Mention was made of the theory that a sharp decline in the fineness of this coinage in the first century AD reflected a downturn in the Nabataean economy which itself was caused by the loss of the aromatics trade passing through Petra.[1] It was pointed out, however, that the decline in the silver content of the Nabataean coinage, while indeed sharp, was paralleled by a similar, although far less serious, decline in the silver content of Roman imperial *denarii* over the same period.

The fineness of the Nabataean silver coinage throughout the first century is seen in Table B.1, showing individual coins according to their date, reign and respective fineness.[2] The figures show a far greater fluctuation than do the Roman coins in Table B.2, but this is partially attributable to the far smaller sample, which has allowed individual coins to be recorded in the graph and table. This would have been far too unwieldy in the case of the Roman coins due to the large numbers of coins used to reach an average weight and fineness.

The Roman *denarius* over the same period shows a roughly parallel decline in silver content, although of a much smaller order. While the Nabataean coins decline from over 90 per cent fine to only 20 per cent by the end of the century, the fineness of the Roman coins declines over the same period from around 98 per cent down to a little over 92. This can be seen in Table B.2.[3]

When the two tables are compared, a broad parallel in decline can be discerned. This is not to say, of course, that there is a corresponding trough in the Roman chart for every dip in value in the Nabataean coinage, as this is simply not the case. However, we should bear in mind that most of the fluctuations in the Roman coinage were caused by expenditure problems at Rome. Thus, the devaluation of Nero's reign was necessitated by the profligate expenditure under that emperor, while the dip in value in Vespasian's reign was caused by the massive expenditure of the Jewish war of AD 66–74 and the civil wars of AD 68–69, both of which caused serious economic pressure at Rome.[4]

Table B.1 Nabataean silver coinage 28 BC–AD 100

Coin (Meshorer)	*Reign*	*Year*	*Silver (%)*
21	Obodas II	28 BC	93.5
21	Obodas II	28 BC	85.0
23	Obodas II	25 BC	83.0
28	Obodas II	23 BC	73.0
30A	Obodas II	21 BC (?)	74.0
32	Obodas II	14 BC	72.0
38	Obodas II	11 BC	65.5
40	Obodas II (Syllaeus)	9 BC	74.0
41	Obodas II (Syllaeus)	9 BC	73.5
46	Aretas IV	9 BC	68.0
47A	Aretas IV	9 BC	70.0
49	Aretas IV	9 BC	72.0
51	Aretas IV	8 BC	47.0
52	Aretas IV	7 BC	73.0
53	Aretas IV	6 BC	54.0
65	Aretas IV	4 BC	72.0
94	Aretas IV	AD 7	62.0
94	Aretas IV	AD 7	41.5
94	Aretas IV	AD 7	54.0
96	Aretas IV	AD 18	39.0
100	Aretas IV	AD 21	36.0
103	Aretas IV	AD 25	51.0
103	Aretas IV	AD 25	35.5
104	Aretas IV	AD 26	36.0
105	Aretas IV	AD 27	34.0
107	Aretas IV	AD 32	35.0
108	Aretas IV	AD 35	38.0
108	Aretas IV	AD 35	34.0
124	Malchus II	AD 42	40.5
127	Malchus II	AD 45	33.0
130	Malchus II	AD 48	42.0
130	Malchus II	AD 48	25.0
132	Malchus II	AD 50	20.0
134	Malchus II	AD 55	20.0
135	Malchus II	AD 56	20.0
138	Malchus II	AD 61	20.0
142	Rabbel II	AD 70	20.0
144	Rabbel II	AD 72	20.0
144	Rabbel II	AD 72	40.5
145	Rabbel II	AD 72	40.5
147	Rabbel II	AD 75	40.5
148	Rabbel II	AD 78	42.0
149	Rabbel II	AD 80	20.0
151	Rabbel II	AD 86	20.0
152	Rabbel II	AD 89	20.0
156	Rabbel II	AD 93	20.0
159	Rabbel II	AD 99	20.0
160	Rabbel II	AD 100	20.0

Table B.2 Roman imperial *denarii* 30 BC–AD 100

Coin type	*Silver (%)*	*Weight (g)*	*Silver weight*
Augustus, Italian mint, 30–27 BC	96.84	3.64	3.52
Augustus, Emerita, 25–3 BC	97.63	3.73	3.64
Augustus, Spanish mint 1, 25–17 BC	98.08	3.74	3.65
Augustus, Spanish mint 2, 25–16 BC	97.44	3.75	3.51
Mint of Rome, 19–12 BC	96.24	3.72	3.58
Augustus, Lugdunum, 15 BC – AD 14	97.91	3.69	3.65
Tiberius, AD 14–37	98.07	3.72	3.64
Gaius, AD 37–41	97.69	3.68	3.59
Claudius, AD 41–54	98.00	3.65	3.59
Nero, pre-reform, AD 54–64	97.35	3.57	3.47
Nero, post-reform, AD 64–68	93.48	3.18	2.97
Galba, AD 68–69	93.20	3.23	3.01
Otho, AD 69	93.59	3.28	3.06
Vitellius, AD 69	92.47	3.21	2.96
Vespasian, AD 70	88.28	3.20	2.82
Vespasian, AD 70–72	89.29	3.17	2.82
Vespasian, AD 72–73	91.68	3.21	2.94
Vespasian, AD 73	88.65	3.25	2.83
Vespasian, AD 74	90.52	3.19	2.88
Vespasian, AD 75	91.89	3.18	2.91
Vespasian, AD 76	90.86	3.19	2.89
Vespasian, AD 77–78	89.77	3.19	2.85
Vespasian, AD 79	90.78	3.23	2.93
Titus, AD 79	92.69	3.20	2.96
Titus, AD 80	91.73	3.21	2.94
Domitian, AD 81	90.56	3.19	2.89
Domitian, 1st reform, AD 82–85	98.01	3.33	3.26
Domitian, 2nd reform, AD 85–88	93.43	3.23	3.02
Domitian, AD 88–92	93.39	3.28	3.05
Domitian, AD 92–96	93.75	3.26	3.05
Nerva, AD 96	93.08	3.20	2.97
Nerva, AD 97	93.19	3.23	3.01
Trajan, AD 98–99	93.55	3.27	3.05
Trajan, AD 100	92.38	3.22	2.97

These expenditures would not have immediately caused a devaluation of coinage in the Nabataean kingdom, and so we do not find an exact parallel between the devaluations in the two realms. Nonetheless, there is reason to believe that the two gradual devaluations show a link.

The Nabataean kingdom, regardless of the health of its economy or its aromatics trade, would be unable to escape the long-term effects of a silver shortage at Rome, such as is evidenced by the devaluation of the *denarius*. Tables B.1 and B.2 (as has already been seen) show a roughly parallel decline, making it most likely that the decline in the fineness of the Nabataean silver coinage is indeed derived not from the loss of the aromatics trade but from the flow-on effect of the Roman shortage of silver, or indeed of any pressure

Table B.3 Syrian *Tetradrachmae* of Antioch 34 BC–AD 100

Coin type	*Silver (%)*	*Weight (g)*	*Silver weight*
Antony & Cleopatra VII, 34–3 BC	80.66	15.04	12.13
Pseudo-Seleucid, 30–13 BC	72.88	14.16	10.31
Augustus 'Zeus' type, 5 BC	72.75	14.01	10.19
Augustus 'Tyche' type, 5 BC – AD 12	78.43	14.74	11.56
Tiberius, AD 17–37	65.75	14.43	9.48
Gaius, AD 37–41	67.75	14.52	9.83
Claudius, AD 41–50	82.50	13.58	11.20
Nero, AD 56–57	63.16	14.50	9.15
Nero, Tyrian standard, AD 59–63	79.39	14.66	11.63
Nero, AD 65–69	78.00	14.35	11.19
Galba, AD 68–69	85.15	14.45	12.30
Otho, AD 69	85.12	14.57	12.40
Vespasian, AD 70–74	81.00	14.25	11.83
Domitian, AD 81–92	81.50	14.43	11.79
Nerva, AD 96–98	88.79	14.78	13.12
Trajan, AD 98–100	80.50	14.50	11.67

on the Roman silver coinage. The shortage would have been far worse in the Nabataean realm simply because of the fact that the Near East depended on imported silver, and had no reserves of its own.[5] Thus, a decline in value over a few per cent at Rome is translated into a far more severe decline in the Nabataean kingdom. For this reason, we see the Nabataean silver coinage slowly debased to the point that it would have been useless except for internal transactions within the kingdom.[6]

This greater difficulty in obtaining silver in the East is illustrated to some extent by the silver content of the tetradrachms minted at Antioch during the first century. These also show a gradual decline through the first century, again roughly parallel to the Roman imperial coinage and the Nabataean coinage (Table B.3).[7]

Here, although again the decline in the silver content is nowhere near as severe as that under the Nabataean kings, we do see a more severe debasement than at Rome, probably reflecting the greater difficulty of obtaining silver at Antioch. Also, the declines in silver content are generally parallel to the two coinages already surveyed, showing that there was a general decline in the availability of silver at that time, and that it was this that most likely caused the devaluation of the Nabataean coinage.[8]

Indeed, the greater difficulty in gaining silver supplies which the Nabataean kingdom experienced might also account for the debasements of the coinage which occurred in the earlier first century, when the Roman imperial issues were still stable. One possibility is the massive building programme which appears to have been undertaken in the first century at Petra, at which time the majority of the great monuments of the city were constructed.[9] The expenditure undertaken at this time, which must have been immense, could well account for the decline in the silver content seen in the reign of Aretas IV. Again, as with the general silver shortage of the later first century, the coinage of the Nabataeans was greatly devalued at this time due to the difficulty of obtaining silver. Indeed, throughout all the first century, there is no need to link the fineness of the Nabataean silver coinage with the health of the aromatics trade through Petra in any way.

APPENDIX C

INSCRIPTIONS REFERRING TO PALMYRENE MILITARY ACTIVITIES AD 132–225

As discussed in Chapter 4, there is some debate about the nature of the Palmyrene 'caravan police' and its organisation and significance. While the military role of Palmyra after the appearance of Odaenathus is not in doubt, there are several inscriptions which, as discussed in the aforementioned section, appear to speak of an organised Palmyrene military under the direction of the city itself well before the third century. Accordingly, a list of these inscriptions together with a summary of the content of each is provided in this appendix.

1 *Baalshamin* III no. 45, AD 132; Palmyra. A caravan under Hagegu b. Iarhibol and Taimarsu b. Taimarsu, having been saved by So'adu b. Bolyada, honours him with four statues in four sanctuaries; also for helping his fellow citizens in Vologesias, caravans and merchants.
2 *CIS* II. 3973, AD 132; Palmyra. These two altars were set up by 'Obaidu b. 'Anamu, a Nabataean, who was a cavalryman in Hirta and in the camp of 'Ana.
3 Unpublished, from Allat temple, Palmyra (see M. Gawlikowski 'Palmyra as a Trading Centre' *Iraq* 56 [1994] no. 15, p. 32), AD 144; Palmyra. A caravan of all the Palmyrenes returning from Vologesias which was attacked by robbers under 'Abdallat Ahitaya, honours So'adu b. Bolyada with four statues in four sanctuaries.
4 *Dura* VII–VIII, no. 909, *c.* AD 150 (Welles), after AD 164 (M. Gawlikowski 'Palmyre et l'Euphrate' *Syria* 60 [1983], 61); Dura Europos. Dedication of the B'nai Mitha, the archers.
5 *Dura* VII–VIII, no. 845, AD 169; Dura Europos. Dedication of Ethpeni, *strategos* over the archers at Dura.
6 Dura VII–VIII, no. 846, AD 171; Dura Europos. Dedication of Zenobios, *strategos* of the archers.
7 *Baalshamin* III no. 51, after AD 188; Palmyra. Dedication by the cavalrymen of the detachment of 'Ana and Gamla.
8 *SEG* VII. 138, AD 198; Palmyra. Honouring Aelius Boras, *strategos* of the peace.

9 *Inv*. X. 44 = *SEG* VII. 139, AD 199; Palmyra. The Council honours 'Ogielu b. Maqqai, several times *strategos* against the nomads, having assured the security of merchants and of caravans under his leadership.

10 J. Cantineau 'L'inscription de 'Umm es-Salâbih' *Syria* 14 (1933), 178–80, AD 225; Umm es-Selabikh: referring to a *strategos* of 'Ana and Gamla.

11 J. Starcky 'Une inscription Palmyrénienne trouvée près de l'Euphrate' *Syria* 40 (1963), 47–55, no date; T1 (oil pumping station). Abgar b. Shalman came to the limits of the territory under the *strategeia* of Iarhai.

APPENDIX D

THE CAREER OF SEPTIMIUS ODAENATHUS AND THE STATUS OF PALMYRA, AD 251–267

In Chapter 4, the emergence of Palmyra as an independent military power in the mid-third century AD was noted. As was seen in that discussion, one man in particular is especially associated with this rise: Septimius Odaenathus the son of Hairan. During the career of this man, several political changes occurred in the status of Palmyra before its eventual revolt in AD 270. Accordingly, it is proposed to examine the evidence, both literary and inscriptional, which allows us to understand something of the status of Palmyra in this period and the position of Septimius Odaenathus, its chief citizen. With this in mind, it is intended to divide the period into subsections, in which the progress of Odaenathus and Palmyra to some sort of military and perhaps political independence can be understood.

AD 251–257/8

During the first period, the prominence at Palmyra of Septimius Odaenathus is marked by his possession of an unusual title, expressed as *Ras Tadmor* (ruler of Tadmor, i.e. Palmyra) in Palmyrene and as *exarchos Palmurenon* (exarch of the Palmyrenes) in Greek. These are unique titles, and do not appear to correspond to any normal Greek or Roman official positions. Nonetheless, it is possible that they reflect some sort of importance and/or leadership by Odaenathus at Palmyra in this period.

Palmyra itself was at this stage, and had been probably since the reign of Septimius Severus, a Roman *colonia*, administered in the normal Roman way by two magistrates called *duumuiri*, referred to at Palmyra by the normal Greek equivalent of *strategoi*.[1] Prior to 251 there is no indication that there was anything unusual about this particular *colonia*, apart from those things which had characterised Palmyra all along such as its dependence upon the long-distance caravan commerce and its possession of a substantial militia designed to protect the caravan traffic.[2] After this date, however, a series of inscriptions honouring Odaenathus use terms such as those mentioned above which are unusual for a normally functioning Roman *colonia*. In one such inscription, Odaenathus is referred to in Palmyrene simply as *Ras Tadmor* without any indicators of Roman rank.[3] In others, however, Odaenathus is honoured by both this title (and its Greek equivalent) as well as by indicators of Roman senatorial rank. This is seen in the following bilingual inscription recently discovered at Palmyra:

> Σεπτίμιον 'Οδαίνα[θον Αἰ]ράνου Ο[ὐαβ]αλλάθ[ου τοῦ Νασώρου] λα[μ]πρότατον [ἔξαρχον Παλμυ]ρηνῶν 'Ιούλιος Αὐρήλιος 'Αθηακά[βος 'Ο]γήλου Ζαβδιβώ[λου . . . τοῦ καὶ Κωρα, τὸν φίλον στοργῆς ἕνεκεν, ἔτους γξφ´ μηνεὶ [Ξανδ]ικῷ.
>
> ṢLM 'SPṬMYWS '[DYNT BR ḤYRN] BR WHBLT NṢWR RŠ ['] DY [TDMW]R NHYR' D'BD LH 'T'QB BR 'GYLW BR ZBDBWL BR MQYMW DMQR' QR' RḤMH LYQRHWN BRBNWTH BYRḤ NYSN ŠNT 563.
>
> To Septimius Odaenathus, son of Hairan son of Vaballathaus Nasor, the illustrious *exarch* of the Palmyrenes (*Palm.*: ruler of Tadmor), Julius Aurelius Ate'aqab son of Ogeilu son of Zabdibol son of Moqimu, also called Qora (dedicated this) to his friend because of his affection (*Palm.*: to his friend, in his honour, during his presidency) in the year 563 in the month Xandikos (*Palm.*: in the month Nisan in the year 563) (April AD 252).[4]

Similarly, another inscription dated at AD 251 honours Odaenathus' son Septimius Hairan with the same titles (illustrious senator and ruler of Tadmor), indicating that Odaenathus had associated his son with himself in these offices.[5]

The exact significance of these titles has been the occasion of some discussion. As has been noted, the expression *Ras Tadmor* is not parallelled by any term in normal Greek, Roman or for that matter Palmyrene administration.[6] Accordingly, it was suggested by Ingholt that the term in fact refers to Odaenathus' leadership of the Palmyrene militia.[7] He then goes on to explain the obvious objection, that the term for such leaders is elsewhere attested as having been *strategos*,[8] by claiming that Odaenathus had been military leader of the whole Palmyrene army in the wars against Shapur that occurred throughout the AD 250s.[9] This, however, should be rejected because there is absolutely no evidence that Odaenathus or Palmyra played any part in these conflicts at all. Even if it were the case, the title 'ruler of Tadmor' would still seem unusual for a purely military leader.

Millar, on the other hand, states that there is no indication of an overall dominance of the city by Odaenathus, only of his patronage of various guilds and persons within the city.[10] However, the use of a title meaning 'ruler' seems even more extraordinary in such circumstances. On the whole, it would seem, as Potter concludes, that the uniqueness of the title and the fact that it is attested only for members of Odaenathus' family indicates that it is an extraordinary hereditary title conferred upon Odaenathus and his family, indicating his headship of the city.[11] We do not know when this was granted, or indeed what powers (if any) the title conferred, but it would seem most likely that it reflects and officially recognises a position of pre-eminence and great influence held by Odaenathus at Palmyra in this period.

It should still be noted, however, that Odaenathus is referred to by not only his Palmyrene titles but also normal Roman ones as well throughout this period. In most of the inscriptions referring to Odaenathus, he is also described as *lamprotatos*, which is the usual Greek equivalent of the Latin *clarissimus*. This would thus indicate that Odaenathus was a member of the senatorial order, and thus among the very highest elite in Palmyra. Indeed, this rank is often indicated explicitly in the inscriptions by the term *sunkletikos*.[12] There are in fact two more inscriptions which would appear to have come from this period that mention only Odaenathus' Roman rank, without mention of the unusual Palmyrene titles. One of these is a tomb inscription apparently set up by Odaenathus himself:

> τὸ μνημῖον τοῦ ταφεῶνος ἔκτισεν ἐξ ἰδίων Σεπτίμιος 'Οδαίναθος
> ὁ λαμπρότατ[ος συνκλητικὸς]
> Αἱράνου Οὐαβαλλάθου τοῦ Νασώρου αὐτῷ τε καὶ υἱοῖς αὐτοῦ
> καῖ υἱωνοῖς εἰς τὸ παντελὲς αἰώνιον τειμήν.
>
> Septimius Odaenathus the illustrious senator, son of Hairan son of Vaballathus son of Nasor built this funerary monument from his own expense for himself, his children and his grandchildren, in (their) honour, for eternity.[13]

The other was set up in Odaenathus' honour by the city of Tyre, indicating his widespread fame. It is also perhaps significant that this inscription from a city of Roman Syria does not use the unusual Palmyrene titles, but only the Roman ones:

> Σεπτίμ. 'Οδαίναθον τὸν λαμπρότατ. Σεπτιμία Κολ. Τύρος ἡ μητρόπολις.
>
> To the illustrious Septimius Odaenathus, Septimia Colonia Tyros the metropolis (dedicated this).[14]

Whatever the significance of Odaenathus' Palmyrene titles, it should therefore be borne in mind that they were coupled with indicators of Roman rank, and borne in a Roman context. For example, even after the appearance of Odaenathus bearing titles such as 'ruler of Tadmor' the normal government and institutions of Palmyra as a Roman colony continued to function. This can also be seen in inscriptions from this period which do not mention

Odaenathus, but which instead show the normal organs of government active at Palmyra. An example of this is an inscription honouring Aurelius Worod:

> Αὐρήλιον Οὐορώδην
> ἱππικὸν καὶ βουλευτὴν
> Παλμυρηνὸν Βηλά–
> καβος ʽΑρσᾶ τὸν φί–
> [λον] τειμῆς χάριν,
> ἔτους οφ´
>
> To Aurelius Vorodes of the equestrian order and councillor of Palmyra, Bel'aqab son of Harsa (dedicated this) to his friend in his honour, in the year 570 (AD 258/9).[15]

Worod's position as an eminent individual is clear, but what is also clear is that it was still possible at this time to honour an individual in strictly Roman terms, without making reference to Odaenathus or his family. Thus, whatever the significance of the title *Ras Tadmor* or its Greek equivalent, it is clear that such powers were still being exercised in the framework of a city with the normal institutions of Roman provincial government.

AD 257/8–261

In AD 257/8, the titulature of Odaenathus appears to undergo some change, which may reflect his increased dominance in the city. The term *Ras Tadmor* at this time disappears, and is replaced by the expression *lamprotatos hupatikos*, equivalent to the Latin *clarissimus consularis*, 'illustrious consular'. This formula is found in several inscriptions from Palmyra of the late AD 250s, most of which consist of dedications to Odaenathus or his son Hairan by individuals or trade guilds in the city.[16] It has been suggested that this term means that Odaenathus had been made consular governor of Syria Phoenice at this time.[17] However, such an appointment would contradict the law that, according to Dio, had been made after the attempted usurpation of Avidius Cassius in AD 175: namely, that no governor should be appointed to rule over the territory from which he himself came.[18] Another possibility to explain the term and its possible significance at Palmyra has, however, recently come to light. An Aramaic papyrus from Edessa describes the king there, Abgar IX, as 'king who is honoured as a *hupatikos* at Urhai (i.e. Edessa)'.[19] Potter suggests that both Abgar and Odaenathus, powerful eastern dynasts ruling over cities of the Roman East, had been given the *ornamenta consularia* in recognition of their positions of prominence in their respective cities.[20] While Odaenathus himself was not actually a king (yet), the parallel between himself and Abgar, if it is a valid one, would seem to indicate that Odaenathus did hold a position of authority at Palmyra at least roughly analogous to that of Abgar at Edessa.

This is possibly also indicated by another inscription which seems to recognise some sort of overlordship by Odaenathus at Palmyra. In a dedication by the guild of gold and silversmiths at Palmyra in AD 258, Odaenathus' consular rank is mentioned together with terms in both Greek and Palmyrene that indicate rulership:

Σεπ[τίμιον 'Οδαίναθον]
τόν λαμ[πρότατον ὑπατικ]ὸν
συντέ[λεια τῶν χρυσοχ]όων
καὶ ἀργυ[ροκόπων, τ]ὸν δεσπότην
τειμῆς χάριν, [ἔτ]ους θξφ´
μηνεὶ Ξανδικῷ.

ṢLM SPṬMYWS 'DYNT
NHYR' HPṬYQ' MRN DY
'QYM LH TGM' DY QYNY'
'BD' DHB' WKSP' LYQRH
BYRḤ NYSN DY ŠNT 569.

To Septimius Odaenathus the illustrious consular, our lord, the association of goldworkers and silverworkers (dedicated this) in his honour in the year 569 in the month Xandikos (*Palm*: in the month Nisan of the year 569) (April AD 258).[21]

The use of the Palmyrene term MRN, usually used of a reigning prince and here translated by the Greek *despotes*, certainly seems to indicate some sort of rule at Palmyra, as opposed to his simple patronage of the association of gold and silverworkers.[22]

As with the preceding period, it would thus seem that Odaenathus held in the period from AD 257/8 to 261 a position of peculiar prominence at Palmyra, analogous even to that of a reigning king in a dependent kingdom such as Osrhoene. While (as we shall see) it remained possible to set up a commemorative inscription at Palmyra without making reference to Odaenathus during this time, it would seem that Odaenathus was certainly the 'first citizen', and perhaps also the effective ruler, of Palmyra prior to AD 261. Moreover, the granting of the *ornamenta consularia* would seem to indicate that this position was approved, if not even established, by the Roman authorities in Syria.

AD 261–267

In 260 the Roman Emperor Valerian was defeated and captured by the Persian King Shapur I, and the entire Roman East was thrown into turmoil. In these years, Odaenathus and Palmyra came to the fore of affairs in the East, with Odaenathus acting as the representative and enforcer of legitimate Roman government (i.e. Valerian's son Gallienus). In so doing, however, Odaenathus secured further titles for himself, both Roman and Palmyrene, and apparently effective independence for Palmyra. Odaenathus, as discussed in Chapter 4 on Palmyra, defeated Macrianus and Quietus, who attempted to seize power in the East after the defeat of Valerian, and then inflicted a series of defeats upon Shapur, re-establishing Roman authority.

In the inscriptions which come from the period 262–267, it appears that Odaenathus acquired two new titles: *Corrector Totius Orientis* and King of Kings. The royal title is seen in an inscription from Palmyra which appears to commemorate the elevation of Herodianus, a son of Odaenathus who may be the same as the Hairan mentioned earlier,[23] to this dignity. This elevation took place well outside Palmyra's territory, somewhere on the Orontes river, after a victory over the Persians:

> [β]ασιλεῖ βασιλέων πρὸς ['Ορ]όντῃ [. . . βα]σιλείας τὴν κατὰ
> [Π]ε[ρ]σῶν νείκην ἀναδησαμένῳ Σεπ[τιμίῳ Ἡρωδι]ανῷ, 'Ιούλιος Αὐρήλιος
> [Σεπτί]μιος Ο[ὐ]ο[ρ]ώδης [καὶ 'Ιούλιος Αὐρήλιος . . . ἐπίτροπος τῆς δ]εσ–
> (π)οίνης κεντηνά[ροις] ἀμφότεροι στρα[τηγοὶ τῆς λαμ]προτάτης [κ]ολω[ν]είας.
>
> To the King of Kings, near the Orontes . . . crowned for the victory over the Persians, Septimius Herodianus. Julius Aurelius Septimius Vorodes (i.e. Worod) and Julius Aurelius . . . procurator *centenarius* of the Queen, both *strategoi* of the illustrious colony.[24]

Although there are no inscriptions mentioning Odaenathus himself which come from this period, there is a posthumous commemoration dating from Zenobia's reign, which also indicates that he bore the title of King of Kings, as well as that of *Corrector Totius Orientis*. This Palmyrene inscription runs as follows:

> ṢLM SPTMYWS 'DY[NT] MLK MLK'
> WMTQNN' DY MDNḤ' KLH SPṬMY'
> ZBD' RB ḤYL' RB' WZBY RB ḤYL'
> DY TDMWR QRṬSṬ' 'QYM LMRHWN
> BYRḤ'B DY ŠNT 582
>
> To Septimius Odaenathus King of Kings and *Corrector* of the whole region, the Septimii Zabda, commander of the great army, and Zabbai, commander of the army of Tadmor, great men, dedicated this for their lord, in the month of Ab of the year 582 (August AD 271).[25]

In addition to these two inscriptions, there is also the milestone from the reign of Vaballathus which (as has been discussed) most probably represents the titles which Vaballathus inherited from Odaenathus on the latter's death in AD 267, namely King of Kings and *Corrector* of the whole East, as in the previous inscription.[26]

The use of the term 'King of Kings', the title normally worn by the Persian king, by someone who was ostensibly a subject of Rome might at the first glance be thought extraordinary, and indicative of a breach with Rome. However, this need not necessarily be the case. Indeed, the granting of a Roman title (*Corrector*) of some importance at the same time would seem to indicate that Gallienus approved, or at least tolerated, Odaenathus' elevation to royal dignity. Certainly given the situation that was then prevailing, with Odaenathus the only power of significance in the East claiming loyalty to Gallienus, it is probable that Gallienus thought he had little choice but to acquiesce.

However, it is quite possible that Odaenathus' assumption of the royal title *was* intended as a direct challenge, not to the Roman emperor, but to the Persian. If this was the case, it may have been that after the defeat of Shapur by Odaenathus, Gallienus approved of Odaenathus' claim to royal power in opposition to the king of Persia. It may be that after the defeat of Shapur, Odaenathus was claiming that *he*, not Shapur, was the legitimate King of Kings. In such circumstances, the approval of Gallienus is not surprising. Indeed, it is possible that there was a parallel to this action in the fourth century, when in the terms of Constantine's will his nephew Hannibalianus was created King of Kings in Armenia and given responsibility over the Persian frontier. Hannibalianus thus was to wear the royal title but would still be considered as functionary of the Roman Empire. It may have been just such a position that Odaenathus held in the later third century.

This then brings us to the question of the status of Palmyra. David Kennedy has suggested that Palmyra had by this time effectively become an allied kingdom of Rome rather than a provincial city,[27] and no doubt this is, in practice at least, true. Odaenathus had by this time total control of Palmyra and effective control of much of the Roman East acting as Gallienus' deputy. There was presumably little that Gallienus could have done to influence affairs in the East at this time, had he chosen to do so. Nonetheless, there is some indication that the situation according to the law was different. Despite Odaenathus' holding the royal dignity, it seems that at Palmyra at least the appearance of Roman 'normality' continued. This is seen in several commemorative inscriptions from this time from Palmyra, which show that it was still possible to be honoured there even as late as AD 266 with Roman and municipal Palmyrene terms, and with no reference to Odaenathus and his family. One of these, honouring Septimius Worod with such titles as *procurator ducenarius*, *iuridicus*, *strategos* and *agoranomos* has already been quoted in the discussion of Palmyra's social structure earlier in this work.[28] These terms are either Roman or municipal posts. The only indication that the situation might be somewhat unusual is the use of the term *metrocolonia* for the usual *colonia*, which may indicate that Palmyra was claiming a status higher than that normally occupied by a Roman *colonia*.[29] Exactly what that status might be, however, is entirely unclear: what *is* clear is that the city still was, at least legally, a part of the Roman world in general, and of the Roman provincial system of government in particular.

This continuing 'Romanness' is also seen in the other of Odaenathus' titles: that of *Corrector Totius Orientis*. There has been considerable discussion concerning whether Odaenathus' title was that of *Corrector*, which is generally taken to mean that he had the overall command of all Roman troops in the region,[30] or a more honorary title with no practical meaning, such as *Restitutor*. The discussion centres upon two inscriptions which have both been quoted in this work: the statue base from Palmyra erected in Zenobia's reign which commemorates Odaenathus' career, and is quoted above; and the milestone from the earlier part of Vaballathus' reign which was quoted earlier in the work.[31]

The former of these two describes Odaenathus as the MTQNN' of the whole East, an Aramaic term derived from the verb TQN, 'to set right, set in order'.[32] Vaballathus, however, is described as the 'PNRTṬ' of the whole East, a direct transliteration of the Greek *epanorthotes*, which is itself the usual Greek translation for *Corrector*. The difference between the two inscriptions has been taken to mean that while Vaballathus had taken (or been given) the title of *Corrector*, Odaenathus himself had held only the less significant title of *Restitutor*.[33] However, as Potter has pointed out, the titles borne by Vaballathus on the milestone are likely to be those which he inherited from Odaenathus: the difference between 'PNRTṬ' and MTQNN' is simply that between expressing the office with a Greek transliteration in one case and with an Aramaic term in the other.[34] In any case, as Millar points out, the definition attached to the term *Corrector* may be misleading: there is every reason to believe that this office too was quite imprecise in its application.[35]

Whatever the actual title which Odaenathus bore, the fact remains that it was a Roman honour, indicating that he was still considered a functionary of the Roman government. Whatever the technical implications of his title, if indeed there were any, the reality of the situation in the Roman East in the AD 260s was that Odaenathus ruled the Roman East as the deputy of Gallienus, and that he led the only effective military resistance to the Persians at that time. The fact that he remained the loyal adherent of Gallienus, and was never in any sense a rebel against Roman rule, is clearly indicated by the fact that he never minted coins in his own name.[36]

Palmyra therefore at this time was still considered a part of the Roman Empire, as is clearly seen in the inscription honouring Septimius Worod mentioned above. The only evidence that the city claimed higher rank than others due to the extraordinary prominence of its chief citizen is the use of the unusual term *metrocoloneia*. Odaenathus himself, however, appears to have held the effective if not official command of the armies of the Roman East, and to have taken or been given the title of King of Kings in order to threaten the position of Shapur. As such, he was effectively the ruler of the Roman East as the deputy of Gallienus: the evidence indicates that he maintained this loyalty throughout.

The situation of Palmyra and of its chief citizen in the period between 251 and 267 is therefore a quite unusual one which conforms to no normal pattern of Roman rule. This perhaps explains the difficulties which many commentators have experienced with these events, but considering the extraordinary situation in the Roman East at the time, we should perhaps hardly be surprised that an unorthodox solution emerged. As we have seen, Palmyra was a *colonia* of the Roman Empire, yet at the same time it was effectively acting as an independent allied state. Similarly, Odaenathus was at once the commander of Roman forces in the East as the loyal deputy of the emperor, yet at the same time he wore the title King of Kings and effectively ruled the East with little more than lip-service to his titular master Gallienus, who was powerless to affect the outcome of events. To search for any kind of regularity or normality in such a situation is clearly pointless.

NOTES

1 INTRODUCTION

1 E.H. Warmington *The Commerce between the Roman Empire and India* (Cambridge 1928), 15; M.P. Charlesworth *Trade-Routes and Commerce of the Roman Empire* (Cambridge 1926), 63, 98–111; J. Starcky 'The Nabataeans: a Historical Sketch' *BA* 18 (1955), 94; J.I. Miller *The Spice Trade of the Roman Empire* (Oxford 1969), 15, 119–41; J.R. Thorley 'The Development of Trade between the Roman Empire and the East under Augustus' *G & R* 16 (1969), 209–23; J.R. Thorley 'The Silk Trade between China and the Roman Empire at its Height' *G & R* 18 (1971), 71–80; G.W. Bowersock 'A Report on Arabia Provincia' *JRS* 61 (1971), 228; A. Negev 'The Nabataeans and the Provincia Arabia' *ANRW* II, 8 (1977), 561–2; J.-P. Rey-Coquais 'Syrie romaine, de Pompée à Dioclétien' *JRS* 68 (1978), 54; D.F. Graf 'The Saracens and the Defence of the Arabian Frontier' *BASOR* 229 (1978), 6–7; W. Schmitthenner 'Rome and India: Aspects of Universal History during the Principate' *JRS* 69 (1979), 90–106; J.-P. Rey-Coquais 'L'Arabie dans les routes de commerce entre le monde Mediterranéen et les côtes Indiennes' in T. Fahd (ed.) *L'Arabie préislamique et son environnement historique et culturel* (Leiden 1989), 225–39.

2 S.E. Sidebotham *Roman Economic Policy in the Erythra Thalassa 30 BC – AD 217* (Leiden 1986).

3 M.G. Raschke 'New Studies in Roman Commerce with the East' *ANRW* II, 9, 2 (1978), 604–1378.

4 Ibid., and see also B. Isaac *The Limits of Empire: The Roman Army in the East* (Oxford 1990).

5 See Chapter 3 (Arabia) and 4 (Palmyra) for these discussions.

6 L. Casson *The Periplus Maris Erythraei: Text with Introduction, Translation and Commentary* (Princeton 1989), 5–10.

7 Ibid., 8. See e.g. *Periplus* 20 for explicit claims of first-hand experience of the route.

8 *Periplus* 29.

9 Casson *The Periplus Maris Erythraei*, 7–8.

10 For the various dates proposed see Raschke 'New Studies in Roman Commerce with the East', 979–80.

11 *Periplus* 19.

12 Bowersock 'A Review of Arabia Provincia', 223; Casson *The Periplus Maris Erythraei*, 7.

13 *Periplus* 23.

14 C. Robin 'L'Arabie du Sud et la date du *Périple de la mer Erythrée* (nouvelles données)' *JA* 289 (1991), 24.

15 A. Dihle *Umstrittene Daten: Untersuchungen zum Auftreten der Griechen am Roten Meer* (Köln 1965), 9–35.
16 W.H. Schoff *The Parthian Stations of Isidore of Charax* (Philadelphia 1914), 17.
17 For a discussion of this archive see A. Fuks 'Notes on the Archive of Nicanor' *Journal of Juristic Papyrology* 5 (1951), 207–16. Substantial additions to this archive are now coming to light in the excavations at Berenike in Egypt. See R.S. Bagnall *et al.* 'The Ostraka' in S.E. Sidebotham and W.Z. Wendrich (eds) *Report of the 1997 Excavations at Berenike and the Survey of the Egyptian Eastern Desert, including Excavations at Shenshef* (Leiden 1999), 201–7. More ostraka will be published in succeeding reports in this series.
18 R.S. Bagnall 'Papyri and Ostraka from Quseir al-Qadim' *BASP* 23 (1986), 1–60.
19 For these papyri see pp. 54–74.
20 J. Cantineau *et al.* (eds) *Inventaire des inscriptions de Palmyre* I–XI (Beirut 1930–). For the other publications relevant to this book see Chapter 4.
21 See pp. 138–43. For a recent listing of the inscriptions relevant to the caravan trade, see M. Gawlikowski 'Palmyra as a Trading Centre' *Iraq* 56 (1994), 32–3.
22 A. Bernand *Le Paneion d'El-Kanais: Les inscriptions grecques* (Leiden 1972); A. Bernand *De Koptos à Kossier* (Leiden 1972); A. Bernand *Les Portes du désert: Recueil d'inscriptions grecques d'Antinoupolis, Tentyris, Koptos, Apollinopolis Parva et Apollinopolis Magna* (Paris 1984).
23 See pp. 132–4.
24 For these field notes and their application to this area of study see pp. 69–74.
25 A. Negev 'The Date of the Petra – Gaza Road' *PEQ* 98 (1966), 89–98, cf. R. Cohen 'New Light on the date of the Petra – Gaza Road' *BA* 45 (1982), 240–7. See pp. 106–7.
26 For Quseir al-Qadim see D.S. Whitcomb and J.H. Johnson (eds) *Quseir al-Qadim, 1978 Preliminary Report* (Princeton 1979); D.S. Whitcomb and J.H. Johnson (eds) *Quseir al-Qadim, 1980 Preliminary Report* (Malibu 1982); D.S. Whitcomb and J.H. Johnson '1982 Season of Excavation at Quseir al-Qadim' *NARCE* 120 (1982), 24–30. For 'Abu Sha'ar see S.E. Sidebotham 'Fieldwork on the Red Sea Coast: the 1987 Season' *JARCE* 26 (1989), 127–66; S.E. Sidebotham 'Preliminary Report on the 1990–1991 Seasons of Fieldwork at 'Abu Sha'ar (Red Sea Coast)' *JARCE* 31 (1994), 133–58; S.E. Sidebotham 'University of Delaware Archaeological Project at 'Abu Sha'ar: The 1992 Season' *NARCE* 161/162 (1993), 1–9. For Berenike see S.E. Sidebotham and W.Z. Wendrich (eds) *Berenike '94. Preliminary Report of the Excavations at Berenike (Egyptian Red Sea Coast) and the Survey of the Eastern Desert* (Leiden 1995); S.E. Sidebotham and W.Z. Wendrich (eds) *Berenike '95. Preliminary Report of the Excavations at Berenike (Egyptian Red Sea Coast) and the Survey of the Eastern Desert* (Leiden 1996); S.E. Sidebotham and W.Z. Wendrich (eds) *Berenike '96: Report of the Excavations at Berenike (Egyptian Red Sea Coast) and the Survey of the Egyptian Eastern Desert* (Leiden 1998); Sidebotham and Wendrich (eds) *Berenike 1997*, and other forthcoming reports on the ongoing Berenike excavation.
27 For the most detailed work of this type, attempting to identify all items of the ancient trade and provide a modern equivalent see Miller *Spice Trade*, 30–118, although one must be cautious about Miller's conclusions. See also Sidebotham *Roman Economic Policy in the Erythra Thalassa*, 14–24 for a survey of the items of the Indian and Arabian trades, and Casson *The Periplus Maris Erythraei*, 39–43 for a survey of the goods of the Arabian, Indian and African trades as revealed in the *Periplus Maris Erythraei*.
28 Warmington *Commerce*, 315–18; Miller *Spice Trade*, 219–23, 229–30; Thorley 'The Development of Trade between the Roman Empire and the East under Augustus', 209.

29 See e.g. the complaints of Scipio Aemilianus about the 'degeneracy' of the youth in his day who were being affected by Greek and Asiatic customs (Scipio fr. 17–26, 30 *ORF*).
30 See e.g. Propertius III. 13. 1–15, 59–60; Ovid *Ars Amatoria* III. 129–30.
31 For this debate see e.g. J. Griffin *Latin Poets and Roman Life* (London 1985); D.F. Kennedy *The Arts of Love* (Cambridge 1993), 1–23.
32 Pliny *NH* XII. 28.
33 Pliny *NH* XII. 44.
34 Pliny *NH* XII. 43. See Pliny *NH* XII *passim* for further references, summarised in Appendix A and Miller *Spice Trade*, 26–8.
35 See Appendix A.
36 Sidebotham *Roman Economic Policy in the Erythra Thalassa*, 15. See this reference also for a list of the references in Roman literature to the use of myrrh and frankincense.
37 For detailed studies of the uses of these incenses and the ancient trade involving them see N. Groom *Frankincense and Myrrh: A Study of the Arabian Incense Trade* (London 1981); A. Avanzini (ed.) *Profumi d'Arabia: Atti del convego* (Rome 1997).
38 Pliny *NH* XII. 41.
39 Indeed, it is likely that the ability to use incense in large quantities was seen as a mark of special prestige, especially in rulers. See G.W. Bowersock 'Perfumes and Power' in Avanzini (ed.) *Profumi d' Arabia*, 543–56.
40 For these and other prices recorded in Pliny see Appendix A.
41 For lists of these references and the various medicinal uses to which the goods were put see Miller *Spice Trade*, 4–8; Raschke 'New Studies in Roman Commerce with the East', 1013.
42 Dioscorides *De Materia Medica* I, 1–27, 52–76.
43 Miller *Spice Trade*, 4–8.
44 Celsus *De Medicina* V. 23. 3.
45 Theophrastus *HP* IX. 20. 1.
46 Rey-Coquais 'L'Arabie dans les routes de commerce', 227.
47 Diodurus Siculus XIX. 94. 5
48 See p. 138.
49 Incense was indeed transported from southern Arabia to Gerrha near the Persian Gulf, and thence into the Parthian Empire, and it is possible that some of this incense may have found its way into the Roman Empire. However, this is far too circuitous a route to have existed in opposition to the more direct route through Petra.
50 For commerce in the Red Sea under the Achaemenids, Seleucids and Ptolemies see now J.-F. Salles 'Achaemenid and Hellenistic Trade in the Indian Ocean' in J. Reade (ed.) *The Indian Ocean in Antiquity* (London 1996), 251–67; J.-F. Salles 'Hellenistic Seafaring in the Indian Ocean: a Perspective from Arabia' in H.P. Ray and J.-F. Salles (eds) *Tradition and Archaeology: Early Maritime Contacts in the Indian Ocean* (New Delhi 1996), 293–309.
51 Strabo *Geog.* XVII. 1. 13.
52 *Periplus* 26.
53 Casson *The Periplus Maris Erythraei*, 158–9. It should be noted, however, that the kingdoms of South Arabia continued to trade with India, most probably to supply their own local market for Indian goods (see p. 35).
54 For the various opinions put forward see Raschke 'New Studies in Roman Commerce with the East', 660–3; Casson *The Periplus Maris Erythraei*, 11–12.
55 M.P. Charlesworth 'Some Notes on the *Periplus Maris Erythraei*' *CQ* 22 (1928), 99; G.W. Van Beek 'Frankincense and Myrrh' *BA* 28, 3 (1960), 80; R. Mauny

'Le Périple de la Mer Erythrée et le problème du commerce romain en Afrique au Sud du Limes' *JSocAfr* 38 (1968), 25; Miller *Spice Trade*, 153–72.

56 Raschke 'New Studies in Roman Commerce with the East', 654.

57 Miller *Spice Trade*, 154–5.

58 Agatharchides frag. 97 *GGM* I, 186; Strabo *Geog*. I. 4. 2; II. 5. 35; XV. 1. 22; XVI. 4. 14, 19; XVII. 1. 1 citing Eratosthenes, Hipparchus, Onesicritus and Artemidorus; Pliny *NH* XII. 42.

59 Groom *Frankincense and Myrrh*, 85. See now also F. De Romanis *Cassia, cinnamomo, ossidiana: uomini e merci tra Oceano Indiano e Mediterraneo* (Rome 1996), 97–117.

60 Sidebotham cites Pliny *NH* XII. 42 as evidence for the importation of Indian cinnamon by the Arabs before the 'breaking of their monopoly' in the Roman era (*Roman Economic Policy*, 38), for which see also L. Casson 'Cinnamon and Cassia in the Ancient World', in L. Casson *Ancient Trade and Society* (Detroit 1984), 225–46. However, as noted above, the cinnamon Pliny refers to at this reference comes from East Africa and it is most likely that it is a different commodity from the spice we call cinnamon today. It is certainly true that Arab ships trading out of Muza and Kanê did trade with northern Indian ports in the first century AD (*Periplus* 21, 27), but this must have been only for local consumption, not through traffic, as Indian trade goods are not listed among the items of merchandise available for sale at those ports (*Periplus* 24, 28).

61 See e.g. the description of Muza in *Periplus* 21.

62 *Periplus* 23, 31.

63 *Periplus* 31.

64 A.V. Sedov 'New Archaeological and Epigraphical Material from Qana (South Arabia)' *AAE* 3 (1992), 110–37; A.V. Sedov 'Sea-trade of the Hadramawt Kingdom from the 1st to the 6th Centuries AD' in Avanzini (ed.) *Profumi d'Arabia*, 365–83; J. Pirenne 'The Incense Port of Moscha (Khor Rori) in Dhofar' *JOS* 1 (1975), 81–96; A.F.L. Beeston 'The Settlement at Khor Rori' *JOS* 2 (1976), 39–42.

65 Rey-Coquais 'L'Arabie dans les routes de commerce', 227.

66 Gawlikowski 'Palmyra as a Trading Centre', 27.

67 Strabo *Geog*. XVI. 1. 27.

68 While Strabo wrote later than this, his sources date from no later than this time. See Gawlikowski 'Palmyra as a Trading Centre', 27.

69 M. Chaumont 'Etudes d'histoire Parthe V. La route royale des Parthes de Zeugma à Séleucie du Tigre d'après l'itinéraire d'Isidore de Charax' *Syria* 61 (1984), 66.

70 Ibid., 106.

71 M. Gawlikowski 'La route de l'Euphrate d'Isidore à Julien' in P.-L. Gatier *et al.* (eds) *Géographie historique au Proche-Orient (Syrie, Phénicie, Arabie, grecques, romaines, byzantines)* (Paris 1988), 91.

72 Gawlikowski 'Palmyra as a Trading Centre', 27.

73 Appian *BC* V. 9.

74 Cicero *In Pisonem* 24–25. For *unguentarii* at Capua see *CIL* I. 1594; X. 3968, 3974, 3979, 3982.

75 *Edictum de Pretiis Maximis* XXIII. 1–2 (undyed white silk, 12,000 d.c./pound); XXIV. 1–1a (dyed purple and fine-spun, 150,000 d.c./pound).

76 L. Richardson *A New Topographical Dictionary of Ancient Rome* (Baltimore 1992), 340.

77 Ovid *Ars Amatoria* II. 265–6; *Amores* I. 8. 100; Propertius II. 24. 13–14.

78 Dio LXXIII. 24. 1–2.

79 Richardson *Topographical Dictionary*, 194–5.

80 For some details of the financial arrangements involved in the Egyptian Red Sea trade see pp. 55–8.
81 India: Pliny *NH* VI. 26; India, Arabia and China: Pliny *NH* XII. 41.
82 F. Hirth *China and the Roman Orient* (Shanghai 1885), 227–8; Warmington *Commerce*, 274–8; A.C. Johnson 'Roman Egypt' *ESAR* II, 345; T. Frank 'Rome and Italy of the empire' *ESAR* V, 283; S.J. de Laet *Portorium* (Brugge 1949), 304; Miller *Spice Trade*, 222–5.
83 See p. 23. On the probable inaccuracy of Pliny's figures see M.I. Finley *The Ancient Economy* (London 1973), 132, 206; Raschke 'New Studies in Roman Commerce with the East', 634–7; Sidebotham *Roman Economic Policy in the Erythra Thalassa*, 36–7.
84 K. Harl *Coinage in the Roman Economy* (Baltimore 1996), 303.
85 Strabo *Geog.* II. 5. 12.
86 Strabo *Geog.* XVII. 1. 13.
87 S. Jameson 'Chronology of the Campaigns of Aelius Gallus and C. Petronius' *JRS* 58 (1968), 71–84.
88 Pliny *NH* XII. 32.

2 THE RED SEA TRADE IN EGYPT

1 G.W. Murray 'Trogodytica: the Red Sea Littoral in Ptolemaic Times' *GJ* 113 (1967), 25–7; S.E. Sidebotham *Roman Economic Policy in the Erythra Thalassa 30 BC – AD 217* (Leiden 1986), 4; R.S. Bagnall *et al.* 'A Ptolemaic Inscription from Bir 'Iayyan' *CE* 71 (1996), 317–30.
2 Sidebotham *Roman Economic Policy in the Erythra Thalassa*, 4–6.
3 See pp. 19–20.
4 For Rome's Red Sea commerce in general see Sidebotham *Roman Economic Policy in the Erythra Thalassa*; L. Casson *The Periplus Maris Erythraei: Text with Introduction, Translation and Commentary* (Princeton 1989); V. Begley and R. De Puma (eds) *Rome and India: The Ancient Sea Trade* (Madison 1991).
5 *Periplus* 39, 49, 56.
6 Casson *The Periplus Maris Erythraei*, 289.
7 Pliny *NH* VI. 26.
8 *Periplus* 39, 49.
9 See pp. 140–3. For the name Scythia for this region see *Periplus* 38.
10 M.G. Raschke 'New Studies in Roman Commerce with the East' *ANRW* II, 9, 2 (1978), 630.
11 See pp. 195–8.
12 *Periplus* 53.
13 Pliny *NH* VI. 26.
14 *Periplus* 56. In addition, a Tamil poem from this time describes western ships 'arriving with gold and leaving with pepper'. See P. Meile 'Les Yavanas dans l'Inde tamoule' *JA* 232 (1940), 90–2.
15 *Periplus* 56.
16 Indeed, these coins were most probably imported into India after Nero's debasement of the coinage in AD 64: after this date, merchants would have deliberately chosen earlier coins for trade as they would have greater value in India (where the coins were considered bullion) due to their higher silver content compared to post-reform coinage. See D. MacDowall 'Numismatic Evidence for the Date of Kaniska' in A.L. Basham (ed.) *Papers on the Date of Kaniska* (Leiden 1968), 137–8; Raschke 'New Studies in Roman Commerce with the East', 665–71.

For the coins see P.J. Turner *Roman Coins from India* (London 1989), 1–6, 20–6, 120–2; D. MacDowall 'Finds of Roman Coins in South Asia: the Problem of Interpretation' *Ancient Ceylon* 9 (1990), 49–74.

17 Tacitus *Annales* III. 53; Pliny *NH* VI. 26.

18 See pp. 201–4.

19 For the *Tabula Peutingeriana* see E. Weber (ed.) *Tabula Peutingeriana Codex Vindobondensis 324. Vollständige Faksimile-Ausgabe im Originalformat* (Graz 1976).

20 *TP* XI. 5.

21 E.H. Warmington *The Commerce between the Roman Empire and India* (Cambridge 1928), 18; Casson *The Periplus Maris Erythraei*, 24.

22 That the lender was probably a Roman and not an Indian is indicated by the fact that the papyrus is in Greek and refers to agents maintained by the lender at the Red Sea ports, at Coptos and at Alexandria. It is most likely that he was a resident of Roman Egypt like the borrower, but who had established himself at Muziris.

23 L. Casson 'P. Vindob. G 40822 and the Shipping of Goods from India' *BASP* 23 (1986), 76.

24 *Periplus* 56.

25 Casson *The Periplus Maris Erythraei*, 24.

26 For the excavations at Arikamedu see R.E.M. Wheeler *et al.* 'Arikamedu: an Indo-Roman Trading Station on the East Coast of India' *Ancient India* 2 (1946), 17–124; J.M. Casal *Fouilles de Virampatnam – Arikamedu* (Paris 1949); R.E.M. Wheeler *Rome Beyond the Imperial Frontiers* (London 1954), 172–9; K.S. Ramachandran *Archaeology of South India Tamil Nadu* (Delhi 1980), 90–140; V. Begley 'Arikamedu Reconsidered' *AJA* 87 (1983), 461–81; Begley and De Puma (eds) *Rome and India*; V. Begley 'New Investigations at the Port of Arikamedu' *JRA* 6 (1993), 93–108; V. Begley (ed.) *The Ancient Port of Arikamedu: New Investigations and Researches 1989–1992*, I (Pondicherry 1996).

27 H. Comfort 'Terra Sigillata at Arikamedu' in Begley and De Puma (eds) *Rome and India*, 134–50; E.L. Will 'Mediterranean Shipping Amphoras from the 1941–50 Excavations' in Begley (ed.) *The Ancient Port of Arikamedu*, 317–49; K.W. Slane 'Other Ancient Ceramics Imported from the Mediterranean' in Begley (ed.) *The Ancient Port of Arikamedu*, 351–68.

28 Begley 'New Investigations at the Port of Arikamedu', 105 (Coin of Constantine); I. Mahadevan 'Pottery Inscriptions in Brahmi and Tamil-Brahmi' in Begley (ed.) *The Ancient Port of Arikamedu*, 287–315.

29 Begley 'Arikamedu Reconsidered', 476.

30 Wheeler *et al.* 'Arikamedu', 17, 34–49, 95–102; Casal *Fouilles de Virampatnam – Arikamedu*, 35–7; Begley 'New Investigations at the Port of Arikamedu', 102. V. Begley and S.E. Sidebotham 'Field Investigations 1989–92' in Begley (ed.) *The Ancient Port of Arikamedu*, 41–66; Will, 'Mediterranean Shipping Amphoras', 317–49; Slane 'Other Ancient Ceramics', 351–68. These remains have generally been accepted as evidence for a permanent colony, as the quantity of the artefacts is far greater than would be expected if there had been only occasional visits by western traders.

31 Although Arikamedu is mentioned in the *Periplus* under the name Podukê (60), and is also noted by Claudius Ptolemy (VII. 1), who calls it Podukê Emporion.

32 *Periplus* 51.

33 Casson *The Periplus Maris Erythraei*, 24.

34 Ibid., 25.

35 *Periplus* 56 (sale at Muziris and Nelkynda) and 63 (origin at Ganges mouth).

36 Begley 'Arikamedu Reconsidered', 479. There is considerable doubt about the

significance of these coin hoards, however. It may well be that the hoards are associated with the formation of states in this area of southern India. See R. Thapar 'Early Mediterranean Contacts with India: an Overview' in F. De Romanis and A. Tchernia (eds) *Crossings: Early Mediterranean Contacts with India* (New Delhi 1997), 18–20.

37 *Periplus* 61. See Casson *The Periplus Maris Erythraei*, 230–2.

38 For Roman and Greek contacts with Sri Lanka see now P.M. Weerakkody *Taprobanê: Ancient Sri Lanka as Known by Greeks and Romans* (Turnhout 1996).

39 Pliny *NH* VI. 24.

40 A. Dihle 'Die entdeckungsgeschichtlichen Voraussetzungen des Indienhandels der römischen Kaiserzeit' *ANRW* II, 9, 2 (1978), 571–3; O. Bopearachchi 'Le commerce maritime entre Rome et Sri Lanka d'après les données numismatiques' *REA* 94 (1992), 107–21.

41 See pp. 195–7.

42 Raschke 'New Studies in Roman Commerce with the East', 641–2.

43 D.F. Graf 'The Roman East from the Chinese Perspective' in *International Colloquium on Palmyra and the Silk Road, AAS* 42 (1996), 199–216. The first attempt to provide an analysis of the place names in the Chinese records and to equate them with western names, thus accepting the records' basic reliability, was that of F. Hirth *China and the Roman Orient* (Shanghai 1885), followed by K. Shiratori *Memoirs of the Research Department of the Toyo Bunko* 15 (1956), 1–163. These works generally accept the accuracy of the Chinese records. As noted, Raschke has criticised these works and the reliability of the Chinese records when dealing with western affairs generally, but in the paper cited at the beginning of this note Graf shows that the Chinese annals can be shown to be a reasonably accurate account.

44 Graf 'The Roman East from the Chinese Perspective', 200.

45 *HHS* 88. Abbreviations of Chinese annals throughout this book are those used by Hirth.

46 Hirth *China and the Roman Orient*, 173–8.

47 Ibid., M.P. Charlesworth *Trade Routes and Commerce of the Roman Empire* (Cambridge 1924), 72; Warmington *Commerce*, 131, 394; J. Ferguson 'China and Rome' *ANRW* II, 9, 2, 594.

48 E. Chavannes *'Seng Hou' T'oung Pao* 10 (1909), 199–212; Graf 'The Roman East from the Chinese Perspective', 204.

49 *Liang shu* 54. 22 a–b.

50 Graf 'The Roman East from the Chinese Perspective', 204.

51 Ptolemy *Geog.* I. 14. 1. For the identification of the 'Golden Chersonese' and Kattigara see P. Wheatley *The Golden Khersonese: Studies in the Historical Geography of the Malay Peninsula before A.D. 1500* (Kuala Lumpur 1961), 120–59; Raschke 'New Studies in Roman Commerce with the East', 1047.

52 G. Coedès 'Fouilles en Cochinchine: le site de Go Oc Eo, ancien port du royaume de *Fou-nan' Artibus Asiae* 10/3 (1947), 199.

53 I.C. Glover 'Early Trade between India and Southeast Asia' in J. Reade (ed.) *The Indian Ocean in Antiquity* (London 1996), 373–8.

54 *Periplus* 24.

55 *Periplus* 23. For the political geography of the *Periplus* see Casson *The Periplus Maris Erythraei*, 45–7.

56 No coin hoards have been found in South Arabia of the sort that have been discovered in southern India. However, some Himyarite coins of the first century appear to be copies of Augustan issues similar to those found in India: such coins were most likely imported into South Arabia in trade and copied locally. As with

the coins imported into India, the use of Augustan coins is likely to be because of their superior purity rather than an indication of the date of their importation. See D.T. Potts 'Augustus, Aelius Gallus and the Periplus: a Re-Interpretation of the Coinage of San'a' Class B' in N. Nebes (ed.) *Arabia Felix: Beiträge zur Sprache und Kultur des vorislamischen Arabien. Festschrift Walter W. Müller zum 60. Geburtstag* (Wiesbaden 1994), 218–21.

57 L. Casson 'South Arabia's Maritime Trade in the First Century AD' in T. Fahd (ed.) *L'Arabie préislamique et son environnement historique et culturel* (Leiden 1989), 190.

58 *Periplus* 24.

59 *Periplus* 21, 24.

60 Casson *The Periplus Maris Erythraei*, 157–60.

61 Ptolemy *Geog.* VI. 7. 7 (Ocelis); VI. 7. 9 (Eudaimon Arabia, under the name of Arabia Emporion).

62 *Periplus* 28.

63 *Periplus* 32.

64 J.-F. Breton 'L'orient gréco-romain et le Hadhramawt' in Fahd (ed.) *L'Arabie préislamique*, 173–6; A. Sedov 'New Archaeological and Epigraphical Material from Qana (South Arabia)' *AAE* 3 (1992), 110–37; A. Sedov 'Qana' (Yemen) and the Indian Ocean: the Archaeological Evidence' in H.P. Ray and J.-F. Salles (eds) *Tradition and Archaeology: Early Maritime Contacts in the Indian Ocean* (New Delhi 1996), 11–35.

65 Sedov 'New Archaeological and Epigraphical Material from Qana', 116.

66 Casson *The Periplus Maris Erythraei*, 12.

67 *Periplus* 3–6.

68 For some archaeological remains from this area see J. Desanges *et al. Sur les routes antiquies de l'Azanie et de l'Indie: Le fonds Réviol du musée de l'homme (Heïs et Damo, en Somalie)* (Paris 1993).

69 Archaeological work in this area has revealed the remains of two settlements at Ras Hafun in Somalia, which could be the remains of Oponê. These settlements appear to be no more than campsites where crews in the African commerce stopped and perhaps traded with the local people. The earlier site (Hafun West) was occupied mainly in the first century BC to first century AD. The ceramic assemblage shows contact with the Nile valley and other western sites at this time. However, the later settlement (Hafun Main Site) was occupied in the later second and third centuries AD and shows little Mediterranean contact, but contains ceramics from Arabia and South Asia. This perhaps demonstrates that the commerce was largely in the hands of Axumites or Arabians during this period. For these investigations see M.C. Smith and H.T. Wright 'The Ceramics from Ras Hafun in Somalia: Notes on a Classical Maritime Site' *Azania* 23 (1988), 115–41.

70 *Periplus* 7–14.

71 See Raschke 'New Studies in Roman Commerce with the East', 933; B. Datoo 'Rhapta: the Location and Importance of East Africa's First Port' *Azania* 5 (1970), 65–75; L. Kirwan 'Rhapta, Metropolis of Azania' *Azania* 21 (1986), 99–104; Casson *The Periplus Maris Erythraei*, 141–2.

72 *Periplus* 16–18.

73 *Periplus* 27.

74 *Periplus* 7–12.

75 A.C. Johnson 'Roman Egypt to the Reign of Diocletian' *ESAR* II, 345; Raschke 'New Studies in Roman Commerce with the East', 868.

76 Philostratus *Vit. Apoll. Ty.* VI. 2.

77 Juvenal *Satire* XIII. 124.
78 Pliny *NH* V. 10.
79 Ptolemy *Geog.* IV. 5. 8.
80 S.E. Sidebotham 'Ports of the Red Sea and the Arabia–India Trade' in Begley and De Puma (eds) *Rome and India*, 15–16.
81 Ibid. For the excavations at this site see B. Bruyère *Fouilles de Clysma-Qolzoum (Suez), 1930–1932* (Cairo 1966).
82 See pp. 75–7.
83 Sidebotham 'Ports of the Red Sea and the Arabia–India Trade', 19–20. The ancient sources do not even agree as to its location relative to other ports: Strabo and Pliny both place it north of Myos Hormos (Strabo *Geog.* XVI. 4. 5; Pliny *NH* VI. 33), whereas Ptolemy places it to the south (Ptolemy *Geog.* IV. 5. 8).
84 *Periplus* 1.
85 Strabo *Geog.* XVII. 1. 45.
86 For a summary of the debate and the issues involved see D. Whitcomb 'Quseir al-Qadim and the Location of Myos Hormos' *Topoi* 6 (1996), 747–72.
87 G.W. Murray 'The Roman Roads and Stations in the Eastern Desert of Egypt' *JEA* 11 (1925), 141–2; L.A. Tregenza *The Red Sea Mountains of Egypt* (London 1955), 89–108; D. Meredith 'The Roman Remains in the Eastern Desert of Egypt' *JEA* 38 (1952), 102–4; Sidebotham *Roman Economic Policy*, 50–1; Casson *The Periplus Maris Erythraei*, 96.
88 S.E. Sidebotham 'Preliminary Report on the 1990–1991 Seasons of Fieldwork at 'Abu Sha'ar (Red Sea Coast)' *JARCE* 31 (1994), 133–58; R.S. Bagnall and J.A. Sheridan 'Greek and Latin Documents from 'Abu Sha'ar, 1990–1991' *JARCE* 31 (1994), 159–68; Sidebotham 'Ports of the Red Sea and the Arabia–India Trade', 19.
89 See pp. 11–13 for the publications concerning these excavations.
90 J.H. Johnson 'Inscriptional Material' in D.S. Whitcomb and J.H. Johnson (eds) *Quseir al-Qadim, 1980 Preliminary Report* (Malibu 1982), 264.
91 R.S. Bagnall 'Papyri and Ostraka from Quseir al-Qadim' *BASP* 23 (1986), no. 18, pp. 21–2.
92 Ibid., no. 54, p. 40.
93 F. Kayser 'Nouveaux textes grecs du Ouadi Hammamat' *ZPE* 98 (1993), 145.
94 M. Reddé and J.-C. Golvin 'Du Nil à la Mer Rouge: Documents anciens et nouveaux sur les routes du désert oriental d'Egypte' *Karthago* 21 (1986–1987), 61–3; D.P.S. Peacock 'The Site of Myos Hormos: a View from Space' *JRA* 6 (1993), 226–32.
95 S.E. Sidebotham *et al.* 'Survey of the 'Abu Sha'ar–Nile Road' *AJA* 95 (1991), 573.
96 W.R. Johnson and D.S. Whitcomb 'Pottery: Roman Pottery – Islamic Pottery' in D.S. Whitcomb and J.H. Johnson (eds) *Quseir al-Qadim, 1978 Preliminary Report* (Princeton 1979), 67–8.
97 A.E.P. Weigall *Travels in the Upper Egyptian Deserts* (London 1909), 61, 81.
98 Peacock 'The Site of Myos Hormos', 232.
99 Ibid., 231; Sidebotham 'Ports of the Red Sea and the Arabia–India Trade', 17.
100 *Periplus* 1.
101 R.E. Zitterkopf and S.E. Sidebotham 'Stations and Towers on the Quseir-Nile Road' *JEA* 75 (1989), 155–89.
102 M. Reddé and T. Bauzou 'Pistes caravanières de Syrie, d'Arabie et d'Egypte: Quelques éléments de comparaison' in Fahd (ed.) *L'Arabie préislamique*, 486.
103 A. Bernand *De Koptos à Kosseir* (Leiden 1972).
104 *I. Koptos* 3, 38, 39 (Augustus); 40, 41, 42, 43, 44, 45, 46, 47, 48, 49 (Tiberius); 1 (Claudius); 50 (Nero); 51 (Titus); 52, 53 (Domitian); 4, 5, 54, 55 (Hadrian); 56 (Antoninus); 57 (Maximinus Thrax).

105 *Periplus* 1.
106 Casson *The Periplus Maris Erythraei*, 272–3.
107 Peacock 'The Site of Myos Hormos', 231.
108 Casson *The Periplus Maris Erythraei*, 96–7.
109 The *Periplus* dates from between AD 40 and AD 70 (see I. 2 above), so the port at Quseir al-Qadim must already have been in use when the *Periplus* was written.
110 Agatharchides frag. (x) *GGM* I. See also Diodorus Siculus III. 39. 1–2, citing this passage but also adding the information about the winding entrance to the harbour as contained in Strabo's account.
111 Strabo *Geog*. XVI. 4. 5.
112 Reddé and Golvin 'Du Nil à la Mer Rouge', 61.
113 Peacock 'The Site of Myos Hormos', 229.
114 Ibid., 229–30.
115 Ibid.
116 Reddé and Golvin 'Du Nil à la Mer Rouge', 63.
117 Bagnall 'Papyri and Ostraka from Quseir al-Qadim', nos. 45, 57; pp. 36, 41. In addition, the recent archaeological work at the road station of el-Zarqa on the Coptos–Quseir road has uncovered several papyri referring to Myos Hormos as the terminus of the road, thus strengthening the identification of Quseir al-Qadim (or a site near it) as Myos Hormos. See A. Bülow-Jacobsen *et al.* 'The Identification of Myos Hormos: New Papyrological Evidence' *BIFAO* 94 (1994), 27–42.
118 Peacock 'The Site of Myos Hormos', 231.
119 S.E. Sidebotham 'Caravans across the Eastern Desert of Egypt: Recent Discoveries on the Berenike – Apollinopolis Magna – Coptos Roads' in A. Avanzini (ed.) *Profumi d'Arabia: Atti del Convego* (Rome 1997), 385–94; S.E. Sidebotham 'The Survey of the Hinterland' in S.E. Sidebotham and W.Z. Wendrich (eds) *Report of the 1997 Excavations at Berenike and the Survey of the Egyptian Eastern Desert, including Excavations at Shenshef* (Leiden 1999), 364–8.
120 Strabo *Geog*. II. 5. 12; XVI. 4. 24; XVII. 1. 45.
121 Casson *The Periplus Maris Erythraei*, 97.
122 Ibid.; Sidebotham *Roman Economic Policy in the Erythra Thalassa*, 51–2.
123 S.E. Sidebotham 'Excavations' in S.E. Sidebotham and W.Z. Wendrich (eds) *Berenike '94: Preliminary Report of the 1994 Excavations at Berenike (Egyptian Red Sea Coast) and Survey of the Eastern Desert* (Leiden 1995), 23–7; S.E. Sidebotham 'The Excavations' in S.E. Sidebotham and W.Z. Wendrich (eds) *Berenike '95: Preliminary Report of the 1995 Excavations at Berenike (Egyptian Red Sea Coast) and Survey of the Eastern Desert* (Leiden 1996), 25–31; S.E. Sidebotham and W.Z. Wendrich 'Interpretative Summary and Conclusion' in Sidebotham and Wendrich (eds) *Berenike '95*, 441–2.
124 The excavations so far published indicate that activity at the port peaked in the first century AD and the fourth through to late fifth centuries. See Sidebotham 'The Excavations' in *Berenike '95*, 94–7. This is reflected in the numismatic evidence from the excavation, in which twenty-one of the thirty-four attributable coins found in the 1994 and 1995 seasons were from the first century, and eleven of them were from the fourth and fifth centuries (see S.E. Sidebotham and J.A. Seeger 'The Coins' in Sidebotham and Wendrich (eds) *Berenike '95*, 179–85). The pottery evidence shows a similar pattern, with 80 per cent of the material found dating to the first century, and much of the remainder to the fourth and fifth centuries. See J.W. Hayes 'The Pottery' in Sidebotham and Wendrich (eds) *Berenike '95*, 147–78.

125 R. Cavenaile 'Prosopographie de l'armée romaine d'Egypte d'Auguste à Diocletien' *Aegyptus* 50 (1970), no. 132, p. 220; no. 299, p. 227; no. 528, p. 236; no. 601, p. 239; nos. 1295 and 1307, p. 269; no. 1715, p. 286; no. 1962, p. 296; no. 2068, p. 301.
126 Sidebotham *Roman Economic Policy in the Erythra Thalassa*, 53.
127 *I.Koptos* 41. See Kayser 'Noveaux textes grecs du Ouadi Hammamat', 113.
128 Sidebotham and Wendrich 'Interpretative Summary and Conclusion', 448–9. For glass at Quseir al-Qadim see C. Meyer *Glass from Quseir al-Qadim and the Indian Ocean Trade* (Chicago 1992).
129 For this road see Zitterkopf and Sidebotham 'Stations and Towers on the Quseir – Nile Road', 155–89. For the inscriptions on this route see Bernand *De Koptos à Kosseir.*
130 Sidebotham *Roman Economic Policy in the Erythra Thalassa*, 63–4; Zitterkopf and Sidebotham 'Stations and Towers on the Quseir – Nile Road', 168.
131 Zitterkopf and Sidebotham 'Stations and Towers on the Quseir – Nile Road', 168.
132 Pliny *NH* VI. 26; *Itinerarium Antoniniana* 171.5–173.4; *TP* VIII.
133 S.E. Sidebotham and R.E. Zitterkopf 'Routes through the Eastern Desert of Egypt' *Expedition* 37, 2 (1995), 39–51.
134 Ibid., 50.
135 Ibid.
136 *ILS* I. 2483.
137 H. Dessau *Inscriptiones Latinae Selectae* I (Chicago 1979), 494–49, dates it to the reign of Tiberius; A. Bernand *Les Portes du désert* (Paris 1984), 178–84, no. 56 dates it to the reign of Augustus; F. De Romanis *Cassia, cinnamomo, ossidiana: Uomini e merci tra oceano Indiano e Mediterraneo* (Rome 1996), 219–24 dates it to before 4 BC . See also D.L. Kennedy 'The Composition of a Military Work Party in Egypt (*ILS* 2483: Coptos)' *JEA* 71 (1985), 156–60.
138 For this route see Sidebotham 'The Survey of the Hinterland' in *Berenike 1997*, 364–8.
139 Sidebotham *Roman Economic Policy in the Erythra Thalassa*, 79–82.
140 See pp. 55–7.
141 For this papyrus see H. Harrauer and P. Sijpesteijn 'Ein neues Dokument zu Roms Indienhandel, P. Vindob. G 40822' *AnzWien*, phil.-hist. Kl. 122 (1985), 124–55; Casson 'P.Vindob. G 40822 and the Shipping of Goods from India', 73–9; G. Thür 'Hypotheken-Urkunde eines Seedarlehens für eine Reise nach Muziris und Apographe für die Tetarte in Alexandreia (zu P. Vindob. G. 40.822)' *Tyche* 2 (1987), 229–45; G. Thür 'Zum Seedarlehen κατὰ Μουζεῖριν P. Vindob. G 40822' *Tyche* 3 (1988), 229–33; L. Casson 'New Light on Maritime Loans: P. Vindob. G 40822' *ZPE* 84 (1990), 195–206.
142 *P.Vindob.* G 40822 recto, col. 2, 4–6
143 For a discussion of these officials see pp. 66–8.
144 Sidebotham *Roman Economic Policy in the Erythra Thalassa*, 80–1.
145 *OGIS* 674 = *IGRR* I. 1183.
146 W. Uxkull-Gyllenband *Der Gnomon des Idios Logos*, II, *der Kommentar. Griechische Urkunden* V. 2 (Berlin 1934), 64. S.L. Wallace *Taxation in Egypt from Augustus to Diocletian* (Princeton 1938), 468. See Sidebotham *Roman Economic Policy in the Erythra Thalassa*, 79–81 for the different passes required to leave and to travel in certain areas of Roman Egypt.
147 Raschke 'New Studies in Roman Commerce with the East', 851. Coptos appears to have been involved in textile manufacture from the evidence of several ostraka: see WO II. 1081–2; 1084–90; 1616. The type of coarse textile

mentioned in these ostraka may be similar to those which were exported in the Red Sea commerce, for which see *Periplus* 6. For the role of Coptos in the trade in general, see now K. Ruffing 'Einige Uberlegungen zu Koptos: Ein Handelsplatz Oberägyptens in römischer Zeit' *MBAH* 14 (1995), 17–42.

148 *P.Giss.* 47.

149 For the city of Alexandria see P.M. Fraser *Ptolemaic Alexandria* 3 vols (Oxford 1972); A. Bernand *Alexandrie la Grande* (Paris 1966); E.G. Huzar 'Alexandria ad Aegyptum in the Julio-Claudian Age' *ANRW* II, 10, 1 (1988), 619–68; A.K. Bowman 'Egypt' *CAH* X, 699–701. For the role of the merchants of Alexandria see Johnson *ESAR* II, 344.

150 See e.g. Strabo *Geog.* XVII. 1. 13; *HA* Quad. Tyr. 8; Diodorus Siculus XVII. 52. 2; Aristides *Or.* XIV. 321. Strabo describes the city as 'the greatest market of the inhabited world' (XVII. 1. 13).

151 Strabo *Geog.* II. 5. 12.

152 Dio Chrysostom XXXII. 36.

153 Presumably the goods would normally be placed under the seal of their owner, but in this case the goods have become security for the loan. See Casson 'New Light on Maritime Loans', 202–206.

154 *P.Vindob.* G 40822 recto, col. 2, 7–9.

155 Casson 'New Light on Maritime Loans', 205.

156 See e.g. Cicero *Pro Rab. Post.* 40. For industry in general at Alexandria see M. Rostovtzeff *Social and Economic History of the Roman Empire* I (Oxford 1957), 73–5; Johnson *ESAR* II, 335–42; Bernand *Alexandrie la Grande*, 267–77; Fraser *Ptolemaic Alexandria* I, 135–43; II, 238–51; Raschke 'New Studies in Roman Commerce with the East', 762–4; 901–3; Huzar 'Alexandria ad Aegyptum', 646–56; Bowman 'Egypt', 699–701.

157 Pliny *NH* XII. 32.

158 Pliny *NH* VIII. 74.

159 For the textile industry of Roman Egypt see E. Wipszycka *L'Industrie textile dans l'Egypte romaine* (Warsaw 1965).

160 *Periplus* 6–8, 24, 28, 39, 49, 56.

161 For the Alexandrian glass industry see Johnson *ESAR* II, 336; Rostovtzeff *Social and Economic History of the Roman Empire*, 71; A.K. Bowman *Egypt after the Pharaohs* (London 1986), 221–2.

162 *Periplus* 6–7, 17, 39.

163 See pp. 5–8.

164 Strabo *Geog.* II. 5. 12.

165 U. Wilcken 'Punt-Fahrten in der Ptolemäerzeit' *Zeitschrift für ägyptische Sprache und Altertumskunde* 60 (1925), 86–102 = *SB* 7169.

166 In the Ptolemaic period there was a royal monopoly on the luxury trade, so the purchase would have been made by government agents at fixed rates. Under the Romans, however, the entire trade seems to have been left in the hands of private individuals. See Raschke 'New Studies in Roman Commerce with the East', 901.

167 Casson *The Periplus Maris Erythraei*, 34–5.

168 See pp. 47–8.

169 *P.Vindob.* G 40822 recto, col. 2, 1–26 – col. 3, 1 as emended in Casson 'New Light on Maritime Loans', 196–7.

170 Casson 'New Light on Maritime Loans', 202–6.

171 *P.Vindob. G 40822* verso, col. 2, 27–9.

172 P. Jouguet 'Dédicace grecque de Médamoud' *BIFAO* 31 (1931), 1–29.

173 *SB* 7539 = *SEG* VIII. 703.

174 L. Casson *Ships and Seamanship in the Ancient World* (Princeton 1971), 314–15.

175 Rostovtzeff *The Social and Economic History of the Roman Empire*, 131–2.

176 A. Wilhelm 'Griechische Inschrift aus Medamut' *AnzWien* 69 (1932), 25–7.

177 Sidebotham *Roman Economic Policy in the Erythra Thalassa*, 87.

178 B. Holtheide 'Matrona Stolata – Femina Stolata' *ZPE* 38 (1980), 127–34.

179 *O.Petrie* 228, 229 (Myos Hormos), 231 (Berenike).

180 *IGRR* I. 1172.

181 Sidebotham *Roman Economic Policy in the Erythra Thalassa*, 84.

182 E.g. Gaius Norbanus (*O.Petrie* 244, 257), whose name is also found on amphora plugs discovered at Coptos (A.J. Reinach 'Rapport sur les fouilles de Koptos. Deuxième campagne, janvier–février 1911' *BSFFA* 3 [1912], p. 80 nos. 1471, 1472, 1603), indicating that this individual maintained business interests in both Coptos and Myos Hormos; Tiberius Claudius Agathocles (*O.Petrie* 275, 276); Gaius Julius Bachyllus (*O. Petrie* 228, 291). For others see A. Fuks 'Notes on the Archive of Nicanor' *Journal of Juristic Papyrology* 5 (1951), 207–16; Sidebotham *Roman Economic Policy in the Erythra Thalassa*, 83–6; Raschke 'New Studies in Roman Commerce with the East', 847–9.

183 On the status of merchants in the Roman world see J.H. D'Arms *Commerce and Social Standing in Ancient Rome* (Cambridge, Mass. 1981), esp. 159–79; M.I. Finley *The Ancient Economy* (London 1973), 60, 144–5; D. Earl *The Moral and Political Tradition of Rome* (London 1967), 31–2. Generally speaking, commerce was not considered a fit activity for one of senatorial class, and mercantile activity in particular was looked down upon by members of upper-class society. Such attitudes seem for the most part to be mirrored by local aristocracies in individual cities throughout the empire, although Finley notes that exceptions could arise where merchant activity was peculiarly important to a local economy, as at Palmyra and Alexandria (*The Ancient Economy*, 59).

184 *O.Petrie* 252, 266, 267, 271, 282.

185 Fuks 'Notes on the Archive of Nicanor', 214–16; J. Schwartz 'Note sur la famille de Philon d' Alexandrie' *AIPHOS* 13 (1953), 597–8.

186 Pliny *NH* VI. 24.

187 Raschke 'New Studies in Roman Commerce with the East', 644.

188 D. Meredith 'Annius Plocamus: Two Inscriptions from the Berenice Road' *JRS* 43 (1953), 38–40.

189 Raschke 'New Studies in Roman Commerce with the East', 644. For another possible example of an Italian family involved in this commerce see A. Tchernia 'Le dromadaire des *Peticii* et le commerce oriental' *Mélanges de l'Ecole Française de Rome (Antiquité)* 104 (1992), 293–301. For these and other Italian merchants active in the Red Sea trade see De Romanis *Cassia, cinnamomo, ossidiana*, 241–59.

190 *HA* Quadr. Tyr. III. 3

191 Sidebotham *Roman Economic Policy in the Erythra Thalassa*, 48–68, 113–74.

192 Ibid., 136. The ostraka are *O.Petrie* 237, 238, 239, 242 (Tiberius); 258 (Caligula); 290 (Nero). For the amphora plugs, one of which seems to mention an imperial freedman from the Flavian period, see R.S. Bagnall 'Epigraphy' in Whitcomb and Johnson (eds) *Quseir al-Qadim 1978 Preliminary Report*, 243–4.

193 Casson *The Periplus Maris Erythraei*, 38.

194 Dio Chrysostom XXXII. 40.

195 Xenophon of Ephesus 3.

196 I. Mahadevan 'Tamil-Brahmi Graffito' in Sidebotham and Wendrich (eds) *Berenike '95*, 205–8.

197 Johnson 'Inscriptional Material', 263–4. For this and other epigraphic evidence of Indian traders in Egypt see R. Salomon 'Epigraphic Remains of Indian Traders in Egypt' *JAOS* 111 (1991), 731–6.
198 Begley 'New Investigations at the Port of Arikamedu', 104; Mahadevan 'Pottery Inscriptions in Tamil-Brahmi', 287–315.
199 G. Wagner 'Une dédicace à Isis et à Héra de la part d'un négociant d'Aden' *BIFAO* 76 (1976), 277–81.
200 Sidebotham *Roman Economic Policy in the Erythra Thalassa*, 99.
201 Ibid.
202 See pp. 100–3.
203 For general information concerning shipping in the Roman world see Casson *Ships and Seafaring in the Ancient World, passim.*
204 S.E. Sidebotham 'The Ship Graffito' in Sidebotham and Wendrich (eds) *Berenike '95*, 315–17. The graffito is dated to *c.* AD 40–70.
205 *OGIS* 674 = *IGRR* I. 1183.
206 *SB* 7539 = *SEG* VIII. 703.
207 *AE* LV (1912), no. 171. For these Palmyrene merchants in Egypt see pp. 80–2.
208 Fuks 'Notes on the Archive of Nicanor', 207–16; Sidebotham *Roman Economic Policy in the Erythra Thalassa*, 83. Isidora's role is unclear: she was herself unable to write, as is clear from three ostraka which mention her requiring someone else to sign on her behalf (*O.Petrie* 244, 257; *O.Brussel-Berlin* 7). She may perhaps have been the wife of one of the men in the family, although in an ostracon found at el-Heita on the Myos Hormos road she appears to address one . . .ροδιτῳ, in terms which would indicate he was her husband (D. Meredith 'The Myos Hormos Road: Inscriptions and Ostraca' *CE* 31 [1956], 356–8). Her role, although established, therefore remains unclear.
209 Fuks 'Notes on the Archive of Nicanor', 212–13.
210 Casson *The Periplus Maris Erythraei*, 13–14.
211 Bagnall 'Papyri and Ostraka from Quseir al-Qadim', 6, nos. 2, 21, 24, 28, 44; R. Bagnall *et al.* 'The Ostraka' in Sidebotham and Wendrich (eds) *Berenike 1997*, 201–5.
212 *P.Vindob.* G 40822 recto, col. 2, 2.
213 Fuks 'Notes on the Archive of Nicanor', 213.
214 See pp. 19–20.
215 E. Littmann and D. Meredith 'Nabataean Inscriptions from Egypt' *BSOAS* 15 (1953), 1–28; E. Littmann and D. Meredith 'Nabataean Inscriptions from Egypt' *BSOAS* 16 (1954), 211–46; P.C. Hammond 'Nabataean' in Whitcomb and Johnson *Quseir al-Qadim 1978 Preliminary Report*, 245–7; C. Toll 'Two Nabataean Ostraka from Egypt' *BIFAO* 94 (1994), 381–2.
216 J. Lesquier *L'Armée romaine d'Egypte d' Auguste à Dioclétien* (Cairo 1918), 421–7.
217 *P. Vindob.* G 40822 verso, col. 2, 11–15; 22–6. See Thür 'Hypotheken-Urkunde eines Seedarlehens für eine Reise nach Muziris', 238–445; Casson 'New Light on Maritime Loans', 198–202.
218 See e.g. the Coptos tariff (*OGIS* 674). See also *OGIS* 685, which mentions Claudius Geminus who was both *arabarch* and *epistrategos* of the Thebaid, and *OGIS* 202 concerning Apollonios the son of the *arabarch* Ptolemaios. In addition, Juvenal *Satire* I. 130 refers to an *Aegyptius Arabarches.*
219 *P. Vindob.* G 40822 verso, col. 2, 1–3; 10; 14; 20–5.
220 Bagnall *et al.* 'The Ostraka' in *Berenike 1997*, 201–5. The goods are for the most part wine, including Italian, Laodicean, Rhodian and Aminaean varieties. While some of these may have been provisions for the ships, Laodicean and Italian wines are also mentioned as exports from Egypt (*Periplus* 49).

221 Bagnall *et al.* 'The Ostraka' in *Berenike 1997*, 203.
222 See pp. 48–50.
223 Cavenaile 'Prosopographie de l'armée romaine d'Egypte', 220, 227, 236, 239, 269, 286, 301.
224 Josephus *AJ* XVIII. 159, 259; XIX. 276; XX. 100. For another Jew, Demetrius, as *alabarch* see Josephus *AJ* XX. 147.
225 Lesquier *L'Armée romaine d'Egypte*, 421–7; E.G. Turner 'Tiberius Iulius Alexander' *JRS* 44 (1954), 54; E. Courtney *A Commentary on the Satires of Juvenal* (London 1980), 110–11.
226 Juvenal *Satires* I. 130. See Turner 'Tiberius Iulius Alexander', 59, 63; Courtney *A Commentary on the Satires of Juvenal*, 110–11.
227 The date is not certain but must date from no later than Augustus' time.
228 *OGIS* 202. See O. Hirschfeld *Die kaiserlichen Verwaltungsbeamten bis auf Diocletian* (Berlin 1905), 82.
229 See pp. 46–7.
230 Pliny *NH* VI. 24.
231 Zitterkopf and Sidebotham 'Stations and Towers on the Quseir – Nile Road', 166.
232 For these towers see ibid., 180–8. Zitterkopf and Sidebotham observed that the construction techniques of the towers and *hydreumata* on the Coptos–Quseir route are similar, suggesting that they are contemporaneous.
233 Ibid., 182–8. Not all the towers are actually intervisible, but enough of them are to indicate that the remaining gaps were probably filled by towers which are no longer extant.
234 *O.Amst* 8–14; Bagnall and Sheridan 'Greek and Latin Documents from 'Abu Sha'ar', 166–7.
235 J.R. Rea 'Vestigationes' *ZPE* 82 (1990), 126–8.
236 Bagnall and Sheridan 'Greek and Latin Documents from 'Abu Sha'ar', 167.
237 R.S. Bagnall 'Upper and Lower Guard Posts' *CE* 57 (1982), 125–8.
238 Ibid., 126.
239 See e.g. Raschke 'New Studies in Roman Commerce in the East', 648; Sidebotham *Roman Economic Policy in the Erythra Thalassa*, 63.
240 *I.Kanais* 3, 8, 13, 18, 43, 47, 62, 82, 90.
241 See pp. 85–7.
242 R. Alston *Soldier and Society in Ancient Egypt* (London 1995), 84.
243 R.S. Bagnall 'Army and Police in Roman Upper Egypt' *JARCE* 14 (1977), 67–86.
244 *P.Fay* 38, 108.
245 Alston *Soldier and Society in Ancient Egypt*, 83.
246 Ibid. See *P.Thmouis* 98, 104, 116. This demographic disruption may well be attributable to the effects of the plague which ravaged Egypt after AD 166. See R. Duncan-Jones 'The Impact of the Antonine Plague' *JRA* 9 (1996), 108–36.
247 See e.g. *BGU* I. 372; *P.Oxy* XII 1408; XLVII 3364, for which see J.D. Thomas 'A Petition to the Prefect of Egypt and Related Imperial Edicts' *JEA* 61 (1975), 201–21.
248 Xenophon of Ephesus 4.
249 Sidebotham *Roman Economic Policy in the Erythra Thalassa*, 63.
250 Indeed, this may account for the presence of fortifications in the Eastern Desert which have been found near watering points but far from any known caravan routes: these soldiers were there to prevent caravans from leaving the appointed routes and so evading their taxes. For such stations see S.E. Sidebotham and R.E. Zitterkopf 'Survey of the Hinterland' in *Berenike '95*, 372–82.

251 *OGIS* 701 = *IGRR* I. 1142.
252 See pp. 207–11.
253 S.E. Sidebotham and W.Z. Wendrich 'Interpretive Summary and Conclusion' in *Berenike 1997*, 454–6. There is a general lack of numismatic and ceramic evidence from this period at Berenike, but there is nonetheless some evidence of continued activity there, including a Trajanic inscription from the fort at Wadi Kalalat. There is no immediately apparent reason why this decline should have occurred, but it may perhaps have to do with the trade of Palmyra, which seems to have experienced its greatest activity at this time. See pp. 139–48.
254 *I.Koptos* 4, 5 and possibly also 54 and 55.
255 Sidebotham *Roman Economic Policy in the Erythra Thalassa*, 141–7. Interest in and knowledge of the East is shown throughout Arrian's works (*Indica, Parthica, Anabasis Alexandri*); in many allusions in Lucian's works (see Sidebotham *Roman Economic Policy in the Erythra Thalassa*, 142 for a listing of these); and also by Juvenal (*Satires* VI. 337, 466, 585; X. 1; XI. 123–126; XV. 163).
256 Dio Chrysostom XXXII. 36.
257 Aristides *Or.* XIV. 321.
258 Sidebotham *Roman Economic Policy in the Erythra Thalassa*, 102–3.
259 Herodotus II. 158–9; IV. 39, 42; Diodorus Siculus I. 33. 7–12; Strabo *Geog.* XVII. 1. 25–6; Pliny *NH* VI. 33; Ptolemy *Geog.* IV. 5.
260 Plutarch *Antony* 69: Cleopatra intended to get her galleys to the Red Sea by having them dragged; clearly the canal was not serviceable at that time.
261 Ptolemy *Geog.* IV. 5. For Trajan's canal see P.J. Sijpesteijn 'Der ΠΟΤΑΜΟΣ ΤΡΑΙΑΝΟΣ' *Aegyptus* 43 (1963), 70–83; P.J. Sijpesteijn 'Trajan and Egypt' *Papyrologica Lugduno-Batava Papyri Selectae* 13 (1965), 106–13.
262 C.A. Redmount 'Wadi Tumilat Survey' *NARCE* 133 (1986), 20.
263 Lucian *Alexander the False Prophet* 44.
264 Alexandria was considered to be 'next to', not 'in' Egypt. Thus, in leaving Alexandria, Lucian describes the young man as sailing εἰς Αἴγυπτον, that is, 'into Egypt'.
265 AD 287: *SB* V. 7676; AD 332: *P.Oxy.* XII. 1426; AD 420/21: *PSI* 689; AD 423: *PSI* 87: AD 710: *P.Lond.* 1346.
266 Sidebotham *Roman Economic Policy in the Erythra Thalassa*, 57; Sidebotham 'Ports of the Red Sea and the Arabia–India Trade', 16.
267 See pp. 94–6.
268 Sidebotham 'Ports of the Red Sea and the Arabia–India Trade', 17; S.E. Sidebotham 'Roman Interests in the Red Sea and Indian Ocean' in Reade (ed.) *The Indian Ocean in Antiquity*, 292.
269 The bulk of these Julio-Claudian coins would probably have been transported to India after Nero's coinage reform of AD 64. Nonetheless, the supply of these coins would have soon dried up; there were probably few or none of them left by the Antonine period.
270 Bruyère *Fouilles de Clysma-Qolzoum (Suez)*, 90–6.
271 For example, his bridge over the Danube for the Dacian campaign and his canal near Antioch to facilitate the movement of soldiers and supplies in Syria. See D. van Berchem 'Le port de Séleucie de Piérie et l'infrastructure logistique des guerres parthiques' *BJb* 185 (1985), 47–87.
272 For the survey of the *Via Hadriana* see S.E. Sidebotham and R.E. Zitterkopf 'Survey of the Via Hadriana by the University of Delaware: the 1996 Season' *BIFAO* 97 (1997), 221–37; S.E. Sidebotham and R.E. Zitterkopf 'Survey of the Via Hadriana: the 1997 Season' *BIFAO* 98 (1998), 353–65.
273 *OGIS* 701 = *IGRR* I. 1142.

274 Sidebotham and Zitterkopf 'Survey of the Via Hadriana: the 1997 Season', 354–6.
275 Sidebotham and Zitterkopf 'Survey of the Via Hadriana: the 1996 Season', 228.
276 H.I. Bell 'Antinoopolis: A Hadrianic Foundation in Egypt' *JRS* 30 (1940), 133–47; S. Follet 'Hadrien en Egypte et en Judée' *Revue de Philologie* 42 (1968), 54–7; R. Lambert *Beloved and God* (London 1984), 198–208. M. Zahrnt 'Antinoopolis in Agypten: Die hadrianische Gründung und ihre Privilegien in der neueren Forschung' *ANRW* II, 10, 1 (1988), 669–706.
277 See pp. 173–5.
278 *I.Portes* 103, adopting the rereading of J. Bingen 'Une dédicace de marchands palmyréniens à Coptos' *CE* 59 (1984), 355–8. Although undated, the inscription is generally assigned to the mid-second century due to *Terra Sigillata* sherds found with it. See Reinach 'Rapports sur les fouilles de Koptos', 65.
279 *CIS* II. 3910.
280 Reinach 'Rapports sur les fouilles de Koptos', 64.
281 H. Seyrig 'Le prétendu fondouq palmyrénien de Coptos' *Syria* 49 (1972), 120–5.
282 Raschke 'New Studies in Roman Commerce with the East', 644; Bingen 'Une dédicace de marchands palmyréniens à Coptos', 358.
283 *IGRR* I. 1169.
284 M.P. Speidel 'Palmyrenian Irregulars at Koptos' *BASP* 21 (1984), 221–4.
285 A.M.F.W. Veerhoogt 'Greek and Latin Textual Material' in S.E. Sidebotham and W.Z. Wendrich (eds) *Berenike '96: Report of the Excavations at Berenike (Egyptian Red Sea Coast) and the Survey of the Eastern Desert* (Leiden 1998), 193–8.
286 M. Dijkstra and A.M.F.W. Veerhoogt 'The Greek – Palmyrene Inscription' in Sidebotham and Wendrich (eds) *Berenike 1997*, 207–18.
287 Speidel 'Palmyrenian Irregulars at Koptos', 221. See pp. 157–66 for the Palmyrene role in caravan protection in Palmyrene territory.
288 See pp. 58–9.
289 Jouget 'Dédicace grecque de Médamoud', 2. Sidebotham, however, prefers a mid-second-century date, although this is based only on his opinion that the trade had declined in the Severan period. See Sidebotham *Roman Economic Policy in the Erythra Thalassa*, 87.
290 *I.Koptos* 58, 59, 60, 89, 91.
291 Sidebotham *Roman Economic Policy in the Erythra Thalassa*, 163.
292 *HA* Quadr. Tyr. III. 3.
293 Johnson 'Inscriptional Material', 265.
294 Sidebotham and Wendrich 'Interpretive Summary and Conclusion' in *Berenike 1997*, 443–56.
295 For a list of these finds and their publications see Raschke 'New Studies in Roman Commerce with the East', 1037–8.
296 K. Harl *Coinage in the Roman Economy* (Baltimore 1996), 132–4.
297 For unrest in Egypt, see this section; for banditry and other disturbances in Arabia see pp. 132–4; for the Persian invasions of Syria and the Palmyrene revolt see pp. 178–82.
298 J. Schwartz 'L'empire romain et le commerce oriental' *Annales ESC* (1960), 32; A. Dihle *Umstrittene Daten: Untersuchungen zum Auftreten der Griechen am Roten Meer* (Köln 1965), 19–20; Dihle 'Indienhandel der Römischen Kaiserzeit', 573; Raschke 'New Studies in Roman Commerce with the East', 678.
299 The so-called 'Third Century Crisis' seems mainly to have been a time in which the empire was subjected to serious outside pressure from enemies along the Rhine and Danube and in the East, causing emperors to debase the coinage in an effort to pay the soldiers. This debasement caused a public loss of confidence

in the coinage resulting in rampant inflation followed by economic and political instability. For the crisis as it related to Roman coinage see Harl *Coinage in the Roman Economy*, 126–36.

300 See pp. 25–6.

301 Tables 2.1 and 2.2 are based upon D.R. Walker *The Metrology of the Roman Silver Coinage* III (Oxford 1978), 49–51.

302 Ibid., 106–48.

303 C. Howgego 'The Supply and Use of Money in the Roman World 200 BC – AD 300' *JRS* 82 (1992), 24; K. Hopkins 'Taxes and Trade in the Roman Empire' *JRS* 70 (1980), 116–23.

304 Hopkins 'Taxes and Trade in the Roman Empire', 105–6.

305 Alston *Soldier and Society in Roman Egypt*, 81–6. One of the initial causes of this population decline may have been the severe plague which raged through the empire starting in 166. See Duncan-Jones 'The Impact of the Antonine Plague', 108–36.

306 For the Blemmyes in this period see R.T. Updegraff 'The Blemmyes I: the Rise of the Blemmyes and the Roman Withdrawal from Nubia under Diocletian' *ANRW* II, 10, 1 (1988), 44–97.

307 *HA* Probus XVII. 3: Zosimus I. 71. 1.

308 Procopius *Pers.* I. 19. 27–33.

309 *AE* 1934, 7 and 8. See P. Lacau 'Inscriptions latines du temple de Louxor' *ASAE* 34 (1934), 22–9.

310 For the Palmyrene invasion of Egypt see pp. 178–9. For the possible alliance of the Blemmyes with the Palmyrenes (and later with Firmus) see J. Schwartz *BSRAA* 37 (1948), 38, 43.

311 Jerome *Chronicon* a.226; Eutropius *Brev.* IX. 22–3. For the movements of Diocletian at this time and his campaigns in Egypt see S. Williams *Diocletian and the Roman Recovery* (London 1985), 78–88.

312 Harl *Coinage in the Roman Economy*, 312.

313 See pp. 75–8.

314 *Itinerarium Egeriae* VI. 4. 7.

315 Bruyère *Fouilles de Clysma-Qolzoum (Suez)*, 90–4. See now also P. Mayerson 'The Port of Clysma (Suez) in Transition from Roman to Arab Rule' *JNES* 55 (1996), 119–26.

316 Raschke 'New Studies in Roman Commerce with the East', 649. As has been noted previously (p. 44), the prevailing winds in the Red Sea favour the more southerly ports. Presumably, therefore, it was only the greater difficulty of trading with Berenike (due to the destruction of Coptos and the activities of the Blemmyes) which made northern ports such as Clysma a viable option.

317 See p. 128.

318 Sidebotham 'The Excavations' in *Berenike '95*, 96.

319 G. Gragg 'South Arabian/Axumite Dipinto' in Sidebotham and Wendrich (eds) *Berenike '95*, 209–11.

320 S.E. Sidebotham and W.Z. Wendrich 'Interpretative Summary and Conclusion' in *Berenike '94*, 106; S.E. Sidebotham 'The Excavations' in *Berenike '95*, 96.

321 Sidebotham 'Preliminary Report on the 1990–1991 Seasons of Fieldwork at 'Abu Sha'ar', 156.

322 Bagnall and Sheridan 'Greek and Latin Documents from 'Abu Sha'ar 1990–1991', 162. This use may have continued into the Christian period of occupation: a Greek inscription, probably from the sixth century, reads ἐγὼ 'Ανδρέας . . . | ἰνδικοπλεύσ[της] | ἦλθον ὧδε . . . [. ('I Andreas . . . sailor to India came here . . .') (ibid., 115).

323 Ibid., 162–3.
324 Ibid., 159. The fragmentary inscription appears to mention Galerius and Licinius as Augusti and Constantine as *fil. Augg.*, thus dating the inscription between 308 and 311.
325 Bopearachchi 'Le commerce maritime entre Rome et Sri Lanka', 112–13. For late Roman coins in South India see R. Krishnamurthy *Late Roman Copper Coins from South India: Karur and Madurai* (Madras 1994).
326 Harl *Coinage in the Roman Economy*, 307–8.
327 Cosmas Indicopleustes *Christian Topography* 11.
328 For an estimate of the significance of these taxes to overall imperial income see pp. 207–11.

3 THE ARABIAN INCENSE TRADE

1 For general accounts of Nabataean history see J. Starcky 'Petra et la Nabatène' *Supplement au dictionnaire de la Bible* 7 (1966), 886–1017; P.C. Hammond *The Nabataeans: Their History, Culture and Archaeology* (Gothenburg 1973); A. Negev 'The Nabataeans and the Provincia Arabia' *ANRW* II, 8 (1977), 520–686; G.W. Bowersock *Roman Arabia* (Cambridge, Mass. 1983); A. Negev *Nabataean Archaeology Today* (New York 1986); D.F. Graf *Rome and the Arabian Frontier: From the Nabataeans to the Saracens* (Ashgate 1997).
2 Starcky, 'Petra et la Nabatène', 886–1017. For a different view of Nabataean origins see D.F. Graf 'The Origin of the Nabataeans' *Aram* 2 (1990), 45–75.
3 Diodorus Siculus XIX. 94. 4–5.
4 See pp. 18–19.
5 *Periplus* 26.
6 P. Crone *Meccan Trade and the Rise of Islam* (Oxford 1987), 18.
7 That the Nabataean wealth *was* chiefly derived from the proceeds of trade certainly seems to be the opinion of the ancient writers: see pp. 113–15.
8 See e.g. J.I. Miller *The Spice Trade of the Roman Empire 29 BC – AD 641* (Oxford 1969), 133–4, although more recent works are not immune from this error either, e.g. Bowersock *Roman Arabia*, 15, 21.
9 Strabo *Geog.* XVI. 4. 18. On these routes see D.T. Potts 'Trans-Arabian Routes of the Pre-Islamic Period' in J.-F. Salles (ed.) *L'Arabie et ses mers bordières I: Itinéraires et voisinages* (Paris 1988), 129–62; M.C.A. MacDonald 'Trade Routes and Trade Goods at the Northern End of the "Incense Road" in the First Millennium BC' in A. Avanzini (ed.) *Profumi d'Arabia: Atti del Convego* (Rome 1997), 333–49.
10 For the political situation of southern Arabia at this time see N. Groom *Frankincense and Myrrh: A Study of the Arabian Incense Trade* (London 1981), 165–88; L. Casson *The Periplus Maris Erythraei: Text, Translation and Commentary* (Princeton 1989), 44–9. For the route followed by the 'Incense Road' see A. de Maigret 'The Frankincense Road from Najran to Ma'an: a Hypothetical Itinerary' in Avanzini (ed.) *Profumi d'Arabia*, 315–31.
11 Pliny *NH* XII. 32.
12 J.H. Mordtmann 'Ein Nabatäer im Sabäerlande – Dionysos – Orotal' *Klio* 25 (1932), 429–30; A.V. Sedov 'New Archaeological and Epigraphical Material from Qana (South Arabia)' *AAE* 3 (1992), 120.
13 Strabo *Geog.* XVI. 3. 3; Pliny *NH* VI. 32.
14 Strabo *Geog.* XVI. 4. 4. Such a trade route would probably have branched off the Incense Road near Tathlith, about 200 km north of Najran (see Map 3.1),

passing through the trading centre of Qaryat al-Faw and thence to Gerrha. For this route see Groom *Frankincense and Myrrh*, 197; M.C.A. MacDonald 'A Dated Nabataean Inscription from Southern Arabia' in N. Nebes (ed.) *Arabia Felix: Beiträge zur Sprache und Kultur des vorislamischen Arabien. Festschrift Walter W. Müller zum 60. Geburtstag* (Wiesbaden 1994), 134–5; for the trade centre of Qaryat al-Faw see A.A.T. al-Ansary (ed.) *Qaryat al-Faw: Studies in the History of Arabia II: Pre-Islamic Arabia* (Riyadh 1984). It should, however, be noted that most MSS of Strabo actually read *Gabaioi* rather than *Gerrhaioi*, and it has been suggested (A.F.L. Beeston, 'Some Observations on Greek and Latin Data Relating to South Arabia' *BSOAS* 62 [1979], 8) that Strabo is actually referring to Pliny's Gebbanitae, and not to the Gerrhaeans at all. Regardless of whether or not this is the case, however, it is still true that the Gerrhaeans trafficked in Arabian aromatics (Strabo *Geog.* XVI. 3. 3), which they must have brought from the incense-growing regions of southern Arabia by some means.

15 Strabo *Geog.* XVI. 3. 3. For Parthian involvement in this area see D.T. Potts 'The Parthian Presence in the Arabian Gulf' in J. Reade (ed.) *The Indian Ocean in Antiquity* (London 1996), 269–85.

16 Strabo *Geog.* XVI. 4. 18.

17 Pliny *NH* VI. 32.

18 Potts 'Trans-Arabian Routes of the Pre-Islamic Period', 132.

19 Strabo *Geog.* XVI. 3. 3.

20 P.-L. Gatier and J.-F. Salles 'Aux frontières méridionales du domaine Nabatéen' in Salles (ed.) *L'Arabie et ses mers bordières*, 181–3.

21 Ibid., 183.

22 R. Savignac and J. Starcky 'Une inscription nabatéenne provenant du Djôf' *RBibl* 64 (1957), 215; Bowersock *Roman Arabia*, 154–9.

23 L. Kirwan 'Where to Search for the Ancient Port of Leuke Kome' *Second International Symposium on the History of Arabia: Pre-Islamic Arabia* (Riyadh 1979), 7.

24 J.W. Eadie 'Strategies of Economic Development in the Roman East: the Red Sea Trade Revisited' in D.H. French and C.S. Lightfoot (eds) *The Eastern Frontier of the Roman Empire* I (Oxford 1989), 117.

25 Groom *Frankincense and Myrrh*, 207.

26 For Muza see *Periplus* 21, 24; for Kanê, 27–28; for Moscha Limen, 32.

27 Strabo *Geog.* XVI. 4. 23.

28 For the bibliography of this debate up until 1978 see M.G. Raschke 'New Studies in Roman Commerce with the East' *ANRW* II, 9, 2 (1978), 982. Since then, Bowersock *Roman Arabia*, 70 and Casson *The Periplus Maris Erythraei*, 145 have supported the view that the officers were Nabataean while S.E. Sidebotham *Roman Economic Policy in the Erythra Thalassa 30 BC – AD 217* (Leiden 1986), 106–7 states that they could be either Nabataean or Roman.

29 The fact that Leuke Kome was not normally used by Roman vessels is further confirmed by the absence of the *Periplus* writer's usual list of imports and exports for a port of trade: clearly Leuke Kome would not be of interest to a likely reader of the *Periplus*, and so these details are left out.

30 *Periplus* 19.

31 Bowersock *Roman Arabia*, 71.

32 *CIS* II. 1. 217.

33 Raschke 'New Studies in Roman Commerce with the East', 664.

34 G.K. Young 'The Customs-collector at the Nabataean Port of Leuke Kome (*Periplus Maris Erythraei* 19)' *ZPE* 119 (1997), 267.

35 Pliny *NH* VI. 32.

36 F. Frank 'Aus der 'Araba I' *ZDPV* 57 (1934), 191–280; A. Alt 'Aus der 'Araba II–IV' *ZDPV* 58 (1935), 1–78; A. Negev 'The Date of the Petra – Gaza Road' *PEQ* 98 (1966), 89–98; Z. Meshel and Y. Tsafrir 'The Nabataean Road from Avdat to Sha'ar Raman I' *PEQ* 106 (1974), 103–18; Z. Meshel and Y. Tsafrir 'The Nabataean Road from Avdat to Sha'ar Raman II' *PEQ* 107 (1975), 3–21; R. Cohen 'New Light on the date of the Petra–Gaza Road' *BA* 45 (1982), 240–7.

37 Cohen 'New Light on the date of the Petra–Gaza Road', 246.

38 Pliny *NH* XII. 32. See pp. 51–3.

39 F. Zayadine 'Caravan Routes between Egypt and Nabataea and the Voyage of Sultan Baibars to Petra in 1276' in A. Hadidi (ed.) *Studies in the History and Archaeology of Jordan* II (Amman 1985), 159–71.

40 Ibid., 159–62.

41 Strabo *Geog.* XVI. 2. 20.

42 D.F. Graf 'A Preliminary Report on a Survey of Nabataean–Roman Military Sites in Southern Jordan' *ADAJ* 23 (1979), 126; J.P. Oleson *et al.* 'Preliminary Report of the Humeima Excavation Project, 1993' *Echos du monde classique/Classical Views* 38 (1994), 141–79.

43 D.F. Graf 'The Via Nova Traiana in Arabia Petraea' in *The Roman and Byzantine Near East: Some Recent Archaeological Research* (Ann Arbor 1995), 264.

44 Strabo *Geog.* XVI. 4. 24.

45 Negev 'The Nabataeans and the Provincia Arabia', 561–2; A. Negev 'Numismatics and Nabataean Chronology' *PEQ* 113 (1981), 124–6.

46 Negev 'The Date of the Petra–Gaza Road', 89–98; Negev 'The Nabataeans and the Provincia Arabia', 620–34.

47 Y. Meshorer *Nabataean Coins* (Jerusalem 1975), 73–4; Negev 'Numismatics and Nabataean Chronology', 122–4.

48 Negev 'The Nabataeans and the Provincia Arabia', 639.

49 Negev 'Numismatics and Nabataean Chronology', 126.

50 M.P. Charlesworth *Trade Routes and Commerce of the Roman Empire* (Cambridge 1924), 63; E.H. Warmington *The Commerce between the Roman Empire and India* (Cambridge 1928), 15; J. Starcky 'The Nabataeans: A Historical Sketch' *BA* 18 (1955), 94; Miller *Spice Trade*, 15; J.R. Thorley 'The Development of Trade between the Roman Empire and the East under Augustus' *G & R* 16 (1969), 210–12; Negev 'The Nabataeans and the Provincia Arabia', 561–2; D.F. Graf 'The Saracens and the Defence of the Arabian Frontier' *BASOR* 229 (1978), 6–7; G.W. Bowersock 'A Report on Arabia Provincia' *JRS* 61 (1971), 228; Hammond *The Nabataeans*, 22; Crone *Meccan Trade and the Rise of Islam*, 18–23.

51 For the expedition see Strabo *Geog.* XVI. 4. 22–4; *Res Gestae* V. 26; Pliny *NH* VI. 32; Dio Cassius LIII. 29. 3–8. For modern works on the subject see E.S. Gruen 'The Expansion of the empire under Augustus' *CAH* X, 149; H. Von Wissman 'Die Geschichte des Sabäerreichs und der Feldzug des Aelius Gallus' *ANRW* II, 9, 1 (1978), 308–544; J. Desanges 'Les relations de l'empire romain avec l'Afrique nilotique et érythréene, d'Auguste à Probus' *ANRW* II, 10, 1 (1988), 4–12.

52 P. Mayerson 'Aelius Gallus at Cleopatris (Suez) and on the Red Sea' *GRBS* 36 (1995), 17–24.

53 M.I. Rostovtzeff *Social and Economic History of the Roman Empire* (Oxford 1957) 53, 66; Warmington *Commerce*, 14–15; A. Sarasin *Der Handel zwischen Indien und Rom zur Zeit der römischen Kaiser* (Basel 1930), 17; G.F. Hourani *Arab Seafaring in the Indian Ocean in Ancient and Early Medieval Times* (Princeton 1951), 294; J. Schwartz 'L'empire romain, l'Egypte, et le commerce orientale' *Annales ESC*

(1960), 23–4; Miller *Spice Trade*, 13–14; J.-P. Rey-Coquais 'L'Arabie dans les routes de commerce entre le monde Mediterranéen et les côtes Indiennes' in T. Fahd (ed.) *L'Arabie préislamique et son environnement historique et culturel* (Leiden 1989), 229.

54 See *Periplus* 26, which states clearly that the transit trade ceased as soon as the direct crossing to India became common. That the monsoon passage was in fact commonly used in Gallus' time is made clear by Strabo, who stated that vast fleets sailed to India from the very beginning of Roman occupation in Egypt (Strabo *Geog*. II. 5. 12).

55 Strabo *Geog*. XVI. 4. 22.

56 G.W. Bowersock 'Perfumes and Power' in Avanzini (ed.) *Profumi d'Arabia*, 543–56.

57 Pliny *NH* II. 67.

58 Miller *Spice Trade*, 15; Thorley 'The Development of Trade between the Roman Empire and the East under Augustus', 212–13.

59 Pliny *NH* VI. 32.

60 Bowersock 'A Report on Arabia Provincia', 227–8; F.E. Romer 'Gaius Caesar's Military Diplomacy in the East' *TAPA* 109 (1979), 205.

61 *Periplus* 26.

62 For a discussion of these suggested dates see Raschke 'New Studies in Roman Commerce with the East', 647 with notes. Briefly, Aelius Gallus' expedition did not reach Aden, and was too far in the past in the mid-first century AD to be called 'not long before our own time'; Gaius Caesar (as noted above) did not campaign in Arabia proper but only near to the Gulf of 'Aqaba; Claudius and Nero lack any Imperial salutations or indeed any other evidence to suggest they embarked on such expeditions; and the case for Septimius Severus rests upon a third-century date for the *Periplus* which must itself be rejected (see p. 6).

63 Warmington *Commerce*, 15; Miller *Spice Trade*, 15.

64 *Periplus* 26.

65 Casson *The Periplus Maris Erythraei*, 160.

66 K. Wellesley 'The Fable of a Roman Attack on Aden' *La Parola del Passato* 9 (1954), 401–5. It is also possible that the word 'Caesar' is in fact a corruption of the name of a local king such as Charibael, Elisar or Eleazus. See Sidebotham *Roman Economic Policy in the Erythra Thalassa*, 130–1.

67 Strabo *Geog*. XVI. 4. 24.

68 *Periplus* 19.

69 See p. 6.

70 Pliny *NH* VI. 26 (sea traffic), XII. 32 (land traffic).

71 Crone *Meccan Trade and the Rise of Islam*, 18–23.

72 Pliny *NH* XII. 32.

73 *Periplus* 27, 31.

74 On the site of Medain Saleh see A. Jaussen and R. Sauvignac *Mission archéologique en Arabie* I (Paris 1909) and II (Paris 1914); A. Negev 'The Nabataean Necropolis at Egra' *RBibl* 83 (1976), 203–36 and J. Bowsher 'The Frontier Post of Medain Saleh' in P. Freeman and D. Kennedy (eds) *The Defence of the Roman and Byzantine East* I (Oxford 1986), 23–9.

75 Negev 'The Nabataean Necropolis at Egra', 207–8.

76 Bowersock *Roman Arabia*, 57.

77 Bowsher 'The Frontier Post of Medain Saleh', 27.

78 F.V. Winnett 'The Revolt of Damasi: Safaitic and Nabataean Evidence' *BASOR* 211 (1973), 54–7.

79 Ibid., 57.

80 Bowsher 'The Frontier Post of Medain Saleh', 25–7.
81 Groom *Frankincense and Myrrh*, 146–8, 212–13.
82 Pliny *NH* XII. 32.
83 Groom *Frankincense and Myrrh*, 213.
84 *Periplus* 39, 49, 56.
85 *Periplus* 32.
86 *Periplus* 24, 28.
87 Groom *Frankincense and Myrrh*, 213.
88 Ibid. On this trading and transport cycle see the table in Groom *Frankincense and Myrrh*, 147. Note that the 'autumn crop' had to be stored at the place of harvest during the summer as the heavy rains of the south-west monsoon made the tracks and waterways of south-west Arabia impassable until September.
89 Negev 'The Date of the Petra–Gaza Road', 97.
90 Cohen 'New Light on the Date of the Petra–Gaza Road', 242–4.
91 Ibid.
92 Ibid., 243–4.
93 Ibid., 246.
94 Negev surmises that nomadic tribes threatened the Nabataean realm after the middle of the first century AD, and that the large garrison at Hegra was designed to hold them off. He states that the failure of the Nabataeans to contain the nomads resulted in the abandonment of Hegra and a large-scale nomadic invasion which resulted in the destruction of the Nabataean sites in the Negev. See Negev 'The Nabataean Necropolis at Egra', 229–30.
95 Negev 'Numismatics and Nabataean Chronology', 126.
96 Ibid.
97 Ibid.
98 M. Vickers 'Nabataea, India, Gaul and Carthage: Reflections on Hellenistic and Roman Gold vessels and Red-Gloss Pottery' *AJA* 98 (1994), 233, 240.
99 J. McKenzie *The Architecture of Petra* (Oxford 1990), 56.
100 Negev 'Numismatics and Nabataean Chronology', 126.
101 See Appendix B.
102 K.W. Harl *Coinage in the Roman Economy* (Baltimore 1996), 103, who also points out that the client king of Osrhoene in northern Mesopotamia also minted heavily debased *drachmae* over the same period.
103 Negev 'The Date of the Petra–Gaza Road', 97; Negev 'The Nabataeans and the Provincia Arabia', 639.
104 See Negev 'The Nabataeans and the Provincia Arabia', 660–8.
105 Bowersock *Roman Arabia*, 21; J.F. Matthews 'The Tax Law of Palmyra: Evidence for Economic History in a City of the Roman East' *JRS* 74 (1984), 171; Rey-Coquais 'L'Arabie dans les routes de commerce', 233.
106 F. Zayadine 'L'espace urbain du grand Pétra: les routes et les stations caravanières' *ADAJ* 36 (1992), 217–39.
107 Ibid., 217. For another example of such a station see M. Lindner 'Abu Khusheiba – a Newly Described Nabataean Settlement and Caravan Station Between Wadi 'Arabah and Petra' in M. Zaghloul *et al.* (eds) *Studies in the History and Archaeology of Jordan* IV (Amman 1992), 263–7.
108 Zayadine 'L'espace urbain du grand Pétra', 224.
109 Pliny *NH* VI. 32.
110 D. Kennedy and D. Riley *Rome's Desert Frontier from the Air* (London 1990), 109.
111 Bowersock *Roman Arabia*, 73; F. Millar *The Roman Near East 31 BC – AD 337* (Cambridge, Mass. 1993), 408.
112 Negev 'The Nabataeans and the Provincia Arabia', 639.

113 See pp. 92–4.
114 Eadie 'Strategies of Economic Development in the Roman East', 118.
115 See pp. 139–48.
116 G. Bowersock 'Syria under Vespasian' *JRS* 63 (1973), 139. For the Decapolis see H. Bietenhard 'Die Dekapolis von Pompeius bis Trajan' *ANRW* II, 8 (1977), 220–61. For excavations at Gerasa see C.H. Kraeling (ed.) *Gerasa: City of the Decapolis* (New Haven 1938); F. Zayadine *Jerash Archaeological Project 1981–1983* (Amman 1986).
117 Bowersock 'Syria under Vespasian', 138.
118 D.F. Graf 'The Nabataeans and the Decapolis' in Freeman and Kennedy (eds) *The Defence of the Roman and Byzantine East* I, 790–1; Kraeling *Gerasa*, 500; F. Zayadine 'Recent Excavations on the Citadel of Amman' *ADAJ* 18 (1973), 25; A. Hadidi 'The Excavation of the Roman Forum at Amman (Philadelphia)' *ADAJ* 19 (1974), 82–5; Zayadine *Jerash Archaeological Project*, 79, 257.
119 J. Starcky 'Nouvelle épitaphe Nabatéenne donnant le nom sémitique de Pétra' *RBibl* 72 (1965), 95–7.
120 H.I. MacAdam 'Ptolemy's *Geography* and the Wadi Sirhan' in P.-L. Gatier, B. Helly, J.-P. Rey-Coquais (eds) *Géographie historique au Proche-Orient (Syrie, Phénicie, Arabie, grecques, romaines, byzantines)* (Paris 1988), 58.
121 Diodorus Siculus II. 48. 1–2; XIX. 94. 2–4, 10.
122 Diodorus Siculus II. 48. 2.
123 On the process of Nabataean sedentarisation see now A.R. Bowes 'The Process of Nabataean Sedentarization: New Models and Approaches' (PhD Diss., Salt Lake City 1998).
124 Diodorus Siculus III. 42. 5; Strabo *Geog.* XVI. 4. 18.
125 Diodorus Siculus XIX. 94. 4–5.
126 See pp. 35–6.
127 Strabo *Geog.* XVI. 4. 22.
128 Negev 'Numismatics and Nabataean Chronology', 126. See pp. 107–9.
129 Vickers 'Nabataea, India, Gaul and Carthage', 233.
130 See pp. 109–10. For these suburbs see Zayadine 'L'espace urbain du Grand Pétra', 217–39.
131 Ibid., 223.
132 Ibid., 230.
133 See pp. 106–7.
134 Graf 'Nabataean–Roman Military Sites in Southern Jordan', 126.
135 Ibid.
136 See pp. 92–4.
137 Diodorus Siculus XIX. 94. 3–4; Strabo *Geog.* XVI. 4. 26.
138 Diodorus Siculus II. 48. 6.
139 See pp. 109–10.
140 Diodorus Siculus XIX. 94. 4–5.
141 See e.g. XVI. 4. 23–4. For the great volume of traders travelling the route between Leuke Kome and Petra see XVI. 4. 23.
142 Strabo *Geog.* XVI. 4. 19.
143 Pliny *NH* VI. 26.
144 McKenzie *The Architecture of Petra*, 56.
145 Dio Cassius LXVIII. 14. 5
146 M. Sartre *Bostra: des origines à l'Islam* (Paris 1985), 76–8.
147 Kennedy and Riley *Rome's Desert Frontier*, 124–5.
148 J.-P. Rey-Coquais 'Syrie romaine, de Pompée à Dioclétien' *JRS* 68 (1978), 54.

149 Tiberius had ordered Vitellius, the governor of Syria, to make war upon Aretas IV because of the latter's attack on Herod Antipas late in Tiberius' reign, but the action ceased upon Tiberius' death (Josephus, *AJ* XVIII. 109–25).
150 For the system of client kingship in general see D. Braund *Rome and the Friendly King: The Character of the Client Kingship* (London 1984).
151 Z.T. Fiema 'The Roman Annexation of Arabia: a General Perspective' *AncW* 15 (1987), 25–35; P. Freeman 'The Annexation of Arabia and Imperial Grand Strategy' in D.L. Kennedy (ed.) *The Roman Army in the East* (Ann Arbor 1996), 93–102.
152 This kingdom may have been annexed prior to the reign of Trajan. See Rey-Coquais 'Syrie romaine', 50; R.D. Sullivan 'The Dynasty of Judaea in the First Century' *ANRW* II, 8 (1977), 344.
153 Graf 'The Saracens and the Defence of the Arabian Frontier', 7; K.H. Waters 'The Reign of Trajan and its Place in Contemporary Scholarship (1960–1972)' *ANRW* II, 2 (1975), 422–3.
154 Freeman 'The Annexation of Arabia', 93–102.
155 Ibid.
156 The existence of this son is attested by numismatic evidence from Rabbel's reign. See Meshorer *Nabataean Coins*, 78. He is also mentioned in papyri from the Archive of Babatha, a collection of legal papyri dating from the reign of Rabbel II and the early years of the province before the Second Jewish War. See Y. Yadin 'Expedition D – The Cave of the Letters' *IEJ* 12 (1962), 239–40; Y. Yadin 'The Nabataean Kingdom, Provincia Arabia, Petra and En-Geddi in the Documents from Nahal Hever' *Ex Oriente Lux* 17 (1963), 230.
157 Sidebotham *Roman Economic Policy in the Erythra Thalassa*, 150.
158 Freeman 'The Annexation of Arabia', 100–2.
159 Josephus *AJ* XIX. 362; *BJ* II. 200
160 It is probable that in these cases the litigants wished to avail themselves of Roman law, and were thus forced to use Greek to make their depositions valid in a Roman court (and, presumably, so that the judge would be able to read them). See M. Goodman 'Babatha's Story' *JRS* 81 (1991), 169–75; H.M. Cotton 'The Guardianship of Jesus Son of Babatha: Roman Law in the Province of Arabia' *JRS* 83 (1993), 94–108.
161 Freeman 'The Annexation of Arabia', 102–13.
162 Graf 'The Via Nova Traiana in Arabia Petraea', 264.
163 Bowersock *Roman Arabia*, 83.
164 The formula *redacta in formam prouinciae* in the inscription probably refers not to a formal organisation of the former kingdom as a province, but rather the creation of a separate Arabian command in *c.* AD 111–114 at the same time as the road was built. The decision to create this command (and build the road) may have been taken *after* the initial military intervention of 106, which might have been intended only as a temporary intervention rather than an annexation. See Freeman 'The Annexation of Arabia', 114. For the governorship of C. Claudius Severus and the provincial *fasti* see W. Eck *Senatoren von Vespasian bis Hadrian: Prosopographie Untersuchungen mit Einschluss der Jahres- und Provinzialfasten der Statthalter* (Munich 1970), 166–7, 235.
165 *CIL* III. 14149. 21
166 N. Glueck 'Exploration in Eastern Palestine II' *AASOR* 15 (1935), 70–1, 75; A. Killick 'Udruh and the Trade Route through Southern Jordan' in A. Hadidi (ed.) *Studies in the History and Archaeology of Jordan* III (Amman 1987), 174–5; S.T. Parker *Romans and Saracens: A History of the Arabian Frontier* (Winona Lake 1986), 87.

167 Graf 'The Via Nova Traiana in Arabia Petraea', 242–4.
168 For the *TP* see p. 30; for the *TP* with respect to Arabia see Bowersock *Roman Arabia*, 164–86.
169 As attested on the inscription from the triumphal arch in Petra. See Bowersock *Roman Arabia*, 84–5 and *JRS* 72 (1982), 198.
170 Attested from AD 125–31 in the Babatha archive. See N. Lewis *The Documents from the Bar Kokhba Period in the Cave of Letters: Greek Papyri* (Jerusalem 1989), nos. 14, 23, 25–6.
171 Graf 'The Via Nova Traiana in Arabia Petraea', 243–4.
172 F. Zayadine and Z.T. Fiema 'Roman Inscriptions from the Siq at Petra' *ADAJ* 30 (1989), 199–205.
173 *P.Mich.* 466.
174 Archaeological evidence indicates that several Nabataean military sites were occupied by the Romans and used as stations on the *Via Nova.* See S.T. Parker 'Archaeological Survey of the *Limes Arabicus*: a Preliminary Report', *ADAJ* 21 (1976), 19–31; Graf 'Nabataean–Roman Military Sites', 123–6; J. Eadie 'The Evolution of the Roman Frontier in Arabia' in Freeman and Kennedy (eds) *The Defence of the Roman and Byzantine East* I, 247.
175 As noted earlier, the roads across the Negev were nonetheless used and garrisoned in this period, which shows that trade was probably still using these routes. See Cohen 'New Light on the Date of the Petra–Gaza Road', 243–6.
176 B. Isaac 'Trade-routes to Arabia and the Roman Army' in W. Hanson and L.J.F. Keppie (eds) *Roman Frontier Studies* III (Oxford 1980), 893.
177 D.F. Graf 'Qura 'Arabiyya and Provincia Arabia' in Gatier *et al.* (eds) *Géographie historique au Proche-Orient*, 173–82. For the Hejaz as part of the Roman province see H. Seyrig 'Postes romaines sur le route de Médine', *Syria* 22 (1941), 218–23; Bowersock *Roman Arabia*, 96–8.
178 The whole question of whether or not this area was formally a part of the province may in fact be unnecessary. Isaac has pointed out the fact that, while the Romans thought of internal boundaries between provinces, they never thought of the area outside frontier provinces as being outside Roman control or outside the 'Roman Empire' (B. Isaac *The Limits of Empire: The Roman Army in the East* (Oxford 1990), 119, 394–7). The idea of Medain Saleh being a place outside the Roman Empire yet garrisoned by Roman troops would probably have been inconceivable to the Romans: if there were Roman troops there then it was part of the *Imperium Romanum* by that fact alone.
179 Jaussen and Savignac *Mission* II, 644–9; Seyrig 'Postes romaines sur le route de Médine', 219–20; T. Barger 'Greek Inscription Deciphered' *Archaeology* 22 (1969), 139–40; M.P. Speidel 'The Roman Army in Arabia' *ANRW* II, 8 (1977), 703–6; M. Sartre *Trois études sur l'Arabie romaine et byzantine* (Brussels 1982), 30–3; Graf 'Qura 'Arabiyya', 192–6.
180 Seyrig 'Postes romaines sur le route de Médine', 223.
181 Speidel 'The Roman Army in Arabia', 706.
182 *ILS* 2544.
183 Bowsher 'The Frontier Post of Medain Saleh', 25–7.
184 Graf 'Qura 'Arabiyya', 194.
185 Jaussen and Savignac *Mission* II, 644–9.
186 Indeed, despite the assertions of many scholars, there appears to have been no 'nomadic threat' of invasion at any time prior to the Islamic conquest. See pp. 128–34.
187 See pp. 69–74.
188 Herodian III. 9. 3.

189 D.L. Kennedy *Archaeological Explorations on the Roman Frontier in North East Jordan* (Oxford 1982), 170–5; D.L. Kennedy and H.I. MacAdam 'Some Latin Inscriptions from the Azraq Oasis' *ZPE* 60 (1985), 105–7.
190 Kennedy *Archaeological Explorations*, 124–6. On this site see also D.A. Welsby 'Qasr al-Uwainid and Da'ajaniya: Two Roman Military Sites in Jordan' *Levant* 30 (1998), 195–8.
191 Kennedy and Riley *Rome's Desert Frontier*, 108–9.
192 D.L. Kennedy 'The Frontier Policy of Septimius Severus: New Evidence from Arabia' in Hanson and Keppie (eds) *Roman Frontier Studies* III, 881–3; Kennedy and Riley *Rome's Desert Frontier*, 161.
193 Speidel 'The Roman Army in Arabia', 694; Bowersock *Roman Arabia*, 98. For the text of the inscription see Kennedy *Archaeological Explorations*, 190, no. 39.
194 M.P. Speidel 'The Roman Road to Dumata (Jawf in Saudi Arabia) and the Frontier Strategy of *Praetensio Colligare*' *Historia* 36 (1987), 215–19. This reading differs from the earlier one (Kennedy and MacAdam 'Some Latin Inscriptions from the Azraq Oasis', 100–4) in several points, the most significant of which are: *concata* for *coligata* in line 6, *Dasianis* for *Basianis* in line 8, *a Basienisa m p XXX* for *a Basienis Amat LXX* in line 9 and *a Bamata-Dumata* for *ab Amata Dumata* in line 10. Essentially, Speidel's reading gives a series of posts along the road, whereas Kennedy and MacAdam's describes distances from one fixed point, Dasianis (Azraq).
195 Speidel 'The Roman Road to Dumata', 218–19.
196 Kennedy and MacAdam 'Some Latin Inscriptions from the Azraq Oasis', 101–3.
197 Speidel 'The Roman Road to Dumata', 219–20.
198 Ibid., 216.
199 S.T. Parker 'Towards a History of the *Limes Arabicus*' in Hanson and Keppie (eds) *Roman Frontier Studies* III, 866; S.T. Parker 'Retrospective on the Arabian Frontier after a Decade of Research' in Freeman and Kennedy (eds) *The Defence of the Roman and Byzantine East* II, 641; Parker *Romans and Saracens*, 15; Sidebotham *Roman Economic Policy in the Erythra Thalassa*, 167.
200 Kennedy *Archaeological Explorations*, 71.
201 Kennedy 'The Frontier Policy of Septimius Severus', 880; Bowersock *Roman Arabia*, 121.
202 See pp. 128–34.
203 For these African posts see R.G. Goodchild 'Oasis Forts of Legio III Augusta on the Routes to the Fezzan' *Proc. Brit. Sch. Rome* 9 (1954), 56–68; A.R. Birley *Septimius Severus: The African Emperor* (London 1971), 216–19; R. Rebuffat 'L'arrivée des romaines à Bu-Ngem' *Libya Antiqua* 9–10 (1972–3), 121–34; E. Fentress *Numidia and the Roman Army* (Oxford 1979), 114–17. For a comparison of these sites with troop deployments in the Roman East see A. Rushworth 'North African Deserts and Mountains: Comparisons and Insights' in Kennedy (ed.) *The Roman Army in the East*, 297–316.
204 See pp. 92–4.
205 Speidel 'The Roman Road to Dumata', 213. It should of course be noted that the same arguments apply to the post at Medain Saleh.
206 See p. 147.
207 D.L. Kennedy *JNES* 50 (1991), 76. Again, we probably should not think of this as an attempt by the Romans to provide an alternative route for the traffic so much as a reaction to the use of the Wadi Sirhan by merchants in need of an alternative to the Palmyrene route. Thus, when the merchants began to use the wadi in greater numbers the Romans simply increased their garrisoning to ensure that the caravans reached Roman territory (and paid their taxes) safely.

208 See pp. 83–5.
209 Graf 'Qura 'Arabiyya', 194.
210 Sartre *Trois études*, 132.
211 P.J. Parr 'The Last days of Petra' in M.A. Bakhit and M. Asfour (eds) *Proceedings of the Symposium on Bilad es-Sham during the Byzantine Period* (Amman 1986), 200, 203.
212 D.F. Graf 'Rome and the Saracens: Reassessing the Nomad Menace' in Fahd (ed.) *L'Arabie préislamique*, 388–9.
213 Eusebius *Onom.*VI. 17–21
214 S.T. Parker 'The Roman 'Aqaba Project: the 1994 Campaign' *ADAJ* 40 (1996), 231–57; S.T. Parker 'Preliminary Report on the 1994 Season of the Roman Aqaba Project' *BASOR* 305 (1997), 19–44.
215 Ibid., 30.
216 For example, datable coins in the 1994 excavations were almost exclusively from the fourth and fifth centuries (Parker 'Preliminary Report', 32–4); important fortification works (probably related to the posting of *X Fretensis* at this site) date from this period (ibid., 35–7, 40); and a small cemetery which was uncovered near the city consists entirely of tombs from the early Byzantine (i.e. fourth to fifth centuries) period (ibid., 32). The coincidence of these results with literary references to commercial activity in the Byzantine period (Eusebius *Onom.* VI. 17–21 [fourth century]; Procopius *BP* I. 19 and Antoninus Placentius *CCSL* 175, p. 149 [both sixth century] all refer to maritime trade between Aila and India) strongly indicates that Aila became a port of major importance in the eastern trade in the fourth century, although there may well have been some trade before that date.
217 See p. 86.
218 For these remains see Parker *Romans and Saracens*; S.T. Parker (ed.) *The Roman Frontier in Central Jordan: Interim Report on the Limes Arabicus Project, 1980–1985* (Oxford 1987); Kennedy and Riley *Rome's Desert Frontier.*
219 Parker *Romans and Saracens*, 143–8, 158.
220 Ibid., 6–8.
221 E.N. Luttwak *The Grand Strategy of the Roman Empire* (Baltimore 1976).
222 For the 'traditional' view, that the Roman Empire possessed a grand strategy which gradually evolved into a system of fixed defensive frontiers, see (with reference to the eastern frontier) Luttwak *Grand Strategy*; Parker *Romans and Saracens*; A. Ferrill *Roman Imperial Grand Strategy* (New York 1991); A. Ferrill 'The Grand Strategy of the Roman Empire' in P. Kennedy (ed.) *Grand Strategy in War and Peace* (New Haven 1991), 71–85; E.L. Wheeler 'Methodological Limits and the Mirage of Roman Strategy' *Journal of Military History* 57 (1993), 215–40. For the more recent view that there was no real 'Grand Strategy', and that the Romans determined strategy in a more *ad hoc* (and generally more aggressive) way, see Isaac *The Limits of Empire*; C.R. Whittaker *Frontiers of the Roman Empire: A Social and Economic Study* (Baltimore 1994); C.R. Whittaker 'Where are the Frontiers Now?' in Kennedy (ed.) *The Roman Army in the East*, 25–40.
223 Parker *Romans and Saracens*, 8.
224 Surface sherding at the sites of Humeima, Khirbet el-Khalde and Khirbet el-Kithara revealed pottery from the early second century through to the Byzantine period, while Humeima and Khirbet el-Khalde also showed evidence of Nabataean occupation. See Graf 'Nabataean–Roman Military Sites in Southern Jordan', 126; Parker *Romans and Saracens*, 104–112; Oleson *et al.* 'Humeima Excavation Project', 141–79.

225 B. Isaac 'Trade Routes to Arabia and the Roman Presence in the Desert' in Fahd (ed.) *L'Arabie préislamique*, 247–8. The road is attested by milestones as far as the Wadi el-Hasa, but Isaac feels that it would have continued further north, linking up the forts in the central part of the province.

226 The site of Muhattet el-Hajj, for example, has sherds from the Nabataean period right through to the Byzantine period. See Parker *Romans and Saracens*, 55–8.

227 Forts at Qasr eth-Thuraiya, Qasr Bshir, Ziza and the legionary fortress at Lejjun (as well as several other sites) all have yielded sherds datable from the third century down to Byzantine times, but show no trace of occupation in the second century AD. See Parker *Romans and Saracens*, 45–58.

228 Parker *Romans and Saracens*, 104–12. For Humeima see Oleson *et al.* 'Preliminary Report of the Humeima Excavation Project, 1993', 141–79.

229 Graf 'Nabataean–Roman Military Sites in Southern Jordan', 126. As Graf points out, these Roman garrisons probably replaced units of Nabataean soldiers.

230 Cohen 'New Light on the Date of the Petra–Gaza Road', 240–7.

231 See pp. 69–74.

232 J. Euting *Sinaitische Inschriften* (Berlin 1891), 61–2, no. 463, a Nabataean inscription referring to the time the Arabs (?) destroyed the land; *Chr. Pasch.* p. 271, a fanciful account of the Emperor Decius releasing lions against the Saracens; *Pan. Lat.* 11 (3). 5. 4; 7. 1, referring to an expedition against the Saracens mounted by Diocletian; Eusebius *Onom.* X, referring to danger in the Arnon gorge, although not specifying its nature; Rufinus *HE* II. 6; Socrates *HE* IV. 36; Sozomen *HE* VI. 38; Theodoret *HE* IV. 23, all speaking of the insurrection of Mavia, 'Queen of the Saracens', a Roman federate who rebelled and then renegotiated a peace in the reign of Valens; and Amm. Marc. XIV. 1. 4–7, a description of the Saracens which describes in them terms common to the Roman description of the 'generic barbarian'.

233 Sartre *Trois études*, 132; Parker *Romans and Saracens*, 132.

234 R.G. Tanner 'Greek Epigraphy in South Jordan' *ZPE* 83 (1990), 183–93.

235 E.B. Banning 'Peasants, Pastoralists and *Pax Romana*: Mutualism in the Southern Highlands of Jordan' *BASOR* 261 (1986), 44–5. See also S.T. Parker 'Peasants, Pastoralists, and *Pax Romana*: a Different View' *BASOR* 265 (1987), 35–51; with Banning's reply '*De Bello Paceque*: a Reply to Parker' *BASOR* 265 (1987), 52–4.

236 Banning 'Peasants, Pastoralists and *Pax Romana*', 37–43.

237 Ibid., 44.

238 Graf 'Rome and the Saracens', 341–400. For a different view see M.C.A. MacDonald 'Nomads and the Hawran in the Late Hellenistic and Roman Periods: a Reassessment of the Epigraphic Evidence' *Syria* 70 (1993), 303–403.

239 'Nabataean–Greek bilinguals from Si': *IGLS* 2366–7, *CIS* II. 163–4; Safaitic inscriptions from the desert: *CIS* V. 3262, WH 1725a. See A.G. Grushevoi 'The Tribe 'Ubaishat in Safaitic, Nabataean and Greek Inscriptions' *Berytus* 33 (1985), 51–4; Graf 'Rome and the Saracens', 360–1.

240 HCH 115, 146–8, 154.

241 *IGLS* 2236, 2393, 2393b. See Sartre *Trois études*, 124–5.

242 Graf 'Rome and the Saracens', 360–8. See WH 402, 3289.

243 *NSIJ* 424.

244 Graf 'Rome and the Saracens', 376.

245 P. Mayerson 'Saracens and Romans: Micro–Macro Relationships' *BASOR* 274 (1989), 71–9.

246 This inscription is cited as *CIL* III. 128 by Rey-Coquais ('Syrie romaine', 66) and Isaac (*Limits of Empire*, 138) although the inscription does not correspond to this reference in the *CIL*.

247 See in particular pp. 194–200.

4 THE TRADE OF PALMYRA

1 M. Gawlikowski 'Palmyra as a Trading Centre' *Iraq* 56 (1994), 27.
2 Pliny NH V. 21; Appian *BC* V. 9.
3 J. Teixidor *Un Port romain du désert: Palmyre et son commerce d'Auguste à Caracalla* (Paris 1984), 9.
4 J.F. Matthews 'The Tax Law of Palmyra' *JRS* 74 (1984), 161.
5 H. Seyrig 'L'incorporation de Palmyre à l'empire romain' *Syria* 13 (1932), 266; J. Starcky and M. Gawlikowski *Palmyre* (Paris 1985), 37.
6 M.A.R. Colledge 'Le temple de Bel à Palmyre: Qui l'a fait, et pourquoi?' in *Palmyre: Bilan et perspectives* (Strasbourg 1976), 51–2.
7 For this very important agricultural and pastoral area north-west of Palmyra see D. Schlumberger *La Palmyrène du Nord-Ouest* (Paris 1951).
8 Pliny *NH* V. 21.
9 The significance of this aristocracy and their role with respect to the caravan trade will be explored fully on pp. 149–57.
10 I.A. Richmond 'Palmyra under the Aegis of Rome' *JRS* 53 (1963), 43.
11 Gawlikowski 'Palmyra as a Trading Centre', 32.
12 Ibid.
13 *Inv.* IX. 6. This inscription of AD 19 was erected by Palmyrene and Greek merchants at Seleucia honouring a benefactor of the Temple of Bel at Palmyra. While it may thus be argued that the Greeks so honoured a benefactor of this temple only because they had interests in Palmyra, it should also be recognised that this inscription dates from the very earliest period of the Palmyrene commerce, and there is no similar mention anywhere else in the Palmyrene corpus. It would thus be extremely dangerous to argue for the participation of Greeks in Palmyrene caravans based upon this reference alone, particularly in view of the absence of any similar references throughout the remainder of Palmyrene history.
14 See e.g. Starcky and Gawlikowski *Palmyre*, 74; J.-P. Rey-Coquais 'Syrie romaine, de Pompée à Dioclétien' *JRS* 68 (1978), 54–6; Teixidor *Un Port romain du désert*, 43.
15 See Chapter 3.
16 Appian *BC* V. 9.
17 For a list of these inscriptions see now Gawlikowski 'Palmyra as a Trading Centre', 32–3.
18 For details of the organisation of the caravans and the caravan trade in general see pp. 149–57.
19 *Inv.* IX. 6 (Seleucia); *Inv.* IX. 11 (Babylon).
20 A. Maricq 'Vologésias, l'emporium de Ctésiphon' *Syria* 36 (1959), 264–76 argued that Vologesias was located on the Tigris in the vicinity of Ctesiphon. However, this has been shown to be incorrect, and the true location of Vologesias has been demonstrated to have been on the Euphrates in the vicinity of Babylon. See M.-L. Chaumont 'Etudes d'histoire parthe III. Les villes fondées par les Vologèse' *Syria* 51 (1974), 76–89.
21 Gawlikowski 'Palmyra as a Trading Centre', 32–3.
22 *Inv.* X. 40.
23 *Inv.* X. 96.
24 See e.g. M.A.R. Colledge *The Art of Palmyra* (London 1976), 76, pl. 103. The presence of Palmyrenes in the Gulf is also attested by the discovery of a Palmyrene tomb on the island of Kharg. See R. Ghirshman 'L'île de Kharg dans le Golfe Persique' *CRAI* (1958), 265–8.

25 Teixidor *Un Port romain du désert*, 38.
26 For this trade see pp. 28–32.
27 See A.-M. Stauffer 'Textiles from Palmyra: Local Production and the Import and Imitation of Chinese Silk Weavings' *International Colloquium on Palmyra and the Silk Road*, *AAS* 42 (1996), 425–30.
28 J.-F. Salles 'La circumnavigation de l'Arabie dans l'antiquité classique' in J.-F. Salles (ed.) *L'Arabie et ses mers bordières I: Itinéraries et voyages* (Lyon 1988), 96.
29 J.-F. Salles 'Découvertes du Golfe Arabo-Persique aux époques grecque et romaine' *REA* 94 (1992), 94.
30 Ibid., 92.
31 L. Casson *The Periplus Maris Erythraei: Text, Translation and Commentary* (Princeton 1989),19.
32 Pliny *NH* V. 21.
33 E. Will 'Pline l'Ancien et Palmyre: un problème d'histoire ou d'histoire littéraire?' *Syria* 62 (1985), 263–9.
34 J. Cantineau 'Textes palmyréniens provenant de la fouille du temple de Bel' *Syria* 12 (1931), 139–41.
35 *Inv.* X. 38, 112; D. Schlumberger 'Palmyre et la Mésène' *Syria* 38 (1961), 256, respectively.
36 J.T. Milik *Dédicaces faites par des dieux* (Paris 1972), 12–14.
37 Teixidor *Un Port romain du désert*, 47–8.
38 S.A. Nodelman 'A Preliminary History of Characene' *Berytus* 13 (1960), 111.
39 F.A. Pennacchietti 'L'inscrizione bilingue greco-parthica dell'Eracle di Seleucia' *Mesopotamia* 22 (1987), 169–86.
40 G.W. Bowersock 'La Mésène (Maisan) antonine' in T. Fahd (ed.) *L'Arabie préislamique et son environnement historique et culturel* (Leiden 1989), 159–68; P. Bernard 'Vicissitudes au gré de l'histoire d'une statue en bronze d'Héraclès entre Séleucie du Tigre et la Mésène' *Journal des Savants* 1990, 3–68.
41 D. Potter 'The Inscription on the Bronze Herakles from Mesene: Vologeses IV's War with Rome and the Date of Tacitus' *Annales*' *ZPE* 88 (1991), 284.
42 Schlumberger 'Palmyre et la Mésène', 256.
43 Dio LXVIII. 28
44 Bowersock 'La Mésène (Maisan) antonine', 166.
45 Ibid.
46 Ibid., 167.
47 Teixidor *Un Port romain du désert*, 49–54.
48 M. Gawlikowski 'Le commerce de Palmyre sur terre et sur eau' in Salles (ed.) *L'Arabie et ses mers bordières*, 169.
49 Ibid. For the excavations at 'Ana, see A. Northedge *et al.* (eds) *'Ana, Excavations of the British Archaeological Expedition at Qal'a Island 1981–2* (Warminster 1988); for those at Bijan see M. Gawlikowski 'Bijan in the Euphrates' *Sumer* 42 (1985), 15–21.
50 For this road and the installations on it see R. Mouterde and A. Poidebard 'La voie antique des caravanes entre Palmyre et Hit au IIème Siècle ap. J.C.' *Syria* 12 (1931), 111–15; D.L. Kennedy and D.S. Riley *Rome's Desert Frontier from the Air* (London 1990), 80–1, 89–93, 212.
51 Gawlikowski 'Palmyra as a Trading Centre', 31.
52 *Inv.* X. 29. For the *tetarte* see pp. 95–6.
53 Gawlikowski 'Palmyra as a Trading Centre', 32–3.
54 M.I. Rostovtzeff 'Les inscriptions caravanières de Palmyre' in *Mélanges Gustave Glotz* II (Paris 1932), 792–811.
55 E. Will 'Marchands et chefs de caravanes à Palmyre' *Syria* 34 (1957), 262–77.

56 See e.g. Starcky and Gawlikowski *Palmyre*, 80; Matthews 'The Tax Law of Palmyra', 169; Teixidor *Un Port romain du désert*, 18; R. Stoneman *Palmyra and its Empire* (Ann Arbor 1991), 63; Gawlikowski 'Palmyra as a Trading Centre', 31.
57 Will 'Marchands et chefs de caravanes a Palmyre', 268.
58 Ibid., 269–70.
59 Ibid., 270.
60 Ibid., 271–3.
61 Schlumberger *La Palmyrène du Nord-Ouest*; Will 'Marchands et chefs de caravanes a Palmyre', 271.
62 J. Teixidor 'Deux inscriptions palmyréniennes du musée de Bagdad' *Syria* 40 (1963), 33–4.
63 *Baalshamin* III. no. 45; see also the unpublished inscription from the Allat temple at Palmyra noted by Gawlikowski ('Palmyra as a Trading Centre', no. 15, p. 32) for a similar occurrence. For summaries of these inscriptions see Appendix C.
64 *Inv*. X. 112.
65 *Inv*. X. 81.
66 *Inv*. X. 29.
67 For a recent list of these inscriptions see Gawlikowski 'Palmyra as a Trading Centre', 32–3.
68 See pp. 144–5.
69 E.g. Iarhai, Satrap of Tylos for the king of Mesene (*Inv*. X. 38); the archon of Mesene (M. Rostovtzeff, *Berytus* 2, 143): both of these were apparently Palmyrenes who held important positions within the kingdom of Mesene and who assisted the merchants of their native city.
70 *Inv*. X. 107.
71 *Inv*. III. 13.
72 This would appear to be indicated by the absence of the mention of a *synodiarch* in this inscription and the fact that the *archemporos* appears to be fulfilling the role normally taken by the *synodiarch*.
73 Will 'Marchands et chefs de caravanes a Palmyre', 270.
74 *Inv*. X. 44.
75 As in the case of Septimius Worod, procurator and *argapet* of the city who is cited for bringing caravans back at his own expense (*Inv*. III. 7). See also *Inv*. III. 28 for another example of a caravan leader assuming costs normally borne by the caravan itself: on this occasion it is specified as being an expense of 300 'old gold *denarii*'.
76 M. Gawlikowski 'Comptes d'un homme d'affaires dans une tour funéraire à Palmyre' *Semitica* L36 (1986), 87–99.
77 See pp. 55–8.
78 A list of these inscriptions and a short summary of each is provided in Appendix C.
79 *Inv*. III. 29; X. 44, 47, 107, 111, 127. Most of these simply state that the honorand 'helped the caravan in every way' without supplying any more specific information. For the interpretation of these inscriptions as referring to military protection see Rostovtzeff *Mélanges Glotz* II, 805; Will 'Marchands et chefs de caravanes a Palmyre', 265–7; Bowersock 'La Mésène (Maisan) antonine', 159; Starcky and Gawlikowski *Palmyre*, 48; Teixidor *Un Port romain du désert*, 31; Matthews 'The Tax Law of Palmyra', 168.
80 See p. 72.
81 Rostovtzeff *Mélanges Glotz* II, 805–7.
82 Will 'Marchands et chefs de caravanes a Palmyre', 267.
83 Ibid., 266. See also Teixidor *Un Port romain du désert*, 31.

84 *CIS* II. 3973.
85 *Baalshamin* III. no. 51.
86 J. Cantineau 'L'inscription de 'Umm es-Salâbih' *Syria* 14 (1933), 178–80. Gamla was identified by Cantineau with the modern Gmeyla, which is 4 km downstream from 'Ana.
87 Gawlikowski 'Palmyre et l'Euphrate', 62.
88 D.L. Kennedy 'Ana on the Euphrates in the Roman Period' *Iraq* 48 (1986), 104.
89 *Dura* VII–VIII, no. 909: Dedication of the 'B'nai Mitha, the archers'; *Dura* VII–VIII, no. 845, AD 169: Dedication of Ethpeni, *strategos* over the archers at Dura; *Dura* VII–VIII, no. 846, AD 171: Dedication of Zenobios, *strategos* of the archers.
90 See e.g. F. Millar *The Roman Near East 31 BC – AD 337* (Cambridge, Mass. 1993), 115.
91 Most notable in this regard is the long series of Palmyrene inscriptions from the city, for which see C. du Mesnil du Buisson *Inventaire des inscriptions Palmyréniennes de Doura-Europos (32 avant J.-C. à 256 après J.-C.)* (Paris 1939).
92 F.E. Brown in *Dura Preliminary Report* VII–VIII (New Haven 1939), 264, 279–81.
93 Gawlikowski 'Palmyre et l'Euphrate', 61.
94 *Inv.* III. 22. For a discussion of this inscription and other examples of strategoi as *duumuiri coloniae* at Palmyra see H. Ingholt 'Varia Tadmorea' in *Palmyre: Bilan et perspectives*, 124–6.
95 Gawlikowski 'Le commerce de Palmyre sur terre et sur eau', 165.
96 *SEG* VII. 138.
97 Matthews 'The Tax Law of Palmyra', 168.
98 *Inv.* X. 44 = *SEG* VII. 139.
99 Will 'Marchands et chefs de caravanes a Palmyre', 265. Matthews ('The Tax Law of Palmyra', 168), along with Will at this reference, consider that Ogeilu's caravan commands in the latter inscription are the same as raising an expedition against the nomads, thus excluding a separate role or regularised command of '*strategos* against the nomads' or '*strategos* of the peace'. However, *Inv.* X. 44 seems to separate the caravan commands and the expeditions against the nomads, indicating that these were two different positions.
100 *Baalshamin* III. 45 (AD 132) and an unpublished inscription from the Allat temple at Palmyra (AD 144, see Gawlikowski 'Palmyra as a Trading Centre', 32).
101 See p. 81.
102 Starcky and Gawlikowski *Palmyre*, 41–3; Millar *The Roman Near East*, 328, 333–4.
103 J.F. Gilliam 'The Roman Army in Dura' in C.B. Welles *et al.* (eds) *The Excavations at Dura Europus: Final Report* V. 1, *The Parchments and Papyri* (New Haven 1959), 24–7; D.L. Kennedy 'The Cohors XX Palmyrenorum at Dura Europos' in E. Dabrowa (ed.) *The Roman and Byzantine Army in the East* (Krakow 1994), 89–98.
104 Ibid., 26–7.
105 B. Isaac *The Limits of Empire: The Roman Army in the East* (Oxford 1990), 225.
106 For this garrison see H. Seyrig 'Textes relatifs à la garnison romaine de Palmyre' *Syria* 14 (1933), 152–68; M.P. Speidel 'Numerus or Ala Vocontiorum at Palmyra?' in *Roman Army Studies* I (Amsterdam 1984), 167–9.
107 Will 'Marchands et chefs de caravanes a Palmyre', 266.
108 Josephus *BJ* II. 18. 9; V. 1. 6; Tacitus *Annales* XII. 49; XV. 3; Ovid *Ex Ponto* I. 2. 808; 8. 5–6; IV. 14. 28. See E. Birley 'Local Militias in the Roman Empire'

in *Bonner Historia-Augusta Colloquium 1972/1974* (Bonn 1976), 65–73; D. van Berchem 'Le port de Seleucie de Pierie et l'infrastructure logistique des guerres parthiques' *BJb* 185 (1985), 47–87; Isaac *The Limits of Empire*, 326.

109 Speidel 'Numerus or Ala Vocontiorum', 169.

110 *Inv.* X. 29.

111 Kennedy 'Ana on the Euphrates in the Roman Period', 103.

112 Ibid., 104.

113 Gawlikowski 'Palmyre et l'Euphrate', 60.

114 Gilliam 'The Roman Army in Dura', 24–7.

115 See pp. 173–5.

116 Gawlikowski 'Palmyre et l'Euphrate', 62.

117 E. Honigmann and A. Maricq *Recherches sur les Res Gestae Divi Saporis* (Brussels 1953), 12, 146.

118 *Inv.* III. 13 (AD 257/258), 7 (AD 260).

119 See pp. 150–1, 154–7.

120 For the text of the Tariff see *CIS* II. 3913. Comprehensive discussions of this text are found in I. Shifman *Palmirskij Poshlinnyj Tarif* (Moscow 1980); Teixidor *Un Port romain du désert*; Matthews 'The Tax Law of Palmyra'.

121 Matthews 'The Tax Law of Palmyra', 172–3.

122 Ibid., 171.

123 Caravan inscriptions dedicated by the Council and/or People include: *Inv.* X. 127 (AD 86); X. 114 (AD 138); Milik *Dédicaces* 12–14 (AD 145/146); *Inv.* X. 44 (AD 199); III. 13 (AD 257/258); IX. 30 (early third century AD); III. 7 (AD 266).

124 This is seen chiefly in the inscriptional evidence from these cities, for which see Millar *The Roman Near East, passim*. Ball now argues, however, that this tendency is only superficial, and that the architecture of eastern cities betrays an underlying 'easternness' with only a veneer of Hellenism. See W. Ball *Rome in the East: The Transformation of an Empire* (London 2000).

125 Millar *The Roman Near East*, 321–30. For Palmyrene religious practices see M. Gawlikowski 'Les dieux de Palmyre' *ANRW* II, 18, 4 (1990), 2605–58.

126 M.I. Rostovtzeff 'Dura and the Problem of Parthian Art' *YCS* 5 (1935), 157–304.

127 Millar *The Roman Near East*, 329.

128 Ibid., 335–6. See K. As'ad and M. Gawlikowski 'New Honorific Inscriptions in the Great Colonnade of Palmyra' *AAS* 37 (1987), 164, nos. 7–8.

129 See pp. 59–60.

130 *Inv.* III. 7.

131 *Inv.* III. 6, 8, 9. For the translation of *argapet* see J. Cantineau's commentary to these inscriptions in the *Inventaire*.

132 The *cursus honorum* at Palmyra in these years is very difficult to reconstruct, particularly as there seem to have been numerous local posts such as *argapet* existing alongside the regular Roman posts common to all *coloniae*. For the known political structure of Palmyra see Millar *The Roman Near East*, 324–7.

133 *Inv.* III. 28.

134 Will 'Marchands et chefs de caravanes a Palmyre', 270.

135 H. Devijver 'Equestrian Officers from the East' in P. Freeman and D. Kennedy (eds) *The Defence of the Roman and Byzantine East* I (Oxford 1986),179–83.

136 E.g. *PME* A7, A8; C165; G29bis; Inc.71.

137 Devijver 'Equestrian Officers from the East', 183.

138 Ibid., 205.

139 Ibid., 184; Isaac *The Limits of Empire*, 225.

140 Herodian VI. 2. 6–7.

141 *Inv*. III. 21.
142 Starcky and Gawlikowski *Palmyre*, 53.
143 For the various sources describing Shapur's invasions see M.H. Dodgeon and S.N.C. Lieu *The Roman Eastern Frontier and the Persian Wars (AD 226–363)* (London 1991), 34–67.
144 The name 'Anatha appears in the list of places conquered by Shapur in his invasion of 256. See Honigmann and Maricq *Recherches sur les Res Gestae Divi Saporis*, 12, 146.
145 Ingholt ('Varia Tadmorea', 123) suggests that this title may refer to the commander of the Palmyrene militia. It is only ever held by members of the family of Odaenathus. For a discussion of this office see Appendix D.
146 G.W. Bowersock *Roman Arabia* (Cambridge, Mass. 1983), 132–7.
147 Al-Tabari 745–761. In this account, Jadhima is killed by al-Zabba (i.e. Zenobia) who is then defeated by 'Amr ibn 'Adi, the nephew of Jadhima, and kills herself.
148 *PAES* IV. A, no. 41.
149 R. Dussaud and F. Macler 'Rapport sur une mission scientifique dans les régions désertiques de la Syrie moyenne' *Nouvelles archives des missions scientifiques et littéraires* 10 (1902), 409–21.
150 See pp. 123–8.
151 For the campaigns of Odaenathus against the Persians and against Roman usurpers see *HA* Valer. IV. 2–4; Gall. III. 1–5; X. 1–8; Trig. Tyr. XV. 1–5; XVIII. 1–3; *Orac. Syb*. XIII. 155–171; *IGRR* III. 1032; Festus *Brev*. XXIII. 64. 13–18; Eutropius IX. 10; Jerome *Chron*. a. 266; Orosius *Adv. Pag*. VII. 22. 12; Continuator of Dio Cassius (*FHG* IV. 197) III. 744; Zosimus I. 39. 1–2; Zonaras XII. 24.
152 For this position see Ingholt 'Varia Tadmorea', 115–36.
153 M. Gawlikowski 'Les princes de Palmyre' *Syria* 62 (1985), 251–61; D. Potter *Prophecy and History in the Crisis of the Roman Empire: A Historical Commentary on the Thirteenth Sibylline Oracle* (Oxford 1990), 381–8.
154 For Odaenathus' titles and their significance see Appendix D.
155 *HA* Gall. 10. 6–8; 12. 1; Trig. Tyr. 15. 4; Festus *Brev*. XXIII. 64. 13–18; Eutropius IX. 10; Jerome *Chron*. a. 266; Orosius *Adv. Pag*. VII. 22. 12; Zosimus I. 39. 2.
156 Festus *Brev*. XXIII. 64. 13–18; Jerome *Chron*. a. 226; Orosius *Adv. Pag*. VII. 22. 12; Continuator of Dio Cassius (*FHG* IV. 197) III. 744.
157 Zosimus I. 39. 1.
158 D.L. Kennedy *JNES* 50 (1991), 76; *JRS* 85 (1995), 243.
159 Kennedy *JRS* 85, 243.
160 Potter *Prophecy and History in the Crisis of the Roman Empire*, 393. See Appendix D.
161 *CIS* II. 3971.
162 *IGLS* XIII. 1. 9107.
163 Malalas XII. 299. 3–10.
164 *HA* Div. Claud. XI. 1–2; Probus IX. 5; Zosimus I. 44. 1–2.
165 Zosimus I. 50.
166 Stoneman *Palmyra and its Empire*, 117–18.
167 *P.Oxy* 1264. 20–7.
168 *ILS* 8924.
169 Zosimus I. 50–6, 59–61; *HA* Aurel. 25–31.
170 J. Schwartz 'L'empire romain et le commerce oriental' *Annales* (Jan.–Feb. 1960), 18–44.

171 J. Schwartz 'Palmyre et l'opposition à Rome en Egypte' in *Palmyre: Bilan et perspectives*, 139–51. For Palmyrenes in Egypt and the disturbances in third-century Egypt see pp. 80–6.
172 Stoneman *Palmyra and its Empire*, 161.
173 *ILS* 8924. See Millar *The Roman Near East*, 220–1.
174 J. Eadie 'One Hundred Years of Rebellion: the Eastern Army in Politics, AD 175–272' in D.L. Kennedy (ed.) *The Roman Army in the East* (Ann Arbor 1996), 135–51.
175 *CIS* II. 3971; T. Bauzou 'Deux milliaires inédits de Vaballath en Jordanie du Nord' in Freeman and Kennedy (eds) *The Defence of the Roman and Byzantine East* I, 1–8.
176 Potter *Prophecy and History in the Crisis of the Roman Empire*, 394.
177 Eadie 'One Hundred Years of Rebellion', 150.
178 Schwartz 'Palmyre et l'opposition à Rome en Egypte', 145–9.
179 Bowersock *Roman Arabia*, 136.
180 For a discussion of the commerce in Roman Syria and Mesopotamia see Chapter 5.
181 Amm. Marc. XIV. 4. 3.
182 Stoneman *Palmyra and its Empire*, 19, 48. See pp. 188–90 for discussion.
183 *HA* Prob. 17.
184 As'ad and Gawlikowski 'New Honorific Inscriptions in the Great Colonnade of Palmyra', 164, nos. 7–8.
185 M. Gawlikowski 'Inscriptions de Palmyre' *Syria* 48 (1971), 407, 412–21.
186 Millar *The Roman Near East*, 335.
187 D. Graf 'Rome and the Saracens: Reassessing the Nomadic Menace' in Fahd (ed.) *L'Arabie préislamique*, 392–400.

5 TRADE IN SYRIA AND THE NORTH

1 Amm. Marc. XIV. 3. 3.
2 R. Stoneman *Palmyra and its Empire: Zenobia's Revolt against Rome* (Ann Arbor 1991), 19.
3 J. Wagner *Seleucia am Euphrat/Zeugma* (Wiesbaden 1976), 71–82.
4 Strabo *Geog.* XVI. 1. 27.
5 Pliny *NH* VI. 31.
6 See pp. 144–7.
7 Josephus *AJ* XX. 3. 34.
8 D.L. Kennedy 'Parthia and Rome: Eastern Perspectives' in D.L. Kennedy (ed.) *The Roman Army in the East* (Ann Arbor 1996), 72.
9 *Inv.* IX. 6 = *CIS* II. 3924.
10 Judging from their inscriptions, which never mention Seleucia again.
11 Midrash Samuel 10. 3.
12 Petr. Patric. frag. 13–14 *FHG* 4.188–9.
13 J. Thorley 'The Silk Trade between China and the Roman Empire at its Height, circa AD 90–130' *G & R* 18 (1971), 71.
14 M. Cary 'Maes, Qui et Titianus' *CQ* n.s. 6 (1956), 130.
15 Ptolemy *Geog.* I. 11. 6–7.
16 M.G. Raschke 'New Studies in Roman Commerce with the East' *ANRW* II, 9, 2 (1978), 630; W. Ball *Rome in the East: The Transformation of an Empire* (London 2000), 133–9.
17 Strabo *Geog.* XVI. 1. 27.

18 H.J.W. Drijvers 'Hatra, Palmyra und Edessa' *ANRW* II, 8 (1977), 819.
19 M.I. Rostovtzeff identified it as such in his *Caravan Cities* (Oxford 1932); see also M.A. Stein 'The Ancient Trade Route past Hatra and its Roman Posts' *JRAS* (1941), 299–316.
20 Drijvers 'Hatra, Palmyra und Edessa', 815.
21 Dio Cassius LXXVI. 12. 2.
22 A. Caquot 'Nouvelles inscriptions araméennes de Hatra V' *Syria* 40 (1963), 12–14; J. Teixidor 'Notes hatréennes 1: l'inscription de Sa'adiya' *Syria* 41 (1964), 273–9.
23 J. Teixidor 'Notes hatréennes 2: l'inscription de Hatra no. 79' *Syria* 41 (1964), 280–4.
24 D. Oates 'A Note on Three Latin Inscriptions from Hatra' *Sumer* 11 (1955), 39–43; A. Maricq 'Classica et Orientalia 2: Les dernières années de Hatra: l'alliance romaine' *Syria* 34 (1957), 288–96.
25 Rostovtzeff *Caravan Cities*, 32.
26 *Inv.* X. 29. See p. 152.
27 For this procedure in Alexandria see p. 52.
28 J.B. Segal *Edessa: The Blessed City* (Oxford 1970), 44, 79, 137.
29 Strabo *Geog.* XVI. 2. 23; Pliny *NH* V. 12.
30 Many scholars have made the assumption that the Parthians deliberately channelled and monopolised the trade with the East in order to increase their own revenues. See W.H. Schoff *The Parthian Stations of Isidore of Charax* (Philadelphia 1914), 18–19; E.H. Warmington *The Commerce between the Roman Empire and India* (Cambridge 1928), 20; J.I. Miller *The Spice Trade of the Roman Empire 29 BC – AD 641* (Oxford 1969), 139, 235; Thorley 'The Silk Trade between China and the Roman Empire at its Height', 75. From this point it has been postulated that Trajan wished to destroy the Parthian monopoly on the trade, and that this was therefore the major reason for his war on Parthia, for which see Warmington *Commerce*, 91–2; J.-P. Rey-Coquais 'Syrie Romaine, de Pompée à Dioclétien' *JRS* 68 (1978), 54; J.-P. Rey-Coquais 'L'Arabie dans les routes de commerce entre le monde Mediterranéen et les côtes Indiennes' in T. Fahd (ed.) *L'Arabie préislamique et son environnement historique et culturel* (Leiden 1989), 235.
31 For references see the previous note.
32 *HHS* 118. 5a.
33 Miller *Spice Trade*, 133–6.
34 *HHS* 88.
35 Ptolemy *Geog.* I. 11. 6–7.
36 This fact has caused some disquiet among scholars who hold to the view that the Parthians prevented any such contact between Romans and Chinese for the purposes of maintaining a trade monopoly. See J. Thorley 'The Development of Trade between the Roman Empire and the East under Augustus' *G & R* 16 (1969), 214; J. Ferguson 'China and Rome' *ANRW* II, 9, 2 (1978), 594, who both note that Maes' expedition seems to be anomalous. There is, of course, no anomaly when it is realised that there were no significant attempts by the Parthians to control or monopolise traffic over the overland route to Central Asia.
37 See pp. 33–4 for these records.
38 Graf 'The Roman East from the Chinese Perspective', 206. See pp. 144–7.
39 *Periplus* 39 (Barbarikon); 49 (Barygaza); 56 (Nelkynda); 64 (The Ganges region).
40 Raschke 'New Studies in Roman Commerce with the East', 642.
41 Ibid., 820–1.
42 Isidore of Charax *Parthian Stations* 1.

43 M.-L. Chaumont 'Etudes d'histoire Parthe V: la route royale des Parthes de Zeugma à Séleucie du Tigre d'après l'itinéraire d'Isidore de Charax' *Syria* 61 (1984), 68.
44 N.C. Debevoise *A Political History of Parthia* (Chicago 1938), 143–78.
45 For the case of Mesene see S.A. Nodelman 'A Preliminary History of Characene' Berytus 13 (1960), 83–121; G.W. Bowersock 'La Mésène (Maisan) antonine' in Fahd (ed.) *L'Arabie préislamique*, 159–68 and the discussion on pp. 143–8. For Susa and Elymais see G. Le Rider *Suse sous les Séleucides et les Parthes* (Paris 1965), 426–30.

6 THE LONG-DISTANCE TRADE AND IMPERIAL GOVERNMENT

1 For these arguments see pp. 1–2.
2 Tacitus *Annales* III. 53.
3 Pliny *NH* VI. 26.
4 Pliny *NH* XII. 41.
5 L. Casson *The Periplus Maris Erythraei: Text, Translation and Commentary* (Princeton 1989), 29–31. Such financial transactions may well have been made in Roman *denarii* as opposed to local currency, as the superior fineness and uniformity of Roman coins probably made them the preferred trade coin. See K. Harl *Coinage in the Roman Economy* (Baltimore 1996), 298–307.
6 See pp. 23–4.
7 M.G. Raschke 'New Studies in Roman Commerce with the East' *ANRW*, II, 9, 2 (1978), 643.
8 C. Howgego 'The Supply and Use of Money in the Roman World' *JRS* 82 (1992), 5; Harl *Coinage in the Roman Economy*, 309–12.
9 Harl *Coinage in the Roman Economy*, 313–14.
10 Ovid *Ars Amatoria* III. 129–30.
11 Ovid *De Medicamine Faciei* 88–94.
12 D. Earl *The Moral and Political Tradition of Rome* (London 1967), 30–2; C. Edwards *The Politics of Immorality in Ancient Rome* (Cambridge 1993), 20–32.
13 Edwards *Politics of Immorality*, 68–9. See e.g. Pliny *NH* XIII. 18–25.
14 For the special significance of the tax-collector at Leuke Kome see Raschke 'New Studies in Roman Commerce with the East', 664; G.K. Young 'The Customs Collector at the Nabataean Port of Leuke Kome (*Periplus Maris Erythraei* 19)' *ZPE* 119 (1997), 266–8; and see pp. 95–6.
15 See pp. 14–16.
16 Pliny *NH* XII. 32.
17 *Dig.* XXXIX. 4. 16. 7.
18 See pp. 66–9.
19 For these ostraka see R.S. Bagnall *et al.* 'The Ostraka' in S.E. Sidebotham and W.Z. Wendrich (eds) *Report of the 1997 Excavations at Berenike and the Survey of the Egyptian Eastern Desert, including Excavations at Shenshef* (Leiden 1999), 201–5. The full publication of these ostraka is eagerly awaited.
20 For the *portoria* levied upon goods being conveyed within Roman Egypt see S.J. de Laet *Portorium* (Brugge 1949), 297–330; A.C. Johnson *ESAR* II, 590–609; S.L. Wallace *Taxation in Egypt from Augustus to Diocletian* (Princeton 1938), 255–76, 460–70.
21 Suetonius *Diu. Iul.* 25.
22 It is regrettable that no more accurate comparison is possible to determine the scale of income from these duties. For example, the Gross National Product of

the Roman Empire, which would be perhaps the most obvious comparison, is impossible to determine given the paucity of our data. Thus, to say that the income derived from the duties levied upon long-distance international trade was probably roughly equivalent to the direct tax income from a reasonably wealthy province is as far as we can legitimately go in describing the scale of the indirect tax income from the long-distance commerce.

23 For a summary of the Ptolemaic trade and its taxes see S.E. Sidebotham *Roman Economic Policy in the Erythra Thalassa 30 BC – AD 217* (Leiden 1986), 2–12.

7 CONCLUSION

1 Annius Plocamus seems to have been one such example: see Pliny *NH* VI. 24 and p. 60.
2 *P.Vindob.* G 40822 recto, col. 2, 1–26 – col. 3, 1.
3 See pp. 211–12.
4 See pp. 123–8.
5 See pp. 100–3, 117–19.
6 Strabo *Geog.* II. 5. 12.
7 See pp. 25–6.
8 See pp. 210–11.
9 See pp. 37–8 (South Arabia) and pp. 195–8 (Parthia).
10 For the discussions of these expeditions see pp. 100–1 (Gallus' Arabian expedition); pp. 117–19 (annexation of the Nabataean kingdom) and pp. 195–8 (Trajan's Parthian war).
11 B. Isaac *The Limits of Empire: The Roman Army in the East* (Oxford 1990), 101–218.
12 For the current state of research on the Roman military presence in the East see D.L. Kennedy 'The Roman Army in the East' in D.L. Kennedy (ed.) *The Roman Army in the East* (Ann Arbor 1996), 9–24.
13 See pp. 147, 173.
14 Isaac *The Limits of Empire*, 19–33.
15 See pp. 167–73.
16 M.I. Finley *The Ancient Economy* (London 1973), 59.
17 See pp. 167–73.
18 See pp. 112–17.

APPENDIX A

1 See pp. 15–17.
2 Pliny *NH* XII. 42
3 R. Duncan-Jones *The Economy of the Roman Empire: Quantitative Studies* 2nd ed. (Cambridge 1982), 146. See *ILS* 2267, 8379.
4 Pliny *NH* XVIII. 90 (prices at Rome); Tacitus *Annales* XV. 39 (controlled price). See Duncan-Jones *The Economy of the Roman Empire*, 145–7; 345–7.
5 An example of such a subsistence level might be the allowance paid to an urban slave in the first century: HS 20 plus 5 modii of grain per month; see Seneca *Ep. Mor.* LXXX. 7. Goods such as frankincense and pepper would certainly have been an unaffordable luxury to such a person.
6 See pp. 15–16.

APPENDIX B

1 A. Negev 'Numismatics and Nabataean Chronology' *PEQ* 114 (1982), 124–6.
2 Table B.1 is based upon Y. Meshorer *Nabataean Coins* (Jerusalem 1975), 73–4.
3 Table B.2 is based upon D.R. Walker *The Metrology of the Roman Silver Coinage* I (Oxford 1976), 5–18, 84–108; and II (Oxford 1977), 3–5.
4 D.R. Walker *The Metrology of the Roman Silver Coinage* III (Oxford 1978), 138.
5 K. Harl *Coinage in the Roman Economy* (Baltimore 1996), 103.
6 Negev 'Numismatics and Nabataean Chronology', 126.
7 Table B.3 is based upon Walker *The Metrology of the Roman Silver Coinage* I, 56–69, 133–7; and II, 91–3.
8 An exception to the general pattern is found in the Nero tetradrachms beginning in AD 59, when the fineness jumps from 63 per cent to about 80. However, the fine tetradrachms of Tyre which had been nearly 95 per cent fine had ceased production in AD 58, and the revaluation of the Antiochene tetradrachm and its retariffing from three *denarii* to four at this time was probably designed to take over the role of this coin.
9 J. McKenzie *The Architecture of Petra* (Oxford 1990), 56.

APPENDIX D

1 F. Millar *The Roman Near East 31 BC – AD 337* (Cambridge, Mass. 1993), 327.
2 See pp. 157–66.
3 J.T. Milik *Dédicaces faites par des dieux* (Paris 1972), 317.
4 M. Gawlikowski 'Les princes de Palmyre' *Syria* 62 (1985), 257. As reproduced here, Gawlikowski provided no indication of line breaks in this preliminary publication.
5 *Inv*. III. 16.
6 D.S. Potter *Prophecy and History in the Crisis of the Roman Empire: A Historical Commentary on the Thirteenth Sybilline Oracle* (Oxford 1990), 389.
7 H. Ingholt 'Varia Tadmorea' in *Palmyre: Bilan et perspectives* (Strasbourg 1976), 123.
8 See pp. 159–62.
9 Ingholt 'Varia Tadmorea', 127–8.
10 Based on the inscription dedicated by a soldier mentioned above (*Inv*. III. 16) and those dedicated by trade associations mentioned below. See Millar *The Roman Near East*, 165.
11 Potter *Prophecy and History in the Crisis of the Roman Empire*, 389.
12 Referring to his adlection to the senatorial order. See *Inv*. VIII. 55; III. 16.
13 *Inv*. VIII. 55
14 Milik *Dédicaces*, 317.
15 Millar *The Roman Near East*, 165.
16 Gawlikowski 'Les princes de Palmyre', 254–5. These inscriptions describe Odaenathus only as 'illustrious consular', however: Hairan is described as 'illustrious son of Odaenathus the illustrious consular'.
17 Millar *The Roman Near East*, 165.
18 Dio Cassius LXXI. 22. 2; 24–6; 31. 1
19 J. Teixidor 'Les derniers rois d'Edesse d'après deux noveaux documents syriaques' *ZPE* 76 (1989), 219–22.
20 Potter *Prophecy and History in the Crisis of the Roman Empire*, 389.
21 *Inv*. III. 17
22 Potter *Prophecy and History in the Crisis of the Roman Empire*, 389.

23 The number and names of the sons of Odaenathus are still subjects of considerable discussion. For a summary of the debate see Potter *Prophecy and History in the Crisis of the Roman Empire*, 386–8.
24 D. Schlumberger 'L'inscription d'Hérodien: Remarques sur l'historie des princes de Palmyre' *Bulletin d'études orientales* 11 (1942–3), 36–50.
25 *Inv*. III. 19.
26 For this inscription and the discussion of Vaballathus' titulature see pp. 178–81.
27 D.L. Kennedy *JNES* 50 (1991), 76; *JRS* 85 (1995), 243.
28 *Inv*. III. 7. See pp. 170–1.
29 J. Cantineau, commentary to *Inv*. III. 7 (p.11).
30 Potter *Prophecy and History in the Crisis of the Roman Empire*, 392.
31 See p. 178.
32 C. Clermont-Ganneau 'Odeinat et Vaballat: Rois de Palmyre, et leur titre romain de *corrector*' *RBibl* 29 (1920), 387–8.
33 J. Cantineau 'Un *Restitutor Orientis* dans le inscription de Palmyre' *JA* 222 (1933), 217; F. Millar 'Paul of Samosata, Zenobia and Aurelian: the Church, Local Culture and Political Allegiance in Third-Century Syria' *JRS* 61 (1971), 9–10; S. Swain 'Greek into Palmyrene: Odenathus as "Corrector Totius Orientis"?' *ZPE* 99 (1993), 157–64.
34 Potter *Prophecy and History in the Crisis of the Roman Empire*, 392–3.
35 Millar *The Roman Near East*, 171.
36 J. Eadie 'One Hundred Years of Rebellion: the Eastern Army in Politics' in D.L. Kennedy (ed.) *The Roman Army in the East* (Ann Arbor 1996), 148.

BIBLIOGRAPHY

al-Ansary, A.A.T. (ed.) *Qaryat al-Faw: Studies in the History of Arabia II: Pre-Islamic Arabia*. Riyadh, 1984.

al-Megdad, S. 'Le role de la ville de Bosra aux époques nabatéenne et romaine.' In Hadidi (ed.) *Studies in the History and Archaeology of Jordan*, I, 267–73.

Alston, R. *Soldier and Society in Roman Egypt: A Social History*. London, 1995.

Alt, A. 'Aus der 'Araba II–IV.' *ZDPV* 58 (1935): 1–78.

Altheim, F., and R. Stiehl. *Die Araber in der alten Welt*, II. Berlin, 1965.

As'ad, K., and M. Gawlikowski. 'New Honorific Inscriptions in the Great Colonnade of Palmyra.' *AAS* 37 (1987): 164.

Avanzini, A. (ed.) *Profumi d'Arabia: Atti del Convego*. Saggi di Storia Antica 11. Rome, 1997.

Bagnall, R.S. 'Army and Police in Roman Upper Egypt.' *JARCE* 14 (1977): 67–86.

Bagnall, R.S. 'Epigraphy: Greek and Latin.' In Whitcomb and Johnson (eds) *Quseir al-Qadim, 1978 Preliminary Report*, 243–4.

Bagnall, R.S. 'Upper and Lower Guard Posts.' *CE* 57 (1982): 125–8.

Bagnall, R.S. 'Papyri and Ostraka from Quseir al-Qadim.' *BASP* 23 (1986): 1–60.

Bagnall, R.S., and J.A. Sheridan. 'Greek and Latin Documents from 'Abu Sha'ar, 1990–1991.' *JARCE* 31 (1994): 159–68.

Bagnall, R.S., and J.A. Sheridan. 'Greek and Latin Documents from 'Abu Sha'ar, 1992–1993.' *BASP* 31 (1994): 109–20.

Bagnall, R.S., C.C. Helms and A.M.F.W. Veerhoogt. 'The Ostraka.' In Sidebotham and Wendrich (eds) *Berenike 1997*, 201–5.

Bagnall, R.S., J.G. Manning, S.E. Sidebotham and R.E. Zitterkopf. 'A Ptolemaic Inscription from Bir 'Iayyan.' *CE* 71 (1996): 317–30.

Baldini, A. 'Roma e Palmira, Note storico-epigrafiche.' *Epigraphica* 36 (1974): 109–33.

Ball, W. *Rome in the East: The Transformation of an Empire*. London, 2000.

Banning, E.B. 'Peasants, Pastoralists and Pax Romana: Mutualism in the Southern Highlands of Jordan.' *BASOR* 261 (1986): 25–50.

Banning, E.B. 'De Bello Paceque: a Reply to Parker.' *BASOR* 265 (1987): 52–4.

Barger, T. 'Greek Inscription Deciphered.' *Archaeology* 22 (1969): 139–40, 325.

Baur, P.V.C. and M.I. Rostovtzeff (eds) *The Excavations at Dura Europos: Preliminary Report*, 11 vols. New Haven, 1929–1946.

Bauzou, T. 'Deux milliaires inédits de Vaballath en Jordanie du Nord.' In Freeman and Kennedy (eds) *The Defence of the Roman and Byzantine East*, I, 1–8.

Beeston, A.F.L. 'The Settlement at Khor Rori.' *JOS* 2 (1976): 39–42.

Beeston, A.F.L. 'Some Observations on Greek and Latin Data Relating to South Arabia.' *BSOAS* 62 (1979): 7–12.

Begley, V. 'Arikamedu Reconsidered.' *AJA* 87 (1983): 461–81.

Begley, V. 'New Investigations at the Port of Arikamedu.' *JRA* 6 (1993): 93–108.

Begley, V. (ed.) *The Ancient Port of Arikamedu: New Investigations and Researches 1989–1992*, I. Pondicherry, 1996.

Begley, V. and R. De Puma (eds) *Rome and India: The Ancient Sea Trade.* Madison, 1991.

Begley, V. and S.E. Sidebotham. 'Field Investigations 1989–92.' In Begley (ed.) *The Ancient Port of Arikamedu*, 41–66.

Beitenhard, H. 'Die Syrische Dekapolis von Pompeius bis Trajan.' *ANRW* II, 8 (1977): 220–61.

Bell, H.I. 'Antinouopolis: a Hadrianic Foundation.' *JRS* 30 (1940): 133–47.

Berchem, D. van. 'Le port de Séleucie de Piérie et l'infrastructure logistique des guerres parthiques.' *BJb* 185 (1985): 47–87.

Bernand, A. *Alexandrie la Grande.* Paris, 1966.

Bernand, A. *Le Paneion d'El-Kanais: Les inscriptions grecques.* Leiden, 1972.

Bernand, A. *De Koptos à Kossier.* Leiden, 1972.

Bernand, A. *Les Portes du désert: Recueil d'inscriptions grecques d'Antinonopolis, Tentyris, Koptos, Apollinopolis Parva et Apollinopolis Magna.* Paris, 1984.

Bernand, P. 'Vicissitudes au gré de l'histoire d'une statue en bronze d'Héraclès entre Séleucie du Tigre et la Mésène.' *Journal des Savants* (1990): 3–68.

Bingen, J. 'Un dédicace de marchands palmyréniens à Coptos.' *CE* 59 (1984): 355–8.

Birley, A.R. *Septimius Severus: The African Emperor.* London, 1971.

Birley, E. 'Local Militias in the Roman Empire.' In *Bonner Historia-Augusta Colloquium 1972/1974*, 65–73. Bonn, 1976.

Black, R. 'The History of Parthia and Characene in the 2nd Century AD.' *Sumer* 43 (1984): 230–4.

Bopearachchi, A. 'Le commerce maritime entre Rome et Sri Lanka d'après les données numismatiques.' *REA* 94 (1992): 107–21.

Bowersock, G.W. 'A Report on Arabia Provincia.' *JRS* 61 (1971): 219–42.

Bowersock, G.W. 'Syria under Vespasian.' *JRS* 63 (1973): 133–40.

Bowersock, G.W. 'The Greek–Nabataean Bilingual Inscription at Ruwwafa, Saudi Arabia.' In *Le Monde grec: Hommages à Claire Preaux*, ed. J. Bingen, G. Cambrier, and G. Nachtegael, 513–22. Brussels, 1975.

Bowersock, G.W. *Roman Arabia.* Cambridge, Mass., 1983.

Bowersock, G.W. 'La Mésène (Maisan) antonine.' In Fahd (ed.) *L'Arabie préislamique*, 159–68.

Bowersock, G.W. 'Perfumes and Power.' In Avanzini (ed.) *Profumi d'Arabia*, 543–56.

Bowes, A.R. 'The Process of Nabataean Sedentarization: New Models and Approaches.' PhD Diss., Salt Lake City, 1998.

Bowman, A.K. *Egypt after the Pharaohs 732 BC – AD 642: From Alexander to the Arab Conquest.* London, 1986.

Bowman, A.K. 'Egypt.' In *CAH* X, 676–702.

Bowsher, J. 'The Frontier Post of Medain Saleh.' In Freeman and Kennnedy (eds) *The Defence of the Roman and Byzantine East*, I, 23–9.

Bowsher, J. 'The Nabataean Army.' In French and Lightfoot (eds) *The Eastern Frontier of the Roman Empire*, I, 19–30.

Braund, D. *Rome and the Friendly King: The Character of the Client Kingship.* London, 1984.

Breton, J.-F. 'L'orient gréco-romain et le Hadramawt.' In Fahd (ed.) *L'Arabie préislamique*, 173–85.

Browning, I. *Petra.* London, 1977.

Browning, I. *Palmyra.* London, 1979.

Browning, I. *Jerash and the Decapolis.* London, 1982.

Brunnow, R.E., and A. von Domazewski. *Die Provincia Arabia*, 3 vols. Strasbourg, 1904–9.

Brunt, P.A. (ed.) *The Roman Economy: Studies in Ancient Economic and Administrative History.* Oxford, 1974.

Brunt, P.A. 'Did Imperial Rome Disarm her Subjects?' *Phoenix* 29 (1975): 260–70.

Bruyère, B. *Fouilles de Clysma – Qolzoum (Suez), 1930–1932.* Cairo, 1966.

Bülow-Jacobsen, A., H. Cuvigny and J.-L. Fournet. 'The Identification of Myos Hormos: New Papyrological Evidence.' *BIFAO* 94 (1994): 27–42.

Cantineau, J. 'Textes palmyréniens provenant de la fouille du temple de Bel.' *Syria* 12 (1931): 116–41.

Cantineau, J. 'L'inscription de 'Umm es-Salâbih.' *Syria* 14 (1933): 178–80.

Cantineau, J. 'Un Restitutor Orientis dans le inscription de Palmyre.' *JA* 222 (1933): 219–34.

Cantineau, J., J. Starcky and M. Gawlikowski (eds) *Inventaire des inscriptions de Palmyre*, 11 vols. Beirut, Paris, Damascus, 1930–.

Caquot, A. 'Nouvelles inscriptions araméennes de Hatra (II).' *Syria* 30 (1953): 234–46.

Caquot, A. 'Nouvelles inscriptions araméennes de Hatra (V).' *Syria* 40 (1963): 1–16.

Cary, M. 'Maes, Qui et Titianus.' *CQ* n.s. 6 (1956): 130–4.

Casal, J.M. *Fouilles de Virampatnam – Arikamedu.* Paris, 1949.

Caskel, W. 'The Bedouinization of Arabia.' *Studies in Islamic Cultural History*, ed. G.E. von. Grunebaum. In *The American Anthropologist* 56 (1954): 36–46.

Casson, L. *Ships and Seamanship in the Ancient World.* Princeton, 1971.

Casson, L. *Travel in the Ancient World.* London, 1974.

Casson, L. *Ancient Trade and Society.* Detroit, 1984.

Casson, L. 'Egypt, Africa, Arabia and India: Patterns of Seaborne Trade in the First Century AD.' *BASP* 21 (1984): 39–47.

Casson, L. 'P. Vindob. G 40822 and the Shipping of Goods from India.' *BASP* 23 (1986): 73–9.

Casson, L. 'Rome's Trade with the Eastern Coast of India.' *CH* 33 (1988): 303–8.

Casson, L. *The Periplus Maris Erythraei: Text, Translation and Commentary.* Princeton, 1989.

Casson, L. 'South Arabia's Maritime Trade.' In Fahd (ed.) *L'Arabie préislamique*, 187–94.

Casson, L. 'New Light on Maritime Loans: P. Vindob. G 40822.' *ZPE* 84 (1990): 195–206.

Casson, L. 'Ancient Naval Technology and the Route to India.' In Begley and De Puma (eds) *Rome and India: The Ancient Sea Trade*, 8–11.

Cavenaile, R. 'Prosopographie de l'armée romaine d'Egypte d'Auguste à Dioclétien.' *Aegyptus* 50 (1970): 213–320.

Charlesworth, M.P. *Trade-Routes and Commerce of the Roman Empire.* Cambridge, 1926.

Charlesworth, M.P. 'Some Notes on the Periplus Maris Erythraei.' *CQ* 22 (1928): 92–100.

Chaumont, M.-L. 'Etudes d'histoire Parthe III: Les villes fondées par les Vologèse.' *Syria* 51 (1974): 76–89.

Chaumont, M.-L. 'Etudes d'histoire Parthe V: La route royale des Parthes de Zeugma à Séleucie du Tigre d'après l'itinéraire d'Isidore de Charax.' *Syria* 61 (1984): 63–107.

Chavannes, E. 'Seng Houe.' *T'oung Pao* 10 (1909): 199–212.

Clark, V.A. 'A Study of New Safaitic Inscriptions from Jordan.' PhD Diss. University of Melbourne, 1980.

Clarysse, W., and P. Sijpesteijn. 'A Military Roster on a Vase in Amsterdam.' *Anc.Soc.* 19 (1988): 71–96.

Clermont-Ganneau, C. 'Odeinat et Vaballat: Rois de Palmyre, et leur titre romain de corrector.' *RBibl* 29 (1920): 382–419.

Coedès, G. 'Fouilles en Cochinchine: le site de Go Oc Eo, ancien port du royaume de Fou-nan.' *Artibus Asiae* 10/3 (1947): 193–9.

Cohen, R. 'New Light on the Date of the Petra–Gaza Road.' *Biblical Archaeologist* 45 (1982): 240–7.

Colledge, M.A.R. *The Art of Palmyra*. London, 1976.

Colledge, M.A.R. 'Le temple de Bel à Palmyre: Qui l'a fait, et pourquoi?' In *Palmyre: Bilan et perspectives*, 46–52.

Comfort, H. 'Terra Sigillata at Arikamedu.' In Begley and De Puma (eds) *Rome and India*, 134–50.

Cotton, H.M. 'The Guardianship of Jesus Son of Babatha: Roman Law in the Province of Arabia.' *JRS* 83 (1993): 94–108.

Courtney, E. *A Commentary on the Satires of Juvenal*. London, 1980.

Crone, P. *Meccan Trade and the Rise of Islam*. Oxford, 1987.

Curtin, P.D. *Cross-Cultural Trade in World History*. Cambridge, 1984.

Dabrowa, E. (ed.) *The Roman and Byzantine Army in the East*. Krakow, 1994.

D'Arms, J.H. *Commerce and Social Standing in Ancient Rome*. Cambridge, Mass., 1981.

Datoo, B. 'Rhapta: the Location and Importance of East Africa's First Port.' *Azania* 5 (1970): 65–75.

Debevoise, N.C. *A Political History of Parthia*. Chicago, 1938.

De Laet, S.J. *Portorium*. Brugge, 1949.

De Maigret, A. 'The Frankincense Road from Najran to Ma'an: a Hypothetical Itinerary.' In Avanzini (ed.) *Profumi d'Arabia*, 315–31.

Dentzer, J.-M., and F. Zayadine. 'L'espace urbain de Petra.' In Zaghloul *et al.* (eds) *Studies in the History and Archaeology of Jordan*, IV, 233–51.

De Romanis, F. *Cassia, Cinnamomo, Ossidiana: Uomini e merci tra oceano Indiano e Mediterraneo*. Saggi di Storia Antica 9. Rome, 1996.

De Romanis, F., and A. Tchernia (eds) *Crossings: Early Mediterranean Contacts with India*. New Delhi, 1997.

Desanges, J. 'Les relations de l'empire romain avec l'Afrique nilotique et érythréenne, d'Auguste à Probus.' *ANRW* II,10, 1 (1988): 4–12.

Desanges, J., E.M. Stern and P. Ballet. *Sur les routes antiques de l'Azanie et de l'Indie: Le fonds Révoil du musée de l'homme (Heïs et Damo en Somalie)*. Memoires de l'académie des inscriptions et belles-lettres n.s. 13. Paris, 1993.

Devijver, H. 'Equestrian Officers from the East.' In Freeman and Kennedy (eds) *The Defence of the Roman and Byzantine East*, I, 109–225.

Dihle, A. *Umstrittene Daten: Untersuchungen zum Auftreten der Griechen am Roten Meer.* Köln, 1965.

Dihle, A. 'Die Entdeckungsgeschichtlichen Voraussetzungen des Indienshandels der römischen Kaiserzeit.' *ANRW* II, 9, 2 (1978): 546–80.

Dijkstra, M. and A.M.F.W. Veerhoogt 'The Greek–Palmyrene Inscription.' In Sidebotham and Wendrich (eds) *Berenike 1997*, 207–18.

Dodgeon, M.H., and S.N.C. Lieu. *The Roman Eastern Frontier and the Persian Wars* AD *226–323*. London, 1991.

Downey, G. *A History of Antioch in Syria from Seleucus to the Arab Conquest.* Princeton, 1961.

Drijvers, H.J.W. 'Hatra, Palmyra und Edessa.' *ANRW* II, 8 (1977): 799–906.

Du Mesnil du Buisson, C. *Inventaire des inscriptions Palmyréniennes de Doura-Europos (32 avant J.-C. à 256 après J.-C.).* Paris, 1939.

Dunant, C. *Le Sanctuaire de Baalshamin à Palmyre III: Les inscriptions.* Rome, 1971.

Duncan-Jones, R. *The Economy of the Roman Empire: Quantitative Studies*, 2nd edn. Cambridge, 1982.

Duncan-Jones, R. *Structure and Scale in the Roman Economy.* Cambridge, 1990.

Duncan-Jones, R. 'The Impact of the Antonine Plague.' *JRA* 9 (1996): 108–36.

Dussaud, R., and F. Macler. 'Rapport sur une mission scientifique dans les régions désertiques de la Syrie moyenne.' *Nouvelles archives des missions scientifiques et littéraires* 10 (1902): 409–21.

Eadie, J.W. 'The Evolution of the Roman Frontier in Arabia.' In Freeman and Kennedy (eds) *The Defence of the Roman and Byzantine East*, I, 243–52.

Eadie, J.W. 'Strategies of Economic Development in the Roman East: the Red Sea Trade Revisited.' In French and Lightfoot (eds) *The Eastern Frontier of the Roman Empire*, I, 113–20.

Eadie, J.W. 'One Hundred Years of Rebellion: the Eastern Army in Politics, AD 175–272.' In Kennedy (ed.) *The Roman Army in the East*, 135–51.

Earl, D. *The Moral and Political Tradition of Rome.* London, 1967.

Eck, W. *Senatoren von Vespasian bis Hadrian: Prosopographie Untersuchungen mit Einschluss der Jahres- und Provinzialfasten der Statthalter.* Munich, 1970.

Edwards, C. *The Politics of Immorality in Ancient Rome.* Cambridge, 1993.

Euting, J. *Sinaitische Inschriften.* Berlin, 1891.

Fahd, T. (ed.) *L'Arabie préislamique et son environnement historique et culturel.* Leiden, 1989.

Fentress, E. *Numidia and the Roman Army.* Oxford, 1979.

Ferguson, J. 'China and Rome.' *ANRW* II, 9, 2 (1978): 581–603.

Ferrill, A. *Roman Imperial Grand Strategy.* New York, 1991.

Ferrill, A. 'The Grand Strategy of the Roman Empire.' In *Grand Strategy in War and Peace*, ed. P. Kennedy, 71–85. New Haven, 1991.

Fiema, Z.T. 'The Roman Annexation of Arabia: a General Perspective.' *AncW* 15 (1987): 25–35.

Finley, M.I. *The Ancient Economy.* London, 1973.

Follet, S. 'Hadrien en Egypte et en Judée.' *Revue de Philologie* 42 (1968): 54–77.

Frank, A. 'Aus der 'Araba I: Reisberichte.' *ZDPV* 57 (1934): 270–6.

Frank, T. (ed.) *Economic Survey of Ancient Rome*, 5 vols. Baltimore, 1936–1939.

Frank, T. 'Rome and Italy of the Empire.' In Frank (ed.) *An Economic Survey of Ancient Rome*, V.

Fraser, P.M. *Ptolemaic Alexandria*, 3 vols. Oxford, 1972.

Freeman, P. 'The Annexation of Arabia and Imperial Grand Strategy.' In Kennedy (ed.) *The Roman Army in the East*, 91–118.

Freeman, P. and D.L. Kennedy (eds) *The Defence of the Roman and Byzantine East.* BAR Int. Ser. 297, 2 vols. Oxford, 1986.

French, D.H. and C.S. Lightfoot (eds) *The Eastern Frontier of the Roman Empire.* BAR Int. Ser. 553, 3 vols. Oxford, 1989.

Fuks, A. 'Notes on the Archive of Nikanor.' *Journal of Juristic Papyrology* 5 (1951): 207–16.

Galazzi, C. 'Un nuovo frammento del vaso di Amsterdam *O.Amst* 8.' *Anc.Soc.* 20 (1989): 185–92.

Garnsey, P., K. Hopkins and C.R. Whittaker. *Trade in the Ancient Economy*. London, 1983.

Gatier, P.-L., and J.-F. Salles. 'Aux frontières méridionales du domaine Nabatéen.' In Salles (ed.) *L'Arabie et ses mers bordières*,173–90.

Gatier, P.-L., B. Helly, and J.-P. Rey-Coquais (eds) *Géographie historique au Proche-Orient (Syrie, Phénicie, Arabie, grecques, romaines, byzantines)*. Paris, 1988.

Gawlikowski, M. 'Inscriptions de Palmyre.' *Syria* 48 (1971): 407–26.

Gawlikowski, M. 'Palmyre et l'Euphrate.' *Syria* 60 (1983): 53–68.

Gawlikowski, M. 'Hadita, Began Island.' *Archiv für Orientforschung* 29–30 (1983–1984): 207.

Gawlikowski, M. 'Les Princes de Palmyre.' *Syria* 62 (1985): 251–61.

Gawlikowski, M. 'Bijan in the Euphrates.' *Sumer* 42 (1985): 15–21.

Gawlikowski, M. 'Comptes d'un homme d'affaires dans une tour funéraire à Palmyre.' *Semitica* L36 (1986): 87–99.

Gawlikowski, M. 'Le commerce de Palmyre sur terre et sur eau.' In Salles (ed.) *L'Arabie et ses mers bordières*, 163–72.

Gawlikowski, M. 'La route de l'Euphrate d'Isidore à Julien.' In Gatier *et al.* (eds) *Géographie historique au Proche-Orient*, 77–98.

Gawlikowski, M. 'Les dieux de Palmyre.' *ANRW* II, 18, 4 (1990): 2605–58.

Gawlikowski, M. 'Palmyra as a Trading Centre.' *Iraq* 56 (1994): 27–33.

Ghirshman, R. 'L'île de Kharg dans le Golfe Persique.' *CRAI* (1958): 265–8.

Gilliam, J.F. 'The Roman Army in Dura.' In Welles *et al.* (eds) *The Excavations at Dura-Europos V.1: The Parchments and Papyri*, 22–7.

Glover, I.C. 'Early Trade between India and Southeast Asia.' In Reade (ed.) *The Indian Ocean in Antiquity*, 373–8.

Glueck, N. 'Exploration in Eastern Palestine II.' *AASOR* 15 (1935).

Glueck, N. 'Wadi Sirhan in North Arabia.' *BASOR* 96 (1944): 7–17.

Glueck, N. *Deities and Dolphins: The Story of the Nabataeans*. New York, 1965.

Goodchild, R.G. 'Oasis Forts of Legio III Augusta on the Routes to the Fezzan.' *Proc. Brit. Sch. Rome* 9 (1954): 56–68.

Goodman, M. 'Babatha's Story.' *JRS* 81 (1991): 169–75.

Graf, D.F. 'The Saracens and the Defence of the Arabian Frontier.' *BASOR* 229 (1978): 1–29.

Graf, D.F. 'A Preliminary Report on a Survey of Nabataean–Roman Military Sites in Southern Jordan.' *ADAJ* 23 (1979): 121–7.

Graf, D.F. 'The Nabataeans and the Decapolis.' In Freeman and Kennedy (eds) *The Defence of the Roman and Byzantine East*, II, 785–96.

Graf, D.F. 'The Roman Road System of Arabia Petraea.' *AJA* 91 (1987): 389.

Graf, D.F. 'Qura 'Arabiyya and Provincia Arabia.' In Gatier *et al.* (eds) *Géographie historique au Proche-Orient*, 171–211.

Graf, D.F. 'Rome and the Saracens: Reassessing the Nomadic Menace.' In Fahd (ed.) *L'Arabie préislamique*, 341–400.

Graf, D.F. 'The Origin of the Nabataeans.' *Aram* 2 (1990): 45–75.

Graf, D.F. 'Nabataean Settlements and Roman Occupation in Arabia Petraea.' In Zaghloul *et al.* (eds) *Studies in the History and Archaeology of Jordan*, IV, 253–60.

Graf, D.F. 'The Via Nova Traiana in Arabia Petraea.' In *The Roman and Byzantine Near East: Some Recent Archaeological Research*, 241–65.

Graf, D.F. 'The Roman East from the Chinese Perspective.' In *International Colloquium on Palmyra and the Silk Road, AAS* 42 (1996): 199–216.

Graf, D.F. *Rome and the Arabian Frontier: From the Nabataeans to the Saracens.* Ashgate, 1997.

Gragg, G. 'South Arabian/Axumite Dipinto.' In Sidebotham and Wendrich (eds) *Berenike '95*, 209–11.

Greene, K. *The Archaeology of the Roman Economy*. Berkeley, 1986.

Gregory, S., and D.L. Kennedy. *Sir Aurel Stein's Limes Report*. BAR Int. Ser. 272. Oxford, 1985.

Griffin, J. *Latin Poets and Roman Life*. London, 1985.

Groom, N. *Frankincense and Myrrh: A Study of the Arabian Incense Trade*. London, 1981.

Groom, N. 'The Periplus, Pliny and Arabia.' *AAE* 6 (1995): 180–95.

Gruen, E.S. 'The Expansion of the Empire under Augustus.' In *CAH* X, 147–97.

Grushevoi, A.G. 'The Tribe 'Ubaishat in Safaitic, Nabataean and Greek Inscriptions.' *Berytus* 33 (1985): 51–4.

Hadidi, A. 'The Excavation of the Roman Forum at Amman (Philadelphia).' *ADAJ* 19 (1974): 82–5.

Hadidi, A. (ed.) *Studies in the History and Archaeology of Jordan*, I–III. Amman, 1982–1987.

Hammond, P.C. *The Nabataeans: Their History, Culture and Archaeology*. Studies in Mediterranean Archaeology 37. Gothenberg, 1973.

Hanson, W.S., and L.J.F. Keppie (eds) *Roman Frontier Studies, 1979: Papers Presented to the 12th International Congress of Roman Frontier Studies*. BAR Int. Ser. 71, 3 vols. Oxford, 1980.

Harel, M. 'The Roman Road at Ma'aleh 'Aqrabbim (Scorpion's Ascent).' *IEJ* 9 (1959): 175–9.

Harl, K.W. *Coinage in the Roman Economy*. Baltimore, 1996.

Harrauer, H., and P.J. Sijpesteijn. 'Ein neues Dokument zu Roms Indienhandel P.Vindob. G 40822.' *AnzWien* phil.-hist. Kl.122 (1985): 124–55.

Hayes, J.W. 'The Pottery.' In Sidebotham and Wendrich (eds) *Berenike '95*, 147–78.

Heichelheim, F.M. 'Roman Syria.' In Frank (ed.) *An Economic Survey of Ancient Rome*, IV, 121–258.

Hillers, D.R., and E. Cussin. 'Two Readings in the Caravan Inscription Dunant, Baalshamin, No. 45.' *BASOR* 286 (1992): 35–7.

Hirschfeld, O. *Die kaiserlichen Verwaltungsbeamten bis auf Diocletian*. Berlin, 1905.

Hirth, F. *China and the Roman Orient: Researches into their Ancient and Medieval Relations as Represented in Old Chinese Records*. Shanghai, 1885.

Hodgson, N. 'The East as Part of the Wider Roman Imperial Frontier Policy.' In French and Lightfoot (eds) *The Eastern Frontier of the Roman Empire*, I, 177–89.

Holtheide, B. 'Matrona Stolata – Femina Stolata.' *ZPE* 38 (1980): 127–34.
Honigmann, E., and A. Maricq. *Recherches sur les Res Gestae Divi Saporis*. Brussels, 1953.
Hopkins, K. 'Taxes and Trade in the Roman Empire.' *JRS* 70 (1980): 101–25.
Hopkins, K. 'Introduction.' In Garnsey *et al. Trade in the Ancient Economy*.
Hourani, G.F. *Arab Seafaring in the Indian Ocean in Ancient and Early Medieval Times*. Princeton, 1951.
Howgego, C. 'The Supply and Use of Money in the Roman World 200 BC – AD 300.' *JRS* 82 (1992): 1–31.
Huzar, E.G. 'Alexandria ad Aegyptum in the Julio-Claudian Age.' *ANRW* II, 10, 1 (1988): 619–68.
Ingholt, H. *Studier over palmyrensk Skulptur*. Copenhagen, 1928.
Ingholt, H. 'Varia Tadmorea.' In *Palmyre: Bilan et perspectives*, 101–37.
Isaac, B. 'Trade Routes to Arabia and the Roman Army.' In Hanson and Keppie (eds) *Roman Frontier Studies*, III, 889–901.
Isaac, B. 'Bandits in Judaea and Arabia.' *HSCP* 88 (1984): 171–203.
Isaac, B. 'The Meaning of the Terms Limes and Limitanei.' *JRS* 78 (1988): 125–47.
Isaac, B. 'Trade Routes to Arabia and the Roman Presence in the Desert.' In Fahd (ed.) *L'Arabie préislamique*, 241–25.
Isaac, B. *The Limits of Empire: The Roman Army in the East*. Oxford, 1990.
Jalalbert, L. and R. Mouterde (eds) *Inscriptions grecques et latines de Syrie*, 21 vols. Paris, 1929–.
Jameson, S. 'Chronology of the Campaigns of Aelius Gallus and C. Petronius.' *JRS* 58 (1968): 71–84.
Janvier, Y. 'La Mer Rouge, lien entre deux mondes dans l'Antiquité.' *CH* 21 (1976): 335–52.
Jaussen, P., and M. Savignac. *Mission archéologique en Arabie*, 2 vols. Paris, 1909–1914.
Johnson, A.C. 'Roman Egypt to the Reign of Diocletian.' In Frank (ed.) *An Economic Survey of Ancient Rome*, II.
Johnson, J.H. 'Inscriptional Material.' In Whitcomb and Johnson (eds) *Quseir al-Qadim, 1980 Preliminary Report*, 263–6.
Johnson, W.R., and D.S. Whitcomb. 'Pottery: Roman Pottery – Islamic Pottery.' In Whitcomb and Johnson (eds) *Quseir al-Qadim, 1978 Preliminary Report*, 64–143.
Jones, A.H.M. *The Cities of the Eastern Roman Empire*, 2nd edn. Oxford, 1971.
Jones, A.H.M. *The Roman Economy: Studies in Ancient Economic and Administrative History*. Oxford, 1974.
Jouguet, P. 'Dédicace grecque de Médamoud.' *BIFAO* 31 (1931): 1–29.
Kayser, F. 'Nouveaux textes grecs du Ouadi Hammamat.' *ZPE* 98 (1993): 111–56.
Kennedy, D.F. *The Arts of Love*. Cambridge, 1993.
Kennedy, D.L. 'The Frontier Policy of Septimius Severus: New Evidence from Arabia.' In Hanson and Keppie (eds) *Roman Frontier Studies*, III, 879–87.
Kennedy, D.L. *Archaeological Explorations on the Roman Frontier in North-East Jordan*. BAR Int. Ser. 134. Oxford, 1982.
Kennedy, D.L. 'The Composition of a Military Work Party in Egypt (*ILS* 2483: Coptos).' *JEA* 71 (1985): 156–60.
Kennedy, D.L. 'Ana on the Euphrates in the Roman Period.' *Iraq* 48 (1986): 103.
Kennedy, D.L. 'The Roman Frontier in Arabia (Jordanian Sector).' *JRA* 5 (1992): 473–89.

Kennedy, D.L. 'The Cohors XX Palmyrenorum at Dura Europos.' In Dabrowa (ed.) *The Roman and Byzantine Army in the East*, 89–98.

Kennedy, D.L. (ed.) *The Roman Army in the East. JRA* Supp. 18. Ann Arbor, 1996.

Kennedy, D.L. 'The Roman Army in the East.' In Kennedy (ed.) *The Roman Army in the East*, 9–24.

Kennedy, D.L. 'Parthia and Rome: Eastern Perspectives.' In Kennedy (ed.) *The Roman Army in the East*, 67–90.

Kennedy, D.L., and H.I. MacAdam. 'Some Latin Inscriptions from the Azraq Oasis.' *ZPE* 60 (1985): 97–107.

Kennedy, D.L., and D.S. Riley. *Rome's Desert Frontier from the Air*. London, 1990.

Khouri, R.G. *Jerash: Frontier City of the Roman East*. London, 1986.

Khouri, R.G., and D. Whitcomb. *Aqaba – Port of Palestine on the China Sea*. Amman, 1988.

Killick, A.C. 'Udruh – the Frontier of an Empire: 1980 and 1981 Seasons, a Preliminary Report.' *Levant* 15 (1983): 110–31.

Killick, A.C. 'Udruh and the Southern Frontier.' In Freeman and Kennedy (eds) *The Defence of the Roman and Byzantine East*, 431–46.

Killick, A.C. *Udruh: Caravan City and Desert Oasis*. Romsey, 1987.

Killick, A.C. 'Udruh and the Trade Route through Southern Jordan.' In Hadidi (ed.) *Studies in the History and Archaeology of Jordan*, III, 174–5.

Kilpatrick, G.D. 'Dura-Europos: the Parchments and Papyri.' *GRBS* 5 (1964): 215–25.

Kirwan, L.P. 'Where to Search for the Ancient Port of Leuke Kome.' In *Second International Symposium on the History of Arabia: Pre-Islamic Arabia*, 55–61. Riyadh, 1976.

Kirwan, L.P. 'Rhapta, Metropolis of Azania.' *Azania* 21 (1986): 99–104.

Kraeling, C.H. (ed.) *Gerasa: City of the Decapolis*. New Haven, 1938.

Krishnamurthy, R. *Late Roman Copper Coins from South India: Karur and Madurai*. Madras, 1994.

Lacau, P. 'Inscriptions latines du temple de Louxor.' *ASAE* 34 (1934): 17–46.

Lambert, R. *Beloved and God*. London, 1984.

Le Rider, G. *Suse sous les Séleucides et les Parthes*. Paris, 1965.

Lesquier, J. *L'Armée romaine d'Egypte d' Auguste à Dioclétien*. Cairo, 1918.

Lewis, N. *The Documents from the Bar Kokhba Period in the Cave of Letters: Greek Papyri*. Jerusalem, 1989.

Lindner, M. 'Abu Khusheiba – a Newly Described Nabataean Settlement and Caravan Station Between Wadi 'Arabah and Petra.' In Zaghloul *et al.* (eds) *Studies in the History and Archaeology of Jordan*, IV, 263–7.

Littman, E., and D. Meredith. 'Nabataean Inscriptions from Egypt.' *BSOAS* 15 (1953): 1–28.

Littman, E., and D. Meredith. 'Nabataean Inscriptions from Egypt.' *BSOAS* 16 (1954): 211–46.

Luttwak, E.N. *The Grand Strategy of the Roman Empire from the First Century AD to the Third*. Baltimore, 1976.

MacAdam, H.I. *Studies in the History of the Roman Province of Arabia: The Northern Sector*. BAR Int. Ser. 295. Oxford, 1986.

MacAdam, H.I. 'Ptolemy's Geography and the Wadi Sirhan.' In Gatier *et al.* (eds) *Géographie historique au Proche-Orient*, 55–75.

MacDonald, B. 'A Nabataean and/or Roman Military Monitoring Zone along the South Bank of the Wadi el-Hasa in Southern Jordan.' *Echos du Monde Classique/Classical Views* 28 (1984): 219–34.

MacDonald, M.C.A. 'Nomads and the Hawran in the Late Hellenistic and Roman Periods: a Reassessment of the Epigraphic Evidence.' *Syria* 70 (1993): 303–403.

MacDonald, M.C.A. 'A Dated Nabataean Inscription from Southern Arabia.' In Nebes (ed.) *Arabia Felix*, 134–5.

MacDonald, M.C.A. 'Trade Routes and Trade Goods at the Northern End of the "Incense Road" in the First Millennium BC.' In Avanzini (ed.) *Profumi d'Arabia*, 333–49.

MacDowell, D.W. 'Numismatic Evidence for the Date of Kaniska.' In *Papers on the Date of Kaniska*, ed. A.L. Basham, 134–49. Leiden, 1968.

MacDowell, D.W. 'Finds of Roman Coins in South Asia: Problems of Interpretation.' *Ancient Ceylon* 9 (1990): 49–73.

McKenzie, J. *The Architecture of Petra*. British Academy Monographs in Archaeology 1. Oxford, 1990.

Mahadevan, I. 'Tamil-Brahmi Graffito.' In Sidebotham and Wendrich (eds) *Berenike '95*, 205–8.

Mahadevan, I. 'Pottery Inscriptions in Brahmi and Tamil-Brahmi.' In Begley (ed.) *The Ancient Port of Arikamedu*, 287–315.

Mann, J.C. 'A Note on the Inscription from Kurnub.' *IEJ* 19 (1969): 211–14.

Maricq, A. 'Classica et Orientalia 2: les dernières années de Hatra: l'alliance romaine.' *Syria* 34 (1957): 288–96.

Maricq, A. 'Vologésias, l'emporium de Ctésiphon.' *Syria* 36 (1959): 264–76.

Matthews, J.F. 'The Tax Law of Palmyra.' *JRS* 74 (1984): 157–80.

Mauny, R. 'Le Périple de la Mer Erythrée et le problème du commerce romain en Afrique au Sud du Limes.' *JSocAfr* 38 (1968): 19–34.

Mayerson, P. 'Saracens and Romans: Micro–Macro Relationships.' *BASOR* 274 (1989): 71–9.

Mayerson, P. 'Aelius Gallus at Cleopatris (Suez) and on the Red Sea.' *GRBS* 36 (1995): 17–24.

Mayerson, P. 'The Port of Clysma (Suez) in Transition from Roman to Arab Rule.' *JNES* 55 (1996): 119–26.

Meile, P. 'Les Yavanas dans l'Inde tamoule.' *JA* 232 (1940): 85–123.

Meredith, D. 'The Roman Remains in the Eastern Desert of Egypt.' *JEA* 38 (1952): 94–111.

Meredith, D. 'Annius Plocamus: Two Inscriptions from the Berenice Road.' *JRS* 43 (1953): 38–40.

Meredith, D. 'The Myos Hormos Road: Inscriptions and Ostraka.' *CE* 31 (1956): 356–62.

Meredith, D. 'Berenice Troglodytica.' *JEA* 43 (1957): 56–70.

Meredith, D., and L.A. Tregenza. 'Notes on Roman Roads and Stations in the Eastern Desert, I.' *Bull. Faculty of Arts, Fouad I University* 11 (1949): 1–30.

Meshel, Z., and Y. Tsafrir. 'The Nabataean Road from Avdat to Sha'ar Raman I.' *PEQ* 106 (1974): 103–18.

Meshel, Z., and Y. Tsafrir. 'The Nabataean Road from Avdat to Sha'ar Raman II.' *PEQ* 107 (1975): 3–21.

Meshorer, Y. *Nabataean Coins*. Jerusalem, 1975.

Meyer, C. *Glass from Quseir al-Qadim and the Indian Ocean Trade*. Chicago, 1992.
Michalowski, K. *Palmyra*. London, 1960.
Milik, J.T. *Dédicaces faites par des dieux*. Paris, 1972.
Millar, F. 'Paul of Samosata, Zenobia and Aurelian: the Church, Local Culture and Political Allegiance in Third-Century Syria.' *JRS* 61 (1971): 1–17.
Millar, F. *The Roman Near East 31 BC – AD 337*. Cambridge, Mass., 1993.
Miller, J.I. *The Spice Trade of the Roman Empire 29 BC – AD 641*. Oxford, 1969.
Mordtmann, J.H. 'Ein Nabatäer im Sabäerlande – Dionysos – Orotal.' *Klio* 25 (1932): 429–30.
Mouterde, R., and A. Poidebard. 'La voie antique des caravanes entre Palmyre et Hit au IIème Siècle ap. J.C.' *Syria* 12 (1931): 111–15.
Murray, G.W. 'The Roman Roads and Stations in the Eastern Desert of Egypt.' *JEA* 11 (1925): 138–50.
Murray, G.W. 'Trogodytica: the Red Sea Littoral in Ptolemaic Times.' *GJ* 133 (1967): 24–33.
Nebes, N. (ed.) *Arabia Felix: Beiträge zur Sprache und Kultur des vorislamischen Arabia*. Wiesbaden, 1994.
Negev, A. 'Avdat, a Caravan Halt in the Negev.' *Archaeology* 14 (1961): 122–30.
Negev, A. 'The Date of the Petra–Gaza Road.' *PEQ* 98 (1966): 89–98.
Negev, A. 'Oboda, Mampsis and Provincia Arabia.' *IEJ* 17 (1967): 46–55.
Negev, A. 'The Nabataean Necropolis at Egra.' *RBibl* 83 (1976): 203–36.
Negev, A. 'The Nabataeans and the Provincia Arabia.' *ANRW* II, 8 (1977): 520–686.
Negev, A. 'Numismatics and Nabataean Chronology.' *PEQ* 114 (1982): 119–27.
Negev, A. *Nabataean Archaeology Today*. New York, 1986.
Nodelman, A. 'A Preliminary History of Characene.' *Berytus* 13 (1960): 83–121.
Northedge, A., A. Bamber, and M. Roaf (eds) *Ana, Excavations of the British Archaeological Expedition at Qal'a Island 1981–2*. Warminster, 1988.
Oates, D. 'A Note on Three Latin Inscriptions from Hatra.' *Sumer* 11 (1955): 39–43.
Oertel, F. 'Das Problem des antiken Suezkanals.' In *Speigel der Geschichte. Festgabe für Max Braubach zum 10 April 1964*, ed. K. Repgen and S. Skalwelt, 18–52. Munster-Westfalen, 1964.
Oleson, J.P., K. 'Amr, R. Foote and R. Schick. 'Preliminary Report of the Humeima Excavation Project, 1993.' *Echos du Monde Classique/Classical Views* 38 (1994): 141–79.
Palmyre: Bilan et perspectives. Colloque de Strasbourg 18–20 Octobre 1973. Strasbourg, 1976.
Parker, S.T. 'Archaeological Survey of the Limes Arabicus: a Preliminary Report.' *ADAJ* 21 (1976): 19–31.
Parker, S.T. 'Towards a History of the Limes Arabicus.' In Hanson and Keppie (eds) *Roman Frontier Studies*, III, 865–78.
Parker, S.T. *Romans and Saracens: A History of the Arabian Frontier*. ASOR Dissertation Series. Winona Lake, 1986.
Parker, S.T. 'Retrospective on the Arabian Frontier after a Decade of Research.' In Freeman and Kennedy (eds) *The Defence of the Roman and Byzantine East*, II, 633–60.
Parker, S.T. (ed.) *The Roman Frontier in Central Jordan: Interim Report on the Limes Arabicus Project 1980–1985*. BAR Int. Ser. 340, 2 vols. Oxford, 1987.
Parker, S.T. 'Peasants, Pastoralists, and Pax Romana: a Different View.' *BASOR* 265 (1987): 35–51.

Parker, S.T. 'The Roman 'Aqaba Project: the 1994 Campaign.' *ADAJ* 40 (1996): 231–57.

Parker, S.T. 'Preliminary Report on the 1994 Season of the Roman Aqaba Project.' *BASOR* 305 (1997): 19–44.

Parr, P.J. 'The Last Days of Petra.' In M.A. Bakhit and M. Asfour (eds) *Proceedings of the Symposium on Bilad es-Sham during the Byzantine Period*, 192–205. Amman, 1986.

Peacock, D.P.S. 'The Site of Myos Hormos: a View from Space.' *JRA* 6 (1993): 226–32.

Pennachietti, F.A. 'L'inscrizione bilingue greco-parthica dell' Eracle di Seleucia.' *Mesopotamia* 22 (1987): 169–85.

Peters, F.E. 'The Nabataeans in the Hawran.' *JAOS* 97 (1977): 263–77.

Pirenne, J. 'The Incense Port of Moscha (Khor Rori) in Dhofar.' *JOS* 1 (1975): 81–96.

Poidebard, A. *La Trace de Rome dans le désert Syrie*, 2 vols. Paris, 1934.

Potter, D.S. *Prophecy and History in the Crisis of the Roman Empire: A Historical Commentary on the Thirteenth Sybilline Oracle*. Oxford, 1990.

Potter, D.S. 'The Inscription on the Bronze Herakles from Mesene: Vologeses IV's War with Rome and the Date of Tacitus' *Annales*.' *ZPE* 88 (1991): 277–90.

Potts, D.T. 'Trans-Arabian Routes of the Pre-Islamic Period.' In Salles (ed.) *L'Arabie et ses mers bordières*, 129–62.

Potts, D.T. 'Augustus, Aelius Gallus and the Periplus: a Re-interpretation of the Coinage of San'a Class B.' In Nebes (ed.) *Arabia Felix*, 212–22.

Potts, D.T. 'The Parthian Presence in the Arabian Gulf.' In Reade (ed.) *The Indian Ocean in Antiquity*, 269–85.

Preaux, C. 'Une source nouvelle sur l'annexation de l'Arabie par Trajan: les papyrus de Michigan 465 et 466.' *Phoibos* 5 (1950–1951): 123–39.

Ramachandran, K.S. *Archaeology of South India Tamil Nadu*. Delhi, 1980.

Raschke, M.G. 'Papyrological Evidence for Ptolemaic and Roman Trade with India.' In *Proceedings of the XIV International Congress of Papyrologists*, 241–6. London, 1975.

Raschke, M.G. 'New Studies in Roman Commerce with the East.' *ANRW* II, 9, 2 (1978): 604–1378.

Ray, H.P., and J.-F. Salles (eds) *Tradition and Archaeology: Early Maritime Contacts in the Indian Ocean*. New Delhi, 1996.

Rea, J.R. '*Vestigationes*.' *ZPE* 82 (1990): 126–8.

Reade, J. (ed.) *The Indian Ocean in Antiquity*. London, 1996.

Rebuffat, R. 'L'arrivée des romaines à Bu-Ngem.' *Libya Antiqua* 9–10 (1972–1973): 121–34.

Reddé, M., and T. Bauzou. 'Pistes caravanières de Syrie, d'Arabie et d'Egypte: Quelques éléments de comparaison.' In Fahd (ed.) *L'Arabie préislamique*, 485–97.

Reddé, M., and J.-C. Golvin. 'Du Nil à la mer rouge: Documents anciens et nouveaux sur les routes du désert oriental d'Egypt.' *Karthago* 21 (1986–1987): 5–64.

Redmount, C.A. 'Wadi Tumilat Survey.' *NARCE* 133 (1986): 19–23.

Reinach, A.J. 'Rapport sur les fouilles de Koptos: Deuxième campagne, janvier–février 1911.' *BSFFA* 3 (1912): 47–82.

Rey-Coquais, J.-P. 'Syrie romaine, de Pompée à Dioclétien.' *JRS* 68 (1978): 44–73.

Rey-Coquais, J.-P. 'L'Arabie dans les routes de commerce entre le monde Mediterranéen et les côtes Indiennes.' In Fahd (ed.) *L'Arabie préislamique*, 225–39.

Richardson, L. *A New Topographical Dictionary of Ancient Rome*. Baltimore, 1992.

Richmond, I.A. 'Palmyra under the Aegis of Rome.' *JRS* 53 (1963): 43–54.

Robin, C. 'L'Arabie du Sud et la date du Périple de la mer Erythrée (nouvelles données).' *JA* 289 (1991): 13–17.

The Roman and Byzantine Near East: Some Recent Archaeological Research. JRA Supp. 14. Ann Arbor, 1995.

Romer, F.E. 'Gaius Caesar's Military Diplomacy in the East.' *TAPA* 109 (1979): 199–214.

Rostovtzeff, M.I. *Caravan Cities*. Translated by D. and T. Talbot-Rice. Oxford, 1932.

Rostovtzeff, M.I. 'Les inscriptions caravanières de Palmyre.' In *Mélanges Gustave Glotz*, II, 792–811. Paris, 1932.

Rostovtzeff, M.I. 'Dura and the Problem of Parthian Art.' *YCS* 5 (1935): 157–304.

Rostovtzeff, M.I. *Social and Economic History of the Roman Empire*. Rev. by P.M. Fraser, rev. edn. Oxford, 1957.

Ruffing, K. 'Einige Uberlegungen zu Koptos: Ein Handelsplatz Oberägyptens in römischer Zeit.' *MBAH* 14 (1995): 17–42.

Rushworth, A. 'North African Deserts and Mountains: Comparisons and Insights.' In Kennedy (ed.) *The Roman Army in the East*, 297–316.

Salles, J.-F. (ed.) *L'Arabie et ses mers bordières I: Itinéraries et voyages*. Lyon, 1988.

Salles, J.-F. 'La circumnavigation de l'Arabie dans l'antiquité classique.' In Salles (ed.) *L'Arabie et ses mers bordières*, 75–102.

Salles, J.-F. 'Découvertes du golfe arabo-persique aux époques grecque et romaine.' *REA* 94 (1992): 79–97.

Salles, J.-F. 'Achaemenid and Hellenistic Trade in the Indian Ocean.' In Reade (ed.) *The Indian Ocean in Antiquity*, 251–67.

Salles, J.-F. 'Hellenistic Seafaring in the Indian Ocean: a Perspective from Arabia.' In Ray and Salles (eds) *Tradition and Archaeology*, 293–309.

Salomon, R. 'Epigraphic Remains of Indian Traders in Egypt.' *JAOS* 111 (1991): 731–6.

Sarasin, A. *Der Handel zwischen Indien und Rom zur Zeit der römischen Kaiser*. Basel, 1930.

Sartre, M. 'Rome et les Nabatéens à la fin de la République (65–30 av. J.-C.).' *REA* 81 (1979): 37–53.

Sartre, M. *Trois études sur l'Arabie romaine et byzantine*. Brussels, 1982.

Sartre, M. *Bostra, des origines à l'Islam*. Paris, 1985.

Sartre, M. *L'Orient romaine: Provinces et sociétés en Méditeranée orientale d' Auguste aux Sévères (31av. J.C. – 235 ap. J.C.)*. Paris, 1991.

Savignac, R., and J. Starcky. 'Une inscription nabatéenne provenant du Djôf.' *RBibl* 64 (1957): 215.

Schlumberger, D. 'L'inscription d'Hérodien: Remarques sur l'histoire des princes de Palmyre.' *Bulletin d'études orientales* 11 (1942–1943): 36–50.

Schlumberger, D. *La Palmyrène du Nord-Ouest*. Paris, 1951.

Schlumberger, D. 'Palmyre et la Mésène.' *Syria* 38 (1961): 258–60.

Schmitthenner, W. 'Rome and India: Aspects of Universal History during the Principate.' *JRS* 69 (1979): 90–106.

Schoff, W.H. *The Parthian Stations of Isidore of Charax*. Philadelphia, 1914.

Schwartz, J. 'Les Palmyréniens et l'Egypte.' *BSAA* 40 (1953): 63–87.

Schwartz, J. 'Note sur la famille de Philon d'Alexandrie.' *AIPHOS* 13 (1953): 591–602.

Schwartz, J. 'L'empire romaine et le commerce oriental.' *Annales* (Jan.–Feb. 1960): 18–44.

Schwartz, J. 'Palmyre et l'opposition à Rome en Egypte.' In *Palmyre: Bilan et perspectives*, 138–51.

Sedov, A.V. 'New Archaeological and Epigraphical Material from Qana (South Arabia).' *AAE* 3 (1992): 110–37.

Sedov, A.V. 'Qana (Yemen) and the Indian Ocean.' In Ray and Salles (eds) *Tradition and Archaeology*, 11–35.

Sedov, A.V. 'Sea-trade of the Hadramawt Kingdom from the 1st to the 6th Centuries AD.' In Avanzini (ed.) *Profumi d'Arabia*, 365–83.

Segal, J.B. *Edessa, the Blessed City*. Oxford, 1970.

Seyrig, H. 'L'incorporation de Palmyre à l'empire romain.' *Syria* 13 (1932): 266–77.

Seyrig, H. 'Textes relatifs à la garnison romaine de Palmyre.' *Syria* 14 (1933): 152–68.

Seyrig, H. 'Postes romaines sur le route de Médine.' *Syria* 22 (1941): 219–23.

Seyrig, H. 'Inscriptions grecques de l'agora de Palmyre.' *Syria* 22 (1941): 223–70.

Seyrig, H. 'Palmyra and the East.' *JRS* 40 (1950): 1–7.

Seyrig, H. 'Caractères de l'histoire d'Emèse.' *Syria* 36 (1959): 190–2.

Seyrig, H. 'Le prétendu fondouq palmyrénien de Coptos.' *Syria* 49 (1972): 120–5.

Shifman, I. *Palmirskij Poshlinnyj Tarif*. Moscow, 1980.

Shiratori, K. 'A Study of T'iao-chih.' *Memoirs of the Research Department of the Toyo Bunko* 15 (1956): 1–23.

Shiratori, K. 'Chinese Ideas Reflected in the Ta-Ch'in Accounts.' *Memoirs of the Research Department of the Toyo Bunko* 15 (1956): 25–72.

Shiratori, K. 'The Geography of the Western Region Studied on the Basis of the Ta-Ch'in Accounts.' *Memoirs of the Research Department of the Toyo Bunko* 15 (1956): 73–163.

Sidebotham, S.E. *Roman Economic Policy in the Erythra Thalassa 30 BC – AD 217*. Leiden, 1986.

Sidebotham, S.E. 'Aelius Gallus and Arabia.' *Latomus* 45 (1986): 590–602.

Sidebotham, S.E. 'Fieldwork on the Red Sea Coast: the 1987 Season.' *JARCE* 26 (1989): 127–66.

Sidebotham, S.E. 'Ports of the Red Sea and the Arabia–India Trade.' In Begley and De Puma (eds) *Rome and India: The Ancient Sea Trade*, 12–38.

Sidebotham, S.E. 'Römische Strassen in der ägyptischen Wüste.' *AW* 22 (1991): 177–89.

Sidebotham, S.E. 'University of Delaware Archaeological Project at 'Abu Sha'ar: the 1992 Season.' *NARCE* 161/162 (1993): 1–9.

Sidebotham, S.E. 'Preliminary Report on the 1990–91 Seasons of Fieldwork at 'Abu Sha'ar (Red Sea Coast).' *JARCE* 31 (1994): 133–58.

Sidebotham, S.E. 'University of Delaware Fieldwork in the Eastern Desert of Egypt, 1993.' *DOP* 48 (1994): 263–75.

Sidebotham, S.E. 'Excavations.' In Sidebotham and Wendrich (eds) *Berenike '94*, 21–8.

Sidebotham, S.E. 'The Excavations.' In Sidebotham and Wendrich (eds) *Berenike '95*, 7–98.

Sidebotham, S.E. 'The Ship Graffito.' In Sidebotham and Wendrich (eds) *Berenike '95*, 315–17.

Sidebotham, S.E. 'Caravans across the Eastern Desert: Recent Discoveries on the Berenike – Apollinopolis Magna – Coptos Roads.' In Avanzini (ed.) *Profumi d'Arabia*, 385–94.

Sidebotham, S.E. 'Roman Interests in the Red Sea and Indian Ocean.' In Reade (ed.) *The Indian Ocean in Antiquity*, 290–2.

Sidebotham, S.E. 'Survey of the Hinterland.' In Sidebotham and Wendrich (eds) *Berenike 1997*, 349–69.

Sidebotham, S.E., and J.A. Seeger. 'The Coins.' In Sidebotham and Wendrich (eds) *Berenike '95*, 179–96.

Sidebotham, S.E., and W.Z. Wendrich (eds) *Berenike '94: Preliminary Report of the 1994 Excavations at Berenike (Egyptian Red Sea Coast) and Survey of the Eastern Desert.* Leiden, 1995.

Sidebotham, S.E., and W.Z. Wendrich. 'Interpretative Summary and Conclusion.' In Sidebotham and Wendrich (eds) *Berenike '94*, 103–6.

Sidebotham, S.E., and W.Z. Wendrich (eds) *Berenike '95: Preliminary Report of the 1995 Excavations at Berenike (Egyptian Red Sea Coast) and Survey of the Eastern Desert.* Leiden, 1996.

Sidebotham, S.E., and W.Z. Wendrich. 'Interpretative Summary and Conclusion.' In Sidebotham and Wendrich (eds) *Berenike '95*, 441–52.

Sidebotham, S.E., and W.Z. Wendrich (eds) *Berenike '96: Report of the Excavations at Berenike (Egyptian Red Sea Coast) and the Survey of the Eastern Desert.* Leiden, 1998.

Sidebotham, S.E., and W.Z. Wendrich (eds) *Report of the 1997 Excavations at Berenike and the Survey of the Egyptian Eastern Desert, including Excavations at Shenshef.* Leiden, 1999.

Sidebotham, S.E., and W.Z. Wendrich. 'Interpretive Summary and Conclusion.' In Sidebotham and Wendrich (eds) *Berenike 1997*, 445–56.

Sidebotham, S.E., and R.E. Zitterkopf. 'Routes through the Eastern Desert of Egypt.' *Expedition* 37.2 (1995): 39–52.

Sidebotham, S.E., and R.E. Zitterkopf. 'Survey of the Via Hadriana by the University of Delaware: the 1996 Season.' *BIFAO* 97 (1997): 221–37.

Sidebotham, S.E., and R.E. Zitterkopf. 'Survey of the Via Hadriana: the 1997 Season.' *BIFAO* 98 (1998): 353–65.

Sidebotham, S.E., R.E. Zitterkopf, and J.A. Riley. 'Survey of the 'Abu Sha'ar – Nile Road.' *AJA* 95 (1991): 571–622.

Sijpesteijn, P.J. 'Der ΠΟΤΑΜΟΣ ΤΡΑΙΑΝΟΣ.' *Aegyptus* 43 (1963): 70–83.

Sijpesteijn, P.J. 'Trajan and Egypt.' *Papyrologica Lugduno-Batava Papyri Selectae* 13 (1965): 106–13.

Slane, K.W. 'Other Ancient Ceramics Imported from the Mediterranean.' In Begley (ed.) *The Ancient Port of Arikamedu*, 351–68.

Smith, M.C., and H.T. Wright. 'The Ceramics from Ras Hafun in Somalia: Notes on a Classical Maritime Site.' *Azania* 23 (1988): 115–41.

Speidel, M.P. 'The Roman Army in Arabia.' *ANRW* II, 8 (1977): 687–730.

Speidel, M.P. 'Palmyrenian Irregulars at Koptos.' *BASP* 21 (1984): 22–4.

Speidel, M.P. *Roman Army Studies*, 2 vols. Amsterdam, 1984.

Speidel, M.P. 'Numerus or Ala Vocontiorum at Palmyra?' In *Roman Army Studies*, I, 167–9.

Speidel, M.P. 'The Roman Road to Dumata (Jawf in Saudi Arabia) and the Frontier Strategy of *Praetensione Colligare.' Historia* 36 (1987): 213–21.

Starcky, J. 'The Nabataeans: a Historical Sketch.' *BA* 18 (1955): 84–106.

Starcky, J. 'Nouvelle épitaphe Nabatéen donnant le nom sémitique de Pétra.' *RBibl* 72 (1965): 95–7.

Starcky, J. 'Pétra et la Nabatène.' In *Supplément au Dictionnaire de la Bible*, VII, 886–1017. Paris, 1966.

Starcky, J., and M. Gawlikowski. *Palmyre*, 2nd edn. Paris, 1985.

Stauffer, A.-M. 'Textiles from Palmyra: Local Production and the Import and Imitation of Chinese Silk Weavings.' *International Colloquium on Palmyra and the Silk Road*, *AAS* 42 (1996): 425–30.

Stein, M.A. 'The Ancient Trade Route past Hatra and its Roman Posts.' *JRAS* (1941): 299–316.

Stoneman, R. *Palmyra and its Empire: Zenobia's Revolt against Rome*. Ann Arbor, 1991.

Strobel, K. 'Zu Fragen der frühen Geschichte der römischen Provinz Arabia und zu einigen Problemen des Imperium Romanum zu Beginn der 2. Jh. n. Chr.' *ZPE* 71 (1988): 251–80.

Sullivan, R.D. 'The Dynasty of Judaea in the First Century.' *ANRW* II, 8 (1977): 296–354.

Swain, S. 'Greek into Palmyrene: Odenathus as "Corrector Totius Orientis".' *ZPE* 99 (1993): 157–64.

Tanner, R.G. 'Greek Epigraphy in South Jordan.' *ZPE* 83 (1990): 183–93.

Tchernia, A. 'Le dromadaire des Peticii et le commerce oriental.' *Mélanges de l'Ecole Française de Rome (Antiquité)* 104 (1992): 293–301.

Teixidor, J. 'Deux inscriptions palmyréniennes du musée de Bagdad.' *Syria* 40 (1963): 33–46.

Teixidor, J. 'Notes hatréennes 1: l'inscription de Sa'adiya.' *Syria* 41 (1964): 273–9.

Teixidor, J. 'Notes hatréennes 2: l'inscription de Hatra no. 79.' *Syria* 41 (1964): 280–4.

Teixidor, J. *Un Port romain du désert: Palmyre et son commerce d'Auguste à Caracalla*. Paris, 1984.

Teixidor, J. 'Les derniers rois d'Edesse d'après deux nouveaux documents syriaques.' *ZPE* 76 (1989): 219–22.

Thapar, R. 'Early Mediterranean Contacts with India: an Overview.' In De Romanis and Tchernia (eds) *Crossings*,11–40.

Thomas, J.D. 'A Petition to the Prefect of Egypt and Related Imperial Edicts.' *JEA* 61 (1975): 201–21.

Thorley, J. 'The Development of Trade between the Roman Empire and the East under Augustus.' *Greece & Rome* 16 (1969): 209–23.

Thorley, J. 'The Silk Trade between China and the Roman Empire at its Height, circa AD 90–130.' *Greece & Rome* 18 (1971): 71–80.

Thür, G. 'Hypotheken-Urkunde eines Seedordehens für eine Reise nach Muziris und Apographe für die Tetarte in Alexandreia (zu P. Vindob. G. 40. 822).' *Tyche* 2 (1987): 229–45.

Thür, G. 'Zum Seedarlehen κατὰ μουζεῖριν P. Vindob. G 40822.' *Tyche* 3 (1988): 229–33.

Toll, C. 'Two Nabataean Ostraka from Egypt.' *BIFAO* 94 (1994): 381–2.

Tregenza, L.A. *The Red Sea Mountains of Egypt*. London, 1955.

Turner, E.G. 'Tiberius Iulius Alexander.' *JRS* 44 (1954): 54–64.

Turner, P.J. *Roman Coins from India*. London, 1989.

Updegraff, R.T. 'The Blemmyes I: the Rise of the Blemmyes and the Roman Withdrawal from Nubia under Diocletian.' *ANRW* II, 10, 1 (1988): 44–97.

Uxcull-Gyllenbrand, W. *Der Gnomon des Idios Logos, II, der Kommentar. Griechische Urkunden*, V.2. Berlin, 1934.

Van Beek, G.W. 'Frankincense and Myrrh in Ancient South Arabia.' *JAOS* 78 (1958): 141–52.

Van Beek, G.W. 'Frankincense and Myrrh.' *BA* 28, 3 (1960): 70–95.

Veerhoogt, A.M.F.W. 'Greek and Latin Textual Material.' In Sidebotham and Wendrich (eds) *Berenike '96*, 193–8.

Vickers, M. 'Nabataea, India, Gaul and Carthage: Reflections on Hellenistic and Roman Gold Vessels and Red-Gloss Pottery.' *AJA* 98 (1994): 231–48.

Wagner, G. 'Une dédicace à Isis et à Héra de la part d'un négociant d'Aden.' *BIFAO* 76 (1976): 277–81.

Wagner, J. *Seleucia am Euphrat/Zeugma*. Wiesbaden, 1976.

Walker, D.R. *The Metrology of the Roman Silver Coinage*, 3 vols. BAR Supp. Ser. 5. Oxford, 1976–1978.

Wallace, S.L. *Taxation in Egypt from Augustus to Diocletian*. Princeton, 1938.

Warmington, E.H. *The Commerce between the Roman Empire and India*. Cambridge, 1928.

Waters, K.H. 'The Reign of Trajan and its Place in Contemporary Scholarship (1960–1972).' *ANRW* II, 2 (1975): 381–431.

Weber, E. *Tabula Peutingeriana: Codex Vindobondensis 324, Vollständige Faksimile-Ausgabe im Originalformat*. Graz, 1976.

Weerakkody, P.M. *Taprobanê: Ancient Sri Lanka as Known by Greeks and Romans*. Turnhout, 1996.

Weigall, A.E.P. *Travels in the Upper Egyptian Deserts*. London, 1909.

Welles, C.B., R.O. Fink, and J.F. Gilliam. *The Excavations at Dura-Europos V.1: The Parchments and Papyri*. New Haven, 1959.

Wellesley, K. 'The Fable of a Roman Attack on Aden.' *La Parola del Passato* 9 (1954): 401–5.

Welsby, D.A. 'Qasr al-Uwainid and Da'ajaniya: Two Roman Military Sites in Jordan.' *Levant* 30 (1998):195–8.

Wheatley, P. *The Golden Khersonese: Studies in the Historical Geography of the Malay Peninsula before AD 1500*. Kuala Lumpur, 1961.

Wheeler, E.L. 'Methodological Limits and the Mirage of Roman Strategy.' *Journal of Military History* 57 (1993): 7–41, 215–40.

Wheeler, R.E.M. *Rome Beyond the Imperial Frontiers*. London, 1954.

Wheeler, R.E.M., A. Ghosh, and K. Deva. 'Arikamedu: an Indo-Roman Trading Station on the East Coast of India.' *Ancient India* 2 (1946): 17–125.

Whitcomb, D.S. 'Quseir al-Qadim and the Location of Myos Hormos.' *Topoi* 6 (1996): 747–72.

Whitcomb, D.S., and J.H. Johnson (eds) *Quseir al-Qadim, 1978 Preliminary Report*. Princeton, 1979.

Whitcomb, D.S., and J.H. Johnson (eds) *Quseir al-Qadim, 1980 Preliminary Report*. Malibu, 1982.

Whitcomb, D.S., and J.H. Johnson. '1982 Season of Excavation at Quseir al-Qadim.' *NARCE* 120 (1982): 24–30.

Whittaker, C.R. *Frontiers of the Roman Empire: A Social and Economic Study*. Baltimore, 1994.

Whittaker, C.R. 'Where are the Frontiers Now?' In Kennedy (ed.) *The Roman Army in the East*, 25–40.

Wilcken, U. 'Punt-Fahrten in der Ptolemäerzeit.' *Zeitschrift für ägyptische Sprache und Altertumskunde* 60 (1925): 86–102.

Wilhelm, A. 'Griechische Inschrift aus Medamut.' *AnzWein* 69 (1932): 25–7.

Will, E. 'Marchands et chefs de caravannes à Palmyre.' *Syria* 34 (1957): 262–77.

Will, E. 'Pline l'Ancien et Palmyre: un problème d'histoire ou d'histoire littéraire?' *Syria* 62 (1985): 263–9.

Will, E.L. 'Mediterranean Shipping Amphoras from the 1941–50 Expeditions.' In Begley (ed.) *The Ancient Port of Arikamedu*, 317–49.

Williams, S. *Diocletian and the Roman Recovery*. London, 1985.

Winnett, F.V. 'The Revolt of Damasi: Safaitic and Nabataean Evidence.' *BASOR* 211 (1973): 54–7.

Winnett, F.V. and G.L. Harding. *Fifty Safaitic Cairns*. Toronto, 1978.

Wipszycka, E. *L'Industrie textile dans l'Egypte romaine*. Warsaw, 1965.

Wissman, H. von. 'Die Geschichte des Sabäerreichs und der Feldzug des Aelius Gallus.' *ANRW* II, 9, 1 (1978): 308–544.

Yadin, Y. 'Expedition D: the Cave of Letters.' *IEJ* 12 (1962): 227–57.

Yadin, Y. 'The Nabataean Kingdom, Provincia Arabia, Petra and En-Geddi in the Documents from Nahal Hever.' *Ex Oriente Lux* 17 (1963): 227–41.

Young, G.K. 'The Customs-collector at the Nabataean Port of Leuke Kome (*Periplus Maris Erythraei* 19).' *ZPE* 119 (1997): 266–8.

Zaghloul, M. *et al.* (eds) *Studies in the History and Archaeology of Jordan*, IV. Amman, 1992.

Zahrnt, M. 'Antinoopolis in Ägypten: Die hadrianische Gründung und ihre Privilegien in der neueren Forschung.' *ANRW* II, 10, 1 (1988): 669–706.

Zayadine, F. 'Recent Excavations on the Citadel of Amman.' *ADAJ* 18 (1973): 25.

Zayadine, F. 'Caravan Routes between Egypt and Nabataea and the Voyage of Sultan Baibars to Petra in 1276.' In Hadidi (ed.) *Studies in the History and Archaeology of Jordan*, II, 159–74.

Zayadine, F. *Jerash Archaeological Project 1981–83*. Amman, 1986.

Zayadine, F. 'L'espace urbain du Grand Pétra: les routes et les Stations caravanières.' *ADAJ* 36 (1992): 217–39.

Zayadine, F. ''Ayla-'Aqaba in the Light of Recent Excavations.' *ADAJ* 38 (1994): 485–501.

Zayadine, F., and Z.T. Fiema. 'Roman Inscriptions from the Siq at Petra.' *ADAJ* 30 (1986): 199.

Zitterkopf, R.E., and S.E. Sidebotham. 'Stations and Towers on the Quseir – Nile Road.' *JEA* 75 (1989): 155–89.

INDEX